IRISH PLANNING LAW AND PRACTICE

SUPPLEMENT 2001

GW00728782

IRISH PLANNING LAW
AND PRACTICE

SUPPLEMENT 2001

THE PLANNING AND DEVELOPMENT ACT 2000

By

Planning and Environmental Law Unit

Consultant Editors
Michael O'Donnell, BA, MRUP, LLB,
Barrister-at-Law
The Hon Mr Justice Philip O'Sullivan

Ireland	Butterworth (Ireland) Ltd, 26 Upper Ormond Quay, Dublin 7
United Kingdom	Butterworths, a Division of Reed Elsevier (UK) Ltd, Halsbury House, 35 Chancery Lane, London WC2A 1EL and 4 Hill Street, Edinburgh EH2 3JZ
Australia	Butterworths, a Division of Reed International Books Australia Pty Ltd, Chatswood, New South Wales
Canada	Butterworths Canada Ltd, Markham, Ontario
Hong Kong	Butterworths Hong Kong, a division of Reed Elsevier (Greater China) Ltd, Hong Kong
India	Butterworths India, New Delhi
Malaysia	Malaysian Law Journal Sdn Bhd, Kuala Lumpur
New Zealand	Butterworths of New Zealand Ltd, Wellington
Singapore	Butterworths Asia, Singapore
South Africa	Butterworths Legal Publishers (Pty) Ltd, Durban
USA	Lexis Law Publishing, Charlottesville, Virginia

ISBN 1–85475–2243

Typeset by Phoenix Photosetting, Chatham, Kent
Printed by Hobbs the Printers Ltd, Totton, Hampshire

Visit us at our website: **http://www.butterworthsireland.com**

Abbreviations

EPAA 1992	Environmental Protection Agency Act 1992
LG(PD)A 1963	Local Government (Planning and Development) Act 1963
LG(PD)A 1976	Local Government (Planning and Development) Act 1976
LG(PD)A 1982	Local Government (Planning and Development) Act 1982
LG(PD)A 1983	Local Government (Planning and Development) Act 1983
LG(PD)A 1990	Local Government (Planning and Development) Act 1990
LG(PD)A 1992	Local Government (Planning and Development) Act 1992
LG(PD)A 1993	Local Government (Planning and Development) Act 1993
LG(PD)A 1998	Local Government (Planning and Development) Act 1998
LG(PD)A 1999	Local Government (Planning and Development) Act 1999
LG(PD)R 1994	Local Government (Planning and Development) Regulations 1994
PDA 2000	Planning and Development Act 2000
WMA 1996	Waste Management Act 1996

s	Section (of an Act)
Sub-s	Sub-section (of an Act)
Sch	Schedule (to an Act)
Pt	Part (of an Act)
SI	Statutory Instrument

Planning and Development Act 2000

Number 30 of 2000

Introductory note

The Planning and Development Act 2000 was signed into law on 28 August 2000 after several years in preparation. It was delayed following the Supreme Court's adjudication on the constitutionality of the provisions dealing with social and affordable housing. Those provisions having been passed, that part (Pt V of the Act), is now immune to further constitutional challenge.

The Act seeks to assemble in one piece of legislation all of the provisions of planning legislation that are still to apply and were previously comprised in nine earlier planning acts. The Act also seeks to make a number of significant changes, and introduces new concepts such as the social and affording housing provisions and the provisions dealing with strategic development zones (Pt IX).

The purpose of this annotated text is to demonstrate, section by section, what is a restatement of the pre-existing position; what changes have been made; and what provisions are new. We have also indicated what parts, as at the time of writing, have been commenced and what parts are still awaiting commencement. The Act is becoming operational in stages.

Overall, it can be seen that a considerable number of additional powers have been given to An Bord Pleanála, and a significant number of new obligations are placed on local authorities (for example in making local plans and regional planning guidelines). The Act also provides a new system for reporting and reviewing the performance of local authorities. It will be interesting to see how those organisations cope with their additional roles in view of their already stretched resources.

Efforts have been made in the control of development section (Pt III) to tighten the time limits applying to the planning application process and it will remain to be seen how this operates, and what effect it has, in practice.

The provisions relating to social and affordable housing have been commenced, and will start to take effect once the housing strategies for particular areas are in place – they must be in place by August 2001.

The government has yet to designate any strategic development zones and this is likely to happen in the foreseeable future.

Regulations have been published in relation to the holding of concerts, the impetus being the prospect of a second U2 concert in Slane – see Pt XVI.

The status of outline planning permission has been bolstered as a result of the provisions in Pt III (s 36) such that local authorities are now to be entitled to reject planning applications on the basis of failure to comply with previous permissions (with the sanction of the High Court only); and where they are satisfied that the development will have significant adverse environmental effects. This blurs the distinction between the roles of the planning authorities and the Environmental Protection Agency. Planning authorities/the Board will still be precluded from imposing conditions of an environmental nature in planning permissions.

The previous provisions for materially contravening development plans – s 4 Motions – have been left virtually unamended. The level of penalties has been increased and the principle of "*polluter pays*" has been incorporated such that the costs that can be awarded against an offender can now include all costs associated with investigating offences.

The provisions in Pt IV relating to protected structures are virtually identical to the provisions under the 1999 Act. There are also new provisions under Pt XVIII of the Act dealing with the control of quarries – again it will be interesting to see how effective these will be.

Enforcement action must now be taken within seven (as opposed to five) years but there is still no amnesty for an unauthorised development – once unauthorised, it remains unauthorised which can have implications relative to funding and further development. Perhaps this was an opportunity missed.

A number of Regulations and guidelines have been passed pursuant to this Act as are referred to in the relevant parts described below. Further, extensive, regulations can be expected in the next few months.

A&L Goodbody
16 May 2001

ARRANGEMENT OF SECTIONS

PART I PRELIMINARY AND GENERAL

1. Short title   **[1]**
2. Interpretation   **[2]**
3. Development   **[3]**
4. Exempted development   **[4]**
5. Declaration and referral on development and exempted development   **[5]**
6. Power of examination, investigation and survey   **[11]**
7. Planning register   **[12]**
8. Obligation to give information to local authority   **[13]**

PART II PLANS AND GUIDELINES

Chapter I   Development Plans
9. Obligation to make development plan   **[14]**
10. Content of development plans   **[15]–[20]**
11. Preparation of draft development plan   **[21]**

12. Making of development plan   **[22]**
13. Variation of development plan   **[23]**
14. Public rights of way in development plans   **[24]**
15. General duty of planning authority to secure objectives of development plan   **[25]**–**[30]**
16. Copies of development plans   **[31]**
17. Evidence of development plans   **[32]**

Chapter II   Local Area Plans
18. Local area plans   **[33]**
19. Application and content of local area plans   **[34]**
20. Consultation and adoption of local area plans   **[35]**–**[40]**

Chapter III   Regional Planning Guidelines
21. Power to make the regional planning guidelines   **[41]**
22. Co-operation of planning authorities with regional authority   **[42]**
23. Content and objectives of regional planning guidelines   **[43]**
24. Consultation regarding regional planning guidelines   **[44]**
25. Procedure for making regional planning guidelines   **[45]**–**[50]**
26. Review of regional guidelines   **[51]**
27. Regional planning guidelines and development plans   **[52]**

Chapter IV   Guidelines and Directives
28. Ministerial guidelines   **[53]**
29. Ministerial policy directives **[54]**
30. Limitation on Ministerial power   **[55]**–**[60]**
31. Ministerial directions regarding development plans   **[61]**

PART III   CONTROL OF DEVELOPMENT
32. General obligations to obtain permission   **[62]**
33. Regulations regarding applications for permission   **[63]**
34. Permission for development   **[64]**
35. Refusal of planning permission for past failures to comply   **[65]**–**[70]**
36. Outline permission   **[71]**
37. Appeal to Board   **[72]**
38. Availability of documents relating to planning applications   **[73]**
39. Supplemental provisions as to grant of permission   **[74]**
40. Limit of duration of permission.   **[75]**–**[80]**
41. Power to vary appropriate period   **[81]**
42. Power to extend additional period   **[82]**
43. Regulations regarding sections 40, 41, 42   **[83]**
44. Revocation or modification of permission   **[84]**
45. Acquisition of land for open spaces   **[85]**–**[90]**
46. Requiring removal or alteration of structure or discontinuance of use   **[91]**
47. Agreements regulating development or use of land   **[92]**
48. Development contributions   **[93]**

49. Supplementary development contribution schemes   **[94]**
50. Judicial review of appeals, referrals and other matters   **[95]–[100]**

PART IV   ARCHITECTURAL HERITAGE

Chapter I   Protected Structures
51. Record of protected structures   **[101]**
52. Guidelines by Minister for Arts Heritage, Gaeltacht and the
        Islands   **[102]**
53. Recommendations to planning authorities concerning specific
        structures   **[103]**
54. Additions to deletions from record of protected structures   **[104]**
55. Procedure for to making additions or deletions   **[105]–[110]**
56. Registration under Registration of Title Act 1964   **[111]**
57. Works affecting character of protected structures or proposed protected
        structures   **[112]**
58. Duty of owners and occupiers to protect structure from
        endangerment   **[113]**
59. Notice to require works to be carried out in relation to endangerment of
        protected structures   **[114]**
60. Notice to require restoration of character of protected structures and other
        places   **[115]–[120]**
61. Appeals against notices   **[121]**
62. Effective date of notices   **[122]**
63. Offence relating to endangerment of protected structures   **[123]**
64. Owners' powers in relation to notices concerning endangerment
        restoration of structures   **[124]**
65. Application to District Court for necessary consent   **[125]–[130]**
66. Jurisdiction of District Court   **[131]**
67. Application to court for contribution to cost of carrying out works on
        endangered structures   **[132]**
68. Carrying out of certain works to be exempted development   **[133]**
69. Planning authority's power to carry out works to protected structures and
        other places   **[134]**
70. Recovery by planning authority of expenses for carrying out works on
        endangered structures   **[135]–[140]**
71. Power to acquire protected structure   **[141]**
72. Notice of intention to acquire protected structure compulsorily   **[142]**
73. Objection to compulsory acquisition of protected structure   **[143]**
74. Vesting order for protected structures   **[144]**
75. Form and effect of vesting order   **[145]–[150]**
76. Registration of acquired title and amendment of vesting order   **[151]**
77. Compensation for interest in protected structure   **[152]**
78. Use of protected structure acquired by planning authority   **[153]**
79. Obligations of sanitary authorities in respect of protected
        structures   **[154]**
80. Grants to planning authorities in respect of functions under this
        Part   **[155]–[160]**

Chapter II   Architectural Conservation Areas and Areas of Special Planning Control
81.   Architectural conservation areas   **[161]**
82.   Development in architectural conservation areas   **[162]**
83.   Power to acquire structure or other land in architectural conservation area   **[163]**
84.   Area of special planning control   **[164]**
85.   Special planning control scheme   **[165]–[170]**
86.   Variation and review of scheme   **[171]**
87.   Development in special planning control area   **[172]**
88.   Service of notice relating to structures or other land in an area of special planning control   **[173]**
89.   Implementation of the notice under section 88   **[174]**
90.   Court may compel compliance with notice under section 88   **[175]–[180]**
91.   Offence to fail to comply with notice under section 88   **[181]**
92.   Permission not required for any development required under this Chapter   **[182]**

PART V   HOUSING SUPPLY

93.   Interpretation   **[183]**
94.   Housing strategies   **[184]**
95.   Housing strategies and development plans   **[185]–[190]**
96.   Provision of social and affordable housing etc   **[191]**
97.   Development to which section 96 does not apply   **[192]**
98.   Allocation of affordable housing   **[193]**
99.   Controls on resale of certain houses   **[194]**
100.   Regulations under this Part   **[195]–[200]**
101.   Housing and planning authority under this section   **[201]**

PART VI   AN BORD PLEANÁLA

Chapter I   Establishment and Constitution
102.   Continuation of Bord Pleanála   **[202]**
103.   Board to be body corporate, etc   **[203]**
104.   Board to consist of chairperson and 7 other members   **[204]**
105.   Appointment of chairperson   **[205]–[210]**
106.   Appointment of ordinary members   **[211]**
107.   Appointment of deputy chairperson   **[212]**
108.   Board's quorum vacancies, etc   **[213]**

Chapter II   Organisation, Staffing, etc
109.   Performance of Board   **[214]**
110.   Chairperson ensure efficient discharge of business of Board etc   **[215]–[220]**
111.   Meetings and procedure of Board   **[221]**
112.   Divisions of Board   **[222]**
113.   Prohibition on disclosure of information relating to functions of Board   **[223]**
114.   Prohibition of certain communications in relation to appeals etc   **[224]**

115. Indemnification of members and employees of Board and other persons   **[225]–[230]**
116. Grants to Board   **[231]**
117. Accounts and audits of Board   **[232]**
118. Annual report and information to Minister   **[233]**
119. Superannuation of members of Board   **[234]**
120. Employees of Board   **[235]–[240]**
121. Superannuation of employees of Board   **[241]**
122. Provision of services by Minister to Board   **[242]**
123. Membership of either House Oireachtas etc   **[243]**
124. Consultants and advisers to Board   **[244]**

Chapter III   Appeal Procedures, etc.
125. Appeals and referrals with which the Board is concerned   **[245]–[250]**
126. Duty and objective of Board in relation to appeals and referrals   **[251]**
127. Provisions as to making of appeals and referrals   **[252]**
128. Submission of documents, etc. to Board by planning authorities.   **[253]**
129. Submissions or observations by other parties   **[254]**
130. Submissions or observations by persons other than parties   **[255]–[260]**
131. Power of Board to request submissions or observations   **[261]**
132. Power of Board to require submission of documents etc   **[262]**
133. Powers of Board where notice is served under section 131 or 132   **[263]**
134. Oral hearings of appeals and referrals   **[264]**
135. Supplemental provisions relating to oral hearings   **[265]–[270]**
136. Convening of meetings on referrals   **[271]**
137. Matters other than those raised by parties   **[272]**
138. Board may dismiss appeals or referrals if vexatious, etc   **[273]**
139. Appeals against conditions   **[274]**
140. Withdrawal of appeals, applications and referrals   **[275]–[280]**
141. Time for decisions and appeals etc   **[281]**
142. Regulations regarding appeals and referrals   **[282]**
143. Board to have regard to certain objectives   **[283]**
144. Fees payable to Board   **[284]**
145. Expenses of appeal or referral   **[285]–[290]**
146. Reports and documents of the Board   **[291]**

PART VII   DISCLOSURE OF INTERESTS, ETC.

147. Declaration by members, etc. of certain interests   **[292]**
148. Requirements affecting members etc who have certain beneficial interests   **[293]**
149. Supplemental provisions relating to sections 147 and 148   **[294]**
150. Codes of conduct   **[295]–[300]**

PART VIII   ENFORCEMENT

151. Offence   **[301]**
152. Warning letter   **[302]**
153. Decision on enforcement   **[303]**

154.   Enforcement notice   **[304]**
155.   Issue of enforcement notice in cases of urgency   **[305]–[310]**
156.   Penalties for offences   **[311]**
157.   Prosecution of offences   **[312]**
158.   Offences by bodies corporate   **[313]**
159.   Payment of fines to planning authorities   **[314]**
160.   Injunctions in relation to unauthorised development   **[315]–[320]**
161.   Costs of prosecutions and applications for injunctions   **[321]**
162.   Evidence of permission   **[322]**
163.   Permission not required for any works required under this Act   **[323]**
164.   Transitional arrangements for offences   **[324]**

PART IX   STRATEGIC DEVELOPMENT ZONES

165.   Interpretation   **[325]–[330]**
166.   Designation of sites for strategic development zones   **[331]**
167.   Acquisition of site for strategic development zone   **[332]**
168.   Planning scheme for strategic development zones   **[333]**
169.   Making of planning scheme   **[334]**
170.   Application for development in strategic development zone   **[335]–[340]**
171.   Revocation of planning scheme   **[341]**

PART X   ENVIRONMENTAL IMPACT ASSESSMENT

172.   Requirement for environmental impact statement   **[342]**
173.   Permission for development requiring environmental impact
           assessment   **[343]**
174.   Transboundary environmental impacts   **[344]**
175.   Environmental impact assessment of certain development carried out by
           or on behalf of local authorities   **[345]–[350]**
176.   Prescribed classes of development requiring assessment   **[351]**
177.   Prescribed information regarding environmental impact
           statements   **[352]**

PART XI   DEVELOPMENT BY LOCAL AND STATE AUTHORITIES, ETC.

178.   Restrictions on development by certain local authorities   **[353]**
179.   Local authority own development   **[354]**
180.   Taking in charge of estates   **[355]–[360]**
181.   Development by State authorities   **[361]**
182.   Cables, wires and pipelines   **[362]**

PART XII   COMPENSATION

Chapter I   Compensation generally
183.   Compensation claims: time limits   **[363]**
184.   Determination of compensation claim   **[364]**
185.   Regulations in relation to compensation   **[365]–[370]**
186.   Prohibition of double compensation   **[371]**

187. Recovery of compensation from planning authority **[372]**
188. Registration of compensation **[373]**
189. Recovery by planning authority of compensation on subsequent development **[374]**

Chapter II   Compensation in relation to decisions under Part III
190. Right to compensation **[375]–[380]**
191. Restriction of compensation **[381]**
192. Notice preventing compensation **[382]**
193. Special provision for structures substantially replacing structures demolished or destroyed by fire **[383]**
194. Restriction on assignment of compensation under section 190 **[384]**
195. Compensation where permission is revoked or modified **[385]–[390]**

Chapter III   Compensation in relation to sections 46, 85, 88, 182, 207 and 252
196. Compensation regarding removal or alteration of structure **[391]**
197. Compensation regarding discontinuance of use **[392]**
198. Compensation claim relating to area of special planning control **[393]**
199. Compensation regarding cables, wires and pipelines **[394]**
200. Compensation regarding creation of public rights of way **[395]–[400]**
201. Compensation regarding entry on land **[401]**

PART XIII   AMENITIES

202. Area of special amenity **[402]**
203. Confirmation of order under section 202 **[403]**
204. Landscape conservation areas **[404]**
205. Tree preservation orders **[405]–[410]**
206. Creation of public rights of way agreement **[411]**
207. Compulsory powers for creation of pubic rights of way **[412]**
208. Supplemental provisions with respect to public right of way **[413]**
209. Repair and tidying of advertisement structures and advertisement **[414]**

PART XIV   ACQUISITION OF LAND, ETC.

210. Appropriation of land for local authority purposes **[415]–[420]**
211. Disposal of land by local authority **[421]**
212. Development by planning authority etc **[422]**
213. Land acquisition by local authorities **[423]**
214. Transfer of Minister's functions in relation to compulsory acquisition of land to Board **[424]**
215. Transfer of Ministerial functions under Road Acts 1993 and 1998 to Board **[425]–[430]**
216. Confirmation of compulsory purchase order objections **[431]**
217. Certain time limits in respect of purchase of land. etc **[432]**
218. Oral hearings in relation to compulsory acquisition of land **[433]**
219. Power to direct payment of certain costs in relation to oral hearing **[434]**
220. Certain procedures to run in parallel **[435]–[440]**
221. Objective of the Board in relation to transferred functions **[441]**

222. Amendment of section 10 of Local Government (No. 2) Act, 1960 **[442]**
223. References to transferred function in regulations etc **[443]**

PART XV DEVELOPMENT ON THE FORESHORE

224. Definition **[444]**
225. Obligation to obtain permission in development on foreshore **[445]–[450]**
226. Local authority development on foreshore **[451]**
227. Acquisition of land etc on foreshore **[452]**
228. Entering on foreshore for certain purposes **[453]**

PART XVI EVENTS AND FUNFAIRS

229. Interpretation **[454]**
230. Obligation to obtain a licence for holding of an event **[455]–[460]**
231. Grant of licence **[461]**
232. Codes of practice in relation to events **[462]**
233. Service of notice in relation to events **[463]**
234. General obligations with regard to safety at events **[464]**
235. Powers of inspection in connection with events **[465]–[470]**
236. Limitation of civil proceedings **[471]**
237. Consequential provisions for offences **[472]**
238. Holding of event by local authority **[473]**
239. Control of funfairs **[474]**
240. Exclusion of events and funfairs from planning control **[475]–[480]**
241. Regulations for event **[481]**

PART XVII FINANCIAL PROVISIONS

242. Expenses of administration of Minister **[482]**
243. Charging of expenses of planning authority that is council of a county **[483]**
244. Apportionment of joint expenses of planning **[484]**
245. Power to set-off **[485]–[490]**
246. Fees payable to planning authorities **[491]**

PART XVIII MISCELLANEOUS

247. Consultations in relation to proposed development **[492]**
248. Information to be provided in electronic form **[493]**
249. Additional requirements for public notifications **[494]**
250. Service of notices etc **[495]–[500]**
251. Calculation of appropriate period and other time limits over holidays **[501]**
252. Power of authorised person to enter on land **[502]**
253. Powers of entry in relation to enforcement **[503]**
254. Licensing of appliances and cables, etc., on public roads **[504]**
255. Performance of functions by planning authorities **[505]–[510]**
256. Amendment of Environmental Protection Agency Act, 1992 **[511]**
257. Amendment of Waste Management Act 1996 **[512]**

258. Limitation on connection to sanitary authority   **[513]**
259. Limitation of section 53 of Waterworks Clauses Act 1847   **[514]**
260. Saving for national monuments   **[515]–[520]**
261. Control of quarries   **[521]**
262. Regulations generally   **[522]**

PART XIX   COMMENCEMENT, REPEALS AND CONTINUANCE

263. Interpretation   **[523]**
264. Repeals   **[524]**
265. Continuity of repealed enactments   **[525]–[530]**
266. Transitional provisions regarding development plans   **[531]**
267. Transitional provisions respecting acquisition of land   **[532]**
268. Miscellaneous transitional provisions   **[533]**
269. Regulations to remove difficulties   **[534]**
270. Commencement   **[535]–[540]**

PART XX   AMENDMENTS OF ROADS ACT, 1993

271. Amendment of section 57 of Roads Act, 1993   **[541]**
272. Scheme prepared under section 57 of Roads Act 1993 be adopted by road authority   **[542]**
273. Amendment of section 60 of Roads Act 1993   **[543]**
274. Amendment of section 61 of Roads Act, 1993   **[544]**
275. Amendment of section 63 of Roads Act 1993   **[545]–[550]**
276. Amendment of section 65 of Roads Act 1993   **[551]**
277. Further amendment of Part V of Roads Act 1993   **[552]–[580]**

FIRST SCHEDULE: PURPOSES FOR WHICH OBJECTIVES MAY BE INDICATED IN DEVELOPMENT PLAN

Part I   Location and Pattern of Development   **[581]**
Part II   Control of Areas and Structures   **[582]**
Part III   Community Facilities   **[583]**
Part IV   Environment and Amenities   **[584]**
Part V   Infrastructure and Transport   **[585]–[590]**

SECOND SCHEDULE: RULES FOR THE DETERMINATION OF THE AMOUNT OF COMPENSATION   [591]

THIRD SCHEDULE: DEVELOPMENT IN RESPECT OF WHICH A REFUSAL OF PERMISSION WILL NOT ATTRACT COMPENSATION   [592]

FOURTH SCHEDULE: REASONS FOR THE REFUSAL OF PERMISSION WHICH EXCLUDE COMPENSATION   [593]

FIFTH SCHEDULE: CONDITIONS WHICH MAY BE IMPOSED, ON THE GRANTING OF PERMISSION TO DEVELOP LAND, WITHOUT COMPENSATION   [594]

SIXTH SCHEDULE: ENACTMENTS REPEALED   [595]–[800]

ACTS REFERRED TO

Acquisition of Land (Assessment of Compensation) Act, 1919	9 & 10 Geo. c. 5
Air Pollution Act, 1987	1987, No. 6
Capital Acquisitions Tax Act, 1976	1976, No. 8
Casual Trading Act, 1995	1995, No.19
City and County Management (Amendment) Act, 1955	1955, No. 12
Civil Service Regulation Act, 1956	1956, No. 46
Companies Act, 1963	1963, No. 33
Companies Act, 1990	1990, No. 33
Companies Acts, 1963 to 1999	
County Management Acts, 1940 to 1994	
Derelict Sites Act, 1990	1990, No. 14
Dublin Docklands Development Authority Act, 1997	1997, No. 7
Environmental Protection Agency Act, 1992	1992, No. 7
Ethics in Public Office Act, 1995	1995, No. 22
European Communities Act, 1972	1972, No. 27
European Parliament Elections Act, 1997	1997, No. 2
Foreshore Act, 1933	1933, No. 12
Foreshore Acts, 1933 to 1998	
Freedom of Information Act, 1997	1991, No. 13
Harbours Act, 1946	1946, No. 9
Health Act, 1910	1910, No. 1
Holidays (Employees) Act, 1913	1913, No. 25
Housing Act, 1966	1966, No. 21
Housing Act, 1988	1988, No. 28
Housing Acts, 1966 to 1998	
Housing (Miscellaneous Provisions) Act, 1992	1992, No. 18
Housing of the Working Classes Act, 1890	53 & 54 Vict. c. 10
Housing (Traveller Accommodation) Act, 1998	1998, No. 33
Land Reclamation Act, 1949	1949, No. 25
Landlord and Tenant Acts, 1961 to 1994	
Lands Clauses Consolidation Act, 1845	8 Vita c. 18
Local Authorities (Officers and Employees) Act, 1926	1926, No. 39
Local Government Act, 1925	1925, No. 5
Local Government Act, 1941	1941, No. 23
Local Government Act, 1946	1946, No. 24
Local Government Act, 1955	1955, No. 9
Local Government Act, 1991	1991, No. 11
Local Government Act, 1994	1994, No. 8
Local Government (Ireland) Act, 1898	61 & 62 Vict. c. 31
Local Government (No. 2) Act, 1960	1960, No. 40
Local Government (Planning and Development) Act, 1963	1963, No. 28
Local Government (Planning and Development) Act, 1976	1976, No. 20
Local Government (Planning and Development) Act, 1982	1982, No. 21
Local Government (Planning and Development) Act, 1983	1983, No. 28
Local Government (Planning and Development) Act, 1990	1990, No. 11
Local Government (Planning and Development) Act, 1992	1992, No. 14

Local Government (Planning and Development) Act, 1993	1993, No. 12
Local Government (Planning and Development) Act, 1998	1998, No. 9
Local Government (Planning and Development) Act, 1999	1999, No. 11
Local Government (Planning and Development) Acts, 1963 to 1999	
Local Government (Sanitary Services) Act, 1962	1962, No. 26
Local Government (Sanitary Services) Act, 1964	1964, No. 29
Local Government (Sanitary Services) Acts, 1818 to 1995	
Local Government (Water Pollution) Act, 1911	1977, No. I
Mines and Quarries Act, 1965	1965, No. 7
Ministers and Secretaries (Amendment) Act, 1956	1956, No. 21
National Monuments Acts, 1930 to 1994	
National Monuments (Amendment) Act, 1987	1987, No. 17
Petty Sessions (Ireland) Act, 1851	14 & 15 Vict. c. 93
Property Values (Arbitration and Appeals) Act, 1960	1960, No. 45
Public Health (Ireland) Act, 1878	41 & 42 Vict. c. 52
Registration of Title Act, 1964	1964, No. 16
Roads Act, 1993	1993, No. 14
Roads Acts, 1993 and 1998	
Roads (Amendment) Act, 1998	1998, No. 23
State Property Act, 1954	1954, No. 25
Town and Regional Planning Act, 1934	1934, No. 22
Urban Renewal Act, 1998	1998, No. 27
Vocational Education Act, 1930	1930, No. 29
Waste Management Act, 1996	1996, No. 10
Water Supplies Act, 1942	1942, No. I
Waterworks Clauses Act, 1841	10 & 11 Vict. c. 17
Wildlife Act, 1916	1916, No. 39

PLANNING AND DEVELOPMENT ACT, 2000

AN ACT TO REVISE AND CONSOLIDATE THE LAW RELATING TO PLAN-NING AND DEVELOPMENT BY REPEALING AND RE-ENACTING WITH AMENDMENTS THE LOCAL GOVERNMENT (PLANNING AND DEVELOP-MENT) ACTS, 1963 TO 1999; TO PROVIDE, IN THE INTERESTS OF THE COMMON GOOD, FOR PROPER PLANNING AND SUSTAINABLE DEVEL-OPMENT INCLUDING THE PROVISION OF HOUSING; TO PROVIDE FOR THE LICENSING OF EVENTS AND CONTROL OF FUNFAIRS; TO AMEND THE ENVIRONMENTAL PROTECTION AGENCY ACT, 1992, THE ROADS ACT, 1993, THE WASTE MANAGEMENT ACT, 1996, AND CERTAIN OTHER ENACTMENTS; AND TO PROVIDE FOR MATTERS CONNECTED THERE-WITH. [28th August, 2000]

BE IT ENACTED BY THE OIREACHTAS AS FOLLOWS:

PART I   PRELIMINARY AND GENERAL

[1]
1. Short title
This Act may be cited as the Planning and Development Act.

[2]
2. Interpretation
(1) In this Act, except where the context otherwise requires

"acquisition of land" shall be construed in accordance with section 213(2), and cog-nate words shall be construed accordingly;

"the Act of 1919" means the Acquisition of Land (Assessment of Compensation) Act, 1919;

"the Act of 1934" means the Town and Regional Planning Act, 1934;

"the Act of 1963" means the Local Government (Planning and Development) Act, 1963;

"the Act of 1976" means the Local Government (Planning and Development) Act, 1976;

"the Act of 1982" means the Local Government (Planning and Development) Act, 1982;

"the Act of 1983" means the Local Government (Planning and Development) Act, 1983;

"the Act of 1990" means the Local Government (Planning and Development) Act, 1990;

"the Act of 1992" means the Local Government (Planning and Development) Act, 1992;

"the Act of 1993" means the Local Government (Planning and Development) Act, 1993;

"the Act of 1998" means the Local Government (Planning and Development) Act, 1998;

"the Act of 1999" means the Local Government (Planning and Development) Act, 1999;

"advertisement" means any word, letter, model, balloon, inflatable structure, kite, poster, notice, device or representation employed for the purpose of advertisement, announcement or direction;

"advertisement structure" means any structure which is a hoarding, scaffold, framework, pole, standard, device or sign (whether illuminated or not) and which is used or intended for use for exhibiting advertisements or any attachment to a building or structure used for advertising purposes;

"agriculture" includes horticulture, fruit growing, seed growing, dairy farming, the breeding and keeping of livestock (including any creature kept for the production of food, wool, skins or fur, or for the purpose of its use in the farming of land), the training of horses and the rearing of bloodstock, the use of land as grazing land, meadow land, osier land, market gardens and nursery grounds, and "agricultural" shall be construed accordingly;

"alteration" includes—

(a)   plastering or painting or the removal of plaster or stucco, or

(b)   the replacement of a door, window or roof,

that materially alters the external appearance of a structure so as to render the appearance inconsistent with the character of the structure or neighbouring structures;

"appeal" means an appeal to the Board;

"architectural conservation area" shall be construed in accordance with section 81(1);

"area of special planning control" shall be construed in accordance with section 85(8);

"attendant grounds", in relation to a structure, includes land lying outside the cartilage of the structure;

"the Birds Directive" means Council Directive No. 79/409/EEC of 2 April 1979[1] on the conservation of wild birds;

"Board" means An Bord Pleanála;

"chairperson" means the chairperson of the Board;

"Commissioners" means the Commissioners of Public Works in Ireland;

"company", except in section 149(5), means a company within the meaning of section 2 of the Companies Act, 1963, or a company incorporated outside the State;

"Council Directive" means Council Directive No. 85/337/EEC of 27 June 1985[2] on the assessment of the effects of certain public and private projects on the environment, as amended by Council Directive No. 97/11/EC of 3 March 1997[3] and any directive amending or replacing those directives;

"dangerous substance" has the meaning assigned to it by the Major Accidents Directive;

14

"deputy chairperson" means the deputy chairperson of the Board;

"development" has the meaning assigned to it by section 3, and "develop" shall be construed accordingly;

"development plan" means a development plan under section 9(1);

"endangered" means exposed to harm, decay or damage, whether immediately or over a period of time, through neglect or through direct or indirect means;

"enforcement notice" means an enforcement notice under section 154;

"environmental impact statement" means a statement of the effects, if any, which proposed development, if carried out, would have on the environment;

"European site" means—

    (a) a site—

        (i) notified for the purposes of Regulation 4 of the European Communities (Natural Habitats) Regulations, 1997 (S.I. No. 94 of 1997), subject to any amendments made to it by virtue of Regulation 5 of those regulations, or

        (ii) transmitted to the Commission in accordance with Regulation 5(4) of the said regulations, or

        (iii) added by virtue of Regulation 6 of the said regulations to the list transmitted to the Commission in accordance with Regulation 5 (4) of the said Regulations,

      but only until the adoption in respect of the site of a decision by the Commission under Article 21 of the Habitats Directive for the purposes of the third paragraph of Article 4(2) of that Directive,

    (b) a site adopted by the Commission as a site of Community importance for the purposes of Article 4(2) of the Habitats Directive in accordance with the procedure laid down in Article 21 of that Directive,

    (c) a special area of conservation within the meaning of the European Communities (Natural Habitats) Regulations, 1997,

    (d) an area classified pursuant to paragraph (1) or (2) of Article 4 of the Birds Directive;

"exempted development" has the meaning specified in section 4;

"exhibit", in relation to an advertisement, includes affix, inscribe, print, paint, illuminate and otherwise delineate;

"existing establishment" has the meaning that it has in the Major Accidents Directive;

"fence" includes a hoarding or similar structure but excludes any bank, wall or other similar structure composed wholly or mainly of earth or stone;

"functional area" means, in relation to a planning authority—

    (a) in the case of the council of a county, its administrative county, excluding any borough or urban district,

    (b) in the case of any other planning authority, its administrative area;

"functions" includes powers and duties;

"Gaeltacht" means the Gaeltacht within the meaning of the Ministers and Secretaries (Amendment) Act, 1956;

"habitable house" means a house which—

(a) is used as a dwelling,

(b) is not in use but when last used was used, disregarding any unauthorised use, as a dwelling and is not derelict, or

(c) was provided for use as a dwelling but has not been occupied;

"Habitats Directive" means Council Directive No. 92/43/EEC of 21 May 1992[4] on the conservation of natural habitats and of wild fauna and flora;

"house" means a building or part of a building which is being or has been occupied as a dwelling or was provided for use as a dwelling but has not been occupied, and where appropriate, includes a building which was designed for use as 2 or more dwellings or a flat, an apartment or other dwelling within such a building;

"integrated pollution control licence" means a licence under Part IV of the Environmental Protection Agency Act, 1992;

"land" includes any structure and any land covered with water (whether inland or coastal);

"local area plan" means a local area plan under section 18;

"local authority" means a local authority for the purposes of the Local Government Act, 1941;

"major accident" has the meaning assigned to it by the Major Accidents Directive;

"Major Accidents Directive" means Council Directive 96/82/EC of 9 December 1996[5] on the control of major accident hazards involving dangerous substances;

"manager" means—

(a) with respect to the corporation of a county borough, the manager for the purpose of the Acts relating to the management of the county borough, and

(b) with respect to the council of a county, the corporation of a borough or an urban district council, the manager for the purposes of the County Management Acts, 1940 to 1994;

"Minister" means the Minister for the Environment and Local Government;

"new establishment" has the meaning that it has in the Major Accidents Directive;

"occupier", in relation to a protected structure or a proposed protected structure, means—

(a) any person in or entitled to immediate use or enjoyment of the structure,

(b) any person entitled to occupy the structure, and

(c) any other person having, for the time being, control of the structure;

"ordinary member" means a member of the Board other than the chairperson;

"owner", in relation to land, means a person, other than a mortgagee not in possession, who, whether in his or her own right or as trustee or agent for any other person, is entitled to receive the rack rent of the land or, where the land is not let at a rack rent, would be so entitled if it were so let;

"party to an appeal or referral" means the planning authority and any of the following persons, as appropriate—

(a) the appellant,

(b) the applicant for any permission in relation to which an appeal is made by another person (other than a person acting on behalf of the appellant),

(c) in the case of a referral under section 5, the person making the referral, and any other person notified under subsection (2) of that section,

(d) in the case of a referral under section 34(5), the applicant for the permission which was granted,

(e) in the case of a referral under section 37(5), the person who made the application for permission which was returned by the planning authority,

(f) any person served or issued by a planning authority with a notice or order, or copy thereof, under sections 44, 45, 46, 88 and 207,

(g) in the case of a referral under section 96(5), a prospective party to an agreement under section 96(2),

(h) in the case of an appeal under section 169, the development agency,

(i) in the case of a referral under section 193, the person by whom the application for permission for erection of the new structure was made,

(j) the applicant for a licence under section 254 in relation to which an appeal is made by another person (other than a person acting on behalf of the appellant),

and "party" shall be construed accordingly;

"permission regulations" means regulations under section 33, 172(2) or 174;

"planning application" means an application to a planning authority in accordance with permission regulations for permission for the development of land required by those regulations;

"planning authority" means—

(a) in the case of a county, exclusive of any borough or urban district therein, the council of the county,

(b) in the case of a county or other borough, the corporation of the borough, and

(c) in the case of an urban district, the council of the urban district,

and references to the area of the planning authority shall be construed accordingly and shall include the functional area of the authority;

"prescribed" means prescribed by regulations made by the Minister and "prescribe" shall be construed accordingly;

"proposed protected structure" means a structure in respect of which a notice is issued under section 12(3) or under section 55 proposing to add the structure, or a specified part of it, to a record of protected structures, and, where that notice so indicates, includes any specified feature which is within the attendant grounds of the structure and which would not otherwise be included in this definition;

"protected structure" means—

(a) a structure, or

(b) a specified part of a structure,

which is included in a record of protected structures, and, where that record so indicates, includes any specified feature which is within the attendant grounds of the structure and which would not otherwise be included in this definition;

"protection", in relation to a structure or part of a structure, includes conservation, preservation and improvement compatible with maintaining the character and interest of the structure or part;

"public place" means any street, road, seashore or other place to which the public have access whether as of right or by permission and whether subject to or free of charge;

"public road" has the same meaning as in the Roads Act, 1993;

"record of protected structures" means the record included under section 51 in a development plan;

"referral" means a referral to the Board under section 5, 34(5), 37(5), 96(5) or 193(2);

"regional authority" means a body established in accordance with section 43 of the Local Government Act, 1991;

"regional planning guidelines" means regional planning guidelines made under Chapter III of Part II;

"register" means the register kept under section 7;

"registering authority" means a registering authority within the meaning of the Registration of Title Act, 1964;

"reserved function" means—

(a) with respect to the council of a county or an elective body for the purposes of the County Management Acts, 1940 to 1994, a reserved function for the purposes of those Acts, and

(b) with respect to the corporation of a county borough, a reserved function for the purposes of the Acts relating to the management of the county borough;

"risk" has the meaning assigned to it by the Major Accidents Directive;

"road" has the same meaning as in the Roads Act, 1993;

"seashore" has the same meaning as in the Foreshore Act, 1933;

"shares" includes stock and "share capital" shall be construed accordingly;

"special amenity area order" means an order confirmed under section 203;

"State authority" means—

(a) a Minister of the Government, or

(b) the Commissioners;

"statutory undertaker" means a person, for the time being, authorised by or under any enactment or instrument under an enactment to—

(a) construct or operate a railway, canal, inland navigation, dock, harbour or airport,

(b) provide, or carry out works for the provision of, gas, electricity or telecommunications services, or

(c) provide services connected with, or carry out works for the purposes of the carrying on of the activities of, any public undertaking;

"structure" means any building, structure, excavation, or other thing constructed or made on, in or under any land, or any part of a structure so defined, and

(a) where the context so admits, includes the land on, in or under which the structure is situate, and

(b) in relation to a protected structure or proposed protected structure, includes—
   (i) the interior of the structure,
   (ii) the land lying within the curtilage of the structure,
   (iii) any other structures lying within that curtilage and their interiors, and
   (iv) all fixtures and features which form part of the interior or exterior of any structure or structures referred to in subparagraph (i) or (iii);

"substratum of land" means any subsoil or anything beneath the surface of land required—

(a) for the purposes of a tunnel or tunnelling or anything connected therewith, or

(b) for any other purpose connected with a scheme within the meaning of the Roads Act, 1993;

"Transboundary Convention" means the United Nations Economic Commission for Europe Convention on Environmental Impact Assessment in a Transboundary Context, done at Espoo (Finland), on 25 February, 1991;

"traveller" means a traveller within the meaning of section 2 of the Housing (Traveller Accommodation) Act, 1998;

"unauthorised development" means, in relation to land, the carrying out of any unauthorised works (including the construction, erection or making of any unauthorised structure) or the making of any unauthorised use;

"unauthorised structure" means a structure other than—

(a) a structure which was in existence on 1 October 1964, or

(b) a structure, the construction, erection or making of which was the subject of a permission for development granted under Part IV of the Act of 1963 or deemed to be such under section 92 of that Act or under section 34 of this Act, being a permission which has not been revoked, or which exists as a result of the carrying out of exempted development (within the meaning of section 4 of the Act of 1963 or section 4 of this Act);

"unauthorised use" means, in relation to land, use commenced on or after 1 October 1964, being a use which is a material change in use of any structure or other land and being development other than—

(a) exempted development (within the meaning of section 4 of the Act of 1963 or section 4 of this Act), or

(b) development which is the subject of a permission granted under Part IV of the Act of 1963 or under section 34 of this Act, being a permission which has not been revoked,

and which is carried out in compliance with that permission or any condition to which that permission is subject;

"unauthorised works" means any works on, in, over or under land commenced on or after 1 October 1964, being development other than—

(a) exempted development (within the meaning of section 4 of the Act of 1963 or section 4 of this Act), or

(b) development which is the subject of a permission granted under Part IV of the Act of 1963 or under section 34 of this Act, being a permission which has not been revoked, and which is carried out in compliance with that permission or any condition to which that permission is subject;

"use", in relation to land, does not include the use of the land by the carrying out of any works thereon;

"warning letter" means a notification in writing under section 152(1);

"waste licence" means a waste licence under Part V of the Waste Management Act, 1996;

"works" includes any act or operation of construction, excavation, demolition, extension, alteration, repair or renewal and, in relation to a protected structure or proposed protected structure, includes any act or operation involving the application or removal of plaster, paint, wallpaper, tiles or other material to or from the surfaces of the interior or exterior of a structure.

(2) In this Act—

(a) a reference to a section, Schedule, Chapter or Part is to a section, Schedule, Chapter or Part of this Act, unless it is indicated that reference to some other enactment is intended, and

(b) a reference to a subsection, paragraph or subparagraph is to the subsection, paragraph or subparagraph of the provision in which the reference occurs, unless it is indicated that reference to some other provision is intended.

(3) In this Act, a reference to the carrying out of development on behalf of a State authority shall, where that authority is a Minister of the Government, be construed as including a reference to the carrying out of development by the Commissioners on behalf of the Minister.

(4) A reference in this Act to contravention of a provision includes, where appropriate, a reference to refusal or failure to comply with that provision.

(5) A reference in this Act to performance of functions includes a reference to the exercise of powers and the performance of duties.

(6) A reference in this Act to any other enactment shall, except where the context otherwise requires, be construed as a reference to that enactment as amended by or under any other enactment, including this Act.

(7) The doing of anything that is required under this Act to be done by resolution shall be a reserved function.

Notes

There are 92 defined terms in this section. A considerable number of these terms are new, at least to planning legislation. Some of these newly defined terms in this section have previously been defined in other, related, legislation, or in the body of planning legislation but are nevertheless new to the interpretation section. The following terms are new to the interpretation section of planning legislation:

Acquisition of land;
Area of special planning control;
The Birds Directive;
Council Directive;
Dangerous substances;
Enforcement notice;
Environmental Impact Statement;
European Site;
Foreshore;
Functional area;
Gaeltacht;
Habitats Directive;
House;
Integrated Pollution Control Licence;
Local area plan;
Manager;
Permission Regulations;
Referral;
Regional authority;
Regional planning guidelines;
Risk;
Special Immunity Area Order;
Sub-stratum of land;
Trans-boundary convention;
Traveller;
Unauthorised development;
Unauthorised structure;
Unauthorised use;
Unauthorised works;
Warning letter;
Waste Licence;

The following definitions have appeared in interpretation sections of planning legislation previously, but have now been amended as detailed:

'Advertisement structure' – The words '. . . or any attachment to a building or structure used for advertising purposes' are added.

'Agriculture' – This definition no longer includes turbary and forestry. The training of horses and the rearing of bloodstock have been added. (See Exempted Development at s 4 below.)

'Alteration' – (b) is added.

'Architectural conservation area' – Amended from s 1 of LG(PD)A 1992. Section 81(1) of the PDA 2000 amends the previous definition by the insertion of the words at s 81(1) of 'a development plan shall include an objective to preserve the character of . . .'.

'Company' – The words 'except in Section 149(5)' added to original definition, s 1 of LG(PD)A 1976.

'Development' – See s 3 below.

'Development plan' – Newly defined from interpretation in LG(PD)A 1963, s 19(9)(a) and (b).

'Exempted development' – See s 4 below.

'Exhibit' – Word 'illuminate' added from LG(PD)A 1963.

'Fence' – Additional words added as follows '. . . but excludes any bank, wall or other similar structure composed wholly or mainly of earth or stone' from LG (PD)A 1963 interpretation.

'Habitable House' – Now excludes a derelict house.

'Land' – The definition no longer includes the acquisition of land, as is contained in the interpretation under the LG(PD)A 1963.

'Party to an appeal or referral' – Words 'or referral' added to interpretation contained in s 1 of the LG(PD)A 1992. (a)-(j) inclusive represent revised wording.

'Reserved function' – The words in s (a) '1940 to 1944' and 'of those Acts' are added.

'State authority' – The interpretation here does not include the detail contained in the definition that first appeared in the LG(PD)A 1993.

'Statutory Undertaker' – This has been extended to include bodies carrying out telecommunications works.

'Structure' – Minor alternations from definition contained in LG(PD)A 1963 and LG(PD)A 1999, the interpretation now refers to Protected Structure and a Proposed Protected Structure, as defined.

'Works' – The following words have been added to the definition in LG(PD)A 1963 '. . . and, in relation to a protected structure or proposed protected structure includes any act or operation involving the application or removal of plaster, paint, wallpaper, tiles or other material to or from the surface of the interior or exterior of a structure'.

1 OJ L103, 25.4.1979, p 1.
2 OJ L175, 5.7.1985, p 40.
3 OJ L73, 14.3.1997, p 5.
4 OJ L206, 22.7.1992, p 7.
5 OJ L10, 14.1.1997, p 13.

[3]
3. Development

(1) In this Act, "development" means, except where the context otherwise requires, the carrying out of any works on, in, over or under land or the making of any material change in the use of any structures or other land.

(2) For the purposes of subsection (1) and without prejudice to the generality of that subsection—

(a) where any structure or other land or any tree or other object on land becomes used for the exhibition of advertisements, or
(b) where land becomes used for any of the following purposes—
  (i) the placing or keeping of any vans, rents or other objects, whether or not moveable and whether or not collapsible, for the purpose of caravanning or camping or habitation or the sale of goods,
  (ii) the storage of caravans or tents, or
  (iii) the deposit of vehicles whether or not usable for the purpose for which they were constructed or last used, old metal, mining or industrial waste, builders' waste, rubbish or debris,

the use of the land shall be taken as having materially changed.

(3) For the avoidance of doubt, it is hereby declared that, for the purposes of this section, the use as two or more dwellings of any house previously used as a single dwelling involves a material change in the use of the structure and of each part thereof which is so used.

Note

Section 3(1)
This is a restatement of s 3(1) of LG(PD)A 1963 save for the addition of the word 'over' as well as on, in and under land.

[4]
4. Exempted development
(1) The following shall be exempted developments for the purposes of this Act—

(a) development consisting of the use of any land for the purpose of agriculture and development consisting of the use for that purpose of any building occupied together with land so used;

(b) development by the council of a county in its functional area, exclusive of any borough or urban district;

(c) development by the corporation of a county or other borough in that borough;

(d) development by the council of an urban district in that district;

(e) development consisting of the carrying out by the corporation of a county or other borough or the council of a county or an urban district of any works required for the construction of a new road or the maintenance or improvement of a road;

(f) development carried out on behalf of, or jointly or in partnership with, a local authority that is a planning authority, pursuant to a contract entered into by the local authority concerned, whether in its capacity as a planning authority or in any other capacity;

(g) development consisting of the carrying out by any local authority or statutory undertaker of any works for the purpose of inspecting, repairing, renewing, altering or removing any sewers, mains, pipes, cables, overhead wires, or other apparatus, including the excavation of any street or other land for that purpose;

(h) development consisting of the carrying out of works for the maintenance, improvement or other alteration of any structure, being works which affect only the interior of the structure or which do not materially affect the external appearance of the structure so as to render the appearance inconsistent with the character of the structure or of neighbouring structures;

(i) development consisting of the thinning, felling and replanting of trees, forests and woodlands, the construction, maintenance and improvement of non-public roads serving forests and woodlands and works ancillary to that development, not including the replacement of broadleaf high forest by conifer species;

(j) development consisting of the use of any structure or other land within the cartilage of a house for any purpose incidental to the enjoyment of the house as such;

(k) development consisting of the use of land for the purposes of a casual trading area (within the meaning of the Casual Trading Act, 1995);

(l) development consisting of the carrying out of any of the works referred to in the Land Reclamation Act, 1949, not being works comprised in the fencing or enclosure of land which has been open to or used by the public within the ten years preceding the date on which the works are commenced

(2) (a) The Minister may by regulations provide for any class of development to be exempted development for the purposes of this Act where he or she is of the opinion that—

   (i) by reason of the size, nature or limited effect on its surroundings, of development belonging to that class, the carrying out of such development would not offend against principles of proper planning and sustainable development, or

   (ii) the development is authorised, or is required to be authorised, by or under any enactment (whether the authorisation takes the form of the grant of a licence, consent, approval or any other type of authorisation) where the enactment concerned requires there to be consultation (howsoever described) with members of the public in relation to the proposed development prior to the granting of the authorisation (howsoever described).

(b) Regulations under paragraph (a) may be subject to conditions and be of general application or apply to such area or place as may be specified in the regulations.

(c) Regulations under this subsection may, in particular and without prejudice to the generality of paragraph (a), provide, in the case of structures or other land used for a purpose of any specified class, for the use thereof for any other purpose being exempted development for the purposes of this Act.

(3) A reference in this Act to exempted development shall be construed as a reference to development which is—

(a) any of the developments specified in subsection (1), or

(b) development which, having regard to any regulations under subsection (2), is exempted development for the purposes of this Act.

(4) The Minister may, in connection with the Council Directive, prescribe development or classes of development which, notwithstanding subsection (1)(a), shall not be exempted development.

(5) Before making regulations under this section, the Minister shall consult with any other State authority where he or she or that other State authority considers that any such regulation relates to the functions of that State authority.

Notes

This section restates s 4 of LG(PD)A 1963. In addition, some significant changes have been made as follows:

(a) As the definition of 'agriculture' no longer includes reference to turbary and forestry, these activities are no longer exempt. However, the felling, filling and maintenance of forests and woodlands are exempt by virtue of (i).

(b) As the definition of 'agriculture' now includes the training of horses and the rearing of blood stock, these two activities are exempted development, s 4(1)(a).

(c) Development by a planning authority within its own functional area is exempt from the requirement to seek planning permission, although it is subject to the requirements of public notification as set out in s 155: see s 4(1)(f). This includes development carried out 'in partnership with' a local authority.

(d) One set of regulations have to date been issued:

LG(PD)R 2000, SI 181/2000 which exempt development within the curtilege of a dwelling house area where same does not exceed 40 sq. mtrs. subject to other stated conditions and limitations.

(e) Further regulations replacing SI 86/1994, SI 69/1995 and SI 100/1996 are awaited and in the meantime, these regulations remain in force.

[5]–[10]
5. Declaration and referral on development and exempted development
(1) If any question arises as to what, in any particular case, is or is not development or is or is not exempted development within the meaning of this Act, any person may, on payment of the prescribed fee, request in writing from the relevant planning authority a declaration on that question, and that person shall provide to the planning authority any information necessary to enable the authority to make its decision on the matter.

(2) (a) Subject to paragraph (b), a planning authority shall issue the declaration on the question that has arisen and the main reasons and considerations on which its decision is based to the person who made the request under subsection (1), and, where appropriate, the owner and occupier of the land in question, within 4 weeks of the receipt of the request.

(b) A planning authority may require any person who made a request under subsection (1) to submit further information with regard to the request in order to enable the authority to issue the declaration on the question and, where further information is received under this paragraph, the planning authority shall issue the declaration within 3 weeks of the date of the receipt of the further information.

(c) A planning authority may also request persons in addition to those referred to in paragraph (b) to submit information in order to enable the authority to issue the declaration on the question.

(3) (a) Where a declaration is issued under this section, any person issued with a declaration under subsection (2)(a) may, on payment to the Board of such fee as may be prescribed, refer a declaration for review by the Board within 4 weeks of the date of the issuing of the declaration.

(b) Without prejudice to subsection (2), in the event that no declaration is issued by the planning authority, any person who made a request under subsection (1) may, on payment to the Board of such fee as may be prescribed, refer the question for decision to the Board within 4 weeks of the date that a declaration was due to be issued under subsection (2).

(4) Notwithstanding subsection (1), a planning authority may, on payment to the Board of such fee as may be prescribed, refer any question as to what, in any particular case, is or is not development or is or is not exempted development to be decided by the Board.

(5) The details of any declaration issued by a planning authority or of a decision by the Board on a referral under this section shall be entered in the register.

(6) (a) The Board shall keep a record of any decision made by it on a referral under this section and the main reasons and considerations on which its decision is based and shall make it available for purchase and inspection.

(b) The Board may charge a specified fee, not exceeding the cost of making the copy, for the purchase of a copy of the record referred to in paragraph (a).

(c) The Board shall, from time to time and at least once a year, forward to each planning authority a copy of the record referred to in paragraph (a)

(d) A copy of the said record shall, at the request of a member of a planning authority, be given to that member by the manager of the planning authority concerned.

(7) A planning authority, before making a declaration under this section, shall consider the record forwarded to it in accordance with subsection (6)(c).

Note
This provision replaces s 5 of LG(PD)A 1963, with significant changes. A declaration can now be sought from the planning authority in the first instance as to whether or not development is exempted. A referral may be made to An Bord Pleanála where there is disagreement on the planning authority's declaration.

[11]
6. Power of examination, investigation and survey
A planning authority and the Board shall each have all such powers of examination, investigation and survey as may be necessary and for the performance of their functions in relation to this Act or to any other Act.

Note
This section restates s 6 of LG(PD)A 1963.

[12]
7. Planning register
(1) A planning authority shall keep a register for the purposes of this Act in respect of all land within its functional area, and shall make all such entries and corrections therein as may be appropriate in accordance with subsection (2), and the other provisions of this Act and the regulations made under this Act.

(2) A planning authority shall enter in the register—

(a) particulars of any application made to it under this Act for permission for development, for retention of development or for outline permission for development (including the name and address of the applicant, the date of receipt of the application and brief particulars of the development or retention forming the subject of the application),

(b) where an environmental impact statement was submitted in respect of an application, an indication of this fact,

(c) where a development, to which an application relates, comprises or is for the purposes of an activity in respect of which an integrated pollution control licence or a waste management licence is required, or a licence under the Local Government (Water Pollution) Act, 1977, is required in respect of discharges from the development, a statement as to that requirement,

(d) where the development to which the application relates would materially affect a protected structure or is situated in an area declared to be an area of special amenity under section 202, an indication of this fact,

(e) the complete decision of the planning authority in respect of any such application, including any conditions imposed, and the date of the decision, the complete decision on appeal of the Board in respect of any such application, including any conditions imposed, and the date of the decision,

(g) where the requirements of section 34(6) in regard to the material contravention of the development plan have been complied with, a statement of this fact,

(h) particulars of any declaration made by a planning authority under section 5 or any decision made by the Board on a referral under that section,

(i) particulars of any application made under section 42 to extend the appropriate period of a permission,

(j) particulars of any decision to revoke or modify a permission in accordance with section 44,

(k) particulars under section 45 of any order, of any decision on appeal or of any acquisition notice for compulsory acquisition of land for open space,

(l) particulars of any notice under section 46 requiring removal or alteration of any structure, or requiring discontinuance of any use or the imposition of conditions on the continuance thereof, including the fact of its withdrawal, if appropriate,

(m) particulars of any agreement made under section 47 for the purpose of restricting or regulating the development or use of the land,

(n) particulars of any declaration issued by the planning authority under section 57, including the details of any review of the declaration,

(o) particulars of any declaration issued by the planning authority under section 87, including the details of any review of the declaration,

(p) particulars of any notice under section 88 in respect of land in an area of special planning control, including, where such notice is withdrawn, the fact of its withdrawal.

(q) particulars of any certificate granted under section 97,

(r) particulars of any warning letter issued under section 152, including the date of issue of the letter and the fact of its withdrawal, if appropriate,

(s) the complete decision made under section 153 on whether an enforcement notice should issue, including the date of the decision,

(t) particulars of any enforcement notice issued under section 154, including the date of the notice and the fact of its withdrawal or that it has been complied with, if appropriate,

(u) particulars of any statement prepared under section 138 concerning a claim for compensation under this Act,

(v) particulars of any order under section 205 requiring the preservation of any tree or trees, including the fact of any amendment or revocation of the order,

(w) particulars of any agreement under section 206 for the creation of a public right of way over land,

(x) particulars of any public right of way created by order under section 207,

(y) particulars of any information relating to the operation of a quarry provided in accordance with section 261, and

(z) any other matters as may be prescribed by the Minister.

(3) The planning authority shall make the entries and corrections as soon as may be after the receipt of any application, the making of any decision or agreement or the issue of any letter, notice or statement, as appropriate.

(4) The register shall incorporate a map for enabling a person to trace any entry in the register.

(5) The planning authority may keep the information on the register, including the map incorporated under subsection (4), in a form in which it is capable of being used to make a legible copy or reproduction of any entry in the register.

(6) (a)   The register shall be kept at the offices of the planning authority and shall be available for inspection during office hours.
(b)   The Minister may prescribe additional requirements in relation to the availability for inspection by members of the public of the register.

(7) Every document purporting to be a copy of an entry in a register maintained by a planning authority under this section and purporting to be certified by an officer of the planning authority to be a true copy of the entry shall, without proof of the signature of the person purporting so to certify or that he or she was such an officer, be received in evidence in any legal proceedings and shall, until the contrary is proved, be deemed to be a true copy of the entry and to be evidence of the terms of the entry.

(8) Evidence of an entry in a register under this section may be given by production of a copy thereof certified pursuant to this section and it shall not be necessary to produce the register itself.

(9) Where an application is made to a planning authority for a copy under this section, the copy shall be issued to the applicant on payment by him or her to the planning authority of the specified fee in respect of each entry.

Note
This section restates with amendments ss 8 and 41 of LG(PD)A 1963. There are additional matters now required to be maintained in the planning register. The register can now be kept in electronic form.

[13]
8. Obligation to give information to local authority
(1) A local authority may, for any purpose arising in relation to its functions under this Act or any other enactment, by notice in writing require the occupier of any structure or other land or any person receiving, whether for himself or herself or for another, rent out of any structure or other land to state in writing to the authority, within a specified time not less than 2 weeks after being so required, particulars of the estate, interest, or right by virtue of which he or she occupies the structure or other land or receives the rent, as the case may be, and the name and address (so far as they are known to him or her) of every person who to his or her knowledge has any estate or interest in, or right over, or in respect of, the structure or other land.

(2) Every person who is required under this section to state in writing any matter or thing to a local authority and either fails so to state the matter or thing within the time appointed under this section or, when so stating any such matter or thing, makes any

statement in writing which is to his or her knowledge false or misleading in a material respect, shall be guilty of an offence.

Note
This section restates s 9 of LG(PD)A 1963.

PART II   PLANS AND GUIDELINES

Note
Part II provides for the making of the development plan and provides for local area plans and regional planning guidelines. It also details the powers of the Minister to issue policy directives and guidelines on planning matters. All of Pt II is now in force.

CHAPTER I   DEVELOPMENT PLANS

[14]
9. Obligation to make development plan
(1) Every planning authority shall every 6 years make a development plan.

(2) Subject to subsection (3), a development plan shall relate to the whole functional area of the authority.

(3) (a) A planning authority which is a county borough corporation, a borough corporation or an urban district council may, with the agreement of one or more planning authorities which are adjoining county councils, or on the direction of the Minister shall, make a single development plan for the area and the environs of the county borough, borough or urban district, as the case may be.
   (b) Where it is proposed to make a development plan under paragraph (a), the planning authorities concerned shall make whatever arrangements they see fit to prepare the plan including the carrying out of the requirements of this Chapter as a joint function of the authorities concerned (and this Chapter shall be construed accordingly) except that where decisions are reserved to the members of the planning authorities concerned the decisions must be made by the members of each authority concerned subject to any agreement which those authorities may make for the resolution of differences between any such reserved decisions.

(4) In making a development plan in accordance with this Chapter, a planning authority shall have regard to the development plans of adjoining planning authorities and shall co-ordinate the objectives in the development plan with the objectives in the plans of those authorities except where the planning authority considers it to be inappropriate or not feasible to do so.

(5) In making a development plan in accordance with this Chapter, a planning authority shall take into account any significant likely effects the implementation of the plan may have on the area of any adjoining planning authority having regard in particular to any observations or submissions made by the adjoining authority.

(6) A development plan shall in so far as is practicable be consistent with such national plans, policies or strategies as the Minister determines relate to proper planning and sustainable development.

(7) (a) The Minister may require 2 or more planning authorities to co-ordinate the development plans for their areas generally or in respect of specified matters and in a manner specified by the Minister.

(b) Any dispute between the planning authorities in question arising out of the requirement under paragraph (a) shall be determined by the Minister.

Notes
Section 9(1)
This section amends s 19(1) of the LG(PD)A 1963.

Section 9(4), (5)
Regard must now be had to the development plans of adjoining planning authorities. This is an attempt at a more integrated planning policy.

[15]–[20]
10. Content of development plans

(1) A development plan shall set out an overall strategy for the proper planning and sustainable development of the area of the development plan and shall consist of a written statement and a plan or plans indicating the development objectives for the area in question.

(2) Without prejudice to the generality of subsection (1), a development plan shall include objectives for—

(a) the zoning of land for the use solely or primarily of particular areas for particular purposes (whether residential, commercial, industrial, agricultural, recreational, as open space or otherwise, or a mixture of those uses), where and to such extent as the proper planning and sustainable development of the area, in the opinion of the planning authority, requires the uses to be indicated;

(b) the provision or facilitation of the provision of infrastructure including transport, energy and communication facilities, water supplies, waste recovery and disposal facilities (regard having been had to the waste management plan for the area made in accordance with the Waste Management Act, 1996), waste water services, and ancillary facilities;

(c) the conservation and protection of the environment including, in particular, the archaeological and natural heritage and the conservation and protection of European sites and any other sites which may be prescribed for the purposes of this paragraph:

(d) the integration of the planning and sustainable development of the area with the social, community and cultural requirements of the area and its population;

(e) the preservation of the character of the landscape where, and to the extent that, in the opinion of the planning authority, the proper planning and sustainable development of the area requires it, including the preservation of views and prospects and the amenities of places and features of natural beauty or interest;

(f) the protection of structures, or parts of structures, which are of special architectural, historical, archaeological, artistic, cultural, scientific, social or technical interest;

(g) the preservation of the character of architectural conservation areas;

(h) the development and renewal of areas in need of regeneration;

(i) the provision of accommodation for travellers, and the use of particular areas for that purpose;

(j)   the preservation, improvement and extension of amenities and recreational amenities;

(k)   the control, having regard to the provisions of the Major Accidents Directive and any regulations, under any enactment, giving effect to that Directive, of—

(i)   siting of new establishments,

(ii)   modification of existing establishments, and

(iii) development in the vicinity of such establishments,

for the purposes of reducing the risk, or limiting the consequences, of a major accident;

(l)   the provision, or facilitation of the provision, of services for the community including, in particular, schools, creches and other education and childcare facilities, and

(m)   the protection of the linguistic and cultural heritage of the Gaeltacht including the promotion of Irish as the community language, where there is a Gaeltacht area in the area of the development plan.

(3) Without prejudice to subsection (2), a development plan may indicate objectives for any of the purposes referred to in the First Schedule.

(4) The Minister may prescribe additional objectives for the purposes of subsection (2) or for the purposes of the First Schedule.

(5) (a) A development plan shall contain information on the likely significant effects on the environment of implementing the plan.

(b)   The Minister may by regulations make further provisions in relation to the manner in which paragraph (a) may be complied with.

(6) Where a planning authority proposes to include in a development plan any development objective the responsibility for the effecting of which would fall on another local authority, the planning authority shall not include that objective in the plan except after consultation with the other local authority.

(7) A development plan may indicate that specified development in a particular area will be subject to the making of a local area plan.

(8) There shall be no presumption in law that any land zoned in a particular development plan (including a development plan that has been varied) shall remain so zoned in any subsequent development plan.

Notes
Section 10(2)
Unlike s 19(2) of the LG(PD)A 1963, there is no distinction now between urban and rural authorities in relation to objectives which must be included in the development plan.

Section 10(2)(l)
'*Facilitation of*' – The inclusion of these new words may well facilitate certain PPP projects for schools, etc.

Section 10(8)
This provision is in line with government policy now to ensure that where land is zoned it is developed without delay.

[21]
11. Preparation of draft development plan

(1) Not later than 4 years after the making of a development plan, a planning authority shall give notice of its intention to review its existing development plan and to prepare a new development plan for its area.

(2) A notice under subsection (1) shall be given to the Minister, any prescribed authorities, any adjoining planning authorities, the Board, any relevant regional authority and any town commissioners and city and county development boards within the functional area of the authority and shall be published in one or more newspapers circulating in the area to which the development plan relates and shall—

(a) state that the planning authority intends to review the existing development plan and to prepare a new development plan,

(b) indicate that submissions or observations regarding the review of the existing plan and the preparation of a new development plan may be made in writing to the planning authority within a specified period (which shall not be less than 8 weeks),

(c) indicate the time during which and the place or places where any background papers or draft proposals (if any) regarding the review of the existing plan and the preparation of the new development plan may be inspected.

(3) (a) As soon as may be after giving notice under this section of its intention to review a development plan and to prepare a new development plan, a planning authority shall take whatever additional measures it considers necessary to consult with the general public and other interested bodies.

(b) Without prejudice to the generality of paragraph (a), a planning authority shall hold public meetings and seek written submissions regarding all or any aspect of the proposed development plan and may invite oral submissions to be made to the planning authority regarding the plan.

(c) In addition to paragraphs (a) and (b), a planning authority shall take whatever measures it considers necessary to consult with the providers of energy, telecommunications, transport and any other relevant infrastructure and of education, health, policing and other services in order to ascertain any long-term plans for the provision of the infrastructure and services in the area of the planning authority and the providers shall furnish the necessary information to the planning authority.

(4) (a) Not later than 16 weeks after giving notice under subsection (1), the manager of a planning authority shall prepare a report on any submissions or observations received under subsection (2) or (3) and the matters arising out of any consultations under subsection (3).

(b) A report under paragraph (a) shall -
  (i) list the persons or bodies who made submissions or observations under this section as well as any persons or bodies consulted by the authority,
  (ii) summarise the issues raised in the submissions and during the consultations, where appropriate,
  (iii) give the opinion of the manager to the issues raised, taking account of the proper planning and sustainable development of the area, the statutory obligations of any local authority in the area, and any relevant policies or

objectives for the time being of the Government or of any Minister of the Government, and

(iv)   state the manager's recommendations on the policies to be included in the draft development plan.

(c)   A report under paragraph (a) shall be submitted to the members of the planning authority, or to a committee of the planning authority, as may be decided by the members of the authority, for their consideration.

(d)   Following the consideration of a report under paragraph (c), the members of the planning authority or of the committee, as the case may be, may issue directions to the manager regarding the preparation of the draft development plan, and any such directions must take account of the statutory obligations of any local authority in the area and any relevant policies or objectives for the time being of the Government or of any Minister of the Government, and the manager shall comply with any such directions.

(e)   Directions under paragraph (d) shall be issued not later than 10 weeks after the submission of a report in accordance with paragraph (c).

(f)   In issuing directions under paragraph (d), the members shall be restricted to considering the proper planning and sustainable development of the area to which the development plan relates.

(5)   (a) The manager shall, not later than 12 weeks following the receipt of any directions under subsection (4)(d), prepare a draft development plan and submit it to the members of the planning authority for their consideration.

(b)   The members of a planning authority shall, as soon as may be, consider the draft development plan submitted by the manager in accordance with paragraph (a).

(c)   Where the draft development plan has been considered in accordance with paragraph (b), it shall be deemed to be the draft development plan, unless, within 8 weeks of the submission of the draft development plan under paragraph (a), the planning authority, by resolution, amends that draft development plan.

Notes
Section 11(2)
The public and certain prescribed bodies are now given an opportunity to put in submissions before the plan is drafted. This is a new provision.

Section 11(3)
Certain bodies/providers must furnish information to the planning authorities before the plan is drafted. Again, these provisions are new and are all with a view to having a more integrated planning policy.

[22]
12. Making of development plan
(1)   Where the draft development plan has been prepared in accordance with section 11, the planning authority shall within 2 weeks of the period referred to in section 11(5)(c)—

(a)   send notice and a copy of the draft development plan to the Minister, the Board, the prescribed authorities, any town commissioners in the area and any city or county development boards in the area, any town commissioners and city and county development boards within the area, and

(b) publish notice of the preparation of the draft in one or more newspapers circulating in its area.

(2) A notice under subsection (1) shall state that—

(a) a copy of the draft may be inspected at a stated place or places and at stated times during a stated period of not less than 10 weeks (and the copy shall be kept available for inspection accordingly), and

(b) written submissions or observations with respect to the draft made to the planning authority within the stated period will be taken into consideration before the making of the plan.

(3) (a) Where the draft includes any provision relating to any addition to or deletion from the record of protected structures, the planning authority shall serve on each person who is the owner or occupier of the proposed protected structure or the protected structure, as the case may be, a notice of the proposed addition or deletion, including the particulars.

(b) A notice under paragraph (a) shall state—

  (i)   that a copy of the proposed addition or deletion may be inspected at a stated place or places and at stated times during a stated period of not less than 10 weeks (and the copy shall be kept available for inspection accordingly),

  (ii)   that written submissions or observations with respect to the proposed addition or deletion made to the planning authority within the stated period will be taken into consideration before the making of the addition or deletion.

  (iii) whether or not the proposed addition or deletion was recommended by the Minister for Arts, Heritage, Gaeltacht and the Islands, and

  (iv) that, if the proposed addition or deletion was recommended by the Minister for Arts, Heritage, Gaeltacht and the Islands, the planning authority shall forward to that Minister for his or her observations a copy of any submission or observation made under subparagraph (ii) (and any such observations shall be taken into consideration accordingly).

(4) (a) Not later than 22 weeks after giving notice under subsection (1) and, if appropriate, subsection (3), the manager of a planning authority shall prepare a report on any submissions or observations received under subsection (2) or (3) and submit the report to the members of the authority for their consideration.

(b) A report under paragraph (a) shall—

  (i)   list the persons or bodies who made submissions or observations under this section,

  (ii)   summarise the issues raised by the persons or bodies in the submissions or observations, and

  (iii) give the response of the manager to the issues raised, taking account of any directions of the members of the authority or the committee under section 11(4), the proper planning and sustainable development of the area, the statutory obligations of any local authority in the area and any relevant policies or objectives of the Government or of any Minister of the Government and, if appropriate, any observations made by the Minister for Arts, Heritage, Gaeltacht and the Islands under subsection (3)(b)(iv).

(5) (a) The members of a planning authority shall consider the draft plan and the report of the manager under subsection (4)

(b) The consideration of a draft plan and the manager's report under paragraph (a) shall be completed within 12 weeks of the submission of the manager's report to the members of the authority.

(6) Where, following the consideration of the draft development plan and the manager's report, it appears to the members of the authority that the draft should be accepted or amended, subject to subsection (7), they may, by resolution, accept or amend the draft and make the development plan accordingly.

(7) (a) In case the proposed amendment would, if made, be a material alteration of the draft concerned, the planning authority shall, not later than 3 weeks after the passing of a resolution under subsection (6), publish notice of the proposed amendment in at least one newspaper circulating in its area.

(b) A notice under paragraph (a) shall state that—
   (i) a copy of the proposed amendment of the draft development plan may be inspected at a stated place and at stated times during a stated period of not less than 4 weeks (and the copy shall be kept available for inspection accordingly), and
   (ii) written submissions or observations with respect to the proposed amendment of the draft made to the planning authority within the stated period shall be taken into consideration before the making of any amendment.

(8) (a) Not later than 8 weeks after giving notice under subsection (7), the manager of a planning authority shall prepare a report on any submissions or observations received under that subsection and submit the report to the members of the authority for their consideration.

(b) A report under paragraph (a) shall—
   (i) list the persons or bodies who made submissions or observations under this section,
   (ii) summarise the issues raised by the persons or bodies in the submissions,
   (iii) give the response of the manager to the issues raised, taking account of the directions of the members of the authority or the committee under section 11(4), the proper planning and sustainable development of the area, the statutory obligations of any local authority in the area and any relevant policies or objectives for the time being of the Government or of any Minister of the Government.

(9) (a) The members of a planning authority shall consider the amendment and the report of the manager under subsection (3).

(b) The consideration of the amendment and the manager's report under paragraph (a) shall be completed not later than 6 weeks after the submission of the manager's report to the members of the authority.

(10) (a) The members of the authority shall, by resolution, having considered the amendment and the manager's report, make the plan with or without the proposed amendment, except that where they decide to accept the amendment they

may do so subject to any modifications to the amendment as they consider appropriate.

(b) The requirements of subsections (7) to (9) shall not apply in relation to modifications made in accordance with paragraph (a).

(11) In making the development plan under subsection (6) or (10), the members shall be restricted to considering the proper planning and sustainable development of the area to which the development plan relates, the statutory obligations of any local authority in the area and any relevant policies or objectives for the time being of the Government or any Minister of the Government.

(12) (a) Where a planning authority makes a development plan, it shall publish a notice of the making of the plan in at least one newspaper circulating in its area.

(b) A notice under this subsection shall state that a copy of the plan is available for inspection at a stated place or places (and the copy shall be kept available for inspection accordingly).

(c) In addition to the requirements of paragraphs (a) and (b), a planning authority shall send a copy of the development plan to the Minister, the prescribed authorities, any adjoining planning authorities, the Board, any town commissioners and city and county development boards within its area.

(13) As soon as may be after making an addition to or a deletion from the record of protected structures under this section, a planning authority shall serve on the owner and on the occupier of the structure concerned a notice of the addition or deletion, including the particulars.

(14) Where a planning authority fails to make a development plan within 2 years of the giving of notice under section 11(1), notwithstanding any other provision of this Part, the manager shall make the plan subject to the proviso that so much of the plan that has been agreed by the members of the planning authority shall be included as part of the plan as made by the manager.

(15) When considering the draft development plan, or amendments thereto, a planning authority may invite such persons as it considers appropriate to make oral submissions regarding such plan or amendment.

(16) A person shall not question the validity of the development plan by reason only that the procedures as set out under subsections (3) to (5) of section 11 and subsections (1), (4), (5), (6), (8) and (9) of this section were not completed within the time required under the relevant subsection.

(17) A development plan made under this section shall have effect 4 weeks from the day that it is made.

Notes
Section 12 is a similar provision to s 21 of LG(PD)A 1963 but there are amendments to time limits for notices, etc. There are also new obligations on County Managers to prepare reports summarising the submissions and observations made, and to make recommendations to the elected members.

Section 12(14)
This is a new provision. It is designed to ensure that development plans are reviewed and adopted within the timescales laid down.

[23]
13. Variation of development plan

(1) A planning authority may at any time, for stated reasons, decide to make a variation of a development plan which for the time being is in force.

(2) Where a planning authority proposes to make a variation in a development plan, it shall—

(a) send notice and copies of the proposed variation of the development plan to the Minister, the Board and, where appropriate, to any adjoining planning authority, the prescribed authorities, any town commissioners and city and county development boards within the area of the development plan,

(b) publish notice of the proposed variation of the development plan in one or more newspapers circulating in that area.

(3) A notice under subsection (2) shall state—

(a) the reason or reasons for the proposed variation,

(b) that a copy of the proposed variation may be inspected at a stated place or places and at stated times during a stated period of not less than 4 weeks (and the copy of the draft variation shall be kept available for inspection accordingly), and

(c) that written submissions or observations with respect to the proposed variation made to the planning authority within the said period will be taken into consideration before the making of the variation.

(4) (a) Not later than 8 weeks after giving notice under subsection (2)(b), the manager of a planning authority shall prepare a report on any submissions or observations received under that subsection and shall submit the report to the members of the authority for their consideration.

(b) A report under paragraph (a) shall—
   (i) list the persons or bodies who made submissions or observations under this section,
   (ii) summarise the issues raised by the persons or bodies in the submissions,
   (iii) give the response of the manager to the issues raised, taking account of the proper planning and sustainable development of the area, the statutory obligations of any local authority in the area and any relevant policies or objectives for the time being of the Government or of any Minister of the Government.

(5) (a) The members of a planning authority shall consider the proposed variation and the report of the manager under subsection (4).

(b) The consideration of the variation and the manager's report under paragraph (a) shall be completed not later than 6 weeks after the submission of the manager's report to the members of the authority.

(6) (a) The members of a planning authority, having considered the proposed variation and manager's report, may, by resolution as they consider appropriate, make the variation, with or without modifications, or they may refuse to make it.

(b) The requirements of subsections (2) to (5) shall not apply in relation to modifications made in accordance with paragraph (a).

(7) In making a variation under this section, the members of the authority shall be restricted to considering the proper planning and sustainable development of the area to which the development plan relates, the statutory obligations of any local authority in the area and any relevant policies or objectives for the time being of the Government or any Minister of the Government.

(8) (a) Where a planning authority makes a variation in a development plan, it shall publish a notice of the making of the variation in at least one newspaper circulating in its area.

(b) A notice under this subsection shall state that a copy of the development plan as varied is available for inspection at a stated place or places (and the copy shall be kept available for inspection accordingly).

(c) In addition to the requirements of paragraphs (a) and (b), a planning authority shall send a copy of the variation to the Minister, the Board and, where appropriate, to the prescribed authorities, any adjoining planning authorities, any town commissioners and city and county development boards within its area.

(9) When considering a variation of a development plan in accordance with this section, a planning authority may invite such persons as it considers appropriate to make oral submissions regarding the variation.

(10) A person shall not question the validity of a variation in a development plan by reason only that the procedures as set out in this section were not completed within the time required.

(11) A variation made to a development plan shall have effect from the day that the variation is made.

Note
Section 13 amends the procedure for varying a development plan under s 21 of LG(PD)A 1963, most notably in relation to the County Manager's obligations.

[24]
14. Public rights of way in development plans
(1) Where a planning authority proposes to include, for the first time, a provision in a development plan relating to the preservation of a specific public right of way, it shall serve notice (which shall include particulars of the provision and a map indicating the right of way) of its intention to do so on any owner and occupier of the land over which the right of way exists.

(2) A notice served under subsection (1) shall state that—

(a) the planning authority proposes to include a provision in the development plan relating to the preservation of the public right of way,

(b) written submissions or observations regarding the proposal may be made to the planning authority within a stated period of not less than 6 weeks and that the submissions or observations will be taken into consideration by the planning authority, and

(c) where, following consideration of any submissions or observations received under paragraph (b), the planning authority considers that the provision should be adopted, or adopted subject to modifications, a right of appeal to the Circuit Court exists in relation to such provision.

(3) The members of a planning authority, having considered the proposal and any submissions or observations made in respect of it, may, by resolution as they consider appropriate, recommend the inclusion of the provision in the development plan, with or without modifications, or may recommend against its inclusion and any person on whom notice has been served under subsection (1) shall be notified of the recommendation accordingly and a copy of such notice shall be published in at least one newspaper circulating in the area.

(4) Any person who has been notified of the recommendation of the planning authority under subsection (3) may, before the expiration of the 21 days next following the notification, appeal to the Circuit Court against the inclusion in the development plan of the proposed provision, and the Court, if satisfied that no public right of way exists, shall so declare and the provision shall accordingly not be included.

(5) (a) The taking of an appeal under subsection (4) shall not prejudice the making of a development plan under section 12 except in regard to the inclusion of the proposed provision which is before the Court.

(b) Where a development plan has been made under section 12 and the Court, having considered an appeal under subsection (4), decides that the public right of way exists, the proposed provision under this section shall be deemed to be part of the development plan.

(6) Where any existing development plan contains any provision relating to the preservation of a public right of way, the provision may be included in any subsequent development plan without the necessity to comply with this section.

(7) (a) Nothing in this section shall affect the existence or validity of any public right of way which is not included in the development plan.

(b) The inclusion of a public right of way in a development plan shall be evidence of the existence of such a right unless the contrary is shown.

[25]–[30]
15. General duty of planning authority to secure objectives of development plan
(1) It shall be the duty of a planning authority to take such steps within its powers as may be necessary for securing the objectives of the development plan.

(2) The manager of a planning authority shall, not more than 2 years after the making of a development plan, give a report to the members of the authority on the progress achieved in securing the objectives referred to in subsection (1).

Notes
Section 15(1)
This sub-section is a restatement of s 22(1) of LG(PD)A 1963.

Section 15(2)
This is a new provision.

[31]
16. Copies of development plans
(1) A planning authority shall make available for inspection and purchase by members of the public copies of a development plan and of variations of a development plan and extracts therefrom.

(2) A planning authority shall make available for inspection and purchase by members of the public copies of a report of a manager of a planning authority prepared under sections 11(4), 12(4) and (3) and 13(4) and extracts therefrom.

(3) Copies of the development plan and of variations of a development plan and reports of the manager referred to in subsection (2) and extracts therefrom shall be made available for purchase on payment of a specified fee not exceeding the reasonable cost of making a copy.

Note
Section 19(8) of LG(PD)A 1963 also provided for regulations in relation to making copies of all development plans available.

[32]
17. Evidence of development plans
(1) A document purporting to be a copy of a part or all of a development plan and to be certified by an officer of a planning authority as a correct copy shall be evidence of the plan or part, unless the contrary is shown, and it shall not be necessary to prove the signature of the officer or that he or she was in fact such an officer.

(2) Evidence of all or part of a development plan may be given by production of a copy thereof certified in accordance with this subsection and it shall not be necessary to produce the plan itself.

Note
Section 17 is a restatement of s 21(6) of LG(PD)A 1963.

CHAPTER II   LOCAL AREA PLANS

[33]
18. Local area plans
(1) A planning authority may at any time, and for any particular area within its functional area, prepare a local area plan in respect of that area.

(2) Two or more planning authorities may co-operate in preparing a local area plan in respect of any area which lies within the combined functional area of the authorities concerned.

(3) (a) When considering an application for permission under section 34, a planning authority, or the Board on appeal, shall have regard to the provisions of any local area plan prepared for the area to which the application relates, and the authority or the Board may also consider any relevant draft local plan which has been prepared but not yet made in accordance with section 20.
  (b) When considering an application for permission, a planning authority, or the Board on appeal, shall also have regard to any integrated area plan (within the meaning of the Urban Renewal Act, 1998) for the area to which the application relates.

(4) (a) A local area plan prepared under this section shall indicate the period for which the plan is to remain in force.
  (b) A local area plan may remain in force in accordance with paragraph (a) notwithstanding the variation of a development plan or the making of a new develop-

ment plan affecting the area to which the local area plan relates except that, where any provision of a local area plan conflicts with the provisions of the development plan as varied or the new development plan, the provision of the local area plan shall cease to have any effect.

(5) A planning authority may at any time amend or revoke a local area plan.

(6) A planning authority may enter into an arrangement with any suitably qualified person or local community group for the preparation, or the carrying out of any aspect of the preparation, of a local area plan.

Notes
Section 18 gives a statutory basis for area action plans which had been around for quite a while under the old planning code.

Section 18(3)(a)
A draft local plan must be taken into account by a local authority or the Board when considering an application for permission, even though there may have been no consultation with the public yet in relation to the draft local plan.

[34]
19. Application and content of local area plans

(1) (a) A local area plan may be prepared in respect of any area, including a Gaeltacht area, or an existing suburb of an urban area, which the planning authority considers suitable and, in particular, for those areas which require economic, physical and social renewal and for areas likely to be subject to large scale development within the lifetime of the plan.
(b) A local area plan shall be made in respect of an area which—
  (i) is designated as a town in the most recent census of population, other than a town designated as a suburb or environs in that census,
  (ii) has a population in excess of 2,000, and
  (iii) is situated within the functional area of a planning authority which is a county council.
(c) Section 20(3)(a) shall be complied with—
  (i) in the case of the first local area plan, not later than 2 years after the making of a development plan under this Part, and
  (ii) notwithstanding section 18(5), at least every 6 years after the making of the previous local area plan.

(2) A local area plan shall be consistent with the objectives of the development plan and shall consist of a written statement and a plan or plans indicating the objectives in such detail as may be determined by the planning authority for the proper planning and sustainable development of the area to which it applies, including detail on community facilities and amenities and on standards for the design of developments and structures.

(3) The Minister may provide in regulations that local area plans shall be prepared in respect of certain classes of areas or in certain circumstances and a planning authority shall comply with any such regulations.

(4) (a) A local area plan shall contain information on the likely significant effects on the environment of implementing the plan.

(b) The Minister may by regulations make further provisions in relation to the manner in which paragraph (a) may be complied with.

Note
Section 19 sets out the requirements of what the plan must include.

[35]–[40]
20. Consultation and adoption of local area plans
(1) A planning authority shall take whatever steps it considers necessary to consult the public before preparing, amending or revoking a local area plan including consultations with any local residents, public sector agencies, non-governmental agencies, local community groups and commercial and business interests within the area.

(2) A planning authority shall consult Udaras na Gaeltachta before making, amending or revoking a local area plan under subsection (3) for an area which includes a Gaeltacht area.

(3) (a) The planning authority shall, as soon as may be after consideration of any matters arising out of consultations under subsections (1) or (2) but before making, amending or revoking a local area plan—
  (i)   send notice of the proposal to make, amend or revoke a local area plan to the Board and to the prescribed authorities (and, where applicable, it shall enclose a copy of the proposed plan or amended plan),
  (ii) publish a notice of the proposal in one or more news papers circulating in its area.
  (b) A notice under paragraph (a) shall state—
  (i)   that the planning authority proposes to make, amend or revoke a local area plan,
  (ii) that a copy of the proposal to make, amend or revoke the local area plan and (where appropriate) the proposed local area plan, or proposed amended plan, may be inspected at such place or places as are specified in the notice during such period as may be so stated (being a period of not less than 6 weeks),
  (iii) that submissions or observations in respect of the proposal made to the planning authority during such period will be taken into consideration in deciding upon the proposal.
  (c) (i)   Not later than 12 weeks after giving notice under paragraph (b), the manager of a planning authority shall prepare a report on any submissions or observations received pursuant to a notice under that paragraph and shall submit the report to the members of the planning authority for their consideration.
  (ii) A report under subparagraph (i) shall—
    (i)   list the persons who made submissions or observations,
    (ii) summarise the issues raised by the persons in the submissions or observations,
    (iii) contain the opinion of the manager in relation to the issues raised, and his or her recommendations in relation to the proposed local area plan, amendment to a local area plan or revocation of a local area

plan, as the case may be, taking account of the proper planning and sustainable development of the area, the statutory obligations of any local authority in the area and any relevant policies or objectives for the time being of the Government or of any Minister of the Government.

(d) (i) The members of a planning authority shall consider the proposal to make, amend or revoke a local area plan and the report of the manager under paragraph (c).

   (ii) Following consideration of the manager's report under subparagraph (i), the local area plan shall be deemed to be made, amended or revoked, as appropriate, in accordance with the recommendations of the manager as set out in his or her report, 6 weeks after the furnishing of the report to all the members of the authority, unless the planning authority, by resolution, varies or modifies the proposal, otherwise than as recommended in the manager's report, or where appropriate decides not to make, amend or revoke, as the case may be, the plan.

(4) The Minister may make regulations or issue guidelines in relation to the preparation of local area plans.

(5) A planning authority shall send a copy of any local area plan made under this Chapter to any bodies consulted under subsection (1), (2) or (3), the Board and. where appropriate, any prescribed body.

Note
Section 20 sets out the procedures for the adoption of the plan.

CHAPTER III   REGIONAL PLANNING GUIDELINES

[41]
21. Power to make the regional planning guidelines
(1) A regional authority may, after consultation with the planning authorities within its region, or shall at the direction of Minister, make regional planning guidelines.

(2) Regional planning guidelines may be made for a whole region or for one or more parts of a region.

(3) (a) The Minister may direct one or more regional authorities to make regional planning guidelines in respect of the combined area of the regional authorities involved or in respect of any particular part or parts of the area which lie within the area of those regional authorities.

(b) Where it is proposed to make regional planning guidelines, the regional authorities concerned shall make whatever arrangements they see fit to prepare the guidelines, including the carrying out of the functions of this Chapter as a joint function of the authorities concerned, and this Chapter shall be construed accordingly.

(4) Notwithstanding any other provision of this Act, the strategic planning guidelines for the greater Dublin area prepared for Dublin Corporation, Dun Laoghaire-Rathdown County Council, Fingal County Council, Kildare County

Council, Meath County Council, South Dublin County Council, Wicklow County Council and the Department of the Environment and Local Government in conjunction with the Dublin Regional Authority and the Mid-East Regional Authority published on 25 March, 1999, shall have effect as if made under this Part.

(5) The Minister may make regulations concerning the making of regional planning guidelines and related matters.

Notes
Section 21 is new.

Section 21(1)
The Local Government (Planning and Development) Act 1993 (Regional Authorities) (Establishment) Order 1993, SI 394/1993 sets out eight regional authorities that have been established.

[42]
22. Co-operation of planning authorities with regional authority
(1) Where a regional authority intends to make regional planning guidelines in accordance with section 24, or to review existing guidelines under section 26, it shall, as soon as may be, consult with all the planning authorities within the region (or part thereof, as the case may be) in order to make the necessary arrangements for making the guidelines.

(2) (a) A planning authority shall assist and co-operate with a regional authority in making arrangements for the preparation of regional planning guidelines and in carrying out the preparation of the guidelines.

(b) The provision of assistance under paragraph (a) shall include the provision of financial assistance, the services of staff and the provision of accommodation, where necessary, and the regional authorities and planning authorities shall agree on such matters based on the proportion of the population of the area for which the regional planning guidelines are prepared resident in the functional areas of the planning authorities concerned.

(c) In the absence of agreement under paragraph (b), a regional authority may request the relevant planning authorities to provide assistance under this section, and the request shall be based on the proportion of the population of the area for which the regional planning guidelines are prepared resident in the functional areas of the planning authorities concerned, and a planning authority shall not refuse a reasonable request for assistance.

Note
Section 22 states that there will be co-operation between planning authorities and regional authorities relative to the regional planning guidelines.

[43]
23. Content and objectives of regional planning guidelines
(1) (a) The objective of regional planning guidelines shall be to provide a long-term strategic planning framework for the development of the region for which the guidelines are prepared.

(b) The planning framework referred to in paragraph (a) shall consider the future development of the region for which the guidelines are prepared for a period of not less than 12 years and not more than 20 years.

(2) The guidelines shall address, for the whole of the region to which the guidelines relate, in accordance with the principles of proper planning and sustainable development, the following matters—

(a) projected population trends and settlement and housing strategies;
(b) economic and employment trends:
(c) the location of industrial and commercial development;
(d) transportation, including public transportation:
(e) water supply and waste water facilities;
(f) waste disposal;
(g) energy and communications networks;
(h) the provision of educational, health care, retail and other community facilities;
(i) the preservation and protection of the environment and its amenities, including the archaeological, architectural and natural heritage:
(j) such other matters as may be prescribed.

(3) (a) Regional planning guidelines shall contain information on the likely significant effects on the environment of implementing the guidelines.
(b) The Minister may by regulation make further provisions in relation to the manner in which paragraph (a) may be complied with.

(4) (a) When making regional planning guidelines the regional authority shall take account of the proper planning and sustainable development of the whole of the region to which the guidelines relate, the statutory obligations of any local authority in the region and any relevant policies or objectives for the time being of the Government or of any Minister of the Government, including any national plans, policies or strategies specified by the Minister to be of relevance to the determination of strategic planning policies.
(b) When making regional planning guidelines which affect the Gaeltacht, the regional authority shall have regard to the need to protect the linguistic and cultural heritage of the Gaeltacht.

(5) Without prejudice to the generality of subsections (2) and (3), the Minister may issue guidelines on the content of regional planning guidelines and regional authorities shall have regard to those guidelines.

Note
Section 23(1)(b)
This section states that the guidelines shall be for a period of twelve to twenty years.

[44]
24. Consultation regarding regional planning guidelines
(1) As soon as may be after agreeing any necessary arrangements under section 21, a regional authority shall give notice of its intention to make the regional planning guidelines.

(2) A notice under subsection (1) shall be given to the Minister, the Board, the prescribed authorities and any town commissioners in the area and shall be published in one or more newspapers circulating in the region for which the regional planning guidelines are prepared and shall—

(a) state that the regional authority intends to make regional planning guidelines,

(b) indicate the matters to be considered in the guidelines, having regard to section 23,

(c) indicate that submissions regarding the making of the regional planning guidelines may be made in writing to the regional authority within a specified period (which shall not be less than 8 weeks).

(3) A regional authority shall consider any submissions received under subsection (2) before preparing the draft regional planning guidelines.

(4) When a regional authority prepares the draft of the regional planning guidelines it shall, as soon as may be—

(a) send notice and copies of the draft guidelines to the Minister, the Board, the prescribed authorities and any town commissioners in its area, and

(b) publish notice of the preparation of the draft in one or more newspapers circulating in its area.

(5) A notice under subsection (4) shall state—

(a) that a copy of the draft guidelines may be inspected at a stated place or places and at stated times during a stated period of not less than 10 weeks (and the copy shall be kept available for inspection accordingly), and

(b) that written submissions or observations with respect to the draft made to the regional authority within the stated period will be taken into consideration before the guidelines are adopted.

(6) Following the consideration of submissions or observations under subsection (5), and subject to section 25, the regional authority shall make the regional planning guidelines subject to any modification considered necessary.

(7) (a) Where a regional authority makes regional planning guidelines, it shall publish a notice of the making of the guidelines in at least one newspaper circulating in the functional area of each planning authority in the region for which the guidelines are prepared.

(b) A notice under this subsection shall state that a copy of the guidelines is available for inspection at a stated place or places (and the copy shall be kept available for inspection accordingly).

[45]–[50]
25. Procedure for making regional planning guidelines
(1) As part of the consultation between a regional authority and the relevant planning authorities under section 22, the authorities concerned shall agree on a procedure for preparing and making the regional planning guidelines under section 24.

(2) Matters to be considered under subsection (1) shall include the establishment of committees to oversee and consider preparation of the guidelines.

(3) The authorities concerned shall agree on the membership of the committees under subsection (2) and shall also agree on the roles of those committees in preparing the draft guidelines, considering submissions or observations under section 24, and drawing up reports in respect of the guidelines.

(4) The making of regional planning guidelines under section 24(6) shall be a matter for the members of the regional authority concerned, following the consideration of any report or reports from the committees referred to in subsection (2).

(5) The Minister may make regulations, or issue guidelines, with regard to the procedures to be adopted under this section, including the number, functions and membership of any committees set up in accordance with subsection (2).

[51]
26. Review of regional guidelines
(1) Where a regional authority has made regional planning guidelines, it shall, not later than 6 years after the making of such guidelines and not less than once in every period of 6 years there after, review such guidelines and when so reviewing, it may revoke the guidelines or make new regional planning guidelines.

(2) Before a regional authority revokes guidelines referred to in subsection (1) (other than for the purpose of making new regional planning guidelines), it shall consult with the planning authorities within its region.

(3) Where the regional authority makes new guidelines, it shall follow the procedures laid down in sections 22, 24 and 25.

(4) Where new guidelines are made under subsection (1), they shall supersede any previous regional planning guidelines for the relevant area.

[52]
27. Regional planning guidelines and development plans
(1) A planning authority shall have regard to any regional planning guidelines in force for its area when making and adopting guidelines and a development plan.

(2) The Minister may, by order, determine that planning authorities shall comply with any regional planning guidelines in force for their area, or any part thereof, when preparing and making a development plan, or may require in accordance with section 31 that an existing development plan comply with any regional planning guidelines in force for the area.

(3) An order under subsection (2) may relate to regional planning guidelines generally, or one or more specified guidelines, or may relate to specific elements of those guidelines.

(4) Following the making of regional planning guidelines for their area, planning authorities shall review the existing development plan and consider whether any variation of the development plan is necessary in order to achieve the objectives of the regional planning guidelines.

(5) For the purposes of this section, a planning authority may have, but shall not be obliged to have, regard to any regional planning guidelines after 6 years from the making of such guidelines.

CHAPTER IV   GUIDELINES AND DIRECTIVES

[53]
28. Ministerial guidelines

(1) The Minister may, at any time, issue guidelines to planning authorities regarding any of their functions under this Act and planning authorities shall have regard to those guidelines in the performance of their functions.

(2) Where applicable, the Board shall have regard to any guidelines issued to planning authorities under subsection (1) in the performance of its functions.

(3) Any planning guidelines made by the Minister and any general policy directives issued under section 7 of the Act of 1982 prior to the commencement of this Part and still in force immediately before such commencement shall be deemed to be guidelines under this section.

(4) The Minister may revoke or amend guidelines issued under this section.

(5) The Minister shall cause a copy of any guidelines issued under this section and of any amendment or revocation of those guidelines to be laid before each House of the Oireachtas

(6) A planning authority shall make available for inspection by members of the public any guidelines issued to it under this section.

(7) The Minister shall publish or cause to be published, in such manner as he or she considers appropriate, guidelines issued under this section.

[54]
29. Ministerial policy directives

(1) The Minister may, from time to time, issue policy directives to planning authorities regarding any of their functions under this Act and planning authorities shall comply with any such directives in the performance of their functions.

(2) Where applicable, the Board shall also comply with any policy directives issued to planning authorities under subsection (1) in the performance of its functions.

(3) The Minister may revoke or amend a policy directive issued under this section.

(4) Where the Minister proposes to issue, amend or revoke a policy directive under this section, a draft of the directive, amendment or revocation shall be laid before both Houses of the Oireachtas and the policy directive shall not be issued, amended or revoked, as the case may be, until a resolution approving the issuing, amending or revocation of the policy directive has been passed by each House.

(5) The Minister shall cause a copy of any policy directive issued under this section to be laid before each House of the Oireachtas.

(6) A planning authority shall make available for inspection by members of the public any policy directive issued to it under this section.

(7) The Minister shall publish or cause to be published, in such manner as he or she considers appropriate, policy directives issued under this section.

[55]–[60]
30. Limitation on Ministerial power
Notwithstanding section 28 or 29, the Minister shall not exercise any power or control in relation to any particular case with which a planning authority or the Board is or may be concerned.

Note
Section 30 restates with some amendments the provisions of s 7(3) of LG(PD)A 1982 and s 23 of LG(PD)A 1983.

[61]
31. Ministerial directions regarding development plans
(1) Where the Minister considers that any draft development plan fails to set out an overall strategy for the proper planning and sustainable development of the area of a planning authority or other wise significantly fails to comply with this Act, the Minister may, for stated reasons, direct the authority to take such specified measures as he or she may require to ensure that the development plan, when made, is in compliance with this Act and, notwithstanding the requirements of Chapter I, the authority shall comply with any such direction.

(2) Where the Minister considers that any development plan fails to set out an overall strategy for the proper planning and sustainable development of the area of the authority or otherwise significantly fails to comply with this Act, the Minister may, for stated reasons, direct the authority to take such specified measures, as he or she may require to review or vary the development plan to ensure compliance with this Act and the authority shall comply with any such direction.

(3) Where the Minister directs a planning authority to take specified measures under subsection (2), he or she may specify any of those provisions of Chapter I which are to apply in respect of such specified measures and any other provisions of that Chapter shall be disregarded.

(4) In exercising any power conferred on them by this Act, neither the manager nor the elected members of any planning authority shall exercise the power in conflict with any direction which the Minister may give under subsection (1) or (2).

(5) The Minister shall cause a copy of any direction issued under this section to be laid before each House of the Oireachtas.

(6) A planning authority shall make available for inspection by members of the public any direction issued to it under this section.

Note
Section 31(1), (2)
This section effectively restates s 22 of LG(PD)A 1963.

PART III   CONTROL OF DEVELOPMENT

Note
Part III has not yet been commenced.

[62]
32. General obligations to obtain permission

(1) Subject to the other provisions of this Act, permission shall be required under this Part—

(a) in respect of any development of land, not being exempted development, and
(b) in the case of development which is unauthorised, for the retention of that unauthorised development.

(2) A person shall not carry out any development in respect of which permission is required by subsection (1), except under and in accordance with a permission granted under this Part.

Note
Section 32
This section is a restatement of s 24 of LG(PD)A 1963.

[63]
33. Regulations regarding applications for permission

(1) The Minister shall by regulations provide for such matters of procedure and administration as appear to the Minister to be necessary or expedient in respect of applications for permission for the development of land.

(2) Without prejudice to the generality of subsection (1), regulations under this section may make provision for the following—

(a) requiring the submission of information in respect of applications for permission for the development of land;
(b) requiring any applicants to publish any specified notices with respect to their applications;
(c) enabling persons to make submissions or observations on payment of the prescribed fee and within a prescribed period;
(d) requiring planning authorities to acknowledge in writing the receipt of submissions or observations;
(e) requiring any applicants to furnish to any specified persons any specified information with respect to their applications;
(f) requiring planning authorities to—
     (i)   (I)   notify prescribed authorities of such proposed development or classes
                 of development as may be prescribed, or
           (II) consult with them in respect thereof,
           and
     (ii) give to them such documents, particulars, plans or other information in
           respect thereof as may be prescribed;
(g) requiring any applicants to submit any further information with respect to their applications (including any information as to any estate or interest in or right over land) or information regarding any effect on the environment which the development may have;
(h) enabling planning authorities to invite an applicant to submit to them revised plans or other drawings modifying, or other particulars providing for the modification of, the development to which the application relates and, in case the plans, drawings or particulars are submitted to a planning authority in response

to such an invitation, enabling the authority in deciding the application to grant a permission for the relevant development as modified by all or any of the plans, drawings or particulars;

(i) requiring the production of any evidence to verify any particulars of information given by any applicants;

(j) requiring planning authorities to furnish to the Minister and to any other speci-fied persons any specified information with respect to applications and the manner in which they have been dealt with;

(k) requiring planning authorities to publish or give notice of their decisions in respect of applications for permission, including the giving of notice thereof to prescribed bodies and to persons who made submissions or observations in respect of such applications:

(l) requiring an applicant to submit specified information to the planning authority with respect to development, or any class of development, carried out by a person to whom section 35(7) applies pursuant to a permission granted to the applicant or to any other person under this Part or under Part IV of the Act of 1963.

(3) (a) Regulations under this section may, for the purposes of securing the attainment of an objective included in a development plan pursuant to section 10(2)(m), require any applicant for permission to provide the planning authority with such informa-tion, in respect of development (including development of a particular class) that the applicant proposes to carry out in a Gaeltacht area, as it may specify.

(b) A requirement to which paragraph (a) applies may relate to development belonging to a particular class.

(c) Before making regulations containing a requirement to which paragraph (a) applies the Minister shall consult with the Minister for Arts, Heritage, Gaeltacht and the Islands.

(4) Regulations under this section may make additional or separate provisions in regard to applications for outline permission within the meaning of section 36.

Notes
Section 33 restates s 25 of LG(PD)A 1963 with some amendments. This section deals with the making of regulations by the Minister. Such regulations are awaited.

In sub-s (2) a number of particular matters which may be provided for by regulation are listed. Note (c), (d) and (e) are new, as is (f)(ii). Sub-sections (2)(k) and (l) represent amendments from the pre-existing provisions and (l) is particularly noteworthy. See also PDA 2000, s 35.

[64]
34. Permission for development

(1) Where—

(a) an application is made to a planning authority in accordance with permission regulations for permission for the development of land, and

(b) all requirements of the regulations are complied with, the authority may decide to grant the permission subject to or with out conditions, or to refuse it.

(2) (a) When making its decision in relation to an application under this section, the planning authority shall be restricted to considering the proper planning and sus-tainable development of the area, regard being had to—

    (i)   the provisions of the development plan,

    (ii) the provisions of any special amenity area order relating to the area,

    (iii) any European site or other area prescribed for the purposes of section 10(2)(c),

    (iv) where relevant, the policy of the Government, the Minister or any other Minister of the Government,

    (v) the matters referred to in subsection (4), and

    (vi) any other relevant provision or requirement of this Act, and any regulations made thereunder.

(b) In considering its decision in accordance with paragraph (a), a planning authority shall consult with any other planning authority where it considers that a particular decision by it may have a significant effect on the area of that authority, and the authority shall have regard to the views of that other authority and, without prejudice to the foregoing, it shall have regard to the effect a particular decision by it may have on any area outside its area (including areas outside the State).

(c) Subject to section 98 (as amended by section 256 of this Act) of the Environmental Protection Agency Act, 1992, and section 54 (as amended by section 257of this Act) of the Waste Management Act, 1996, where an application under this section relates to development which comprises or is for the purposes of an activity for which an integrated pollution control licence or a waste licence is required, a planning authority shall take into consideration that the control of emissions arising from the activity is a function of the Environmental Protection Agency.

(3) A planning authority shall, when considering an application for permission under this section, have regard to—

(a) in addition to the application itself, any information relating to the application furnished to it by the applicant in accordance with the permission regulations,

(b) any written submissions or observations concerning the proposed development made to it in accordance with the permission regulations by persons or bodies other than the applicant.

(4) Conditions under subsection (1) may, without prejudice to the generality of that subsection, include all or any of the following—

(a) conditions for regulating the development or use of any land which adjoins, abuts or is adjacent to the land to be developed and which is under the control of the applicant, so far as appears to the planning authority to be expedient for the purposes of or in connection with the development authorised by the permission;

(b) conditions for requiring the carrying out of works (including the provision of facilities) which the planning authority considers are required for the purposes of the development authorised by the permission;

(c) conditions for requiring the taking of measures to reduce or prevent—

    (i)   the emission of any noise or vibration from any structure or site comprised in the development authorised by the permission which might give reasonable cause for annoyance either to persons in any premises in the neighbourhood of the development or to persons lawfully using any public place in that neighbourhood, or

(ii) the intrusion of any noise or vibration which might give reasonable cause for annoyance to any person lawfully occupying any such structure or site;

(d) conditions for requiring provision of open spaces;

(e) conditions for requiring the planting, maintenance and replacement of trees, shrubs or other plants or the landscaping of structures or other land;

(f) conditions for requiring the satisfactory completion within a specified period, not being less than 2 years from the commencement of any works, of the proposed development (including any roads, open spaces, car parks, sewers, watermains or drains or other public facilities), where the development includes the construction of 2 or more houses;

(g) conditions for requiring the giving of adequate security for satisfactory completion of the proposed development;

(h) conditions for determining the sequence and timing in which and the time at which works shall be carried out;

(i) conditions for the maintenance or management of the proposed development (including the establishment of a company or the appointment of a person or body of persons to carry out such maintenance or management);

(j) conditions for the maintenance, until taken in charge by the local authority concerned, of roads, open spaces, car parks, sewers, watermains or drains and other public facilities or, where there is an agreement with the local authority in relation to such maintenance, conditions for maintenance in accordance with the agreement;

(k) conditions for requiring the provision of such facilities for the collection or storage of recyclable materials for the purposes of the proposed development;

(l) conditions for requiring construction and demolition waste to be recovered or disposed of in such a manner and to such extent as may be specified by the planning authority;

(m) conditions for requiring the provision of roads, including traffic calming measures, open spaces, car parks, sewers, watermains or drains, facilities for the collection or storage of recyclable materials and other public facilities in excess of the immediate needs of the proposed development, subject to the local authority paying for the cost of the additional works and taking them in charge or otherwise entering into an agreement with the applicant with respect to the provision of those public facilities;

(n) conditions for requiring the removal of any structures authorised by the permission, or the discontinuance of any use of the land so authorised, at the expiration of a specified period, and the carrying out of any works required for the re-instatement of land at the expiration of that period;

(o) conditions in relation to appropriate naming and numbering of, and the provision of appropriate signage for, the proposed development;

(p) conditions for requiring, in any case in which the development authorised by the permission would remove or alter any protected structure or any element of a protected structure which contributes to its special architectural, historical, archaeological, artistic, cultural, scientific, social or technical interest—

    (i) the preservation by a written and visual record (either measured architectural drawings or colour photographs and/or audio-visual aids as considered appropriate) of that structure or element before the development authorised by the permission takes place, and

(ii) where appropriate, the architectural salvaging of any element, or the re-instatement of any element in a manner specified by the authority;

(q) conditions for regulating the hours and days during which a business premises may operate.

(5) The conditions under subsection (1) may provide that points of detail relating to a grant of permission may be agreed between the planning authority and the person to whom the permission is granted and that in default of agreement the matter is to be referred to the Board for determination.

(6) (a) In a case in which the development concerned would contravene materially the development plan, a planning authority may, notwithstanding any other provision of this Act, decide to grant permission under this section, provided that the following requirements are complied with before the decision is made, namely—

    (i) notice in the prescribed form of the intention of the planning authority to consider deciding to grant the permission shall be published in at least one daily newspaper circulating in its area and the notice shall specifically state which objective of the development plan would be materially contravened by granting this permission,

    (ii) copies of the notice shall be given to the applicant and to any person who has submitted a submission or observation in writing in relation to the development to which the application relates,

    (iii) any submission or observation as regards the making of a decision to grant permission and which is received by the planning authority not later than 4 weeks after the first publication of the notice shall be duly considered by the authority, and

    (iv) a resolution shall be passed by the authority requiring that a decision to grant permission be made.

(b) It shall be necessary for the passing of a resolution referred to in paragraph (a) that the number of the members of the planning authority voting in favour of the resolution is not less than three-quarters of the total number of the members of the planning authority or where the number so obtained is not a whole number, the whole number next below the number so obtained shall be sufficient, and the requirement of this paragraph is in addition to and not in substitution for any other requirement applying in relation to such a resolution.

(c) Where—

    (i) notice is given pursuant to section 4 of the City and County Management (Amendment) Act, 1955, of intention to propose a resolution which, if passed, would require the manager to decide to grant permission under this section, and

    (ii) the manager is of the opinion that the development concerned would contravene materially the development plan,

he or she shall, within one week of receiving the notice, make, by order, a declaration stating his or her opinion (a copy of which shall be furnished by him or her to each of the signatories of the notice) and thereupon the provisions of subparagraphs (i),(ii) and (iii) of paragraph (a) shall apply and have effect and shall operate to cause the notice to be of no further effect.

(d) If a resolution referred to in subparagraph (iv) of paragraph (a)is duly passed, the manager shall decide to grant the relevant permission.

(7) Notwithstanding section 4 of the City and County Management (Amendment) Act, 1955—

(a) the notice specified in subsection (2) of that section shall, in the case of a resolution under that section relating to a decision of a planning authority under this section or section 42, be signed—

    (i) if the land concerned is situated in a single local electoral area, by not less than three-quarters of the total number of the members who stand elected to the authority for that area, or where the number so obtained is not a whole number, the whole number next below the number so obtained shall be sufficient, and

    (ii) if the land concerned is situated in more than one local electoral area, by not less than three-quarters, as respects each such area, of the total number of the members of the authority who stand elected for that area, or where the number so obtained is not a whole number, the whole number next below the number so obtained shall be sufficient,

and

(b) it shall be necessary for the passing of a resolution under that section relating to a decision referred to in paragraph (a) that the number of the members voting in favour of the resolution is not less than three-quarters of the total number of members of the authority, or where the number so obtained is not a whole number, the whole number next below the number so obtained shall be sufficient.

(8) (a) Subject to paragraphs (b), (c), (d) and (e), where -

    (i) an application is made to a planning authority in accordance with the permission regulations for permission under this section, and

    (ii) any requirements of those regulations relating to the application are complied with,

a planning authority shall make its decision on the application within the period of 8 weeks beginning on the date of receipt by the planning authority of the application.

(b) Where a planning authority, within 8 weeks of the receipt of a planning application, serves notice in accordance with the permission regulations requiring the applicant to give to the authority further information or to produce evidence in respect of the application, the authority shall make its decision on the application within 4 weeks of the notice being complied with, provided that the total period is not less than 8 weeks.

(c) Where, in the case of an application accompanied by an environmental impact statement, a planning authority serves a notice referred to in paragraph (b), the authority shall make its decision within 8 weeks of the notice being complied with.

(d) Where a notice referred to in subsection (6) is published in relation to the application, the authority shall make its decision within the period of 8 weeks beginning on the day on which the notice is first published.

(e) Where, in the case of an application for permission for development that—

    (i) would be likely to increase the risk of a major accident, or

    (ii) is of such a nature as to be likely, if a major accident were to occur, and, having regard to all the circumstances, to cause there to be serious consequences, a planning authority consults, in accordance with the permission regulations, with a prescribed authority for the purpose of obtaining technical advice regarding such risk or consequences, the authority shall make a decision in relation to the application within 4 weeks beginning on the day on which the technical advice is received.

(f) Where a planning authority fails to make a decision within the period specified in paragraph (a), (b), (c), (d) or (e), a decision by the planning authority to grant the permission shall be regarded as having been given on the last day of that period.

(9) Where, within the period of 8 weeks beginning on the date of receipt by the planning authority of the application, the applicant for a permission under this section gives to the planning authority in writing his or her consent to the extension of the period for making a decision under subsection (8), the period for making the decision shall be extended for the period consented to by the applicant.

(10) (a) A decision given under this section or section 37 and the notification of the decision shall state the main reasons and considerations on which the decision is based, and where conditions are imposed in relation to the grant of any permission the decision shall state the main reasons for the imposition of any such conditions, provided that where a condition imposed is a condition described in subsection (4), a reference to the paragraph of subsection (4) in which the condition is described shall be sufficient to meet the requirements of this subsection.

(b) Where a decision by a planning authority under this section or by the Board under section 37 to grant or to refuse permission is different, in relation to the granting or refusal of permission from the recommendation in—

    (i) the reports on a planning application to the manager (or such other person delegated to make the decision) in the case of a planning authority, or

    (ii) a report of a person assigned to report on an appeal on behalf of the Board, a statement under paragraph (a) shall indicate the main reasons for not accepting the recommendation in the report or reports to grant or refuse permission.

(11) (a) Where the planning authority decides under this section to grant a permission—

    (i) in case no appeal is taken against the decision, it shall make the grant as soon as may be after the expiration of the period for the taking of an appeal,

    (ii) in case an appeal or appeals is or are taken against the decision, it shall not make the grant unless, as regards the appeal or, as may be appropriate. each of the appeals—

        (i) it is withdrawn, or

        (ii) it is dismissed by the Board pursuant to section 133 or 138, or

        (iii) in relation to it a direction is given to the authority by the Board pursuant to section 139, and, in the case of the withdrawal or dismissal of an appeal or of all such appeals, as may be appropriate, it shall make the grant as soon as may be after such withdrawal or dismissal and, in the case of such a direction, it shall make the grant, in accordance with the direction, as soon as may be after the giving by the Board of the direction.

(b) Where the Board decides on appeal under section 37 to grant a permission, it shall make the grant as soon as may be after the decision.

(12) An application for development of land in accordance with the permission regulations may be made for the retention of unauthorised development and this section shall apply to such an application, subject to any necessary modifications.

(13) A person shall not be entitled solely by reason of a permission under this section to carry out any development.

Notes
Section 34 restates s 26 of LG(PD)A 1963 with some amendments. Specifically sub-s (2)(c) requires a planning authority to take into consideration that the control of emissions arising from an integrated pollution controlled activity is a function of the Environmental Protection Agency. This is specifically qualified now by reference to s 256 of PDA 2000 which in broad terms allows a planning authority now to refuse to grant planning permission where it considers that the development is unacceptable on environmental grounds. Sub-section (3)(b) puts on a formal footing the obligation of the planning authority to consider submissions made by parties other than the applicant. Note also sub-s (3)(f)–(l) are for the most part new and are to seek to ensure that development is carried out in a controlled way; (m) contains a significant number of amendments to the pre-existing provision; (o)–(q) inclusive are new.

Sub-section (6) sets out the procedure where planning permission sought materially contravenes the development plan. This sub-section repeats with only minor amendments s 39(d) of LG(PD)A 1976 which amended LG(PD)A 1963.

Sub-section (8) sets out the time limits for deciding on planning applications. Essentially, all of the previous time limits have been converted from months to weeks to standardise where previously the Planning Acts provided for time limits in days, weeks and months. Sub-section (8)(d) states that where additional information is sought, the planning authority has a further four weeks to make their decision (whereas previously the period was two months). This period is eight weeks if an environmental impact statement accompanies the planning application. See also the provisions of sub-s (8)(e) in this regard.

Sub-section (10) differs from the provisions of s 26, sub-s (8) of LG(PD)A 1963 as substituted by s 39(d) of LG(PD)A 1976, by the inclusion of sub-s (b).

[65]–[70]
35. Refusal of planning permission for past failures to comply
(1) Where, having regard to—

(a) any information furnished pursuant to regulations made under section 33(2)(1), or

(b) any information available to the planning authority concerning development carried out by a person to whom this section applies, pursuant to a permission (in this subsection and subsection (2) referred to as a "previous permission") granted to the applicant or to any other person under this Part or Part IV of the Act of 1963, the planning authority is satisfied that a person or company to whom this section applies is not in compliance with the previous permission, or with a condition to which the previous permission is subject, the authority may form the opinion—
  (i) that there is a real and substantial risk that the development in respect of which permission is sought would not be completed in accordance with

such permission if granted or with a condition to which such permission if granted would be subject, and

(ii) that planning permission should not be granted to the applicant concerned in respect of that development.

(2) In forming its opinion under subsection (1), the planning authority shall only consider those failures to comply with any previous permission, or with any condition to which that permission is subject, that are of a substantial nature.

(3) An opinion under this subsection shall not be a decision on an application for permission for the purposes of this Part.

(4) Where the planning authority has formed an opinion under subsection (1), the planning authority shall apply, by motion on notice to the person to whom the opinion concerned relates, to the High Court for an authorisation to refuse permission and the High Court, on hearing the application—

(a) may grant an authorisation to the authority to refuse permission for that reason, or

(b) may refuse to grant an authorisation to the authority to refuse permission and shall remit the application to the authority for decision, or

(c) may give such other directions to the authority as the Court considers appropriate.

(5) (a) Subsection (3)(a) in section 34 shall not apply where an application to the High Court under subsection (4) is made within the period of 8 weeks from the date of the making of an application for permission under this section.

(b) Where, under subsection (4)(b), a matter is remitted to the planning authority, a decision on the permission shall be made within the period of 8 weeks from the date of the decision of the High Court, and subsection (8)(b) in section 34 shall be construed and have effect in accordance with this subsection.

(6) Where an authority is granted an authorisation by the Court under subsection (4)(a) to refuse a permission, no appeal shall lie to the Board from that refusal.

(7) In this section, "a person to whom this section applies" means—

(a) the applicant for the permission concerned,

(b) a partnership of which the applicant is or was a member and which, during the membership of that applicant, carried out a development referred to in subsection (1)(b),

(c) in the case where the applicant for permission is a company—

(i) the company concerned is related to a company (within the meaning of section 140(5) of the Companies Act, 1990) which carried out a development referred to in subsection (1)(b), or

(ii) the company concerned is under the same control as a company which carried out a development referred to in subsection (1)(b), where "control" has the same meaning as in section 26(3) of the Companies Act, 1990,

or

(d) a company which carried out a development referred to in subsection (1) (b), which company is controlled by the applicant—

(i) where "control" has the same meaning as in section 26(3) of the Companies Act, 1990, or

(ii) as a shadow director within the meaning of section 27(1) of the Companies Act, 1990.

Note
Section 35 is a new provision and allows a local authority in specified circumstances to refuse to grant planning permission on the basis of previous failures to comply with planning permissions on the part of the applicant. The procedure requires an order from the High Court confirming the local authority's decision.

[71]
36. Outline permission
(1) An application under section 34 may be made to a planning authority in accordance with the permission regulations for out line permission for the development of land.

(2) Where outline permission is granted under section 34, that permission shall not operate to authorise the carrying out of any development to which the outline permission relates until a subsequent permission has been granted under that section.

(3) (a) Where outline permission has been granted by a planning authority, any subsequent application for permission must be made not later than 3 years beginning on the date of the grant of outline permission, or such longer period, not exceeding 5 years, as may be specified by the planning authority.
(b) The outline permission shall cease to have effect at the end of the period referred to in paragraph (a) unless the subsequent application for permission is made within that period.
(c) Sections 40, 41 and 42 shall not apply to the grant of an outline permission.

(4) Where an application for permission is made to a planning authority consequent on the grant of outline permission, the planning authority shall not refuse to grant permission on the basis of any matter which had been decided in the grant of outline permission, provided that the authority is satisfied that the proposed development is within the terms of the outline permission.

(5) No appeal may be brought to the Board under section 37 against a decision of a planning authority to grant permission consequent on the grant of outline permission in respect of any aspect of the proposed development which was decided in the grant of outline permission.

(6) In this section, "outline permission" means permission granted in principle under section 34 for the development of land subject to a subsequent detailed application for permission under that section.

Note
Section 36 provides the basis in primary legislation for outline permission where previously this was dealt with only in regulations. The provisions at sub-s (3)(a) and (b) should be noted. The provisions at sub-ss (4) and (5) will be particularly welcome for developers in circumstances where having obtained outline planning permission, this will significantly limit the opportunity of the planning authority to revisit matters decided in the course of the grant of outline planning permission when considering an application for full planning permission.

Similarly, having outline planning permission will limit the ability for appeals to be brought against decisions on an application based on a previous outline planning permission. This is a significant change to the pre-existing position.

[72]
37. Appeal to Board
(1) (a) An applicant for permission and any person who made submissions or observations in writing in relation to the planning application to the planning authority in accordance with the permission regulations and on payment of the appropriate fee, may, at any time before the expiration of the appropriate period, appeal to the Board against a decision of a planning authority under section 34.

(b) Subject to paragraphs (c) and (d), where an appeal is brought against a decision of a planning authority and is not withdrawn, the Board shall determine the application as if it had been made to the Board in the first instance and the decision of the Board shall operate to annul the decision of the planning authority as from the time when it was given; and subsections (1), (2), (3) and (4) of section 34 shall apply, subject to any necessary modifications, in relation to the determination of an application by the Board on appeal under this subsection as they apply in relation to the determination under that section of an application by a planning authority.

(c) Paragraph (b) shall be construed and have effect subject to sections 133, 138 and 139.

(d) In paragraph (a) and subsection (6), "the appropriate period" means the period of four weeks beginning on the day of the decision of the planning authority.

(2) (a) Subject to paragraph (b), the Board may in determining an appeal under this section decide to grant a permission even if the proposed development contravenes materially the development plan relating to the area of the planning authority to whose decision the appeal relates.

(b) Where a planning authority has decided to refuse permission on the grounds that a proposed development materially contravenes the development plan, the Board may only grant permission in accordance with paragraph (a) where it considers that—
(i) the proposed development is of strategic or national importance,
(ii) there are conflicting objectives in the development plan or the objectives are not clearly stated, insofar as the proposed development is concerned, or
(iii) permission for the proposed development should be granted having regard to regional planning guidelines for the area, guidelines under section 28, policy directives under section 29, the statutory obligations of any local authority in the area. and any relevant policy of the Government, the Minister or any Minister of the Government, or
(iv) permission for the proposed development should be granted having regard to the pattern of development, and permissions granted, in the area since the making of the development plan

(c) Where the Board grants a permission in accordance with paragraph (b), the Board shall, in addition to the requirements of section 34(10), indicate in its decision the main reasons and considerations for contravening materially the development plan.

(3) Subject to section 141(2), the provisions of subsection (1) authorising appeals to be made before the expiration of the appropriate period within the meaning of that subsection shall be construed as including a provision that an appeal received by the Board after the expiration of the appropriate period shall be invalid as not having been made in time.

(4) (a) Notwithstanding subsection (1), where in accordance with the permission regulations any prescribed body is entitled to be given notice of any planning application, that body shall be entitled to appeal to the Board before the expiration of the appropriate period within the meaning of that subsection where the body had not been sent notice in accordance with the regulations.

(b) The Board may dismiss any appeal made under paragraph (a) where it considers the body concerned was not entitled to be sent notice of the planning application in accordance with the permission regulations.

(5) (a) No application for permission for the same development or for development of the same description as an application for permission for development which is the subject of an appeal to the Board under this section shall be made before—
  (i) the Board has made its decision on the appeal,
  (ii) the appeal is withdrawn, or
  (iii) the appeal is dismissed by the Board pursuant to section 133 or 138.

(b) Where an application for permission referred to in paragraph (a) is made to a planning authority, the planning authority shall notify the applicant that the application cannot be considered by the planning authority and return the application and any other information submitted with the application in accordance with the permission regulations, and any fee paid.

(c) A dispute as to whether an application for permission is for the same development or is for development of the same description as an application for permission which is the subject of an appeal to the Board may be referred to the Board for determination.

(6) (a) Notwithstanding subsection (1)(a), a person who has an interest in land adjoining land in respect of which permission has been granted may, within the appropriate period and on payment of the appropriate fee, apply to the Board for leave to appeal against a decision of the planning authority under section 34.

(b) An application under paragraph (a) shall state the name and address of the person making the application, the grounds upon which the application is made, and a description of the person's interest in the land.

(c) The Board shall, within one week from the receipt of an application under paragraph (a), require, by notice in writing, the planning authority concerned to submit to the Board copies of the materials referred to in subparagraph (i) of section 128(a), the report referred to in subparagraph (ii) of that section, and the decision and notification referred to in subparagraph (iii) of that section and the planning authority shall comply with such requirement within one week from the date of receiving the notice.

(d) The Board, or any member or employee of the Board duly authorised by the Board in that behalf, shall, where an applicant under this subsection shows that—
  (i) the development for which permission has been granted will differ materially from the development as set out in the application for permission by

        reason of conditions imposed by the planning authority to which the grant is subject, and

   (ii) that the imposition of such conditions will materially affect the applicant's enjoyment of the land or reduce the value of the land,

        within 4 weeks from the receipt of the application grant the applicant leave to appeal against the decision of the planning authority under subsection (1).

(e) The Board shall notify in writing the applicant and the planning authority of a decision to grant or refuse an application under this subsection within 3 days from its making.

(f) A person to whom leave to appeal has been granted under this subsection shall bring the appeal within 2 weeks from the receipt of the notification under paragraph (e).

(g) Notwithstanding section 34(11)(a)(i), where an application is made under this subsection a planning authority shall not make a grant of permission unless the application is refused.

(h) Where leave to appeal is granted under this subsection, subsection (2) of section 126 shall apply subject to the modification that the reference therein to 18 weeks shall be construed as a reference to 14 weeks.

(i) Where leave to appeal is granted under this section, a planning authority that has complied with paragraph (c) shall, in respect of the appeal, be deemed to have complied with the requirements of section 128.

Note

Section 37 provides for appeals to An Bord Pleanála and again converts the pre-existing time limits from weeks to months and specifies that time runs from the date of the decision and not from notification of it. Note in particular s 37(1)(a) which is new and requires that only persons (other than the applicant) who made submissions and observations in writing in relation to the planning application to the planning authority may appeal. Sub-section (2) limits the ability of the Board to grant permission in circumstances which materially contravene the development plan where the planning authority have refused to grant planning permission on that basis.

[73]
38. Availability of documents relating to planning applications

(1) Where a planning authority gives its decision in respect of a planning application the following documents shall be made available within 3 working days for inspection and purchase by members of the public during office hours at the offices of the authority:

(a) a copy of the planning application and of any particulars, evidence, environmental impact statement, other written study or further information received or obtained by the authority from the applicant in accordance with regulations under this Act;

(b) a copy of any submissions or observations in relation to the planning application which have been received by the authority;

(c) a copy of any report prepared by or for the authority in relation to the planning application;

(d) a copy of the decision of the authority in respect of the planning application and a copy of the notification of the decision given to the applicant; and

(e) a copy of any documents relating to a contribution or other matter referred to in section 34(5).

(2) Without prejudice to the Freedom of Information Act, 1997, and the European Communities Act, 1972 (Access to Information on the Environment) Regulations, 1998 (S.I. No. 125 of 1998), and any regulations amending those regulations, the documents referred to under subsection (1) shall be available for inspection for a period of not less than 7 years after the making of the decision by the authority.

(3) Any document referred to in paragraphs (a) and (b) of subsection (1) which is received or obtained by a planning authority shall be made available for inspection and purchase by members of the public at the office hours of the authority from as soon as may be after receipt of the document until a decision is made on the application.

(4) Copies of documents under this section shall be available for purchase on payment of a specified fee not exceeding the reasonable cost of making such a copy.

(5) At the end of the period for the availability of documents referred to in subsection (2), a planning authority shall retain at least one original copy of each of those documents in a local archive in accordance with section 65 of the Local Government Act, 1994.

(6) The Minister may prescribe additional requirements in relation to the availability for inspection by members of the public of documents relating to planning applications.

(7) This section shall apply in respect of any application made to a planning authority after the commencement of this section.

Note
Section 38 restates ss 5, 6 of LG(PD)A 1992 with some amendments, in particular sub-s (1)(b) and (e), and sub-ss (2)–(7) inclusive.

[74]
39. Supplemental provisions as to grant of permission
(1) Where permission to develop land or for the retention of development is granted under this Part, then, except as may be otherwise provided by the permission, the grant of permission shall enure for the benefit of the land and of all persons for the time being interested therein.

(2) Where permission is granted under this Part for a structure, the grant of permission may specify the purposes for which the structure may or may not be used, and in case the grant specifies use as a dwelling as a purpose for which the structure may be used, the permission may also be granted subject to a condition specifying that the use as a dwelling shall be restricted to use by persons of a particular class or description and that provision to that effect shall be embodied in an agreement under section 47.

(3) (a) Where permission to develop land is granted under this Part for a limited period only, nothing in this Part shall be construed as requiring permission to be obtained thereunder for the resumption, at the expiration of that period, of the use of the land for the purpose for which it was normally used before the permission was granted.

(b) In determining for the purposes of this subsection the purposes for which land was normally used before the grant of permission, no account shall be taken of any use of the land begun in contravention of this Part.

(4) Notwithstanding anything in this Part, permission shall not be required under this Part, in the case of land which, on 1 October, 1964, was normally used for one purpose and was also used on occasions, whether at regular intervals or not, for any other purpose, for the use of the land for that other purpose on similar occasions after 1 October, 1964.

Note
Section 39 restates s 38(5)–(7) of LG(PD)A 1963 save that sub-s (4) is a new provision.

[75]–[80]
40. Limit of duration of permission
(1) Subject to subsection (2), a permission granted under this Part, shall on the expiration of the appropriate period (but without prejudice to the validity of anything done pursuant thereto prior to the expiration of that period) cease to have effect as regards—

(a) in case the development to which the permission relates is not commenced during that period, the entire development, and
(b) in case the development is commenced during that period, so much of the development as is not completed within that period.

(2) (a) Subsection (1) shall not apply—
    (i)   to any permission for the retention on land of any structure,
    (ii) to any permission granted either for a limited period only or subject to a condition which is of a kind described in section 34(4)(n),
    (iii) in the case of a house, shop, office or other building which itself has been completed, in relation to the provision of any structure or works included in the relevant permission and which are either necessary for or ancillary or incidental to the use of the building in accordance with that permission, or
    (iv) in the case of a development comprising a number of buildings of which only some have been completed, in relation to the provision of roads, services and open spaces included in the relevant permission and which are necessary for or ancillary or incidental to the completed buildings.
(b) Subsection (1) shall not affect—
    (i)   the continuance of any use, in accordance with a permission, of land.
    (ii) where a development has been completed (whether to an extent described in paragraph (a) or otherwise), the obligation of any person to comply with any condition attached to the relevant permission whereby something is required either to be done or not to be done.

(3) In this section and in section 42, "the appropriate period" means—

(a) in case in relation to the permission a period is specified pursuant to section 41, that period, and
(b) in any other case, the period of five years beginning on the date of the grant of permission.

Note
Section 40 restates s 2 of LG(PD)A 1982.

[81]
41. Power to vary appropriate period
Without prejudice to the powers conferred on them by this Part to grant a permission to develop land for a limited period only, in. deciding to grant a permission under sections 34 and 37, a planning authority or the Board, as may be appropriate, may, having regard to the nature and extent of the relevant development and any other material consideration, specify the period, being a period of more than 5 years, during which the permission is to have effect, and in case the planning authority exercises, or refuses to exercise, the power conferred on it by this section, the exercise or refusal shall be regarded as forming part of the relevant decision of the authority or the Board under sections 34 and 37.

Note
Section 41 restates s 3 of LG(PD)A 1982.

[82]
42. Power to extend additional period
(1) On application a planning authority shall, as regards a particular permission, extend the appropriate period, by such appropriate period. as the authority considers requisite to enable the development to which the permission relates to be completed, if each of the following requirements is complied with—

(a) the application is in accordance with such regulations under this Act as apply to it;
(b) any requirements of, or made under, those regulations are complied with as regards the application;
(c) the authority is satisfied in relation to the permission that—
    (i) the development to which the permission relates commenced before the expiration of the appropriate period sought to be extended,
    (ii) substantial works were carried out pursuant to the permission during that period, and
    (iii) the development will be completed within a reasonable time;
(d) the application is made prior to the end of the appropriate period.
(2) Where—

(a) an application is duly made under this section to a planning authority,
(b) any requirements of, or made under, regulations under section 43 are complied with as regards the application, and
(c) the planning authority does not give notice to the applicant of its decision as regards the application within the period of 8 weeks beginning on—
    (i) in case all of the requirements referred to in paragraph (b) are complied with on or before the day of receipt by the planning authority of the application, that day, and
    (ii) in any other case, the day on which all of those requirements stand complied with,

subject to section 246(3), a decision by the planning authority to extend, or to further extend, as may be appropriate, the period, which in relation to the relevant permission is the appropriate period, by such additional period as is specified in the application, shall be deemed to have been given by the planning authority on the last day of the 8 week period.

(3) (a) Where a decision to extend an appropriate period is given under subsection (1), or, pursuant to subsection (2), such a decision is deemed to have been given, the planning authority shall not further extend the appropriate period, unless each of the following requirements is complied with—

    (i) an application in that behalf is made to it in accordance with the regulations under section 43;

    (ii) any requirements of, or made under, the regulations are complied with as regards the application;

    (iii) the authority is satisfied that the relevant development has not been completed due to circumstances beyond the control of the person carrying out the development.

(b) An appropriate period shall be further extended under this subsection only for such period as the planning authority considers requisite to enable the relevant development to be completed.

(4) Particulars of any application made to a planning authority under this section and of the decision of the planning authority in respect of the application shall be recorded on the relevant entry in the register.

(5) Where a decision to extend, or further to extend, is given under this section, or, pursuant to subsection (2), such a decision is deemed to have been given, section 40 shall, in relation to the permission to which the decision relates, be construed and have effect subject to and in accordance with the terms of the decision.

Note
Section 42 restates s 4 of LG(PD)A 1982.

[83]
43. Regulations regarding sections 40, 41, 42
(1) The Minister may make regulations providing for any matter of procedure in relation to applications under section 42 and making such incidental, consequential or supplementary provision as may appear to him or her to be necessary or proper to give full effect to any of the provisions of section 40, 41 or 42.

(2) Without prejudice to the generality of subsection (1), regulations under this section may—

(a) specify the time at which applications under section 42 may be made, the manner in which those applications shall be made and the particulars they shall contain,

(b) require applicants to furnish to the planning authority any specified information with respect to their applications (including any information regarding any estate or interest in or right over land),

(c) require applicants to submit to a planning authority any further information relevant to their applications (including any information as to any such estate, interest or right),

(d) require the production of any evidence to verify any particulars or information given by any applicant, and

(e)   require the notification (in a prescribed manner) by planning authorities of decisions on applications.

Note
Section 43 deals with the making of Regulations relative to ss 40–42 inclusive.

[84]
44. Revocation or modification of permission
(1) If the planning authority considers that it is expedient that any permission to develop land granted under this Part should be revoked or modified, it may serve a notice in accordance with subsection (3) on the applicant and on any other person who, in its opinion, will be materially affected by the revocation or modification.

(2) A planning authority shall neither revoke nor modify a permission under this section unless the development to which the permission relates no longer conforms with the provisions of the development plan.

(3) The notice referred to in subsection (1) shall—

(a)   refer to the permission concerned,
(b)   specify the provisions of the development plan to which the permission no longer conforms, and
(c)   invite the person or persons served with the notice to make written submissions or observations to the planning authority within the period specified in the notice (being not less than 4 weeks from the service of the notice) concerning the proposed revocation or modification.

(4) A planning authority may decide to revoke or modify a permission and, when making its decision, shall have regard to any submissions or observations made under subsection (3)(c).

(5) Where a planning authority decides to revoke or modify a permission under subsection (4), it shall specify in the decision the provisions of the development plan to which the permission no longer conforms, and the main reasons and considerations on which the decision is based.

(6) A person served with a notice under subsection (1) may, at any time within 4 weeks of the date of the decision, appeal to the Board against the decision.

(7) Where an appeal is brought under this section against a decision, the Board may confirm the decision with or without modifications, or annul the decision, and it shall specify the main reasons and considerations for its decision.

(8) The power conferred by this section to revoke or modify permission to develop land may be exercised—

(a)   where the permission relates to the carrying out of works, at any time before those works have been commenced or, in the case of works which have been commenced and which, consequent on the making of a variation in the development plan, will contravene the plan, at any time before those works have been completed,
(b)   where the permission relates to a change of the use of any land, at any time before the change has taken place.

but the revocation or modification of permission for the carrying out of works shall not affect so much of the works as have been previously carried out.

(9) A planning authority may at any time, for stated reasons, by notice in writing withdraw a notice served under this section.

(10) Particulars of a decision made under this section shall be entered in the register.

(11) The revocation or modification under this section of a permission shall be a reserved function.

Note
Section 44 restates s 30 of LG(PD)A 1963 with some amendments. Note the addition of sub-ss (2), (3)(c) and (4).

[85]–[90]
45. Acquisition of land for open spaces
(1) Where—

(a) development is being or has been carried out pursuant to a permission under section 34,
(b) (i) a condition requiring the provision or maintenance of land as open space, being open space to which this section applies, was attached to the permission, or
(ii) it was either explicit or implicit. in the application for the permission that land would be provided or maintained as such open space,
(c) the planning authority has served on the owner of the land a written request that, within a period specified in the request (being a period of not less than 8 weeks commencing on the date of the request), he or she will provide, level, plant or otherwise adapt or maintain the land in a manner so specified, being a manner which in its opinion would make it suitable for the purpose for which the open space was to be provided, and
(d) the owner fails to comply or to secure compliance with the request within the period so specified, the planning authority may, if it thinks fit, publish in a newspaper circulating in the district a notice (an "acquisition notice") of its intention to acquire the land by order under this section and the acquisition notice shall specify a period (being a period of not less than 4 weeks commencing on the date on which the notice is published) within which an appeal may be made under this section.

(2) Where a planning authority publishes an acquisition notice, it shall serve a copy of the notice on the owner of the land to which the notice relates not later than 10 days after the date of the publication.

(3) Any person having an interest in the land to which an acquisition notice relates may within the period specified in the notice appeal to the Board.

(4) Where an appeal is brought under this section the Board may—

(a) annul the acquisition notice to which the appeal relates, or
(b) confirm the acquisition notice, with or without modification, in respect of all or such part of the relevant land as the Board considers reasonable.

(5) If a planning authority publishes an acquisition notice and either—

(a) the period for appealing against the notice has expired and no appeal has been taken, or

(b) an appeal has been taken against the notice and the appeal has been withdrawn or the notice has been confirmed whether unconditionally or subject to modifications,

the planning authority may make an order in the prescribed form which order shall be expressed and shall operate to vest the land to which the acquisition notice, or, where appropriate, the acquisition notice as confirmed, relates in the planning authority on a specified date for all the estate, term or interest for which immediately before the date of the order the land was held by the owner together with all rights and liabilities which, immediately before that date, were enjoyed or incurred in connection therewith by the owner together with an obligation to comply with the request made under subsection (1) (c).

(6) Where a planning authority has acquired by an order under this section land which is subject, either alone or in conjunction with other land, to a purchase annuity, payment in lieu of rent, or other annual sum (not being merely a rent under a contract of tenancy) payable to the Minister for Agriculture, Food and Rural Development or to the Commissioners, the authority shall become and be liable, as from the date on which the land is vested in them by the vesting order, for the payment to that Minister or to the Commissioners, as the case may be, of the annual sum or such portion thereof as shall be apportioned by that Minister or by the Commissioners, on the land as if the land had been transferred to the authority by the owner thereof on that date.

(7) When a planning authority makes an order under this section in relation to any land, it shall send the order to the registering authority under the Registration of Title Act, 1964, and thereupon the registering authority shall cause the planning authority to be registered as owner of the land in accordance with the order.

(8) Where a claim is made for compensation in respect of land to which an order under this section relates, the claim shall, in default of agreement, be determined by arbitration under the Acquisition of Land (Assessment of Compensation) Act, 1919, in the like manner in all respects as if such claim arose in relation to the compulsory acquisition of land, but subject to the proviso that the arbitrator shall have jurisdiction to make a nil award and to the following provisions:

(a) the arbitrator shall make a nil award, unless it is shown by or on behalf of the owner that an amount equal to the value of the land to which the relevant permission under section 34 relates, being that value at the time when the application for the permission was made, as a result of the development has not been recovered and as a further such result will not in the future be recoverable by disposing of the land which is land to which the permission relates and which is not land to which the order relates, and

(b) in the assessment of the value of the land to which the order relates, no regard shall be had to its value for use other than as open space and a deduction shall be made in respect of the cost of carrying out such works as may be necessary to comply with the request made pursuant to subsection (1)(c).

(9) A planning authority shall enter in the register—

(a) particulars of any acquisition notice published by it,
(b) the date and effect of any decision on appeal in relation to any such notice, and
(c) particulars of any order made under this section,

and every entry shall be made within the period of 7 days commencing on the day of publication, receipt of notification of the decision or the making of the order, as may be appropriate.

(10) This section applies to any form of open space (whether referred to as open space or by any other description in the relevant application for a permission or in a condition attached to the relevant permission), being land which is not described in the application or condition either as private open space or in terms indicating that it is not intended that members of the public are to have resort thereto without restriction.

Note
Section 45 restates s 25 of LG(PD)A 1976.

[91]
46. Requiring removal or alteration of structure or discontinuance of use
(1) If a planning authority decides that, in exceptional circumstances—

(a) any structure should be demolished, removed, altered or replaced,
(b) any use should be discontinued, or
(c) any conditions should be imposed on the continuance of a use,

the planning authority may serve a notice on the owner and on the occupier of the structure or land concerned and on any other person who, in its opinion, will be affected by the notice.

(2) Subsection (1) shall not apply to any unauthorised development unless the notice under this section is served after seven years from the commencement of the unauthorised development.

(3) A notice referred to in subsection (1) shall—

(a) specify the location of the structure or land concerned,
(b) specify the steps that will be required to be taken within a specified period, including, where appropriate—
    (i) the demolition, removal, alteration or replacement of any structure, or
    (ii) the discontinuance of any use or the continuance of any use subject to conditions,
    and
(c) invite any person served with the notice to make written submissions or observations to the planning authority in respect of the matters referred to in the notice within a specified period (being not less than 4 weeks from the date of service of the notice).

(4) A planning authority may, having regard to any submissions or observations made in accordance with subsection (3)(c), decide to confirm the notice, with or without modifications, or not to confirm the notice.

(5) A planning authority, in deciding whether to confirm a notice pursuant to this section, shall consider—

(a) the proper planning and sustainable development of the area,
(b) the provisions of the development plan,
(c) the provisions of any special amenity area order, any European site or other area designated for the purposes of section 10(2)(c) relating to the area, and
(d) any other relevant provision of this Act and any regulations made thereunder.

(6) Where a notice is confirmed by a planning authority under subsection (4), any person served with the notice may, within 8 weeks of the date of service of the notice, appeal to the Board against the notice.

(7) Where an appeal is brought under this section against a notice, the Board may confirm the notice with or without modifications or annul the notice, and the provisions of subsection (5) shall apply, subject to any necessary modifications, to the deciding of an appeal under this subsection by the Board, as they apply to the making of a decision by the planning authority.

(8) A notice under this section (other than a notice which is annulled) shall take effect—

(a) in case no appeal against it is taken, on the expiration of the period for taking an appeal, or
(b) in case an appeal or appeals are taken against it and not withdrawn, when the appeal or appeals have been either withdrawn or decided.

(9) If, within the period specified in a notice under this section, or within such extended period as the planning authority may allow, any demolition, removal, alteration or replacement required by the notice has not been effected, the planning authority may enter the structure and may effect such demolition, removal, alteration or replacement as is specified in the notice.

(10) Where a notice under this section is complied with, the planning authority shall pay to the person complying with the notice the expenses reasonably incurred by the person in carrying out the demolition, removal, alteration or replacement specified in the notice, less the value of any salvageable materials.

(11) Where any person served with a notice under this section fails to comply with the requirements of the notice, or causes or permits the failure to comply with the requirements, he or she shall be guilty of an offence.

(12) Particulars of a notice served or confirmed under this section shall be entered in the register.

(13) (a) A planning authority may, for stated reasons, by notice in writing withdraw a notice served under this section.
(b) Where a notice is withdrawn pursuant to this subsection by a planning authority, the fact that the notice was withdrawn shall be recorded by the authority in the register.

Note
Section 46 restates ss 36 and 37 of LG(PD)A 1963 with amendments. In particular, note the provisions of sub-s (2) and the statement of the relevant periods in weeks.

[92]
47. Agreements regulating development or use of land

(1) A planning authority may enter into an agreement with any person interested in land in their area, for the purpose of restricting or regulating the development or use of the land, either permanently or during such period as may be specified by the agreement, and any such agreement may contain such incidental and consequential provisions (including provisions of a financial character) as appear to the planning authority to be necessary or expedient for the purposes of the agreement.

(2) A planning authority in entering into an agreement under this section may join with any body which is a prescribed authority for the purposes of section 11.

(3) An agreement made under this section with any person interested in land may be enforced by the planning authority, or any body joined with it, against persons deriving title under that person in respect of that land as if the planning authority or body, as may be appropriate, were possessed of adjacent land, and as if the agreement had been expressed to be made for the benefit of that land.

(4) Nothing in this section, or in any agreement made thereunder, shall be construed as restricting the exercise, in relation to land which is the subject of any such agreement, of any powers exercisable by the Minister, the Board or the planning authority under this Act, so long as those powers are not exercised so as to contravene materially the provisions of the development plan, or as requiring the exercise of any such powers so as to contravene materially those provisions.

(5) Particulars of an agreement made under this section shall be entered in the register.

Note
Section 47 restates s 38 of LG(PD)A 1963 concerning agreements often known as 'sterilisation' agreements.

[93]
48. Development contributions

(1) A planning authority may, when granting a permission under section 34, include conditions for requiring the payment of a contribution in respect of public infrastructure and facilities benefiting development in the area of the planning authority and that is provided, or that it is intended will be provided, by or on behalf of a local authority (regardless of other sources of funding for the infrastructure and facilities).

(2) (a) Subject to paragraph (c), the basis for the determination of a contribution under subsection (1) shall be set out in a development contribution scheme made under this section, and a planning authority may make one or more schemes in respect of different parts of its functional area.

(b) A scheme may make provision for payment of different contributions in respect of different classes or descriptions of development.

(c) A planning authority may, in addition to the terms of a scheme, require the payment of a special contribution in respect of a particular development where specific exceptional costs not covered by a scheme are incurred by any local authority in respect of public infrastructure and facilities which benefit the proposed development.

(3) (a) A scheme shall state the basis for determining the contributions to be paid in respect of public infrastructure and facilities, in accordance with the terms of the scheme.

(b) In stating the basis for determining the contributions in accordance with paragraph (a), the scheme shall indicate the contribution to be paid in respect of the different classes of public infrastructure and facilities which are provided or to be provided by any local authority and the planning authority shall have regard to the actual estimated cost of providing the classes of public infrastructure and facilities, except that any benefit which accrues in respect of existing development may not be included in any such determination.

(c) A scheme may allow for the payment of a reduced contribution or no contribution in certain circumstances, in accordance with the provisions of the scheme.

(4) Where a planning authority proposes to make a scheme under this section, it shall publish in one or more newspapers circulating in the area to which the scheme relates, a notice—

(a) stating that a draft scheme has been prepared,

(b) giving details of the proposed contributions under the draft scheme,

(c) indicating the times at which, the period (which shall be not less than 6 weeks) during which, and the place where, a copy of the draft scheme may be inspected, and

(d) stating that submissions or observations may be made in writing to the planning authority in relation to the draft scheme, before the end of the period for inspection.

(5) (a) In addition to the requirements of subsection (4), a planning authority shall send a copy of the draft scheme to the Minister.

(b) The Minister may make recommendations to the planning authority regarding the terms of the draft scheme, within 6 weeks of being sent the scheme.

(6) (a) Not later than 4 weeks after the expiration of the period for making submissions or observations under subsection (4), the manager of a planning authority shall prepare a report on any submissions or observations received under that subsection, and submit the report to the members of the authority for their consideration.

(b) A report under paragraph (a) shall—

(i) list the persons or bodies who made submissions or observations under this section,

(ii) summarise the issues raised by the persons or bodies in the submissions or observations, and

(iii) give the response of the manager to the issues raised, taking account of the proper planning and sustainable development of the area.

(7) The members of the planning authority shall consider the draft scheme and the report of the manager under subsection (6), and shall have regard to any recommendations made by the Minister under subsection (5).

(8) (a) Following the consideration of the manager's report, and having had regard to any recommendations made by the Minister, the planning authority shall make the scheme, unless it decides, by resolution, to vary or modify the scheme,

otherwise than as recommended in the manager's report, or otherwise decides not to make the scheme.

(b) A resolution under paragraph (a) must be passed not later than 6 weeks after receipt of the manager's report.

(9) (a) Where a planning authority makes a scheme in accordance with subsection (8), the authority shall publish notice of the making, or approving, of the scheme, as the case may be, in at least one newspaper circulating in its area.

(b) A notice under paragraph (a) shall—

    (i) give the date of the decision of the planning authority in respect of the draft scheme,

    (ii) state the nature of the decision, and

    (iii) contain such other information as may be prescribed.

(10) (a) Subject to paragraph (b), no appeal shall lie to the Board in relation to a condition requiring a contribution to be paid in accordance with a scheme made under this section.

(b) An appeal may be brought to the Board where an applicant for permission under section 34 considers that the terms of the scheme have not been properly applied in respect of any condition laid down by the planning authority.

(c) Notwithstanding section 34(11), where an appeal is brought in accordance with paragraph (b), and no other appeal of the decision of a planning authority is brought by any other person under section 37, the authority shall make the grant of permission as soon as may be after the expiration of the period for the taking of an appeal, provided that the person who takes the appeal in accordance with paragraph (b) furnishes to the planning authority security for payment of the full amount of the contribution as specified in the condition.

(11) Where an appeal is brought to the Board in respect of a refusal to grant permission under this Part, and where the Board decides to grant permission, it shall, where appropriate, apply as a condition to the permission the provisions of the contribution scheme for the time being in force in the area of the proposed development.

(12) Where payment of a special contribution is required in accordance with subsection (2) (c), the following provisions shall apply—

(a) the condition shall specify the particular works carried out, or proposed to be carried out, by any local authority to which the contribution relates,

(b) where the works in question—

    (i) are not commenced within 5 years of the date of payment to the authority of the contribution,

    (ii) have commenced, but have not been completed, within 7 years of the date of payment to the authority of the contribution, or

    (iii) where the local authority decides not to proceed with the proposed works or part thereof,

the contribution shall, subject to paragraph (c), be refunded to the applicant together with any interest that may have accrued over the period while held by the local authority,

(c) where under subparagraph (ii) or (iii) of paragraph (b), any local authority has incurred expenditure within the required period in respect of a proportion of the works proposed to be carried out, any refund shall be in proportion to those proposed works which have not been carried out.

(13) (a) Notwithstanding sections 37 and 139, where an appeal received by the Board after the commencement of this section relates solely to a condition dealing with a special contribution, and no appeal is brought by any other person under section 37 of the decision of the planning authority under that section, the Board shall not determine the relevant application as if it had been made to it in the first instance, but shall determine only the matters under appeal.

(b) Notwithstanding section 34(11), where an appeal referred to in paragraph (a) is received by the Board, and no appeal is brought by any other person under section 37, the authority shall make the grant of permission as soon as may be after the expiration of the period for the taking of an appeal, provided that the person who takes the appeal furnishes to the planning authority, pending the decision of the Board, security for payment of the full amount of the special contribution as specified in the condition referred to in paragraph (a).

(14) (a) Money accruing to a local authority under this section shall be accounted for in a separate account, and shall only be applied as capital for public infrastructure and facilities.

(b) A report of a local authority under section 50 of the Local Government Act, 1991, shall contain details of monies paid or owing to it under this section and shall indicate how such monies paid to it have been expended by any local authority.

(15) (a) A planning authority may facilitate the phased payment of contributions under this section, and may require the giving of security to ensure payment of contributions.

(b) Where a contribution is not paid in accordance with the terms of the condition laid down by the planning authority, any outstanding amounts due to the planning authority shall be paid together with interest that may have accrued over the period while withheld by the person required to pay the contribution.

(c) A planning authority may recover, as a simple contract debt in a court of competent jurisdiction, any contribution or interest due to the planning authority under this section.

(16) (a) A planning authority shall make a scheme or schemes under this section within 2 years of the commencement of this section.

(b) Notwithstanding the repeal of any enactment by this Act, the provisions of section 26 of the Act of 1963, in relation to requiring contributions in respect of expenditure by local authorities on works which facilitate development, shall continue to apply pending the making of a scheme under this section, but shall not apply after two years from the commencement of this section.

(17) In this section—

"public infrastructure and facilities" means—

  (a) the acquisition of land,
  (b) the provision of open spaces, recreational and community facilities and amenities and landscaping works,

(c) the provision of roads, car parks, car parking places, sewers, waste water and water treatment facilities, drains and watermains,

(d) the provision of bus corridors and lanes, bus interchange facilities (including car parks for those facilities), infrastructure to facilitate public transport, cycle and pedestrian facilities, and traffic calming measures,

(e) the refurbishment, upgrading, enlargement or replacement of roads, car parks, car parking places, sewers, waste water and water treatment facilities, drains or watermains, and

(f) any matters ancillary to paragraphs (a) to (e);

"scheme" means a development contribution scheme made under this section;

"special contribution" means a special contribution referred to in subsection (2)(c).

Note
Section 48 deals with the inclusion of contributions as conditions attached to planning permissions. This is a new system of levying contributions.

[94]
49. Supplementary development contribution schemes
(1) A planning authority may, when granting a permission under section 34, include conditions requiring the payment of a contribution in respect of any public infrastructure service or project—

(a) specified in a scheme made by the planning authority (hereafter in this section referred to as a "supplementary development contribution scheme"),

(b) provided or carried out, as may be appropriate, by a planning authority or, pursuant to an agreement entered into by a local authority, any other person, and

(c) that will benefit the development to which the permission relates when carried out.

(2) (a) The amount, and manner of payment, of a contribution under subsection (1) shall be determined in accordance with a supplementary development contribution scheme.

(b) A supplementary development contribution scheme shall specify—
 (i) the area or areas within the functional area of the planning authority, and
 (ii) the public infrastructure project or service,
 to which it relates, and more than one such scheme may be made in respect of a particular area.

(c) A supplementary development contribution scheme may make provision for the payment of different contributions in respect of different classes or descriptions of development.

(3) Subsections (3), (4), (5), (6), (7), (8), (9), (10), (11) and (15) of section 48 shall apply to a scheme subject to—

(a) the modification that references in those subsections to a scheme shall be construed as references to a supplementary development contribution scheme,

(b) any other necessary modifications, and

(c) the provisions of this section.

(4) (a) A planning authority may enter into an agreement with any person in relation to the carrying out, or the provision, as may be appropriate, of a public infrastructure project or service.

(b) Without prejudice to the generality of paragraph (a), an agreement may make provision for—

    (i) the manner in which the service or project is to be provided or carried out, as the case may be, including provision relating to construction or maintenance of any infrastructure or operation of any service or facility.

    (ii) arrangements regarding the financing of the project or service and the manner in which contributions paid or owed to a planning authority pursuant to a condition under subsection (1) may be applied in respect of that project or service,

    (iii) the entry into such further agreements as may be necessary with any other person regarding the financing and provision of such service or carrying out of such project,

    (iv) the entry into force, duration and monitoring of the agreement (including the resolution of disputes).

(5) A planning authority shall not, pursuant to a condition under subsection (1), require the payment of a contribution in respect of a public infrastructure project or service where the person concerned has made a contribution under section 48 in respect of public infrastructure and facilities of which the said public infrastructure project or service constituted a part.

(6) A planning authority may, at any time, by resolution, amend a supplementary development contribution scheme for the purpose of modifying the manner of determining a contribution pursuant to a condition under subsection (1) where the cost of carrying out or providing, as the case may be, the public infrastructure project or service is less than the cost that was estimated when the planning authority first determined the amount of the contribution.

(7) In this section, "public infrastructure project or service" means—

(a) the provision of particular rail, light rail or other public transport infrastructure, including car parks and other ancillary development,

(b) the provision of particular new roads,

(c) the provision of particular new sewers, waste, water and water treatment facilities, drains or watermains and ancillary infrastructure.

Note
Section 49 also deals with the inclusion of contributions as conditions attached to planning permissions. This is a new system of levying contributions.

[95]–[100]
50. Judicial review of appeals, referrals and other matters
(1) Where a question of law arises on any appeal or referral, the Board may refer the question to the High Court for decision.

(2) A person shall not question the validity of—

(a) a decision of a planning authority—

(i) on an application for a permission under this Part, or
(ii) under section 179,
(b) a decision of the Board—
    (i) on any appeal or referral,
    (ii) under section 175, or
    (iii) under Part XIV,

otherwise than by way of an application for judicial review under Order 84 of the Rules of the Superior Courts (S.I. No. 15 of 1986) ("the Order").

(3) The Board or any party to an appeal or referral may, at any time after the bringing of an application for leave to apply for judicial review of a decision of a planning authority, apply to the High Court to stay the proceedings pending the making of a decision by the Board in relation to the appeal or referral concerned, and the Court may, where it considers that the matter is within the jurisdiction of the Board, make an order on such terms as it thinks fit.

(4) (a) (i) Subject to subparagraph (iii), application for leave to apply for judicial review under the Order in respect of a decision referred to in paragraph (a)(i) or (b)(i) of subsection (2), shall be made within the period of 8 weeks commencing on the date of the decision of the planning authority or the Board, as the case may be.
    (ii) Subject to subparagraph (iii), application for leave to apply for judicial review under the Order in respect of a decision referred to in paragraph (a)(ii) or (b)(ii) or (iii) of subsection (2), shall be made within the period of 8 weeks commencing on the date on which notice of the decision was first published.
    (iii) The High Court shall not extend the period referred to in subparagraph (i) or (ii) unless it considers that there is good and sufficient reason for doing so.
(b) An application for leave to apply for judicial review shall be made by motion, on notice (grounded in the manner specified in the Order in respect of an ex parte motion for leave)—
    (i) if the application relates to a decision referred to in paragraph (a) of subsection (2), to the planning authority concerned and, with regard to a decision on an application for permission under this Part, to the applicant for the permission where he or she is not the applicant for leave,
    (ii) if the application relates to a decision referred to in subparagraph (i) of subsection (2)(b), to the Board and each party or each other party, as the case may be, to the appeal or referral,
    (iii) if the application refers to a decision referred to in subparagraph (ii) or (iii) of subsection (2)(b), to the Board and the planning or local authority concerned, and
    (iv) to any other person specified for that purpose by order of the High Court,
    and leave shall not be granted unless the High Court is satisfied that there are substantial grounds for contending that the decision is invalid or ought to be quashed, and that the applicant has a substantial interest in the matter which is the subject of the application.

(c) Without prejudice to the generality of paragraph (b), leave shall not be granted to an applicant unless the applicant shows to the satisfaction of the High Court that—

(i) the applicant—

(I) in the case of a decision of a planning authority on an application for permission under this Part, was an applicant for permission or is a prescribed body or other person who made submissions or observations in relation to the proposed development,

(II) in the case of a decision of a planning authority under section 179, is a prescribed body or other person who made submissions or observations in relation to the proposed development,

(III) in the case of a decision of the Board on any appeal or referral, was a party to the appeal or referral or is a prescribed body or other person who made submissions or observations in relation to that appeal or referral,

(IV) in the case of a decision of the Board under section 175, is the planning authority which applied for approval, or is a prescribed authority or other person who made submissions or observations under subsection (4) or (5) of that section, or

(V) in the case of a decision of the Board under Part XIV, is a local authority that proposes to acquire land or to carry out a scheme or proposed road development or is a person who made objections, submissions or observations in relation to that proposal,

or

(ii) in the case of a person (other than a person to whom clause (I), (II), (III), (IV) or (V) applies), there were good and sufficient reasons for his or her not making objections, submissions or observations, as the case may be.

(d) A substantial interest for the purposes of paragraph (b) is not limited to an interest in land or other financial interest.

(e) A Member State of the European Communities or a state which is a party to the Transboundary Convention shall not be required, when applying for leave to apply for judicial review of a decision referred to in paragraph (c), to comply with the requirements of that paragraph.

(f) (i) The determination of the High Court of an application for leave to apply for judicial review, or of an application for judicial review, shall be final and no appeal shall lie from the decision of the High Court to the Supreme Court in either case, except with the leave of the High Court, which leave shall only be granted where the High Court certifies that its decision involves a point of law of exceptional public importance and that it is desirable in the public interest that an appeal should be taken to the Supreme Court.

(ii) This paragraph shall not apply to a determination of the High Court, in so far as it involves a question as to the validity of any law, having regard to the provisions of the Constitution.

(g) Where an application is made for judicial review under this section in respect of part only of a decision referred to in subsection (2), the High Court may, if it thinks fit, declare to be invalid or quash the part concerned or any provision thereof without declaring to be invalid or quashing the remainder of the decision or part of a decision, and if the Court does so, it may make any consequential amendments to the remainder of the decision or part of a decision that it considers appropriate.

(h) References in subsection (2) and this subsection to the Order shall be construed as including references to the Order as amended or re-enacted (with or without modification) by rules of court.

(5) (a) Where an application is made for leave to apply for judicial review, or an application is made for judicial review, in respect of—

  (i)   a decision by a planning authority under section 34 of a class in relation to which the Minister has given a direction under section 126(5),

  (ii) a decision of the Board on an appeal of a decision of a class in relation to which the Minister has given a direction under section 126(5),

  (iii) a decision of a planning authority referred to in subsection (2)(a)(ii), or

  (iv) a decision of the Board referred to in subsection (2) (b) (ii) or (iii),

  the High Court shall, in determining the application, act as expeditiously as possible consistent with the administration of justice.

(b) The Supreme Court shall act as expeditiously as possible consistent with the administration of justice in determining any appeal made in respect of a determination by the High Court of an application referred to in paragraph (a).

(c) Rules of court may make provision for the expeditious hearing of an application referred to in paragraph (a).

Note

Section 50 restates s 82 of LG(PD)A 1963 as substituted by s 19(2) of LG(PD)A 1992, with amendments. Sub-section (3) provides that the High Court may stay proceedings pending the making of a decision by the Board, and is new. Note in particular the provisions of sub-s (4) and the requirement for the High Court to be satisfied prior to granting leave to apply for judicial review that there are substantial grounds, that the applicant has a sufficient interest, and that the applicant has made submissions and observations in relation to the proposed development. These new principles apply only to those decisions of the planning authority and the Board as described in sub-s (4)(a). The period within which an appeal must be brought is eight weeks from the date of An Bord Pleanála's decision, and whereas previously that period could not be extended, the High Court now has the power to extend it in limited circumstances as set out in sub-s (4)(a)(iii). Note the provisions of sub-s (4)(d) also.

PART IV   ARCHITECTURAL HERITAGE

Note

Chapter I of Part IV incorporates the provisions of LG(PD)A 1999 in almost identical terms. The Planning and Development Act, 2000 (Commencement) (No 2) Order 2000, SI 449/2000, brought certain provisions (ie those relating to the acquisition by a local authority of protected structures) of this Part into force on 1 January 2001.

CHAPTER I   PROTECTED STRUCTURES

[101]

51. Record of protected structures

(1) For the purpose of protecting structures, or parts of structures, which form part

of the architectural heritage and which are of special architectural, historical, archaeological, artistic, cultural, scientific, social or technical interest, every development
plan shall include a record of protected structures, and shall include in that record
every structure which is, in the opinion of the planning authority, of such interest
within its functional area.

(2) After consulting with the Minister for Arts, Heritage, Gaeltacht and the Islands,
the Minister shall prescribe the form of a record of protected structures.

(3) Subject to any additions or deletions made to the record, either under this Part or
in the course of a review of the development plan under Part II, a record of protected
structures shall continue to be part of that plan or any variation or replacement of the
plan.

Note
Section 51
'Protected Structure', 'Proposed Protected Structure', 'Structure' and 'Attendant grounds' are
all defined terms in the Act. 'Fixture' and 'Curtillage' are not defined in PDA 2000.

[102]
52. Guidelines by Minister for Arts Heritage, Gaeltacht and the Islands
(1) The Minister for Arts, Heritage, Gaeltacht and the Islands shall, after consulting
with the Minister, issue guidelines to planning authorities concerning development
objectives—

(a) for protecting structures, or parts of structures, which are of special architec-
     tural, historical, archaeological, artistic, cultural, scientific, social or technical
     interest, and
(b) for preserving the character of architectural conservation areas,

and any such guidelines shall include the criteria to be applied when selecting proposed protected structures for inclusion in the record of protected structures

(2) The Minister for Arts, Heritage, Gaeltacht and the Islands may, after consulting
with the authorities of any religious denominations which he or she considers necessary, issue guidelines to planning authorities concerning—

(a) the issue of declarations under section 57 in respect of protected structures
     which are regularly used as places of public worship, and
(b) the consideration by planning authorities of applications for development
     affecting the interior of such protected structures.

(3) In considering development objectives, a planning authority shall have regard to
any guidelines issued under this section.

(4) In this section, "development objective" means an objective which, under section 10, a planning authority proposes to include in its development plan.

Note
Section 52(1)
There are draft guidelines in place, which have been proposed by Dúchas under LG(PD)A
1999 and these have been published. Revised draft guidelines are due to be published and
circulated shortly.

[103]
53. Recommendations to planning authorities concerning specific structures

(1) The Minister for Arts, Heritage, Gaeltacht and the Islands may, in writing, make recommendations to a planning authority concerning the inclusion in its record of protected structures of any or all of the following—

(a) particular structures;
(b) specific parts of particular structures;
(c) specific features within the attendant grounds of particular structures.

(2) A planning authority shall have regard to any recommendations made to it under this section.

(3) A planning authority which, after considering a recommendation made to it under this section, decides not to comply with the recommendation, shall inform the Minister for Arts, Heritage, Gaeltacht and the Islands in writing of the reason for its decision.

[104]
54. Additions to and deletions from record of protected structures

(1) A planning authority may add to or delete from its record of protected structures a structure, a specified part of a structure from a specified feature of the attendant grounds of a structure, where—

(a) the authority considers that—
    (i) in the case of an addition, the addition is necessary or desirable in order to protect a structure, or part of a structure, of special architectural, historical, archaeological, artistic, cultural, scientific, social or technical interest, whether or not a recommendation has been made under section 53, or
    (ii) in the case of a deletion, the protection of the structure or part is no longer warranted,
    and
(b) the addition or deletion is made when making a development plan under Part II or in accordance with section 55.

(2) The making of an addition to, or a deletion from, a record of protected structures shall be a reserved function.

Notes
Section 54 provides that an authority may make an addition or deletion from the record of protected structures when making a development plan or under s 55. It is a reserved function.

It should be noted that structures which were listed buildings under the development plans adopted prior to 1 January 2000 are now protected structures under PDA 2000 and will continue to be so protected unless the planning authority pursuant to s 38(3) of LG(PD)A 1999 or s 54 of PDA 2000 decide that they should no longer have protected status.

[105]–[110]
55. Procedure for making additions or deletions

(1) A planning authority which proposes, at any time other than in the course of making its development plan under Part II, to make an addition to or a deletion from its record of protected structures shall—

(a) serve on each person who is the owner or occupier of the proposed protected structure or the protected structure, as the case may be, a notice of the proposed addition or deletion, including the particulars,

(b) send particulars of the proposed addition or deletion to the Minister for Arts, Heritage, Gaeltacht and the Islands and to any other prescribed bodies, and

(c) cause notice of the proposed addition or deletion to be published in at least one newspaper circulating in its functional area.

(2) A notice under paragraph (a) or (c) of subsection (1) shall state the following—

(a) that particulars of the proposed addition or deletion may be inspected at a specified place, during a specified period of not less than 6 weeks;

(b) that, during such period, any person may make written submissions or observations, with respect to the proposed addition or deletion, to the planning authority, and that any such submissions or observations will be taken into consideration before the making of the addition or deletion concerned;

(c) whether or not the proposed addition or deletion was recommended by the Minister for Arts, Heritage, Gaeltacht and the Islands;

(d) that, if the proposed addition or deletion was recommended by the Minister for Arts, Heritage, Gaeltacht and the Islands, the planning authority shall forward to that Minister for his or her observations a copy of any submission or observation made under paragraph (b).

(3) Before making the proposed addition or deletion, the planning authority shall—

(a) consider any written submissions or observations received under subsection (2)(b), and

(b) have regard to any observations received from the Minister for Arts, Heritage, Gaeltacht and the Islands, concerning those submissions or observations, within 4 weeks after the receipt by that Minister of a copy of the submissions or observations.

(4) Within 12 weeks after the end of the period allowed under subsection (2)(a) for inspection, the planning authority shall decide whether or not the proposed addition or deletion should be made.

(5) Within 2 weeks after making an addition to or a deletion from the record of protected structures, a planning authority shall serve on the owner and on the occupier of the structure concerned a notice of the addition or deletion, including the particulars.

Note
Section 55 sets out the procedure for the addition to or deletion from the record of protected structures other than in the course of making its development plan.

[111]
56. Registration under Registration of Title Act 1964
Where a structure, a specified part of a structure or a specified feature within the attendant grounds of a structure is included in the record of protected structures, its inclusion may be registered under the Registration of Title Act, 1964, in the appropriate register maintained under that Act, as a burden affecting registered land (within the meaning of that Act).

Note
Where a structure is included in the record of protected structures its inclusion may be registered under the Registration of Title Act 1964.

[112]
57. Works affecting character of protected structures or proposed protected structures

(1) Notwithstanding section 4(1) (h), the carrying out of works to a protected structure, or a proposed protected structure, shall be exempted development only if those works would not materially affect the character of—

(a) the structure, or
(b) any element of the structure which contributes to its special architectural, historical, archaeological, artistic, cultural, scientific, social or technical interest.

(2) An owner or occupier of a protected structure may make a written request to the planning authority, within whose functional area that structure is situated, to issue a declaration as to the type of works which it considers would or would not materially affect the character of the structure or of any element, referred to in subsection (1)(b), of that structure.

(3) Within 12 weeks after receiving a request under subsection (2), or within such other period as may be prescribed, a planning authority shall issue a declaration under this section to the person who made the request.

(4) Before issuing a declaration under this section, a planning authority shall have regard to—

(a) any guidelines issued under section 52, and
(b) any recommendations made to the authority under section 53.

(5) If the declaration relates to a protected structure that is regularly used as a place of public worship, the planning authority—

(a) in addition to having regard to the guidelines and recommendations referred to in subsection (4), shall respect liturgical requirements, and
(b) for the purpose of ascertaining those requirements shall—
  (i) comply with any guidelines concerning consultation which may be issued by the Minister for Arts, Heritage, Gaeltacht and the Islands, or
  (ii) if no such guidelines are issued, consult with such person or body as the planning authority considers appropriate.

(6) When considering an application for permission for the development of land under section 34 which—

(a) relates to the interior of a protected structure, and
(b) is regularly used as a place of public worship, the planning authority, and the Board on appeal, shall, in addition to any other requirements of the Act, respect liturgical requirements.

(7) A planning authority may at any time review a declaration issued under this section but the review shall not affect any works carried out in reliance on the declaration prior to the review.

(8) A planning authority shall cause—

(a) the details of any declaration issued by that authority under this section to be entered on the register kept by the authority under section 7, and

(b) a copy of the declaration to be made available for inspection by members of the public during office hours, at the office of the authority, following the issue of the declaration.

(9) A declaration under this section shall not prejudice the application of section 5 to any question that arises as to what, in a particular case, is or is not exempted development.

(10) (a) For the avoidance of doubt, it is hereby declared that a planning authority or the Board on appeal—

    (i) in considering any application for permission in relation to a protected structure, shall have regard to the protected status of the structure, or

    (ii) in considering any application for permission in relation to a proposed protected structure, shall have regard to the fact that it is proposed to add the structure to a record of protected structures.

(b) A planning authority, or the Board on appeal, shall not grant permission for the demolition of a protected structure or proposed protected structure, save in exceptional circumstances.

Notes
Section 57 provides that the carrying out of works to a protected structure or a proposed protected structure shall be exempted development only if the works would not materially affect the character of the structure or any element of the structure which contributes to its special architectural, historical, archaeological, artistic, cultural, scientific, social or technical interest. It is clear therefore, that interior works will not be exempted development where they materially affect the character of the structure. An owner/occupier may make a written request to an authority to issue a declaration as to the type of works it considers would not affect the character of the structure or any element of the structure. The declaration can clarify what works are exempted development in the context of a specific protected structure. Any exemption through this declaration procedure can only apply in respect of works that would be exempted in the normal way if the structure was not protected.

Section 57(8)
Details of the declaration must be entered on the planning register and these details will be revealed in any planning office search.

Section 57(10)
Due to the wide definition of 'structure' under PDA 2000 and given that there is no definition of 'exceptional circumstances' there is concern that s 57(10)(b) may prove to be very onerous.

[113]
58. Duty of owners and occupiers to protect structure from endangerment
(1) Each owner and each occupier shall, to the extent consistent with the rights and obligations arising out of their respective interests in a protected structure or a proposed protected structure, ensure that the structure, or any element of it which contributes to its special architectural, historical, archaeological, artistic, cultural, scientific, social or technical interest, is not endangered.

(2) The duty imposed by subsection (1) in relation to a proposed protected structure arises at the time the owner or occupier is notified, under section 55 or under Part II, of the proposal to add the structure to the record of protected structures.

(3) Neither of the following shall be considered to be a breach of the duty imposed on each owner and each occupier under this section—

(a) development in respect of which permission under section 34 has been granted;
(b) development consisting only of works of a type which, in a declaration issued under section 57(3) to that owner or occupier, a planning authority has declared would not materially affect the character of the protected structure or any element, referred to in subsection (1) of this section, of that structure.

(4) Any person who, without lawful authority, causes damage to a protected structure or a proposed protected structure shall be guilty of an offence.

(5) Without prejudice to any other defence that may be available, it shall be a good defence in any proceedings for an offence under subsection (4) to prove that the damage to the structure resulted from works which were—

(a) urgently required in order to secure the preservation of the structure or any part of it,
(b) undertaken in good faith solely for the purpose of temporarily safeguarding the structure, and
(c) unlikely to permanently alter the structure or any element of it referred to in subsection (1).

Notes
Section 58(1)
There is a *positive* duty on an owner and occupier to ensure that the protected structure is free from endangerment.

Section 58(2)
The duty at s 58(1) is imposed on the owner and occupier from the time the structure is *proposed* for protection. Many commentators have questioned the constitutionality of this provision given that the duty arises before an owner/occupier has an opportunity to put in submissions.

[114]
59. Notice to require works to be carried out in relation to endangerment of protected structures
(1) Where, in the opinion of the planning authority, it is necessary to do so in order to prevent a protected structure situated within its functional area from or continuing to be endangered, the authority shall serve on each person who is the protected owner or occupier of the protected structure a notice—

(a) specifying the works which the planning authority considers necessary in order to prevent the protected structure from becoming or continuing to be endangered, and
(b) requiring the person on whom the notice is being served to carry out those works within a specified period of not less than 8 weeks from the date the notice comes into effect under section 62.

(2) After serving notice under subsection (1) on a person, a planning authority may—

(a) at its discretion, assist the person in carrying out the works required under the notice, and

(b) provide such assistance in any form it considers appropriate, including advice, financial aid, materials, equipment and the services of the authority's staff.

(3) Any person on whom a notice under subsection (1) has been served may, within 4 weeks from the date of service of the notice, make written representations to the planning authority concerning—

(a) the terms of the notice,

(b) the provision of assistance under subsection (2), and

(c) any other material considerations.

(4) After considering any representations made under subsection (3), the planning authority may confirm, amend or revoke the notice, and shall notify the person who made the representations of its decision.

(5) Particulars of a notice served under this section shall be entered in the register.

Note
Section 59(5)
Particulars of the notice must be entered in the planning register and again a planning office search will reveal those details.

[115]–[120]
60. Notice to require restoration of character of protected structures and other places
(1) In this section, "works", in relation to a structure or any element of a structure, includes the removal, alteration or replacement of any specified part of the structure or element, and the removal or alteration of any advertisement structure.

(2) A planning authority may serve a notice that complies with subsection (3) on each person who is the owner or occupier of a structure situated within its functional area, if—

(a) the structure is a protected structure and, in the opinion of the planning authority, the character of the structure or of any of its elements ought to be restored, or

(b) the structure is in an architectural conservation area and, in the opinion of the planning authority, it is necessary, in order to preserve the character of the area, that the structure be restored

(3) A notice under subsection (2) shall—

(a) specify the works required to be carried out for the purposes of restoring the structure or element referred to in the notice,

(b) state that the person on whom the notice is served may, within a specified period of not less than 8 weeks from the date of the service of the notice, make written representations to the planning authority concerning the notice,

(c) invite that person to enter into discussions with the planning authority, within a specified period of not less than 8 weeks from the date of the service of the notice, concerning the notice and in particular concerning—

(i) the provision by the planning authority of advice, materials, equipment, the services of the authority's staff or other assistance in carrying out the works specified in the notice, and

(ii) the period within which the works are to be carried out,

(d) specify the period within which, unless otherwise agreed in the discussions under paragraph (c), the works shall be carried out, being a period of not less than 8 weeks from the end of the period allowed for entering into discussions, and

(e) state that the planning authority shall pay any expenses that are reasonably incurred by that person in carrying out the works in accordance with the notice, other than works that relate to an unauthorised structure which has been constructed, erected or made 7 years or less prior to the service of the notice.

(4) In deciding whether to serve a notice under this section, a planning authority shall have regard to any guidelines issued under section 52 and any recommendations made under section 53.

(5) If the invitation under subsection (3) (c) to enter into discussions is accepted, the planning authority shall facilitate the holding of those discussions.

(6) After considering any representations made under subsection (3)(b) and any discussions held under subsection (5), the planning authority may confirm, amend or revoke the notice and shall notify the person who made the representations of its decision.

(7) Particulars of a notice served under this section shall be entered in the register.

[121]
61. Appeals against notices

(1) Within 2 weeks after being notified under section 59(4) or 60(6) of the confirmation or amendment of a notice, any person who made representations in relation to the notice may appeal against the notice to the District Court, on any one or more of the following grounds:

(a) that the person is not the owner or occupier of the structure in respect of which the notice has been served;

(b) that, in the case of a notice under section 59(1), compliance with the requirements of the notice would involve unreasonable expense, and that the person had stated in representations made to the planning authority under section 59(3) that he or she did not have the means to pay;

(c) that the person has already taken all reasonable steps to—

(i) in the case of a notice under section 59(1), prevent the structure from becoming or continuing to be endangered,

(ii) in the case of a notice under section 60(2) in relation to a protected structure, restore the character of the structure or the element, or

(iii) in the case of a notice under section 60(2) in relation to a structure that forms part of a place, area, group of structures or townscape referred to in paragraph (b) of that subsection, assist in restoring the character of that place, area, group of structures or townscape, as the case may be;

(d)　that the time for complying with the notice is unreasonably short.

(2) Notice of an appeal under subsection (1) shall be given to the planning authority, and it shall be entitled to appear, be heard and adduce evidence on the hearing of the appeal.

(3) On the hearing of the appeal, the District Court may, as it thinks proper—

(a)　confirm the notice unconditionally,
(b)　confirm the notice subject to such modifications or additions as the Court thinks reasonable, or
(c)　annul the notice.

(4) Where the notice is confirmed under subsection (3)(b) subject to modifications or additions, the notice shall have effect subject to those modifications or additions.

[122]
62. Effective date of notices
A notice under section 59(1) or 60(2) shall not have effect until the expiry of 4 weeks from the date of service of the notice, subject to the following exceptions—

(a)　if any representations have been made under section 59 or 60 in relation to the notice, and no appeal is taken within the period allowed under section 61(1), the notice has effect on the expiry of the appeal period;
(b)　if an appeal is taken under section 61(1) and the notice is confirmed, the notice has effect on the date on which the decision of the District Court is pronounced, or the date on which that order is expressed to take effect, whichever is later;
(c)　if an application is made to the District Court under section 65(1) and an order is made under section 65(2)(a), the notice has effect on the date on which the decision of the Court is pronounced, or the date on which that order is expressed to take effect, whichever is later.

[123]
63. Offence relating to endangerment of protected structures
A person who fails to comply with a notice served on him or her under section 59(1) shall be guilty of an offence.

[124]
64. Owners' powers in relation to notices concerning endangerment or restoration of structures
Any person who is the owner of the land or structure in respect of which a notice under section 59(1) or 60(2) has been served, and his or her servants or agents, may enter that land or structure and carry out the works required under the notice.

[125]–[130]
65. Application to District Court for necessary consent
(1) A person served with a notice under section 59(1) or 60(2) may apply to the District Court for an order under subsection (2) of this section if—

(a)　that person is unable, without the consent of another person, to carry out the works required under the notice, and

(b) the other person withholds consent to the carrying out of those works.

(2) If, on hearing an application under subsection (1), the District Court determines that the other person's consent has been unreasonably withheld—

(a) the Court may, at its discretion, deem that consent to have been given, and
(b) in that case, the person making the application shall be entitled to carry out the works required under the notice.

[131]
66. Jurisdiction of District Court
The jurisdiction conferred on the District Court—

(a) by section 61 in relation to an appeal against a notice, or
(b) by section 65 in relation to an application for an order deeming consent to have been given,

shall be exercised by a judge of that Court having jurisdiction in the district in which the structure that is the subject of the appeal or application is situated.

[132]
67. Application to court for contribution to cost of carrying out works on endangered structures
(1) A person who has been served with a notice under section, and who has carried out the works required under the notice, may apply to a court of competent jurisdiction for an order directing that all, or such part as may be specified in the order, of the cost of those works be borne by some other person who has an interest in endangered the structure concerned structures.

(2) On the hearing of an application under subsection (1), the court shall make such order as it considers just, having regard to all the circumstances of the case.

[133]
68. Carrying out of certain works to be exempted development
The carrying out of any works specified in a notice under section 59(1) or 60(2) shall be exempted development.

Note
Any works required to be carried out on foot of a notice to protect or restore a protected structure constitutes exempted development.

[134]
69. Planning authority's power to carry out works to protected structures and other places
Where a person on whom a planning authority has served a notice under section 59(1) or 60(2) fails to comply with the notice, the planning authority may take such steps as it considers reasonable and necessary to give effect to the terms of the notice including—

(a) entry on land by authorised persons in accordance with section 252, and
(b) the carrying out, or arranging the carrying out, of the works specified in the notice.

[135]–[140]
70. Recovery by planning authority of expenses for carrying out works on endangered structures
A planning authority which serves a notice under section 59(1) in respect of a protected structure may—

(a) recover (whether as a simple contract debt in a court of competent jurisdiction or otherwise), from the owner or occupier, any expenses reasonably incurred by the authority under section 69, including any assistance provided under section 59(2), and
(b) secure those expenses by—
    (i)   charging the protected structure under the Registration of Title Act, 1964, or
    (ii) an instrument vesting any interest in the protected structure in the authority subject to a right of redemption by the owner or occupier.

[141]
71. Power to acquire protected structure
(1) A planning authority may acquire, by agreement or compulsorily, any protected structure situated within its functional area if -

(a) it appears to the planning authority that it is necessary to do so for the protection of the structure, and
(b) in the case of a compulsory acquisition, the structure is not lawfully occupied as a dwelling house by any person other than a person employed as a caretaker.

(2) In this section and sections 72 to 77, a reference to a protected structure shall be construed to include a reference to any land which—

(a) forms part of the attendant ground of that structure, and
(b) is, in the planning authority's opinion, necessary to secure the protection of that structure,

whether or not the land lies within the curtilage of the structure or is specified as a feature in the record of protected structures.

Notes
Sections 71–78 were brought into force by the Planning and Development (Commencement Order) (No 2), SI 449/2000.

The Notice of Intention to acquire a protected structure is not required under PDA 2000 to be registered in the planning register.

[142]
72. Notice of intention to acquire protected structure compulsorily
(1) A planning authority intending to acquire any protected structure compulsorily under this Part shall—

(a) publish in one or more newspapers circulating in its functional area a notice—
    (i)   stating its intention to acquire the protected structure compulsorily under this Part,
    (ii) describing the structure to which the notice relates,

    (iii) naming the place where a map showing the location of the protected structure is deposited and the times during which it may be inspected, and

    (iv) specifying the time within which (not being less than 4 weeks), and the manner in which, objections to the acquisition of the structure may be made to the planning authority,

    and

(b) serve on every owner, lessee and occupier (except tenants for one month or a period less than one month) of the structure a notice which complies with paragraph (a).

(2) In this section, "owner", in relation to a protected structure, means—

(a) a person, other than a mortgagee not in possession, who is for the time being entitled to dispose (whether in possession or reversion) of the fee simple of the protected structure, and

(b) a person who, under a lease or agreement the unexpired term of which exceeds 5 years, holds or is entitled to the rents or profits of the protected structure.

[143]
73. Objection to compulsory acquisition of protected structure

(1) Any person, on whom a notice of the proposed compulsory acquisition of a protected structure has been served under section 72(1)(b), may, within the time and in the manner specified in the notice, submit to the planning authority concerned an objection to the proposed compulsory acquisition referred to in the notice.

(2) A person who has submitted an objection under subsection (1) may withdraw the objection by notice in writing sent to the planning authority concerned.

(3) Where an objection submitted to a planning authority under subsection (1) is not withdrawn, the planning authority shall not acquire the protected structure compulsorily without the consent of the Board.

(4) An application for the Board's consent to the compulsory acquisition of a protected structure shall be made within 4 weeks after the expiry of the time allowed, under subsection (1), for submitting an objection to that acquisition, and shall be accompanied by the following—

(a) the relevant map,
(b) a copy of the objection made under subsection (1) to the planning authority,
(c) the planning authority's comments (if any) on the objection, and
(d) such other documents and particulars as may be prescribed.

(5) On receipt of the planning authority's comments (if any) on the objection, the Board shall, by notice served on the person who made the objection, send a copy of the comments to that person who may, within 3 weeks from the date of the service of the notice, make observations to the Board in relation to the comments.

(6) On application under subsection (4), the Board may, as it thinks fit, grant or refuse to grant consent to the compulsory acquisition of all or part of a protected structure referred to in a notice published under section 72.

[144]
74. Vesting order for protected structures

(1) After complying with section 73, a planning authority may, by vesting order, acquire a protected structure if—

(a) no objection is submitted to the planning authority under section 73,

(b) any objection submitted under section 73 is subsequently withdrawn, or

(c) the Board consents to the compulsory acquisition of the structure by the planning authority.

(2) Where a planning authority becomes aware, before making a vesting order in respect of a protected structure, that the structure is subject (whether alone or in conjunction with other land) to—

(a) any annuity or other payment to the Minister for Agriculture, Food and Rural Development or to the Commissioners, or

(b) any charge payable to the Revenue Commissioners on the death of any person,

the planning authority shall forthwith inform the Minister for Agriculture, Food and Rural Development, the Commissioners or the Revenue Commissioners, as the case may be, of its intention to make the vesting order.

(3) Within 2 weeks after making a vesting order, a planning authority shall—

(a) publish, in one or more newspapers circulating within its functional area, a notice—
    (i) stating that the order has been made,
    (ii) describing the protected structure to which it relates, and
    (iii) naming a place where a copy of the order and the attached map may be seen during office hours at the offices of the authority,
    and

(b) serve on every person appearing to the authority to have an interest in the protected structure to which the order relates, a notice stating that the order has been made and the effect of the order.

[145]–[150]
75. Form and effect of vesting order

(1) A vesting order by which a planning authority acquires a protected structure under this Part shall be in the prescribed form, and shall have attached to it a map showing the location of the protected structure.

(2) A vesting order shall be expressed and shall operate to vest the protected structure to which it relates in the planning authority in fee simple, free from encumbrances and all estates, rights, titles and interests of whatsoever kind on a specified date (in this section referred to as the vesting date) not earlier than 3 weeks after the making of the order.

(3) Notwithstanding subsection (2), where a planning authority has acquired by a vesting order a protected structure which is subject, either alone or in conjunction with other land, to an annual sum payable to the Minister for Agriculture, Food and Rural Development or the Commissioners, the planning authority shall become and

be liable, as from the vesting date, for the payment to that Minister or those Commissioners, as the case may be, of—

(a) that annual sum, or

(b) such portion of it as shall be apportioned by the Minister or the Commissioners, as the case may be,

as if the protected structure had been transferred to the authority by the owner on that date.

(4) For the purposes of subsection (3), an "annual sum" means a purchase annuity, a payment in lieu of rent, or any other annual sum that is not merely a rent under a contract of tenancy.

Note

The Planning and Development (No 2) Regulations 2000, SI 457/2000 set out the form of vesting order.

[151]
76. Registration of acquired title and amendment of vesting order

(1) On making a vesting order in relation to a protected structure, a planning authority shall send the order to the registering authority which, on receipt of the order, shall immediately cause the planning authority to be registered as owner of the land in accordance with the order.

(2) On the application of any person, a planning authority may amend a vesting order made by the authority if—

(a) the authority is satisfied that the vesting order contains an error, whether occasioned by it or otherwise, and

(b) the error may be rectified without injustice to any person.

(3) Where a copy of an order under subsection (2), amending a vesting order, is lodged with the registering authority, that authority shall rectify its register in such manner as may be necessary to make the register conform with the amending order.

[152]
77. Compensation for interest in protected structure

(1) Any person who, immediately before a vesting order is protected made, has any estate or interest in, or any right in respect of, the protected structure acquired by the order, may apply to the planning authority within one year (or such other period as the High Court, on application to it, may allow) after the making of the order for compensation in respect of the estate, interest or right.

(2) On application under subsection (1), the planning authority shall, subject to subsection (4), pay to the applicant by way of compensation an amount equal to the value (if any) of the estate, interest or right.

(3) The compensation to be paid by the planning authority under this section in relation to any estate, interest or right in respect of the protected structure shall, in default of agreement, be determined by arbitration under and in accordance with the Acquisition of Land (Assessment of Compensation) Act, 1919.

(4) Where, after a planning authority makes a vesting order in relation to a protected structure, any sum (including a sum for costs) remains due to the authority by any person under an order of a court for payment of an amount due (whether under this Act or any other Act, or whether remaining due after deducting expenses reasonably incurred by the authority under this Act in relation to the structure), the amount of any compensation payable to that person under this section shall be reduced by the amount of that sum.

(5) Sections 69 to 79 of the Lands Clauses Consolidation Act, 1845, as amended or adapted by or under the Second Schedule to the Housing of the Working Classes Act, 1890, or any other Act, shall apply in relation to compensation to be paid by a planning authority under this section as if such compensation were a price or compensation under that Act as so amended

(6) Where money is paid into court by the planning authority under section 69 of the Lands Clauses Consolidation Act, 1845, as applied by this section, no costs shall be payable by that authority to any person in respect of any proceedings for the investment, payment of income. or payment of capital of such money.

[153]
78. Use of protected structure acquired by planning authority
A planning authority may—

(a) use a protected structure acquired by it under this Act or any other enactment for any purpose connected with its functions, or
(b) sell, let, transfer or exchange all or any part of that protected structure, and in so doing shall have regard to its protected status.

[154]
79. Obligations of sanitary authorities in respect of protected structures
(1) Before issuing a notice under section 3(1) of the Local Government (Sanitary Services) Act, 1964, in respect of a protected structure or a proposed protected structure, a sanitary authority shall consider—

(a) the protected status of the structure, and
(b) whether, instead of a notice under section 3(1) of that Act, a notice should be issued under section 59(1) or section 11 of the Derelict Sites Act, 1990.

(2) As soon as practicable after serving or proposing to serve a notice in accordance with section 3(1) of the Local Government (Sanitary Services) Act, 1964, in respect of a protected structure or a proposed protected structure, a sanitary authority shall inform the Minister for Arts, Heritage, Gaeltacht and the Islands of the particulars of the notice if he or she recommended that the structure be protected.

(3) A sanitary authority which carries out works on a protected structure, or a proposed protected structure, under section 3(2) of the Local Government (Sanitary Services) Act, 1964, shall as far as possible preserve that structure (or elements of that structure which may be of special architectural, historical, archaeological, artistic, cultural, scientific, social or technical interest), in as much as the preservation of that structure is not likely to cause a danger to any person or property.

(4) When carrying out works in accordance with section 3(2) of the Local Government (Sanitary Services) Act, 1964, on a protected structure or a proposed protected structure, a sanitary authority shall, as soon as practicable, inform the Minister for Arts, Heritage, Gaeltacht and the Islands of the works if he or she recommended that the structure be protected.

[155]–[160]
80. Grants to planning authorities in respect of functions under this Part

With the consent of the Minister for Finance, the Minister may out of moneys provided by the Oireachtas, make grants to planning authorities in respect of any or all of their functions under this Part, including grants for the purpose of defraying all or part of the expenditure incurred by them in—

(a) assisting persons on whom notice is served under section 59(1) or 60(2) in carrying out works in accordance with the notice, and
(b) assisting any other person in carrying out works to protected structures in accordance with such conditions as may be specified by a planning authority for the receipt of such assistance.

Note

Section 80 states that the grants are available for the carrying out of works where a notice has been served and for works carried out when no such notice has been served.

CHAPTER II   ARCHITECTURAL CONSERVATION AREAS AND AREAS OF
SPECIAL PLANNING CONTROL

[161]
81. Architectural conservation areas

(1) A development plan shall include an objective to preserve the character of a place, area, group of structures or townscape, taking account of building lines and heights, that—

(a) is of special architectural, historical, archaeological, artistic, cultural, scientific, social or technical interest or value, or
(b) contributes to the appreciation of protected structures, if the planning authority is of the opinion that its inclusion is necessary for the preservation of the character of the place, area, group of structures or townscape concerned and any such place, area, group of structures or townscape shall be known as and is in this Act referred to as an "architectural conservation area".

(2) Where a development plan includes an objective referred to in subsection (1), any development plan that replaces the first-mentioned development plan shall, subject to any variation thereof under section 13, also include that objective.

[162]
82. Development in architectural conservation areas

(1) Notwithstanding section 4(1)(h), the carrying out of works to the exterior of a structure located in an architectural conservation area shall be exempted development only if those works would not materially affect the character of the area.

(2) In considering an application for permission for development in relation to land situated in an architectural conservation area, a planning authority, or the Board on appeal, shall take into account the material effect (if any) that the proposed development would be likely to have on the character of the architectural conservation area.

[163]
83. Power to acquire structure or other land in architectural conservation area

(1) A planning authority may acquire, by agreement or compulsorily, any land situated within an architectural conservation area if the planning authority is of the opinion—

(a) that it is necessary to so do in order to preserve the character of the architectural conservation area, and

(b) (i) the condition of the land, or the use to which the land or any structure on the land is being put, detracts, or is likely to detract, to a material degree from the character or appearance of the architectural conservation area, or

    (ii) the acquisition of the land is necessary for the development or renewal of the architectural conservation area or for the provision of amenities in the area.

(2) A planning authority shall not compulsorily acquire any land under subsection (1) that is lawfully occupied as a dwelling house by any person other than a person employed therein as a caretaker.

(3) Sections 71(2) to 78 of this Act shall, subject to any necessary modifications, apply to acquisitions under subsection (1) and references in those provisions to a protected structure shall, for the purposes of this section, be construed as references to a structure or other land situated within an architectural conservation area.

[164]
84. Area of special planning control

(1) A planning authority may, if it considers that all or part of an architectural conservation area is of special importance to, or as respects, the civic life or the architectural, historical, cultural or social character of a city or town in which it is situated, prepare a scheme setting out development objectives for the preservation and enhancement of that area, or part of that area, and providing for matters connected therewith.

(2) Without prejudice to the generality of subsection (1), a scheme prepared under that subsection may include objectives (and provisions for the furtherance or attainment of those objectives) for—

(a) the promotion of a high standard of civic amenity and civic design;

(b) the preservation and protection of the environment, including the architectural, archaeological and natural heritage;

(c) the renewal, preservation, conservation, restoration, development or redevelopment of the streetscape, layout and building pattern, including the co-ordination and upgrading of shop frontages;

(d) the control of the layout of areas, density, building lines and height of structures and the treatment of spaces around and between structures;

(e) the control of the design, colour and materials of structures, in particular the type or quality of building materials used in structures;

(f) the promotion of the maintenance, repair or cleaning of structures;

(g) the promotion of an appropriate mix of uses of structures or other land;

(h) the control of any new or existing uses of structures or other land;

(i) the promotion of the development or redevelopment of derelict sites or vacant sites; or

(j) the regulation, restriction or control of the erection of advertisement structures and the exhibition of advertisements.

(3) A scheme prepared under subsection (1) shall be in writing and shall be consistent with the objectives of the relevant development plan and any local area plan or integrated area plan (within the meaning of the Urban Renewal Act, 1998) in force relating to the area to which the scheme relates.

(4) (a) A scheme prepared under subsection (1) shall indicate the period for which the scheme is to remain in force.

(b) A scheme may indicate the order in which it is proposed that the objectives of the scheme or provisions for their furtherance or attainment will be implemented.

(5) A scheme shall contain information, including information of such class or classes as may be prescribed by the Minister, on the likely significant effects on the environment of implementing the scheme.

(6) In this section, and sections 85 and 36—

"city" means a county borough;

"town" means a borough (other than a county borough), an urban district or a town having town commissioners that has a population in excess of 2,000.

[165]–[170]
85. Special planning control scheme

(1) Subsections (2), (3), (4), (5) and (6) shall, upon the passing of a resolution by the planning authority concerned, be complied with in relation to the scheme specified in the resolution.

(2) The planning authority shall, as soon as may be after the passing of a resolution under subsection (1)—

(a) notify in writing the Minister, the Board and such other persons as may be prescribed, of the preparation of the scheme,

(b) send copies of the scheme to each of the persons referred to in paragraph (a), and

(c) publish a notice of the preparation of the scheme in one or more newspapers circulating in the city or town concerned.

(3) A notice under subsection (2) shall—

(a) indicate the place or places at which, and the period (being not less than 8 weeks) during and times at which, a copy of the scheme may be inspected (and a copy of the scheme shall be kept available for inspection accordingly), and

(b) invite submissions or observations in relation to the scheme within such period (being not less than 8 weeks) as is specified in the notice.

(4) (a) Where the scheme prepared under subsection (1) includes an objective or provision relating to—

 (i) the co-ordination, upgrading or changing of specified shop frontages,

 (ii) the control of the layout of specified areas, the density, building lines and height of specified structures and the treatment of spaces around and between specified structures,

 (iii) the control of the design, colour and materials of specified structures,

 (iv) the promotion of the maintenance, repair or cleaning of specified structures,

 (v) the control of the use or uses of any specified structure or other land in the area,

 (vi) the discontinuance of the existing use of any specified structure or other land,

 (vii) the development or redevelopment of specified derelict or vacant sites, or

 (viii) the control of specified advertisement structures or of the exhibition of specified advertisements,

the planning authority shall, as soon as may be after the making of a resolution under subsection (1), notify in writing each person who is the owner or occupier of land thereby affected, of the objective or provision concerned.

(b) A notice under paragraph (a) shall refer to the land concerned and shall—

 (i) specify the measures that are required to be undertaken in respect of the structure or other land to ensure compliance with the proposed objective or objectives,

 (ii) indicate the place or places at which, and the period (being not less than 8 weeks) during and times at which, a copy of the scheme may be inspected (and the copy shall be kept available for inspection accordingly). and

 (iii) invite submissions or observations in relation to the proposed objective or provision within such period (being not less than 8 weeks) as is specified in the notice.

(5) (a) Not later than 12 weeks after giving notice under subsection (2) and, where appropriate, a notification under subsection (4), whichever occurs later, the manager of a planning authority shall prepare a report on any submissions or observations received in relation to a scheme prepared under subsection (1) and shall submit the report to the members of the authority for their consideration.

(b) A report under paragraph (a) shall—

 (i) list the persons who made submissions or observations in relation to the scheme,

 (ii) give a summary of the matters raised in those submissions or observations, and

 (iii) include the response of the manager to the submissions or observations.

(6) In responding to submissions or observations made in relation to a scheme prepared under subsection (1), the manager of a planning authority shall take account of the proper planning and sustainable development of the area, the statutory obligations of any local authority in the area and any relevant policies or objectives of the Government or of any Minister of the Government.

(7) A planning authority may, after considering a scheme prepared under subsection (1) and the report of the manager under subsection (5), by resolution, approve

the scheme with or without modifications, or refuse to so approve, and a scheme so approved shall be known as and is referred to in this Part as an "approved scheme".

(8) An architectural conservation area, or that part of an architectural conservation area, to which a scheme approved by a planning authority under subsection (7) applies shall be known as and is referred to in this Act as an "area of special planning control".

(9) (a) Where a planning authority approves a scheme under subsection (7), it shall publish a notice thereof in one or more newspapers circulating in the city or town concerned.

(b) A notice under paragraph (a) shall indicate the place or places at which, and times during which, an approved scheme may be inspected (and a copy thereof shall be kept available for inspection accordingly).

(c) A planning authority shall send a copy of the scheme to the Minister, the Board and such other persons as may be prescribed.

[171]
86. Variation and review of scheme
(1) A planning authority shall, from time to time as circumstances require and in any case not later than 6 years after—

(a) its approval under section 85(7), or
(b) it has most recently been reviewed,

review an approved scheme and may by resolution, amend or revoke the scheme.

(2) Where a planning authority proposes to amend an approved scheme under this section, section 85 shall, subject to any necessary modifications, apply as respects any such amendment.

(3) Notice of the revocation of an approved scheme under this section shall be given in one or more newspapers circulating in the city or town concerned.

(4) The amendment or revocation of an approved scheme shall be without prejudice to the validity of anything previously done thereunder.

[172]
87. Development in special planning control area
(1) Notwithstanding section 4 and any regulations made thereunder, any development within an area of special planning control shall not be exempted development where it contravenes an approved scheme applying to that area.

(2) When considering an application for permission in relation to land situated in an area of special planning control, a planning authority, or the Board on appeal, shall, in addition to the matters set out in section 34, have regard to the provisions of an approved scheme.

(3) An owner or occupier of land situated in an area of special planning control may make a written request to the planning authority, within whose functional area the area of special planning control is situated, for a declaration as to—

(a) those developments or classes of development that it considers would be contrary or would not be contrary, as the case may be, to the approved scheme concerned,

(b) the objectives or provisions of the approved scheme that apply to the land, or

(c) the measures that will be required to be undertaken in respect of the land to ensure compliance with such objectives or provisions.

(4) Within 12 weeks of receipt by a planning authority of a request under subsection (3), or within such other period as may be prescribed by regulations of the Minister, a planning authority shall issue a declaration under this section to the person who made the request.

(5) A planning authority may at any time rescind or vary a declaration under this section.

(6) The rescission or variation of a declaration under subsection (5) shall not affect any development commenced prior thereto in reliance on the declaration concerned and that the planning authority has indicated, in accordance with paragraph (a) of subsection (3) would not be contrary to an approved scheme.

(7) A declaration under this section is without prejudice to the application of section 5.

(8) A planning authority shall cause—

(a) the particulars of any declaration issued by that authority under this section to be entered on the register kept by the authority under section 7, and

(b) a copy of the declaration to be made available for inspection by members of the public during office hours, at the principal office of the authority, following the issue of the declaration.

Note
Section 87(3)
This section is similar to s 57(2) for requesting a declaration relating to a protected structure.

[173]
88. Service of notice relating to structures or other land in an area of special planning control
(1) A planning authority may serve a notice that complies with subsection (2) on each person who is the owner or occupier of land to which an objective or provision of an approved scheme applies.

(2) A notice under subsection (1) shall—

(a) refer to the structure or land concerned,

(b) specify the date on which the notice shall come into force,

(c) specify the measures required to be undertaken on the coming into force of the notice including, as appropriate, measures for—

    (i) the restoration, demolition, removal, alteration, replacement, maintenance, repair or cleaning of any structure, or

    (ii) the discontinuance of any use or the continuance of any use subject to conditions,

(d) invite the person on whom the notice is served, within such period as is specified in the notice (being not less than 8 weeks from the date of service of the notice) to make written representations to the planning authority concerning the notice,

(e) invite the person to enter into discussions with the planning authority, within such period as is specified in the notice (being not less than 8 weeks from the date of service of the notice) concerning the matters to which the notice refers and in particular concerning—

    (i) the period within which the measures specified in the notice are to be carried out, and

    (ii) the provision by the planning authority of advice, materials, equipment, the services of the authority's staff or other assistance required to carry out the measures specified in the notice,

(f) specify the period within which, unless otherwise agreed in the discussions entered into pursuant to an invitation in the notice in accordance with paragraph (e), the measures specified in the notice shall be carried out, being a period of not less than 8 weeks from the date of the coming into force of the notice.

(g) state that the planning authority shall pay any expenses that are reasonably incurred by that person in carrying out the steps specified in the notice, other than expenses that relate to unauthorised development carried out not more than 7 years prior to the service of the notice, and

(h) state that the planning authority shall, by way of compensation, pay, to any person who shows that as a result of complying with the notice—

    (i) the value of an interest he or she has in the land or part thereof existing at the time of the notice has been reduced, or

    (ii) he or she, having an interest in the land at that time, has suffered damage by being disturbed in his or her enjoyment of the structure or other land,

a sum equal to the amount of such reduction in value or a sum in respect of the damage suffered.

(3) If the invitation in a notice in accordance with subsection (2)(d) to enter into discussions is accepted, the planning authority shall take all such measures as may be necessary to enable the discussions concerned to take place.

(4) After considering any representations made and any discussions held pursuant to invitations in a notice under subsection (2), the planning authority may confirm, amend or revoke the notice and shall notify in writing the person to whom the notice is addressed.

(5) Any person served with a notice under subsection (1) may, within 8 weeks from the date of notification of the confirmation or amendment of the notice under subsection (4), appeal to the Board against the notice.

(6) Where an appeal is brought under subsection (5) against a notice, the Board may, after taking into account—

(a) the proper planning and sustainable development of the area,

(b) the provisions of the development plan for the area,

(c) any local area plan or integrated area plan (within the meaning of the Urban Renewal Act, 1998) in force relating to the area to which the scheme relates, and

(d) the provisions of the approved scheme concerned,

confirm with or without modification, or annul, the notice.

(7) A notice served by a planning authority under subsection (1) may, for stated reasons, by notice in writing, be withdrawn.

(8) A notice under this section (other than a notice that has been withdrawn) shall not come into force—

(a) until the expiry of any period within which an appeal against the notice may be brought, or
(b) where an appeal is taken against the notice, when the appeal has been withdrawn or decided,

as may be appropriate.

Note
Section 88(2)
This section provides that where a person can show that the value of their interest in land has been diminished (on account of being obliged to comply with a notice to carry out restoration works or discontinuance of a use) or that they have suffered damage by being disturbed in their enjoyment of the structure/land, they are entitled to compensation.

[174]
89. Implementation of the notice under section 88
If, within 8 weeks from the date of the coming into force of the notice or such longer period as may be agreed by the planning authority and the person to whom the notice is addressed, the restoration, demolition, removal, alteration, replacement, maintenance, repair or cleaning required by the notice has not been effected, the planning authority may, subject to section 252, enter the structure or land and may effect such restoration, demolition, removal, alteration, replacement. maintenance. repair or cleaning as is specified in the notice.

[175]–[180]
90. Court may compel compliance with notice under section 88
(1) Where a person served with a notice under section 88 fails to comply with a requirement of the notice, or causes or permits a person to fail to comply with such a requirement, the High Court or the Circuit Court may, on the application of the planning authority, order any person to comply with the notice or to do, or refrain from doing or continuing to do, anything that the Court considers necessary or expedient to ensure compliance with the terms of the said notice.

(2) An order under subsection (1) may, without prejudice to that subsection, require such person as is specified in the order to carry out any works, including the restoration, demolition, removal, alteration, replacement, maintenance, repair or cleaning of any structure or other feature, or the discontinuance of any use, or continuance thereof subject to such conditions as are specified in the order.

(3) (a) An application to the High Court or the Circuit Court for an order under subsection (1) shall be by motion and the Court when considering the matter may make such interim or interlocutory order, if any, as it considers appropriate.

(b) The order by which an application under this section is determined may contain such terms and conditions (if any) as to the payment of costs as the Court considers appropriate.

(4) Rules of Court made in respect of section 27 of the Act of 1976 (inserted by section 19 of the Act of 1992) shall apply with any necessary modifications to an application under this section.

(5) (a) An application under subsection (1) to the Circuit Court shall be made to the judge of the Circuit Court for the circuit in which the land the subject of the application is situated.

(b) The Circuit Court shall have jurisdiction to hear and determine an application under this section where the rateable valuation of the land the subject of the application does not exceed £200.

(c) Where the rateable valuation of any land the subject of the application under this section exceeds £200, the Circuit Court shall, if an application is made to it in that behalf by any person having an interest in the proceedings, transfer the proceedings to the High Court, but any order made or act done in the course of such proceedings before the transfer shall be valid unless discharged or varied by order of the High Court.

[181]
91. Offence to fail to comply with notice under section 88
Where a person served with a notice under section 88 fails to comply with a requirement of the notice, or causes or permits a person to fail to comply with such a requirement he or she shall be guilty of an offence.

[182]
92. Permission not required for any development required under this Chapter
Notwithstanding Part III, permission shall not be required in respect of a development required by a notice under section 88 or an order under section 90.

PART V   HOUSING SUPPLY

Note
The Planning and Development Act (Commencement) Order 2000, SI 349/2000, brought Pt V of the Act into force as and from 1 November 2000. This new Part is probably one of the most controversial and radical elements of the Act. When the Bill had passed both Houses of the Oireachtas, Pt V was referred to the Supreme Court pursuant to art 26 of the Constitution of Ireland, 1937. The Supreme Court on 28 August 2000 upheld the constitutionality of these provisions.

[183]
93. Interpretation
(1) In this Part—

"accommodation needs" means the size of the accommodation required by an eligible person determined in accordance with the regulations made by the Minister under section 100(1)(a);

"affordable housing" means houses or land made available, in accordance with section 96(9) or (10), for eligible persons;

"eligible person" means, subject to subsection (3) and to the regulations, if any, made by the Minister under section 100(1)(b), a person who is in need of accommodation and whose income would not be adequate to meet the payments on a mortgage for the purchase of a house to meet his or her accommodation needs because the payments calculated over the course of a year would exceed 35 per cent of that person's annual income net of income tax and pay related social insurance;

"housing strategy" means a strategy included in a development plan in accordance with section 94(1);

"market value", in relation to a house, means the price which the unencumbered fee simple of the house would fetch if sold on the open market;

"mortgage" means a loan for the purchase of a house secured by mortgage in an amount not exceeding 90 per cent of the price of the house.

(2) For the purposes of this Part, the accommodation needs of an eligible person includes the accommodation needs of any other person who might reasonably be expected to reside with the eligible person.

(3) In determining the eligibility of a person for the purposes of this Part, the planning authority shall take into account—

(a) half the annual income, net of income tax and pay related social insurance, of any other person who might reasonably be expected to reside with the eligible person and contribute to the mortgage payments, and

(b) any other financial circumstances of the eligible person and any other person who might reasonably be expected to reside with the eligible person and contribute to the mortgage payments.

(4) For the avoidance of doubt, it is hereby declared that, in respect of any planning application or appeal, compliance with the housing strategy and any related objective in the development plan shall be a consideration material to the proper planning and sustainable development of the area.

Note
Section 93(1)
'Eligible Person' includes not only those who would be entitled to social housing under the Housing Acts but also those who have accommodation needs and their mortgage repayments to meet those needs would exceed 35% of their annual net income.

[184]
94. Housing strategies
(1) (a) Each planning authority shall include in any development plan it makes in accordance with section 12 a strategy for the purpose of ensuring that the proper planning and sustainable development of the area of the development plan provides for the housing of the existing and future population of the area in the manner set out in the strategy.

(b) (i) Subject to subparagraph (ii), any development plan made by a planning authority after the commencement of this section shall include a housing strategy in respect of the area of the development plan.

    (ii) Where before the commencement of this section a planning authority has given notice under section 21A(2) (inserted by the Act of 1976) of the Act of 1963 of a proposed amendment of a draft development plan, it may proceed in accordance with section 266 without complying with subparagraph (i), but where a development plan is so made, the planning authority shall take such actions as are necessary to ensure that, as soon as possible and in any event within a period of 9 months from the commencement of this section, a housing strategy is prepared in respect of the area of the development plan and the procedures under section 13 are commenced to vary the development plan in order to insert the strategy in the plan and to make such other changes as are necessary arising from the insertion of the strategy in the plan pursuant to this Part.

(c) A planning authority shall take such actions as are necessary to ensure that, as soon as possible and in any event within a period of 9 months from the commencement of this section, a housing strategy is prepared in respect of the area of the development plan and the procedures under section 13 are commenced to vary the development plan in order to insert the strategy in the plan and to make such other changes as are necessary arising from the insertion of the strategy in the plan pursuant to this Part.

(d) A housing strategy shall relate to the period of the development plan or, in the case of a strategy prepared under paragraph (b)(ii) or paragraph (c), to the remaining period of the existing development plan.

(e) A housing strategy under this section may, or pursuant to the direction of the Minister shall, be prepared jointly by 2 or more planning authorities in respect of the combined area of their development plans and such a joint strategy shall be included in any development plan that relates to the whole or any part of the area covered by the strategy and the provisions of this Part shall apply accordingly.

(2) In preparing a housing strategy, a planning authority shall have regard to the most recent housing assessment or assessments made under section 9 of the Housing Act, 1988, that relate to the area of the development plan.

(3) A housing strategy shall take into account—

(a) the existing need and the likely future need for housing to which subsection (4)(a) applies,

(b) the need to ensure that housing is available for persons who have different levels of income,

(c) the need to ensure that a mixture of house types and sizes is developed to reasonably match the requirements of the different categories of households, as may be determined by the planning authority, and including the special requirements of elderly persons and persons with disabilities, and

(d) the need to counteract undue segregation in housing between persons of different social backgrounds.

106

(4) (a) A housing strategy shall include an estimate of the amount of—
   (i) housing for persons referred to in section 9(2) of the Housing Act, 1988, and
   (ii) affordable housing,
   required in the area of the development plan during the period of the development plan and the estimate may state the different requirements for different areas within the area of the development plan.
(b) For the purpose of making an estimate under paragraph (a)(ii), a planning authority may exclude eligible persons who own or have previously owned a house.
(c) Subject to paragraph (d), a housing strategy shall provide that as a general policy a specified percentage, not being more than 20 per cent, of the land zoned for residential use, or for a mixture of residential and other uses, shall be reserved under this Part for the provision of housing for the purposes of either or both subparagraphs (i) and (ii) of paragraph (a).
(d) Paragraph (c) shall not operate to prevent any person (including a local authority) from using more than 20 per cent. of land zoned for residential use, or for a mixture of residential and other uses, for the provision of housing to which paragraph (a) applies.

(5) (a) When making an estimate under subsection (4)(a)(ii), the planning authority shall have regard to the following:
   (i)   the supply of and demand for houses generally, or houses of a particular class or classes, in the whole or part of the area of the development plan;
   (ii) the price of houses generally, or houses of a particular class or classes, in the whole or part of the area of the development plan:
   (iii) the income of persons generally or of a particular class or classes of person who require houses in the area of the development plan;
   (iv) the rates of interest on mortgages for house purchase;
   (v)   the relationship between the price of housing under subparagraph (ii), incomes under subparagraph (iii) and rates of interest under subparagraph (iv) for the purpose of establishing the affordability of houses in the area of the development plan;
   (vi) such other matters as the planning authority considers appropriate or as may be prescribed for the purposes of this subsection.
(b) Regulations made for the purposes of this subsection shall not affect any housing strategy or the objectives of any development plan made before those regulations come into operation.

Notes
Section 94(1)(c)
Housing strategies must be prepared on or before 1 August 2001.

Section 94(4)(a)(c)
A housing strategy must provide that a specified percentage not greater than 20% of lands zoned residential shall be reserved for the provision of social and affordable housing.

[185]–[190]
95. Housing strategies and development plans
(1) (a) In conjunction with the inclusion of the housing strategy in its development plan, a planning authority shall ensure that sufficient and suitable land is zoned

for residential use, or for a mixture of residential and other uses, to meet the requirements of the housing strategy and to ensure that a scarcity of such land does not occur at any time during the period of the development plan.

(b) A planning authority shall include objectives in the development plan in order to secure the implementation of the housing strategy, in particular, any of the matters referred to in section 94(3), including objectives requiring that a specified percentage of land zoned solely for residential use, or for a mixture of residential and other uses, be made available for the provision of housing referred to in section 94(4)(a).

(c) Specific objectives as referred to in paragraph (b) may be indicated in respect of each area zoned for residential use, or for a mixture of residential and other uses, and, where required by local circumstances relating to the amount of housing required as estimated in the housing strategy under section 94(4)(a), different specific objectives may be indicated in respect of different areas, subject to the specified percentage referred to in section 94(4)(c) not being exceeded.

(d) In order to counteract undue segregation in housing between persons of different social backgrounds, the planning authority may indicate in respect of any particular area referred to in paragraph (c) that there is no requirement for housing referred to in section 94(4)(a) in respect of that area, or that a lower percentage than that specified in the housing strategy may instead be required.

(2) Nothing in subsection (1) shall prevent any land being developed exclusively for housing referred to in section 94(4)(a)(i) or (ii).

(3) (a) The report of the manager under section 15(2) shall include a review of the progress achieved in implementing the housing strategy and, where the report indicates that new or revised housing needs have been identified, the manager may recommend that the housing strategy be adjusted and the development plan be varied accordingly.

(b) The manager of a planning authority shall, where he or she considers that there has been a change in the housing market, or in the regulations made by the Minister under section 100, that significantly affects the housing strategy, give a report on the matter to the members of the authority and, where he or she considers it necessary, the manager may recommend that the housing strategy be adjusted and the development plan be varied accordingly.

Note
Section 95(3)
The Department of the Environment Guidelines for Planning Authorities in relation to Pt V of PDA 2000 (December 2000) ("the Guidelines") state that to ensure the housing strategy is kept up to date it must be reviewed within two years of its preparation. The housing strategy must also be reviewed where there is a change in housing requirements or in the housing market that could fundamentally affect the existing strategy.

[191]
96. Provision of social and affordable housing etc
(1) Subject to subsection (14) and section 97, where a development plan objective requires that a specified percentage of any land zoned solely for residential use, or for a mixture of residential and other uses, be made available for housing referred to in section 94(4)(a), the provisions of this section shall apply to an application for per-

mission for the development of houses, or where an application relates to a mixture of developments, to that part of the application which relates to the development of houses, in addition to the provisions of section 34.

(2) A planning authority, or the Board on appeal, may require as a condition of a grant of permission that the applicant, or any other person with an interest in the land to which the application relates, enter into an agreement with the planning authority, concerning the development for housing of land to which a specific objective applies in accordance with section 95(1)(b).

(3) (a) An agreement under this section may provide for—
    (i)   the transfer to the planning authority of the ownership of the land required by the agreement to be reserved for the provision of housing referred to in section 94(4)(a),
    (ii) instead of the transfer of land referred to in subparagraph (i), the building and transfer, on completion, to the planning authority, or to persons nominated by the authority in accordance with this Part, of houses of such number and description as may be specified in the agreement at a price determined on the basis of—
          (I) the site cost of the houses being calculated as if it was equal to the cost of land transferred to the authority under subparagraph (i), and
          (II) the building and attributable development costs as agreed between the authority and the developer, including profit on the costs, or
    (iii) instead of the transfer of land referred to in subparagraph (i), the transfer of such number of fully or partially serviced sites as the agreement may specify to the planning authority, or to persons nominated by the authority in accordance with this Part, at a price determined on the basis of—
          (I) the site cost of the sites being calculated as if it was equal to the cost of land transferred to the authority under subparagraph (i), and
          (II) the attributable development costs as agreed between the authority and the developer, including profit on the costs.
(b) Where an agreement provides for the transfer of land, houses or sites in accordance with paragraph (a), the houses or sites or the land, whether in one or more parts, shall be identified in the agreement.
(c) In so far as it is known at the time of the agreement, the planning authority shall indicate to the applicant its intention in relation to the provision of housing, including a description of the proposed houses, on the land or sites to be transferred in accordance with paragraph (a)(i) or (iii).
(d) Nothing in this subsection shall be construed as requiring the applicant or other person to enter into an agreement to transfer houses or sites in accordance with subparagraphs (ii) or (iii) of paragraph (a) instead of transferring land in accordance with subparagraph (i) of that paragraph.
(e) For the purposes of an agreement under paragraph (a), the planning authority shall have regard to—
    (i) the proper planning and sustainable development of the area to which the application relates,
    (ii) the housing strategy and the specific objectives of the development plan which relate to the implementation of the strategy,

(iii) the need to ensure the overall coherence of the development to which the application relates, and

(iv) the views of the applicant in relation to the impact of the agreement on the development.

(f) Government guidelines on public procurement shall not apply to an agreement made under paragraph (a)(ii) or (iii), except in the case of an agreement which is subject to the requirements of Council Directive No. 93/37/EEC on the co-ordination of procedures relating to the award of Public Works Contracts and any directive amending or replacing that directive.

(4) An applicant for permission shall, when making an application to which this section applies, specify the manner in which he or she would propose to comply with a condition to which subsection (2) relates, were the planning authority to attach such a condition to any permission granted on foot of such application, and where the planning authority grants permission to the applicant subject to any such condition it shall have regard to any proposals so specified.

(5) In the case of a dispute in relation to any matter which may be the subject of an agreement under this section, other than—

(a) a dispute in relation to an agreement under subsection (3)(a)(ii) or (iii),

(b) a dispute as to the amount of compensation payable under subsection (6), or

(c) a dispute as to the sum payable to a planning authority under subsection (12),

the matter may be referred by the planning authority or any other prospective party to the agreement to the Board for determination.

(6) Where ownership of land is transferred to a planning authority pursuant to subsection (3)(a)(i), the planning authority shall, by way of compensation, pay to the owner of the land a sum equal to—

(a) (i) in the case of—

(I) land purchased by the applicant before 25 August 1999, or

(II) land purchased by the applicant pursuant to a legally enforceable agreement entered into before that date or in exercise of an option in writing to purchase the land granted or acquired before that date,

the price paid for the land, or the price agreed to be paid for the land pursuant to the agreement or option, together with such sum in respect of interest thereon (including, in circumstances where there is a mortgage on the land, interest paid in respect of the mortgage) as may be determined by the property arbitrator,

(ii) in the case of land the ownership of which was acquired by the applicant by way of a gift or inheritance taken (within the meaning of the Capital Acquisitions Tax Act, 1976) before 25 August 1999, a sum equal to the market value of the land on the valuation date (within the meaning of that Act) estimated in accordance with section 15 of that Act,

(iii) in the case of—

(i) land purchased before 25 August 1999, or

(ii) land purchased pursuant to a legally enforceable agreement to purchase the land entered into before that date, or in exercise of an option, in writing, to purchase the land granted or acquired before that date, (where the applicant for permission is a mortgagee in possession of the land) the price paid for the land, or the price agreed to be paid for the land pursuant to the agreement or option, together with such sum in respect of interest thereon calculated from that date (including any interest accruing and not paid in respect of the mortgage) as may be determined by the property arbitrator,

or

(b) the value of the land calculated by reference to its existing use on the date of the transfer of ownership of the land to the planning authority concerned on the basis that on that date it would have been, and would thereafter have continued to be, unlawful to carry out any development in relation to that land other than exempted development,

whichever is the greater.

(7) (a) Subject to paragraph (b), a property arbitrator appointed under section 2 of the Property Values (Arbitration and Appeals) Act, 1960, shall (in accordance with the Acquisition of Land (Assessment of Compensation) Act, 1919), in default of agreement, fix the following where appropriate:
   (i)   the number and price of houses to be transferred under subsection (3)(a)(ii);
   (ii) the number and price of sites to be transferred under subsection (3)(a)(iii);
   (iii) the compensation payable under subsection (6) by a planning authority to the owner of land;
   (iv) the sum payable to a planning authority under subsection (12); and
   (v)   the allowance to be made under section 99(3)(d)(i).
(b) For the purposes of paragraph (a), section 2(2) of the Acquisition of Land (Assessment of Compensation) Act, 1919, shall not apply and the value of the land shall be calculated on the assumption that it was at that time and would remain unlawful to carry out any development in relation to the land other than exempted development.
(c) Section 187 shall apply to compensation payable under subsection (6).

(8) Where it is a condition of the grant of permission that an agreement be entered into in accordance with subsection (2) and, because of a dispute in respect of any matter relating to the terms of such an agreement, the agreement is not entered into before the expiration of 8 weeks from the date of the grant of permission, the applicant or any other person with an interest in the land to which the application relates may—

(a) refer to the Board any dispute to which subsection (5) applies. or
(b) refer to the property arbitrator—
   (i)   any dispute to which subsection (3)(a)(ii) or (iii) relates,
   (ii) any dispute as to the amount of compensation payable under subsection (6), or
   (iii) any dispute as to the sum payable to a planning authority under subsection (12),

and the Board or the property arbitrator, as may be appropriate, shall determine the matter as soon as practicable.

111

(9) (a) Where ownership of land or sites is transferred to a planning authority in accordance with subsection (3)(a)(i) or (iii), the authority may—
   (i) provide, or arrange for the provision of, houses on the land or sites for persons referred to in section 94 (4)(a),
   (ii) make land or sites available to those persons for the development of houses by them for their own occupation, or
   (iii) make land or sites available to a body approved for the purposes of section 6 of the Housing (Miscellaneous Provisions) Act, 1992, for the provision of houses on the land for persons referred to in section 94(4)(a).
(b) Pending the provision of houses or sites in accordance with paragraph (a)(i), or the making available of land or sites in accordance with paragraph (a)(ii) or (iii), the planning authority shall maintain the land or sites in a manner which does not detract, and is not likely to detract, to a material degree from the amenity, character or appearance of land or houses in the neighbourhood of the land or sites.

(10) (a) Where a house is transferred to a planning authority or its nominees under subsection (3)(a)(ii), it shall be used for the housing of persons to whom section 94(4)(a) applies.
(b) A nominee of a planning authority may be a person referred to in section 94(4)(a) or a body approved for the purposes of section 6 of the Housing (Miscellaneous Provisions) Act, 1992, for the provision of housing for persons referred to in section 94(4)(a).

(11) Notwithstanding any provision of this or any other enactment, if a planning authority becomes satisfied that land, a site or a house transferred to it under subsection (3) is no longer required for the purposes specified in subsection (9) or (10), it may use the land, site or house for another purpose connected with its functions or sell it for the best price reasonably obtainable and, in either case, it shall pay an amount equal to the market value of the land, site or house or the proceeds of the sale, as the case may be, into the separate account referred to in subsection (13).

(12) (a) Where for reasons of the size, shape or other attribute of the site, the planning authority, or the Board on appeal, considers that an agreement under subsection (3) is not practical, the planning authority, or the Board on appeal, may as a condition of a grant of permission in accordance with section 34 require the payment to the planning authority of an amount equivalent in value to a transfer of land to the authority under paragraph (a) of subsection (3).
(b) The condition specified in paragraph (a) shall provide that the sum shall be agreed between the planning authority and the person to whom the permission is granted and that in default of agreement the sum shall be fixed by a property arbitrator in accordance with subsection (7).

(13) Any amount referred to in subsection (11) and any amount paid to a planning authority in accordance with subsection (12) shall be accounted for in a separate account and shall only be applied as capital for its functions under this Part or by a housing authority for its functions in relation to the provision of housing under the Housing Acts, 1966 to 1998.

(14) This section shall not apply to applications for permission for—

(a) development consisting of the provision of houses by a body standing approved for the purposes of section 6 of the Housing (Miscellaneous Provisions) Act, 1992, for the provision of housing for persons referred to in section 9(2) of the Housing Act, 1988, where such houses are to be made available for letting only,

(b) the conversion of an existing building or the reconstruction of a building to create one or more dwellings, provided that 50 per cent or more of the existing external fabric of the building is retained, or

(c) the carrying out of works to an existing house.

(15) A permission granted under Part IV of the Act of 1963 or under Part III of this Act pursuant to an application made after 25 August 1999 and to which this Part would have applied if the application for permission had been made after the inclusion of a housing strategy in the development plan under section 94(1), shall cease to have effect on 31 December 2002 or on the expiry of a period of 2 years from the date of the grant of permission whichever is the later, as regards—

(a) where the development to which the permission relates is not commenced by that date or the expiry of that period, the entire development, and

(b) where the development to which the permission relates is commenced by that date or the expiry of that period, any portion of the development consisting of buildings the external walls of which have not been completed, but without prejudice to the obligation on the person carrying out the development to fulfil the other requirements of the permission in relation to so much of the development as is not affected by this paragraph.

(16) In this section, "owner" means—

(a) a person, other than a mortgagee not in possession, who is for the time being entitled to dispose (whether in possession or reversion) of the fee simple of the land, and

(b) a person who, under a lease or agreement the unexpired term of which exceeds 5 years, holds or is entitled to the rents or profits of the land.

Notes
Section 96(2), (3)
In an application for planning permission for residential development, a planning authority may require as a condition of the grant of planning permission that the developer enter into an agreement with the planning authority. This agreement may provide for the transfer to the planning authority of land for the provision of housing; the building and transfer of houses; or the transfer of fully or partially serviced sites. A developer cannot be *required* to transfer houses or sites instead of land.

Section 96(5)
A reference may be made to An Bord Pleanála in respect of a dispute as to any matter that may be the subject of an agreement required by a condition pursuant to s 96(2), except those matters that must be referred to the property arbitrator.

Section 96(6)
Where before 25 August 1999 an applicant for planning permission had acquired land or bought land or had entered into a legally enforceable agreement to purchase land then the price to be paid for the land is the actual purchase price of the land together with a sum in respect of interest. Compensation in respect of all other land is paid at the '*existing use*' value as of the date of the transfer to the planning authority and on the basis that it would be unlawful to carry

out any development except exempt development. Most land will be deemed as having an agricultural use value.

Section 96(7)

The property arbitrator can determine issues relating to compensation payable for the land; the number and price of houses to be transferred where the developer has agreed to build houses for the local authority; and the number and price of sites to be transferred where the developer has agreed to provide fully or partially serviced sites.

[192]
97. Development to which section 96 does not apply

(1) In this section

"applicant" includes a person on whose behalf a person applies for a certificate;

"the court" other than in subsections (19) and (21), means the Circuit Court for the circuit in which all or part of the development, to which the application under sub-section (3) relates, is situated.

(2) For the purposes of this section—

(a) 2 or more persons shall be deemed to be acting in concert if, pursuant to an agreement, arrangement or understanding, one of them makes an application under subsection (3) or causes such an application to be made, and

(b) land in the immediate vicinity of other land shall be deemed in any particular case not to include land that is more than 400 metres from the land second-men-tioned in this subsection.

(3) A person may, before applying for permission in respect of a development—

(a) consisting of the provision of 4 or fewer houses, or

(b) for housing on land of 0.2 hectares or less,

apply to the planning authority concerned for a certificate stating that section 96 shall not apply to a grant of permission in respect of the development concerned (in this section referred to as a "certificate"), and accordingly, where the planning authority grants a certificate, section 96 shall not apply to a grant of permission in respect of the development concerned.

(4) Subject to—

(a) subsections (6) and (12), and

(b) compliance by the applicant for a certificate with subsection (8),

a planning authority to which an application has been made under and in accordance with this section may grant a certificate to the applicant.

(5) An application for a certificate shall be accompanied by a statutory declaration made by the applicant—

(a) giving, in respect of the period of 5 years preceding the application, such partic-ulars of the legal and beneficial ownership of the land, on which it is proposed to carry out the development to which the application relates, as are within the applicant's knowledge or procurement,

(b) identifying any persons with whom the applicant is acting in concert,

(c) giving particulars of—
  (i) any interest that the applicant has, or had at any time during the said period, in any land in the immediate vicinity of the land on which it is proposed to carry out such development, and
  (ii) any interest that any person with whom the applicant is acting in concert has, or had at any time during the said period, in any land in the said immediate vicinity, of which the applicant has knowledge,

(d) stating that the applicant is not aware of any facts or circumstances that would constitute grounds under subsection (12) for the refusal by the planning authority to grant a certificate,

(e) giving such other information as may be prescribed.

(6) (a) A planning authority may require an applicant for a certificate to provide it with such further information or documentation as is reasonably necessary to enable it to perform its functions under this section.

(b) Where an applicant refuses to comply with a requirement under paragraph (a), or fails, within a period of 8 weeks from the date of the making of the requirement, to so comply, the planning authority concerned shall refuse to grant the applicant a certificate.

(7) A planning authority may, for the purpose of performing its functions under this section, make such further inquiries as it considers appropriate.

(8) It shall be the duty of the applicant for a certificate, at all times, to provide the planning authority concerned with such information as it may reasonably require to enable it to perform its functions under this section.

(9) The Minister may make regulations in relation to the making of an application under this section.

(10) Where a planning authority fails within the period of 4 weeks from—

(a) the making of an application to it under this section, or

(b) (in the case of a requirement under subsection (6)) the date of receipt by it of any information or documentation to which the requirement relates,

to grant, or refuse to grant a certificate, the planning authority shall on the expiry of that period be deemed to have granted a certificate to the applicant concerned.

(11) Particulars of a certificate granted under this section shall be entered on the register.

(12) A planning authority shall not grant a certificate in relation to a development if the applicant for such certificate, or any person with whom the applicant is acting in concert—

(a) has been granted, not earlier than 5 years before the date of the application, a certificate in respect of a development, and the certificate at the time of the application remains in force, or

(b) has carried out, or has been granted permission to carry out, a development referred to in subsection (3), not earlier than—
  (i) 5 years before the date of the application, and
  (ii) one year after the coming into operation of this section,

in respect of the land on which it is proposed to carry out the first-mentioned development, or land in its immediate vicinity, unless—

(I) the aggregate of any development to which paragraph (a) or (b) relates and the first-mentioned development would not, if carried out, exceed 4 houses, or

(II) (in circumstances where the said aggregate would exceed 4 houses) the aggregate of the land on which any development to which paragraph (a) or (b) relates, and the land on which it is proposed to carry out the first-mentioned development, does not exceed 0.2 hectares.

(13) Where a planning authority refuses to grant a certificate, it shall by notice in writing inform the applicant of the reasons for its so refusing.

(14) (a) Where a planning authority to which an application has been made under subsection (3) refuses to grant a certificate to the applicant, he or she may, not later than 3 weeks from the date on which the applicant receives notification of the refusal by the planning authority to grant the certificate, or such later date as may be permitted by the court, appeal to the court for an order directing the planning authority to grant to the applicant a certificate in respect of the development.

(b) The court may at the hearing of an appeal under paragraph (a)—

(i) dismiss the appeal and affirm the refusal of the planning authority to grant the certificate, or

(ii) allow the appeal and direct the planning authority to grant the applicant a certificate in respect of the development concerned.

(15) A planning authority shall comply with a direction of the court under this section.

(16) (a) Subject to paragraph (b), a planning authority shall revoke a certificate, upon application in that behalf being made to it by the owner of land to which the certificate related, or by any other person acting with the permission of such owner.

(b) A planning authority shall not revoke a certificate under this subsection where permission has been granted in respect of the development to which the certificate relates.

(17) A person who, knowingly or recklessly—

(a) makes a statutory declaration under subsection (5), or

(b) in purported compliance with a requirement under subsection (6), provides a planning authority with information or documentation,

that is false or misleading in a material respect, or who believes any such statutory declaration made, or information or documentation provided in purported compliance with such requirement, by him or her not to be true, shall be guilty of an offence and shall be liable—

(i) on summary conviction to a fine not exceeding £1,500 or to imprisonment for a term not exceeding 6 months, or to both, or

(ii) on conviction on indictment to a fine not exceeding £500,000 or to imprisonment for a term not exceeding 5 years, or to both.

(18) A person who—

(a) forges, or utters, knowing it to be forged, a certificate purporting to have been granted under this section (hereafter in this subsection referred to as a "forged certificate "),

(b) alters with intent to deceive or defraud, or utters, knowing it to be so altered, a certificate (hereafter in this subsection referred to as an "altered certificate"), or

(c) without lawful authority or other reasonable excuse, has in his or her possession a forged certificate or an altered certificate,

shall be guilty of an offence and shall be liable—

(i) on summary conviction to a fine not exceeding £1,500 or imprisonment for a term not exceeding 6 months, or to both, or

(ii) on conviction on indictment to a fine not exceeding £500,000 or imprisonment for a term not exceeding 5 years. or to both.

(19) Where a person is convicted on indictment of an offence under subsection (17) or (18), the court may in addition to any fine or term of imprisonment imposed by the court under that subsection order the payment into court by the person of an amount that in the opinion of the court is equal to the amount of any gain accruing to that person by reason of the grant of a certificate on foot of the statutory declaration, information or documentation, as the case may be, to which the offence relates, and such sum shall, when paid in accordance with such order, stand forfeited.

(20) All sums that stand forfeited under subsection (19) shall be paid to the planning authority that granted the certificate concerned and shall be accounted for in the account referred to in section 96(13) and be applied only for the purposes specified in that section.

(21) Where a person is convicted of an offence under subsection (17), the court may revoke a certificate granted on foot of a statutory declaration, information or documentation to which the offence relates, upon application being made to it in that behalf by the planning authority that granted the certificate.

(22) A person shall not, solely by reason of having been granted a certificate, be entitled to a grant of permission in respect of the development to which the certificate relates.

Note
Section 97(3)
A condition requiring the transfer of land under s 96(2) will not be imposed where the development is for four or less houses or is on 0.2 hectares or less. Section 97(12) seeks to prevent applicants carving up land/sites into smaller sections or applying for planning permission on a piecemeal basis to avoid the imposition of social/affordable housing conditions.

[193]
98. Allocation of affordable housing
(1) Affordable housing may be sold or leased only to eligible persons who qualify in accordance with a scheme established by a planning authority under subsection (2).

(2) For the purposes of subsection (1), each planning authority shall establish a scheme which determines the order of priority to be accorded to eligible persons.

(3) Without prejudice to the generality of subsection (2), when establishing a scheme referred to in that subsection, the planning authority shall have regard to the following:

(a) the accommodation needs of eligible persons, in particular eligible persons who have not previously purchased or built a house for their occupation or for any other purpose;

(b) the current housing circumstances of eligible persons;

(c) the incomes or other financial circumstances of eligible persons (and priority may be accorded to eligible persons whose income level is lower than that of other eligible persons);

(d) the period for which eligible persons have resided in the area of the development plan;

(e) whether eligible persons own houses or lands in the area of the development plan or elsewhere;

(f) distance of affordable housing from places of employment of eligible persons;

(g) such other matters as the planning authority considers appropriate or as may be prescribed for the purposes of this section.

(4) A planning authority—

(a) shall, when making or reviewing a development plan under Part II, and

(b) may, at any other time, review a scheme made under this section and, as it sees fit, make amendments to the scheme or make a new scheme.

(5) The making of a scheme under this section and the making of an amendment to any such scheme shall be reserved functions.

(6) For the purposes of allocation under this section, a planning authority may, from time to time, set aside such specified number or proportion of affordable houses, for such eligible persons or classes of eligible persons, as it considers appropriate.

(7) In this section and section 99, "lease" means a shared owner ship lease within the meaning of section 2 of the Housing (Miscellaneous Provisions) Act, 1992.

Note
Section 98(2)
The Guidelines (December 2000) state that the scheme of allocation of priorities should ensure that the allocation of affordable housing is done in an open and transparent way and should set out clearly the basis for prioritising the allocation of affordable housing.

[194]
99. Controls on resale of certain houses
(1) Where houses are provided or sites made available in accordance with section 96(9) or (10), the sale or lease of those houses or sites shall be subject to such conditions (if any) as may be specified by the planning authority.

(2) Without prejudice to the generality of subsection (1), terms and conditions under those subsections may provide for—

(a) the notification of the planning authority of the resale of any house or land, and

(b) the basis on which any house sold or leased under this Part may be occupied.

(3) (a) Terms and conditions under this section shall require, subject to paragraphs (b) and (c), that where any house or land sold to any person in accordance with subsection (1) is first resold before the expiration of 20 years from the date of purchase, the person selling the house or land shall pay to the planning authority out of the proceeds of the sale an amount equal to a percentage of the proceeds, which percentage is calculated in accordance with the following formula—

$$\frac{Y \times 100}{Z}$$

where—

Y   is the difference between the market value of the house or land at the time of sale to the person and the price actually paid, and

Z   is the market value of the house at the time of sale to the person.

(b)   The amount payable under paragraph (a) shall be reduced by 10 per cent in respect of each complete year after the 10th year during which the person to whom the house or land was sold has been in occupation of the house or land as his or her normal place of residence.

(c)   Where the amount payable under paragraph (a) would reduce the proceeds of the sale (disregarding solicitor and estate agent's fees and costs) below the price actually paid, the amount payable shall be reduced to the extent necessary to avoid that result.

(d)   (i)   In calculating the amount payable under paragraph (a), due allowance shall be made for any material improvements made by the person to whom the house or land was sold.

(ii)   For the purpose of this paragraph, "material improvements" means improvements made to the house (whether for the purpose of extending, enlarging, repairing or converting the house), but does not include decoration, or any improvements carried out on the land including the construction of a house.

(4) Any moneys accruing to a planning authority arising out of the resale of any house or land, subject to terms and conditions in accordance with subsection (1), shall be paid into the separate account referred to in section 96(13) and shall be subject to the other requirements of that subsection.

[195]–[200]
100. Regulations under this Part
(1) The Minister may make regulations—

(a)   specifying the criteria for determining the size of the accommodation required by eligible persons, including minimum and maximum size requirements, having regard to any guidelines specified by the Minister in respect of the provision of housing under the Housing Acts, 1966 to 1998,

(b)   governing the determination of income for the purposes of section 93,

(c)   specifying matters for the purposes of section 94(5) or 98(3), and

(d)   setting out requirements related to terms and conditions

referred to in section 99(1).

(2) Regulations made under subsection (1) may apply either generally or by reference to a specified class or classes of eligible persons or to any other matter as may be considered by the Minister to be appropriate.

Note
The Guidelines (December 2000) will assist local authorities in developing their housing strategies, which are fundamental to realising the social and affordable housing provisions of the Act.

[201]
101. Housing and planning authority under this section
(1) Where a planning authority performing any function under this Part is not the housing authority for the area of the function, the planning authority shall consult with the housing authority for the area with respect to the performance of that function.

(2) In this section, a reference to a "housing authority" means a housing authority as defined pursuant to section 23(2) of the Housing (Miscellaneous Provisions) Act, 1992.

PART VI   AN BORD PLEANÁLA

Note
Part VI concerns the make-up of An Bord Pleanála as well as the rules and procedures for appealing or referring a matter to An Bord Pleanála. These matters were previously provided for in LG(PD)A 1976, LG(PD)A 1982, LG(PD)A 1983, LG(PD)A 1992 and LG(PD)A 1998.

CHAPTER I   ESTABLISHMENT AND CONSTITUTION

[202]
102. Continuation of Bord Pleanála
(1) An Bord Pleanála shall continue in being notwithstanding the repeal of any enactment effected by this Act.

(2) The Board shall perform the functions assigned to it by this Act.

(3) The chairman, deputy chairman and any other member of the Board in office immediately prior to the coming into force of this section under an enactment repealed by this Act shall continue in office as chairperson, deputy chairperson and other member, respectively, for a term ending on the day on which his or her appointment would have expired under the repealed enactment.

Note
Section 102 is a restatement of the previous provision.

[203]
103. Board to be body corporate, etc
(1) The Board shall be a body corporate with perpetual succession and a seal and power to sue and be sued in its corporate name and to acquire, hold and dispose of land.

(2) The seal of the Board shall be authenticated by the signature of the chairperson or of some other member, or of an employee of the Board or of a person whose services are availed of by the Board by virtue of section 122, who is authorised by the Board to act in that behalf.

(3) Judicial notice shall be taken of the seal of the Board and every document purporting to be an instrument made by the Board and to be sealed with the seal (purporting to be authenticated in accordance with subsection (2)) of the Board shall be received in evidence and be deemed to be such an instrument without proof unless the contrary is shown.

Note
Section 103 restates s 2 of LG(PD)A 1982.

[204]
104. Board to consist of chairperson and 7 other members
(1) Subject to subsections (2) and (3) of this section, the Board shall consist of a chairperson and 7 other ordinary members.

(2) The Minister may by order increase the number of ordinary members where he or she is of the opinion that the number of appeals, referrals or other matters with which the Board is concerned is at such a level so as to necessitate the appointment of one or more additional Board members to enable the Board fulfil its duty and objective under section 126.

(3) Where an order is proposed to be made under subsection (2), a draft of the order shall be laid before each House of the Oireachtas and the order shall not be made until a resolution approving of the draft has been passed by each such House.

(4) (a) Notwithstanding subsection (2) of this section or subsection (3) of section 106, where the Minister is of the opinion that one or more than one additional ordinary member should be appointed as a matter of urgency due to the number of appeals, referrals or other matters with which the Board is concerned, the Minister may, pending the making and approval of an order under subsections (2) and (3) of this section, appoint one or more than one person from among the officers of the Minister who are established civil servants for the purposes of the Civil Service Regulation Act, 1956, or from among the employees of the Board, on a temporary basis.
(b) A person shall not be appointed to be an ordinary member under this subsection for a term in excess of 9 months.

(5) An order made under subsection (2) shall have effect for such a period not exceeding 5 years as shall be specified therein.

Note
This is an increase of one on the number of members provided for in s 1 of LG(PD)A 1998. Otherwise, the section is a restatement.

[205]–[210]
105. Appointment of chairperson
(1) The chairperson shall be appointed by the Government.

(2) There shall be a committee ("the committee") consisting of—

(a) the President of the High Court,

(b) the Cathaoirleach of the General Council of County Councils,

(c) the Secretary-General of the Department of the Environment and Local Government,

(d) the Chairperson of the Council of An Taisce—the National Trust for Ireland,

(e) the President of the Construction Industry Federation,

(f) the President of the Executive Council of the Irish Congress of Trade Unions, and

(g) the Chairperson of the National Women's Council of Ireland.

(3) Where—

(a) any of the persons referred to in subsection (2) signifies at any time his or her unwillingness or inability to act for any period as a member of the committee, or

(b) any of the persons referred to in subsection (2) is through ill-health or otherwise unable so to act for any period,

the Minister may, when making a request under subsection (7), appoint another person to be a member of the committee in his or her place and that person shall remain a member of the committee until such time as the selection by the committee pursuant to the request is made.

(4) Where the Minister makes a request under subsection (1) and at the time of making the request any of the offices referred to in subsection (2) is vacant, the Minister may appoint a person to be a member of the committee and that person shall remain a member of the committee until such time as the selection of the committee pursuant to the request is made.

(5) Where, pursuant to subsection (3) or (4), the Minister appoints a person to be a member of the committee, he or she shall, as soon as may be, cause a notice of the appointment to be published in Iris Oifigiúil.

(6) (a) The Minister may by order amend subsection (2).

(b) The Minister may by order amend or revoke an order under this subsection (including an order under this paragraph).

(c) Where an order under this subsection is proposed to be made, the Minister shall cause a draft thereof to be laid before both Houses of the Oireachtas and the order shall not be made until a resolution approving of the draft has been passed by each such House.

(d) Where an order under this subsection is in force, subsection (2) shall be construed and have effect subject to the terms of the order.

(7) (a) The committee shall, whenever so requested by the Minister, select 3 candidates, or if in the opinion of the committee there is not a sufficient number of suitable applicants, such lesser number of candidates as the committee shall determine, for appointment to be the chairperson and shall inform the Minister of the names of the candidates, or, as may be appropriate, the name of the candidate, selected and of the reasons why, in the opinion of the committee, they are or he or she is suitable for the appointment.

(b) In selecting candidates the committee shall have regard to the special knowledge and experience and other qualifications or personal qualities which the committee considers appropriate to enable a person effectively to perform the functions of the chairperson.

(8) Except in the case of a re-appointment under subsection (12), the Government shall not appoint a person to be the chairperson unless the person was selected by the committee under subsection (7) in relation to that appointment but—

(a) if the committee is unable to select any suitable candidate pursuant to a particular request under subsection (7), or

(b) if the Government decides not to appoint to be the chairperson any of the candidates selected by the committee pursuant to a particular request, then either—

    (i) the Government shall appoint a person to be the chairperson who was a candidate selected by the committee pursuant to a previous request (if any) in relation to that appointment, or

    (ii) the Minister shall make a further request to the committee and the Government shall appoint to be the chairperson a person who is selected by the committee pursuant to the request or pursuant to a previous request.

(9) The Minister may make regulations as regards—

(a) the publication of the notice that a request has been received by the committee under subsection (7),

(b) applications for selection by the committee, and

(c) any other matter which the Minister considers expedient for the purposes of this section.

(10) A person who is, for the time being—

(a) entitled under the Standing Orders of either House of the Oireachtas to sit therein,

(b) a member of the European Parliament, or

(c) a member of a local authority,

shall be disqualified from being appointed as the chairperson.

(11) The chairperson shall be appointed in a wholetime capacity and shall not at any time during his or her term of office hold any other office or employment in respect of which emoluments are payable.

(12) Subject to the other provisions of this section, the chairperson shall hold office for a term of 7 years and may be re-appointed by the Government for a second or subsequent term of office, provided that a person shall not be re-appointed under this subsection unless, at the time of his or her re-appointment, he or she is or was the outgoing chairperson.

(13) (a) The chairperson may resign his or her office as chairperson by letter addressed to the Minister and the resignation shall take effect on and from the date of the receipt of the letter by the Minister.

(b) The chairperson shall vacate the office of chairperson on attaining the age of 65 years.

(c) A person shall cease to be the chairperson if he or she—

    (i) is nominated either as a member of Seanad Éireann or for election to either House of the Oireachtas or to the European Parliament,

      (ii) is regarded pursuant to Part XIII of the Second Schedule to the European Parliament Elections Act, 1997, as having been elected to that Parliament to fill a vacancy, or

      (iii) becomes a member of a local authority.

(d) A person shall cease to be the chairperson if he or she—

      (i)   is adjudicated bankrupt,

      (ii) makes a composition or arrangement with creditors,

      (iii) is convicted of any indictable offence in relation to a company,

      (iv) is convicted of an offence involving fraud or dishonesty, whether in connection with a company or not,

      (v) is sentenced by a court of competent jurisdiction to a term of imprisonment,

      (vi) is the subject of an order under section 160 of the Companies Act, 1990, or

      (vii) ceases to be resident in the State.

(14) (a) There shall be paid by the Board to the chairperson the same salary as is paid to a judge of the High Court.

(b) Subject to the provisions of this section, the chairperson shall hold office on such terms and conditions (including terms relating to allowances for expenses) as the Minister, with the consent of the Minister for Finance, determines.

(15) The chairperson may be removed from office by the Government if he or she has become incapable through ill-health of effectively performing his or her functions, or if he or she has committed stated misbehaviour, or if his or her removal appears to the Government to be necessary for the effective performance by the Board of its functions, and in case the chairperson is removed from office under this subsection, the Government shall cause to be laid before each House of the Oireachtas a statement of the reasons for the removal.

Note
Section 105 is a restatement of s 5 of LG(PD)A 1983.

[211]
106. Appointment of ordinary members
(1) The Minister shall appoint 7 ordinary members of the Board as follows:

(a) one member shall be appointed from among persons selected by prescribed organisations which in the Minister's opinion are representative of persons whose professions or occupations relate to physical planning, engineering and architecture;

(b) one member shall be appointed from among persons selected by prescribed organisations which in the Minister's opinion are representative of persons concerned with the protection and preservation of the environment and of amenities;

(c) one member shall be appointed from among persons selected by prescribed organisations which in the Minister's opinion are concerned with economic development, the promotion of and carrying out of development, the provision of infrastructure or the development of land or otherwise connected with the construction industry;

(d) one member shall be appointed from among persons selected by prescribed organisations which in the Minister's opinion are representative of the interests of local government;

(e) one member shall be appointed from among persons nominated by such trade unions, bodies representing farmers and bodies that, in the opinion of the Minister, have a special interest or expertise in matters relating to rural and local community development, as may be prescribed;

(f) one member shall be appointed from among persons nominated by such voluntary bodies, bodies having charitable objects and bodies that, in the opinion of the Minister, have a special interest or expertise in matters relating to the promotion of the Irish language, the promotion of the arts and culture or that are representative of people with disability, as may be prescribed;

(g) one member shall be appointed from among the officers of the Minister who are established civil servants for the purposes of the Civil Service Regulation Act, 1956.

(2) The Minister shall prescribe at least 2 organisations for the purposes of each of paragraphs (a) to (f) of subsection (1).

(3) Where the Minister decides to appoint one or more members to the Board pursuant to an order under section 104(2)—

(a) where not more than 5 additional members are appointed, not more than one shall be appointed from among persons selected by organisations which are prescribed for the purposes of a particular paragraph of subsection (1);

(b) where more than 5 but not more than 10 additional members are appointed, not more than 2 shall be appointed from among persons selected by organisations which are prescribed for the purposes of a particular paragraph of subsection (1).

(4) An organisation prescribed for the purposes of paragraph (a), (b), (c), (d), (e) or (f) of subsection (1), shall, whenever so requested by the Minister, nominate such number of candidates (not being less than two) as the Minister may specify for appointment as an ordinary member and shall inform the Minister of the names of the candidates nominated and of the reasons why, in the opinion of the organisation, they are suitable for appointment.

(5) Except in the case of an appointment pursuant to subsection (1)(g) or a re-appointment under subsection (12) and subject to subsection (6) and section 108(4), the Minister shall not appoint a person to be an ordinary member unless the person was nominated pursuant to a request under subsection (4) in relation to that appointment.

(6) Where—

(a) pursuant to a particular request under subsection (4), an organisation refuses or fails to nominate any candidate, or

(b) the Minister decides not to appoint as an ordinary member any candidate nominated by the organisations pursuant to a particular request under that subsection,

then

    (i) the Minister shall appoint as an ordinary member a person who was among those nominated by such an organisation pursuant to a previous request (if any) under that subsection in relation to that appointment,

   (ii)   the Minister shall make a further request and shall appoint as an ordinary member a person who was among those nominated pursuant to that request or pursuant to another request made in relation to that appointment, or

  (iii)   the Minister shall appoint as an ordinary member a person selected by a committee established under subsection (7).

(7) (a) There shall be a committee ("the committee") consisting of—

     (i)   the chairperson,

    (ii)   the Assistant-Secretary of the Department of the Environment and Local Government with responsibility for planning and sustainable development, and

   (iii)   the Chairperson of the Heritage Council.

(b) The committee shall, whenever so requested by the Minister—

     (i)   by notice in one or more national newspapers, invite applications for appointment as an ordinary member by suitably qualified persons,

    (ii)   select 3 candidates, or if in the opinion of the committee there is not such a sufficient number of suitable applicants, such lesser number of candidates as the committee shall determine, for appointment as an ordinary member, having regard to the knowledge and experience and other qualifications or personal qualities which the committee considers appropriate to enable a person effectively to perform the functions of an ordinary member, and

   (iii)   inform the Minister of the names of the candidates or, as may be appropriate, the name of the candidate, selected and of the reasons why, in the opinion of the committee, they are or he or she is suitable for the appointment.

(8) Where a request is made under subsection (4), failure or refusal by the organisation of whom the request is made to nominate the number of candidates specified in the request shall not preclude the appointment as an ordinary member of a person who was nominated in relation to that appointment either by the organisation or by any other organisation.

(9) The Minister may make regulations as regards—

(a) the period within which the Minister is to be informed in accordance with subsection (4), and

(b) any other matter which the Minister considers expedient for the purposes of this section.

(10) A person who is for the time being—

(a) entitled under the Standing Orders of either House of the Oireachtas to sit therein,

(b) a member of the European Parliament, or

(c) a member of a local authority,

shall be disqualified from being appointed as an ordinary member.

(11) Each of the ordinary members shall be appointed in a wholetime capacity and shall not at any time during his or her term of office hold any other office or employment in respect of which emoluments are payable.

(12) Subject to section 108(4)(b), an ordinary member shall hold office for such term (not exceeding 5 years) as shall be specified by the Minister when appointing him or her to office and may be re appointed by the Minister for a second or sub-

sequent term of office provided that a person shall not be re-appointed under this subsection unless, at the time of his or her re-appointment, he or she is or was an outgoing member of the Board.

(13) (a) An ordinary member may resign his or her membership by letter addressed to the Minister and the resignation shall take effect on and from the date of the receipt of the letter by the Minister.

(b) A person shall vacate the office of ordinary member on attaining the age of 65 years.

(c) A person shall cease to be an ordinary member if he or she—
  (i) is nominated either as a member of Seanad Éireann or for election to either House of the Oireachtas or to the European Parliament,
  (ii) is regarded pursuant to Part XIII of the Second Schedule to the European Parliament Elections Act, 1997, as having been elected to that Parliament to fill a vacancy, or
  (iii) becomes a member of a local authority.

(d) A person shall cease to be an ordinary member of the Board if he or she—
  (i) is adjudicated bankrupt,
  (ii) makes a composition or arrangement with creditors,
  (iii) is convicted of any indictable offence in relation to a company,
  (iv) is convicted of an offence involving fraud or dishonesty, whether in connection with a company or not,
  (v) is sentenced by a court of competent jurisdiction to a term of imprisonment,
  (vi) is the subject of an order under section 160 of the Companies Act, 1990, or
  (vii) ceases to be resident in the State.

(14) (a) There shall be paid by the Board to each ordinary member such remuneration and allowances for expenses as the Minister, with the consent of the Minister for Finance, determines.

(b) Subject to the other provisions of this section, an ordinary member shall hold office on such terms and conditions as the Minister, with the consent of the Minister for Finance, determines.

(15) An ordinary member may be removed from office by the Minister if he or she has become incapable through ill-health of effectively performing his or her functions, or if he or she has committed stated misbehaviour, or if his or her removal appears to the Minister to be necessary for the effective performance by the Board of its functions, and in case an ordinary member is removed from office under this subsection, the Minister shall cause to be laid before each House of the Oireachtas a statement in writing of the reasons for the removal.

Note
Section 106 is a restatement of s 7 of LG(PD)A 1983 with a number of amendments. In particular, the panels from which persons for appointment can be nominated have been modified.

[212]
107. Appointment of deputy chairperson
(1) The Minister shall appoint from among the ordinary members a person to be the deputy chairperson and the appointment shall be for such period as shall be specified in the appointment.

(2) If at any time the deputy chairperson ceases to be an ordinary member of the Board, he or she shall thereupon cease to be the deputy chairperson.

(3) The deputy chairperson shall, in addition to his or her remuneration as an ordinary member, be paid by the Board such additional remuneration (if any) as the Minister, with the consent of the Minister for Finance, determines.

(4) The deputy chairperson may resign his or her office as deputy chairperson by letter addressed to the Minister and the resignation shall take effect on and from the date of the receipt of the letter by the Minister.

Note
Section 107 is a restatement of s 8 of LG(PD)A 1983.

[213]
108. Board's quorum vacancies, etc
(1) The quorum for a meeting of the Board shall be 3.

(2) Subject to subsection (1), the Board may act notwithstanding a vacancy in the office of chairperson or deputy chairperson or among the ordinary members.

(3) Where a vacancy occurs or is due to occur in the office of chairperson or deputy chairperson or among the ordinary members, the Minister shall, as soon as may be, take steps to fill the vacancy.

(4) (a) Where, owing to the illness of the chairperson or of an ordinary member, or for any other reason, a sufficient number of members of the Board is not available to enable the Board effectively to perform its functions, the Minister may, as an interim measure, appoint from among the officers referred to in section 106(1)(g) or the employees of the Board, one or more persons to be an ordinary member.

(b) A person shall not be appointed to be an ordinary member under this subsection for a term in excess of one year.

Note
Section 108 is a restatement of s 12 of LG(PD)A 1983.

CHAPTER II   ORGANISATION, STAFFING, ETC

[214]
109. Performance of Board
(1) The Board shall supply the Minister with such information relating to the performance of its functions as he or she may from time to time request.

(2) (a) The Board shall conduct, at such intervals as it thinks fit or the Minister directs, reviews of its organisation and of the systems and procedures used by it in relation to appeals and referrals.

(b) Where the Minister gives a direction under this section, the Board shall report to the Minister the results of the review conducted pursuant to the direction and shall comply with any directive which the Minister may, after consultation with the Board as regards those results, give in relation to all or any of the matters which were the subject of the review.

(3) The Board may make submissions to the Minister as regards any matter pertaining to its functions.

(4) The Minister may consult with the Board as regards any matter pertaining to the performance of—

(a) the functions of the Board, or
(b) the functions assigned to the Minister by or under this Act or by any other enactment or by any order, regulation or other instrument thereunder.

Note
Section 109 is a restatement of s 9(2) of LG(PD)A 1976 and s 4 of LG(PD)A 1983.

[215]–[220]
110. Chairperson to ensure efficient discharge of business of Board etc
(1) It shall be the function of the chairperson, or, where he to or she is not available or where the office of chairperson is vacant, of the deputy chairperson—.

(a) to ensure the efficient discharge of the business of the Board, and
(b) to arrange the distribution of the business of the Board among its members.

(2) Where the chairperson is of the opinion that the conduct of an ordinary member has been such as to bring the Board into disrepute or has been prejudicial to the effective performance by the Board of all or any one or more of its functions, he or she may in his or her absolute discretion—

(a) require the member of the Board to attend for interview and there interview the member privately and inform him or her of such opinion, or
(b) where he or she considers it appropriate to do so, otherwise investigate the matter,

and, if he or she considers it appropriate to do so, report to the Minister the result of the interview or investigation.

Note
Section 110 is a restatement of s 6 of LG(PD)A 1983.

[221]
111. Meetings and procedure of Board
(1) The Board shall hold such and so many meetings as may be necessary for the performance of its functions.

(2) The chairperson and each ordinary member at a meeting of the Board shall have a vote.

(3) At a meeting of the Board—

(a) the chairperson shall, if present, be chairperson of the meeting,
(b) if the chairperson is not present the deputy chairperson shall, if present. be chairperson of the meeting, and
(c) if neither the chairperson nor the deputy chairperson is present, the ordinary members who are present shall choose one of their number to be chairperson of the meeting.

(4) Every question at a meeting of the Board relating to the performance of its functions shall be determined by a majority of votes of the members present and, in the event that voting is equally divided, the person who is chairperson of the meeting shall have a casting vote.

(5) (a) Subject to this Act, and to any regulations made thereunder, and subject also to any other enactment or order, regulation or other instrument thereunder, which regulates or otherwise affects the procedure of the Board, the Board shall regulate its own procedure and business.

(b) The Minister may require the Board to keep him or her informed of the arrangements made under this subsection for the regulation of its procedure and business.

(6) (a) Subject to paragraphs (b) and (c), the Board may perform any of its functions through or by any member of the Board or other person who has been duly authorised by the Board in that behalf.

(b) Paragraph (a) shall be construed as enabling a member of the Board finally to determine points of detail relating to a decision on a particular case if the case to which an authorisation under that paragraph relates has been considered at a meeting of the Board prior to the giving of the authorisation and that determination shall conform to the terms of that authorisation.

(c) Paragraph (a) shall not be construed as enabling the Board to authorise a person who is not a member of the Board finally to determine any particular case with which the Board is concerned.

(7) The Board shall arrange to keep a written record of all its decisions including the names of those present at a meeting of the Board and the number of those persons who vote for or against those decisions.

Note
Section 111 is a restatement of s 11 of LG(PD)A 1983.

[222]
112. Divisions of Board
(1) Whenever the Minister or the chairperson considers that, for the speedy dispatch of the business of the Board, it is expedient that the Board should act by divisions, he or she may direct accordingly, and until that direction is revoked—

(a) the chairperson shall assign to each division the business to be transacted by it, and

(b) for the purpose of the business so assigned to it, each division shall have all the functions of the Board.

(2) A division of the Board shall consist of not less than 3 members of the Board.

(3) The chairperson, or in his or her absence, a person acting as chairperson of a meeting of a division of the Board, may at any stage before a decision is made, transfer the consideration of any appeal or referral from the division to a meeting of all available members of the Board, where the chairperson considers the appeal or referral to be of particular complexity or significance.

Note
Section 112 is new. It allows the Board to meet in divisions in an effort to allow the Board to meets its workload, increased under this Act, in a more efficient manner. Note the quorum provisions in s 108 above.

[223]
113. Prohibition on disclosure of information relating to functions of Board
(1) No person shall, without the consent of the Board (which may be given to the person, subject to or without conditions, as regards any information, as regards particular information or as regards information of a particular class or description), disclose—

(a) any information obtained by him or her while serving as a member or employee of, or consultant or adviser to, the Board or as a person whose services are availed of by the Board by virtue of section 120(2) or 122, or
(b) any information so obtained relative to the business of the Board or to the performance of its functions.

(2) A person who contravenes subsection (1) shall be guilty of an offence.

(3) Nothing in subsection (1) shall prevent—

(a) disclosure of information in a report made to the Board or in a report made by or on behalf of the Board to the Minister,
(b) disclosure of information by any person in the course of and in accordance with the functions of his or her office,
(c) disclosure of information in accordance with the Freedom of Information Act, 1997, or
(d) disclosure of information in accordance with the European Communities Act, 1972 (Access to Information on the Environment) Regulations, 1998, and any regulations amending or replacing those regulations.

Note
Section 113 is a restatement of s 13 of LG(PD)A 1983 save for the references to the Freedom of Information Act, 1997 and the equivalent regulations relative to environmental information, 1998, at sub-ss (3)(c) and (d).

[224]
114. Prohibition of certain communications in relation to appeals etc
(1) Any person who communicates with the chairperson, an ordinary member, an employee of, or consultant or adviser to, the Board or a person whose services are availed of by the Board by virtue of section 120(2) or 122 for the purpose of influencing etc. improperly the consideration of an appeal or referral or a decision of the Board as regards any matter shall be guilty of an offence.

(2) If the chairperson or an ordinary member or an employee of, or consultant or adviser to, the Board or a person whose services are availed of by the Board by virtue of section 120(2) or 122, becomes of the opinion that a communication is in contravention of subsection (1), it shall be his or her duty not to entertain the communication further and shall disclose the communication to the Board.

Note
Section 114 makes it an offence to seek to influence improperly the Board's decision by communicating with any employee or member of the Board. Section 14 of LG(PD)A 1983 made such communication unlawful.

[225]–[230]
115. Indemnification of members and employees of Board and other persons
Where the Board is satisfied that a member of the Board, an employee of the Board or a person whose services are provided to the Board under section 120(2), 122 or 124(1) has discharged his or her duties in relation to the functions of the Board in a bona fide manner, it shall indemnify the member, employee or person against all actions or claims howsoever arising in respect of the discharge by him or her of his or her duties.

Note
Section 115 is a restatement of s 2 of LG(PD)A 1988.

[231]
116. Grants to Board
There may, subject to such conditions, if any, as the Minister thinks proper, be paid to the Board in each financial year out of moneys provided by the Oireachtas a grant or grants of such amount or amounts as the Minister, with the consent of the Minister for Finance and after consultation with the Board in relation to its programme of expenditure for that year, may fix.

Note
Section 116 is a restatement of s 7 of LG(PD)A 1976.

[232]
117. Accounts and audits of Board
(1) The Board shall keep in such form as may be approved by the Minister, after consultation with the Minister for Finance, all proper and usual accounts of all moneys received or expended by it.

(2) Accounts kept under this section shall be submitted by the Board to the Comptroller and Auditor General for audit at such times as the Minister shall direct and, when audited shall, together with the report of the Comptroller and Auditor General, be presented to the Minister who shall cause copies to be laid before each House of the Oireachtas.

Note
Section 117 is a restatement of s 8 of LG(PD)A 1976.

[233]
118. Annual report and information to Minister
The Board shall, not later than the 30th day of June in each year, make a report to the Minister of its proceedings during the preceding year and the Minister shall cause copies of the report to be laid before each House of the Oireachtas.

Note
Section 118 is a restatement of s 9(1) of LG(PD)A 1976.

[234]
119. Superannuation of members of Board

(1) The Minister may, with the consent of the Minister for Finance, make a scheme or schemes for the granting of pensions, gratuities or other allowances to or in respect of the chairperson and ordinary members ceasing to hold office.

(2) A scheme under this section may provide that the termination of the appointment of the chairperson or of an ordinary member during that person's term of office shall not preclude the award to him or her under the scheme of a pension, gratuity or other allowance.

(3) The Minister may, with the consent of the Minister for Finance, amend a scheme made by him or her under this section.

(4) If any dispute arises as to the claim of any person to, or the amount of, any pension, gratuity, or allowance payable in pursuance of a scheme under this section, the dispute shall be submitted to the Minister who shall refer it to the Minister for Finance, whose decision shall be final.

(5) A scheme under this section shall be carried out by the Board in accordance with its terms.

(6) No pension, gratuity or other allowance shall be granted by the Board to or in respect of any person referred to in subsection (1) ceasing to hold office otherwise than in accordance with a scheme under this section.

(7) Every scheme made under this section shall be laid before each House of the Oireachtas as soon as may be after it is made and if either such House, within the next 21 days on which that House has sat after the scheme is laid before it, passes a resolution annulling the scheme, the scheme shall be annulled accordingly, but without prejudice to the validity of anything previously done thereunder.

Note
Section 119 is a restatement of s 9 of LG(PD)A 1983.

[235]–[240]
120. Employees of Board

(1) The Board shall appoint such and so many persons to be employees of the Board as the Board, subject to the approval of the Minister, given with the consent of the Minister for Finance, as to the number and kind of those employees, from time to time considers appropriate, having regard to the need to ensure that an adequate number of staff are competent in the Irish language so as to be able to provide service through Irish as well as English.

(2) The Board may employ a person in a part-time capacity to be remunerated by the payment of fees in such amounts as the Board may, with the approval of the Minister, given with the consent of the Minister for Finance, from time to time determine.

(3) An employee of the Board shall hold his or her employment on such terms and conditions as the Board, subject to the approval of the Minister, from time to time determines.

(4) There shall be paid by the Board to its employees out of moneys at its disposal such remuneration and allowances as the Board, subject to the approval of the Minister, with the consent of the Minister for Finance, from time to time determines.

Note
Section 120 is a restatement of s 10 of LG(PD)A 1976.

[241]
121. Superannuation of employees of Board

(1) The Board shall prepare and submit to the Minister for his or her approval, a scheme or schemes for the granting of pensions, gratuities and other allowances on retirement or death to or in respect of such whole-time employees of the Board as it considers appropriate.

(2) The Board may, at any time, prepare and submit to the Minister a scheme amending a scheme under this section.

(3) Where a scheme is submitted to the Minister pursuant to this section, the Minister may, with the consent of the Minister for Finance, approve the scheme without modification or with such modification (whether by way of addition, omission or variation) as the Minister shall, with such consent, think proper.

(4) A scheme submitted to the Minister under this section shall, if approved of by the Minister, with the consent of the Minister for Finance, be carried out by the Board in accordance with its terms.

(5) A scheme approved of under this section shall fix the time and conditions of retirement for all persons to or in respect of whom pensions, gratuities or other allowances are payable under the scheme, and different times and conditions may be fixed in respect of different classes of persons.

(6) If any dispute arises as to the claim of any person to, or the amount of, any pension, gratuity or other allowance payable in pursuance of a scheme under this section, the dispute shall be submitted to the Minister who shall refer it to the Minister for Finance, whose decision shall be final.

(7) Every scheme approved of under this section shall be laid before each House of the Oireachtas as soon as may be after it is approved of and if either House within the next 21 days on which that House has sat after the scheme is laid before it, passes a resolution annulling the scheme, the scheme shall be annulled accordingly, but without prejudice to the validity of anything previously done thereunder.

Note
Section 121 is a restatement of s 11 of LG(PD)A 1976.

[242]
122. Provision of services by Minister to Board

(1) For the purposes of enabling the Board to perform its functions, the Minister may provide services (including services of staff) to the Board on such terms and conditions (including payment for such services) as may be agreed and the Board may avail of such services.

(2) The Board may provide services (including services of staff) to the Minister on such terms and conditions (including payment for such services) as may be agreed and the Minister may avail of such services.

Note
Section 122 is a restatement, with some amendments, of s 21 of LG(PD)A 1976. Specifically sub-s (2) now provides for the Board to provide services to the Minister.

[243]
123. Membership of either House Oireachtas etc
(1) Where a person who is an employee of the Board is nominated as a member of Seanad Éireann or for election to either of the House of the Oireachtas or the European Parliament, or is regarded pursuant to Part XIII of the Second Schedule to the European Parliament Elections Act, 1997, as having been elected to that Parliament to fill a vacancy, or becomes a member of a local authority, he or she shall stand seconded from employment by the Board and shall not be paid by, or be entitled to receive from, the Board any remuneration or allowances—

(a) in case he or she is nominated as a member of Seanad Éireann in respect of the period commencing on his or her acceptance of the nomination and ending when he or she ceases to be a member of that House,

(b) in case he or she is nominated for election to either such House or to the European Parliament, or is regarded as having been elected to the European Parliament, in respect of the period commencing on his or her nomination or appointment and ending when he or she ceases to be a member of that House or Parliament or fails to be elected or withdraws his or her candidature, as may be appropriate, or

(c) in case he or she becomes a member of a local authority, in respect of the period commencing on his or her becoming a member of the local authority and ending when he or she ceases to be a member of that authority.

(2) A person who is for the time being entitled under the Standing Orders of either House of the Oireachtas to sit therein or is a member of the European Parliament shall, while he or she is so entitled or is such a member, be disqualified from becoming an employee of the Board.

(3) A person who is for the time being a member of a local authority shall, while holding office as such member, be disqualified from becoming an employee of the Board.

Note
Section 123 is a restatement with some amendments of s 12 of LG(PD)A 1976.

[244]
124. Consultants and advisers to Board
(1) The Board may from time to time engage such consultants or advisers as it considers necessary for the performance of its functions and any fees due to a consultant or adviser engaged pursuant to this section shall be paid by the Board out of moneys at its disposal.

(2) The Board shall include in each report made under section 118 a statement of the names of the persons (if any) engaged pursuant to this section during the year to which the report relates.

Note
Section 124 is a restatement of ss 13(1) and 5 of LG(PD)A 1976 with amendment such that the Board will not in future be required to maintain a list of persons eligible for work.

CHAPTER III   APPEAL PROCEDURES, ETC.

[245]–[250]
125. Appeals and referrals with which the Board is concerned
This Chapter shall apply to appeals and referrals to the which Board except that it will not apply to appeals under section 182(4)(b).

Note
Section 125 applies to all appeals to the Board (save as indicated) and also to all referrals made, which referrals are new in this Act and wording to include referrals is included in all the relevant sections, which previously dealt only with appeals.

[251]
126. Duty and objective of Board in relation to appeals and referrals
(1) It shall be the duty of the Board to ensure that appeals and referrals are disposed of as expeditiously as may be and, for that purpose, to take all such steps as are open to it to ensure that, in so far as is practicable, there are no avoidable delays at any stage in the determination of appeals and referrals.

(2) Without prejudice to the generality of subsection (1) and subject to subsections (3), (4) and (5), it shall be the objective of the Board to ensure that every appeal or referral is determined within—

(a) a period of 18 weeks beginning on the date of receipt by the Board of the appeal or referral, or
(b) such other period as the Minister may prescribe in accordance with subsection (4), either generally or in respect of a particular class or classes of appeals or referrals.

(3) (a) Where it appears to the Board that it would not be possible or appropriate, because of the particular circumstances of an appeal or referral or because of the number of appeals and referrals which have been submitted to the Board, to determine the appeal or referral within the period referred to in paragraph (a) or (b) of subsection (2), as the case may be, the Board shall, by notice in writing served on the parties to the appeal or referral before the expiration of that period, inform those parties of the reasons why it would not be possible or appropriate to determine the appeal or referral within that period and shall specify the date before which the Board intends that the appeal or referral shall be determined, and shall also serve such notice on each person who has made submissions or observations to the Board in relation to the appeal or referral.
   (b) Where a notice has been served under paragraph (a), the Board shall take all such steps as are open to it to ensure that the appeal or referral is determined before the date specified in the notice.

(4) The Minister may by regulations vary the period referred to in subsection (2)(a) either generally or in respect of a particular class or classes of appeals or referrals where it appears to him or her to be necessary, by virtue of exceptional circumstances, to do so and for so long as such regulations are in force this section shall be construed and have effect in accordance therewith.

(5) Where the Minister considers it to be necessary or expedient that—

(a) appeals from decisions (of a specified class or classes) of planning authorities under section 34, or

(b) referrals of a specified class or classes,

relating to development of a class or classes of special strategic, economic or social importance to the State, be determined as expeditiously as is consistent with proper planning and sustainable development, the Minister may give a direction to the Board to give priority to the class or classes of appeals or referrals concerned, and the Board shall comply with such direction.

(6) The Board shall include in each report made under section 118 a statement of the number of appeals and referrals that it has determined within a period referred to in paragraph (a) or (b) of subsection (2) and such other information as to the time taken to determine appeals and referrals as the Minister may direct.

Note
Section 126 restates s 2 of LG(PD)A 1992 with some amendments. The Board now has 18 weeks rather than 4 months within which to seek to make a decision (save where otherwise indicated). All time limits previously expressed in months are now stated in weeks for clarity. Subsection (5), which allows the Minister to direct the Board to treat a particular appeal or referral as a priority matter, is new.

[252]
127. Provisions as to making of appeals and referrals
(1) An appeal or referral shall—

(a) be made in writing,

(b) state the name and address of the appellant or person making the referral and of the person, if any, acting on his or her behalf,

(c) state the subject matter of the appeal or referral,

(d) state in full the grounds of appeal or referral and the reasons, considerations and arguments on which they are based,

(e) in the case of an appeal under section 37 by a person who made submissions or observations in accordance with the permission regulations, be accompanied by the acknowledgement by the planning authority of receipt of the submissions or observations,

(f) be accompanied by such fee (if any) as may be payable in respect of such appeal or referral in accordance with section 144, and

(g) be made within the period specified for making the appeal or referral.

(2) (a) An appeal or referral which does not comply with the requirements of subsection (1) shall be invalid.

(b) The requirement of subsection (1)(d) shall apply whether or not the appellant or person making the referral requests, or proposes to request, in accordance with section 134, an oral hearing of the appeal or referral.

(3) Without prejudice to section 131 or 134, an appellant or person making the referral shall not be entitled to elaborate in writing upon, or make further submissions in writing in relation to, the grounds of appeal or referral stated in the appeal or referral or to submit further grounds of appeal or referral and any such elaboration, submissions or further grounds of appeal or referral that is or are received by the Board shall not be considered by it.

(4) (a) An appeal or referral shall be accompanied by such documents, particulars or other information relating to the appeal or referral as the appellant or person making the referral considers necessary or appropriate.

(b) Without prejudice to section 132, the Board shall not consider any documents, particulars or other information submitted by an appellant or person making the referral other than the documents, particulars or other information which accompanied the appeal or referral.

(5) An appeal or referral shall be made—

(a) by sending the appeal or referral by prepaid post to the Board,
(b) by leaving the appeal or referral with an employee of the Board at the offices of the Board during office hours (as determined by the Board), or
(c) by such other means as may be prescribed.

Note
Section 127 restates s 4 of LG(PD)A 1992 with some amendments. Subsection (4)(b) has been extended by the addition of the words '. . . *or person making the referral and of the person, if any, acting on his or her behalf* . In addition, sub-s (1)(e) is new.

[253]
128. Submission of documents, etc. to Board by planning authorities
Where an appeal or referral is made to the Board the planning authority concerned shall within a period of 2 weeks beginning on the day on which a copy of the appeal or referral is sent to them by the Board, submit to the Board—

(a) in the case of an appeal under section 37—
  (i) a copy of the planning application concerned and of any drawings, maps, particulars, evidence, environmental impact statement, other written study or further information received or obtained by them from the applicant in accordance with regulations under this Act,
  (ii) a copy of any report prepared by or for the planning authority in relation to the planning application, and
  (iii) a copy of the decision of the planning authority in respect of the planning application and a copy of the notification of the decision given to the applicant;
(b) in the case of any other appeal or referral, any information or documents in their possession which is or are relevant to that matter.

Note
Section 128 restates s 6 of LG(PD)A 1992 with some changes merely to the layout of the section.

[254]
129. Submissions or observations by other parties
(1) The Board shall, as soon as may be after receipt of an appeal or referral, give a copy thereof to each other party.

(2) (a) Each other party may make submissions or observations in writing to the Board in relation to the appeal or referral within a period of 4 weeks beginning on the day on which a copy of the appeal or referral is sent to that party by the Board.

(b) Any submissions or observations received by the Board after the expiration of the period referred to in paragraph (a) shall not be considered by the Board.

(3) Where no submissions or observations have been received from a party within the period referred to in subsection (2), the Board may without further notice to that party determine the appeal or referral.

(4) Without prejudice to section 131 or 134, a party shall not be entitled to elaborate in writing upon any submissions or observations made in accordance with subsection (2) or make any further submissions or observations in writing in relation to the appeal or referral and any such elaboration, submissions or observations that is or are received by the Board shall not be considered by it.

Note
Section 129 restates s 7 of LG(PD)A 1992 with some amendments to reflect the time limits now being expressed in weeks and to include referrals.

[255]–[260]
130. Submissions or observations by persons other than parties
(1) (a) Any person other than a party may make submissions or observations in writing to the Board in observations by relation to an appeal or referral, other than a referral under section 96(5).

(b) Without prejudice to subsection (4), submissions or observations may be made within the period specified in subsection (3) and any submissions or observations received by the Board after the expiration of that period shall not be considered by the Board.

(c) A submission or observation shall—
   (i) be made in writing,
   (ii) state the name and address of the person making the submission or observation and the name and address of any person acting on his or her behalf,
   (iii) state the subject matter of the submission or observation,
   (iv) state in full the reasons, considerations and arguments on which the submission or observation is based, and
   (v) be accompanied by such fee (if any) as may be payable in accordance with section 144.

(2) Submissions or observations which do not comply with subsection (1) shall be invalid.

(3) The period referred to in subsection (1)(b) is—

(a) where notice of receipt of an environmental impact statement is published in accordance with regulations under section 172(5), the period of 4 weeks beginning on the day of publication of any notice required under those regulations,

(b) where notice is required by the Board to be given under section 142(4), the period of 4 weeks beginning on the day of publication of the required notice,

(c) in any other appeal under this Act, the period of 4 weeks beginning on the day of receipt of the appeal by the Board or, where there is more than one appeal against the decision of the planning authority, on the day on which the Board last receives an appeal, or

(d) in the case of a referral, the period of 4 weeks beginning on the day of receipt by the Board of the referral.

(4) Without prejudice to section 131 or 134, a person who makes submissions or observations to the Board in accordance with this section shall not be entitled to elaborate in writing upon the submissions or observations or make further submissions or observations in writing in relation to the appeal or other matter and any such elaboration, submissions or observations that is or are received by the Board shall not be considered by it.

(5) Subsections (1)(b) and (4) shall not apply to submissions or observations made by a Member State of the European Communities (within the meaning of the European Communities Act, 1972) or another state which is a party to the Transboundary Convention, arising from consultation in accordance with the Council Directive or the Transboundary Convention, as the case may be, in relation to the effects on the environment of the development to which the appeal under section 37 relates.

Note
Section 130 restates s 8 of LG(PD)A 1992 with the addition of sub-ss (1)(c), (2) and (3)(b).

[261]
131. Power of Board to request submissions or observations
Where the Board is of opinion that, in the particular circumstances of an appeal or referral, it is appropriate in the interests of justice to request—

(a) any party to the appeal or referral.

(b) any person who has made submissions or observations to the Board in relation to the appeal or referral, or

(c) any other person or body,

to make submissions or observations in relation to any matter which has arisen in relation to the appeal or referral, the Board may, in its discretion, notwithstanding section 127(3), 129(4), 130(4) or 137(4)(b), serve on any such person a notice under this section—

(i) requesting that person, within a period specified in the notice (not being less than 2 weeks or more than 4 weeks beginning on the date of service of the notice) to submit to the Board submissions or observations in relation to the matter in question, and

(ii) stating that, if submissions or observations are not received before the expiration of the period specified in the notice, the Board will, after the expiration of that period and without further notice to the person, pursuant to section 133, determine the appeal or referral.

Note
Section 131 restates s 9 of LG(PD)A 1992 with the addition of (a) and (c) and the amendment of the time limits to weeks.

[262]
132. Power of Board to require submission of documents etc

(1) Where the Board is of opinion that any document, particulars or other information may be necessary for the purpose of enabling it to determine an appeal or referral, the Board may, in its absolute discretion, serve on any party, or on any person who has made submissions or observations to the Board in relation to the appeal or referral as appropriate. a notice under this section—

(a) requiring that person, within a period specified in the notice (being a period of not less than 2 weeks beginning on the date of service of the notice) to submit to the Board such document, particulars or other information as is specified in the notice, and

(b) stating that, in default of compliance with the requirements of the notice, the Board will, after the expiration of the period so specified and without further notice to the person, pursuant to section 133, dismiss or otherwise determine the appeal or referral.

(2) Nothing in this section shall be construed as affecting any other power conferred on the Board under this Act to require the submission of further or additional information or documents.

Note
This section restates s 10 of LG(PD)A 1992 with minor conforming amendments regarding time limits going from months to weeks.

[263]
133. Powers of Board to where notice is served under section 131 or 132

Where a notice has been served under section 131 or 132, the Board, at any time after the expiration of the period specified in the notice, may, having considered any submissions or observations or document, particulars or other information submitted by the person on whom the notice has been served, without further notice to that person determine or, in the case of a notice served under section 132, dismiss the appeal or referral.

Note
Section 133 restates s 11 of LG(PD)A 1992 with conforming amendments.

[264]
134. Oral hearings of appeals and referrals

(1) The Board may, in its absolute discretion, hold an oral hearing of an appeal or of a referral under section 5.

(2) (a) A party to an appeal or referral under section 5 may request an oral hearing of the appeal or referral.
(b) (i) A request for an oral hearing of an appeal or referral shall be made in writing to the Board and shall be accompanied by such fee (if any) as may be payable in respect of the request in accordance with section 144.

   (ii) A request for an oral hearing of an appeal or referral which is not accompanied by such fee (if any) as may be payable in respect of the request shall not be considered by the Board.

(c) (i) A request by an appellant for an oral hearing of an appeal under section 37 shall be made within the appropriate period referred to in that section and any request received by the Board after the expiration of that period shall not be considered by the Board.

   (ii) Where a provision of this Act, other than sections 37 and 254(6), authorising an appeal to the Board enables the appeal only to be made within, or before the expiration of, a specified period or before a specified day, a request by an appellant for an oral hearing of an appeal may only be made within, or before the expiration of, the specified period or before the specified day and any request for an oral hearing not so received by the Board shall not be considered by the Board.

   (iii) A request by a person making a referral or by an appellant under section 254(6) for an oral hearing of the referral or appeal, as the case may be, shall accompany the referral or appeal, and any request for an oral hearing received by the Board other than a request which accompanies the referral or appeal, shall not be considered by the Board.

(d) A request by a party to an appeal or referral other than the appellant for an oral hearing of an appeal or referral shall be made within the period referred to in section 129(2)(a) within which the party may make submissions or observations to the Board in relation to the appeal or referral, and any such request received by the Board after the expiration of that period shall not be considered by the Board.

(3) Where the Board is requested to hold an oral hearing of an appeal or referral and decides to determine the appeal or referral without an oral hearing, the Board shall serve notice of its decision on the person who requested the hearing and on each other party to the appeal or referral and on each person who has made submissions or observations to the Board in relation to the appeal or referral.

(4) (a) A request for an oral hearing may be withdrawn at any time.

(b) Where, following a withdrawal of a request for an oral hearing under paragraph (a), the appeal or referral falls to be determined without an oral hearing, the Board shall give notice to each other party to the appeal or referral and to each person who has made submissions or observations to the Board in relation to the appeal or referral.

Note
Section 134 restates s 12 of LG(PD)A 1992 with conforming amendments to deal with referrals. Subsections (2)(c)(ii) and (4) are new.

[265]–[270]
135. Supplemental provisions relating to oral hearings
(1) The Board or an employee of the Board duly authorised by the Board may assign a person to conduct an oral hearing of an appeal or referral on behalf of the Board.

(2) The person conducting an oral hearing of any appeal or referral shall have discretion as to the conduct of the hearing and, in particular, shall—

(a) conduct the hearing without undue formality,

(b) decide the order of appearance of persons at the hearing,

(c) permit any person to appear in person or to be represented by another person,

(d) hear a person other than a person who has made submissions or observations to the Board in relation to the appeal or referral where it is considered appropriate in the interests of justice to allow the person to be heard.

(3) A person conducting an oral hearing of any appeal or referral may require any officer of a planning authority to give to him or her any information in relation to the appeal or referral which he or she reasonably requires for the purposes of the appeal or referral, and it shall be the duty of the officer to comply with the requirement.

(4) A person conducting an oral hearing of any appeal or referral may take evidence on oath or affirmation and for that purpose may administer oaths or affirmations, and a person giving evidence at any such hearing shall be entitled to the same immunities and privileges as if he or she were a witness before the High Court.

(5) (a) Subject to paragraph (b), the Board in relation to an oral hearing of any appeal or referral may, by giving notice in that behalf in writing to any person, require that person to do either or both of the following:

    (i)   to attend at such time and place as is specified in the notice to give evidence in relation to any matter in question at the hearing;

    (ii) to produce any books, deeds, contracts, accounts, vouchers, maps, plans, documents or other information in his or her possession, custody or control which relate to any such matter.

(b) Where a person is given a notice under paragraph (a):

    (i)   the Board shall pay or tender to any person whose attendance is required such reasonable subsistence and travelling expenses to be determined by the Board in accordance with the rates for the time being applicable to senior planning authority officials;

    (ii) any person who in compliance with a notice has attended at any place shall, save in so far as the reasonable and necessary expenses of the attendance have already been paid to him or her, be paid those expenses by the Board, and those expenses shall, in default of being so paid, be recoverable as a simple contract debt in any court of competent jurisdiction.

(6) Every person to whom a notice under subsection (5) has been given who refuses or wilfully neglects to attend in accordance with the notice or who wilfully alters, suppresses, conceals or destroys any document or other information to which the notice relates or who, having so attended, refuses to give evidence or refuses or wilfully fails to produce any document or other information to which the notice relates shall be guilty of an offence.

(7) Where any person—

(a) wilfully gives evidence which is material to the oral hearing and which he or she knows to be false or does not believe to be true,

(b) by act or omission, obstructs or hinders the person conducting the oral hearing in the performance of his or her functions,

(c) refuses to take an oath or to make an affirmation when legally required to do so by a person holding the oral hearing,

(d) refuses to answer any question to which the person conducting an oral hearing may legally require an answer, or

(e) does or omits to do any other thing which, if the inquiry had been by the High Court, would have been contempt of that court,

the person shall be guilty of an offence.

(8) (a) An oral hearing may be conducted through the medium of the Irish or the English language.

(b) Where an oral hearing relates to development within the Gaeltacht, the hearing shall be conducted through the medium of the Irish language, unless the parties to the appeal or referral to which the hearing relates agree that the hearing should be conducted in English.

(c) Where an oral hearing relates to development outside the Gaeltacht, the hearing shall be conducted through the medium of the English language, unless the parties to the appeal or referral to which the hearing relates agree that the hearing should be conducted in the Irish language.

Note
Section 135 restates s 82(4)–(7) of LG(PD)A 1963 as amended by LG(PD)A 1976.

[271]
136. Convening of meetings on referrals
(1) Where it appears to the Board to be expedient or convenient for the purposes of determining a referral under section 34(5), 96(5) or 193(2), the Board may, in its absolute discretion, convene a meeting of the parties.

(2) The Board shall keep a record in writing of a meeting convened in accordance with this section and a copy of the record shall be placed and kept with the documents to which the referral concerned relates and, where the referral is connected with an appeal, with the documents to which the appeal concerned relates.

Note
Section 136 is new. It allows the Board to convene a meeting to discuss issues arising out of a referral.

[272]
137. Matters other than those raised by parties
(1) The Board in determining an appeal or referral may take into account matters other than those raised by the parties or by any person who has made submissions or observations to the Board in relation to the appeal or referral if the matters are matters to which, by virtue of this Act, the Board may have regard.

(2) The Board shall give notice in writing to each of the parties and to each of the persons who have made submissions or observations in relation to the appeal or referral of the matters that it proposes to take into account under subsection (1) and shall indicate in that notice—

(a) in a case where the Board proposes to hold an oral hearing of the appeal or referral, or where an oral hearing of the appeal or referral has been concluded and the Board considers it expedient to re-open the hearing, that submissions in relation to the matters may be made to the person conducting the hearing, or

(b) in a case where the Board does not propose to hold an oral hearing of the appeal or referral, or where an oral hearing of the appeal or referral has been concluded and the Board does not consider it expedient to re-open the hearing, that submissions or observations in relation to the matters may be made to the Board in writing within a period specified in the notice (being a period of not less than 2 weeks or more than 4 weeks beginning on the date of service of the notice).

(3) Where the Board has given notice, in accordance with subsection (2)(a), the parties and any other person who is given notice shall be permitted, if present at the oral hearing, to make submissions to the Board in relation to the matters which were the subject of the notice or which, in the opinion of the person conducting the hearing, are of relevance to the appeal or referral.

(4) (a) Submissions or observations that are received by the Board after the expiration of the period referred to in subsection (2)(b) shall not be considered by the Board.

(b) Subject to section 131, where a party or a person referred to in subsection (1) makes submissions or observations to the Board in accordance with subsection (2)(b), that party or person shall not be entitled to elaborate in writing upon those submissions or observations or make further submissions or observations in writing in relation to the matters referred to in subsection (1) and any such elaboration, submissions or observations that is or are received by the Board shall not be considered by it.

Note
Section 137 restates s 13 of LG(PD)A 1992 with minor changes.

[273]
138. Board may dismiss appeals or referrals if vexatious, etc
(1) The Board shall have an absolute discretion to dismiss an appeal or referral—

(a) where, having considered the grounds of appeal or referral, the Board is of the opinion that the appeal or referral—
  (i) is vexatious, frivolous or without substance or foundation, or
  (ii) is made with the sole intention of delaying the development or the intention of securing the payment of money, gifts, consideration or other inducement by any person,
  or
(b) where, the Board is satisfied that, in the particular circumstances, the appeal or referral should not be further considered by it having regard to—
  (i) the nature of the appeal (including any question which in the Board's opinion is raised by the appeal or referral), or
  (ii) any previous permission which in its opinion is relevant.

(2) A decision made under this section shall state the main reasons and considerations on which the decision is based.

(3) The Board may, in its absolute discretion, hold an oral hearing under section 134 to determine whether an appeal or referral is made with an intention referred to in subsection (1)(a)(ii).

Note
Section 138 restates with amendments s 14 of LG(PD)A 1992 and adds to the powers the Board has to dismiss appeals by the addition of sub-s (1)(a)(ii) and allows the Board to hold an oral hearing. The Board must now give reasons for its decision.

[274]
139. Appeals against conditions
(1) Where—

(a) an appeal is brought against a decision of a planning authority to grant a permission,

(b) the appeal relates only to a condition or conditions that the decision provides that the permission shall be subject to, and

(c) the Board is satisfied, having regard to the nature of the condition or conditions, that the determination by the Board of the relevant application as if it had been made to it in the first instance would not be warranted,

then, subject to compliance by the Board with subsection (2), the Board may, in its absolute discretion, give to the relevant planning authority such directions as it considers appropriate relating to the attachment, amendment or removal by that authority either of the condition or conditions to which the appeal relates or of other conditions.

(2) In exercising the power conferred on it by subsection (1), apart from considering the condition or conditions to which the relevant appeal relates, the Board shall be restricted to considering—

(a) the matters set out in section 34(2)(a), and

(b) the terms of any previous permission considered by the Board to be relevant.

Note
Section 139 restates s 15 of LG(PD)A 1992.

[275]–[280]
140. Withdrawal of appeals, applications and referrals
(1) (a) A person who has made an appeal, a planning application to which an appeal relates or a referral may withdraw, in writing, the appeal, planning application or referral at any time before that appeal or referral is determined by the Board.

(b) As soon as may be after receipt of a withdrawal, the Board shall notify each other party or person who has made submissions or observations on the appeal or referral of the withdrawal

(2) (a) Without prejudice to subsection (1), where the Board is of the opinion that an appeal or a planning application to which an appeal relates, or a referral has been abandoned, the Board may serve on the person who made the appeal, application or referral, as appropriate, a notice stating that opinion and requiring that person, within a period specified in the notice (being a period of not less than two weeks or more than four weeks beginning on the date of service of the notice) to make to the Board a submission in writing as to why the appeal, application or referral should not be regarded as having been withdrawn.

(b) Where a notice has been served under paragraph (a), the Board may, at any time after the expiration of the period specified in the notice, and after considering the submission (if any) made to the Board pursuant to the notice, declare that the appeal, application or referral, as appropriate, shall be regarded as having been withdrawn.

(3) Where, pursuant to this section, a person withdraws a planning application to which an appeal relates, or the Board declares that an application is to be regarded as having been withdrawn, the following provisions shall apply as regards the application:

(a) any appeal in relation to the application shall be regarded as having been withdrawn and accordingly shall not be determined by the Board, and

(b) notwithstanding any previous decision under section 34 by a planning authority as regards the application, no permission shall be granted under that section by the authority on foot of the application.

Note
Section 140 restates s 16 of LG(PD)A 1992 with amendments allowing parties to withdraw appeals or referrals.

[281]
141. Time for decisions and appeals etc

(1) Where a requirement of or under this Act requires a planning authority or the Board to give a decision within a specified period and the last day of that period is a public holiday (within the meaning of the Holidays (Employees) Act, 1973) or any other day on which the offices of the planning authority or the Board are closed, the decision shall be valid if given on the next following day on which the offices of the planning authority or Board, as the case may be, are open.

(2) Where the last day of the period specified for making an appeal or referral is a Saturday, a Sunday, a public holiday (within the meaning of the Holidays (Employees) Act, 1973) or any other day on which the offices of the Board are closed, an appeal or referral shall (notwithstanding any other provision of this Act) be valid as having been made in time if received by the Board on the next following day on which the offices of the Board are open.

(3) Where a requirement of or under this Act requires submissions, observations or a request to be made, or documents, particulars or other information to be submitted, to the Board within a specified period and the last day of that period is a public holiday (within the meaning of the Holidays (Employees) Act, 1973) or any other day on which the offices of the Board are closed, the submissions, observations or request of documents, particulars or other information (as the case may be) shall be regarded as having been received before the expiration of that period if received by the Board on the next following day on which the offices of the Board are open.

Note
Section 141 restates s 17 of LG(PD)A 1992 with clarification of the dates from which time limits are to run.

[282]
142. Regulations regarding appeals and referrals

(1) The Minister may by regulations—

(a) provide for such additional, incidental, consequential or supplemental matters as regards procedure in respect of appeals as appear to the Minister to be necessary or expedient, and

(b) make such provision as regards procedure in respect of referrals as appear to the Minister to be necessary or expedient.

(2) Without prejudice to the generality of subsection (1), regulations under this section may enable the Board where it is determining an appeal under section 37 to invite an applicant and enable an applicant so invited to submit to the Board revised plans or other drawings modifying, or other particulars providing for the modification of, the development to which the appeal relates.

(3) Where plans, drawings or particulars referred to in subsection (2) are submitted to the Board in accordance with regulations under this section, the Board may, in determining the appeal, grant a permission for the relevant development as modified by all or any of the plans, drawings or particulars.

(4) Without prejudice to the generality of subsection (1), the Board may require any party to an appeal or referral to give such public notice in relation thereto as the Board may specify and, in particular, may require notice to be given at the site or by publication in a newspaper circulating in the district in which the land or structure to which the appeal or referral relates is situate.

Note
Section 142 restates s 18 of LG(PD)A 1992 with amendments principally to allow the Board to require a party to publicise an appeal or referral. The regulations that can be made under this section should replace LG(PD)R 1994 currently dealing with these issues.

[283]
143. Board to have regard to certain objectives
(1) The Board shall, in performing its functions, have regard to the policies and objectives for the time being of the Government a State authority, the Minister, planning authorities and any other body which is a public authority whose functions have, or may have, a bearing on the proper planning and sustainable development of cities, towns or other areas, whether urban or rural.

(2) In this section "public authority" means any body established by or under statute which is for the time being declared, by regulation made by the Minister, to be a public authority for the purposes of this section.

Note
Section 143 restates s 5 of LG(PD)A 1976 with amendments to reflect more positively the obligations on the Board to take account of current Government policies and objectives and those of other identified parties. Reference is made to the concept of sustainable development for the first time.

[284]
144. Fees payable to Board
(1) Subject to the approval of the Minister, the Board may determine fees in relation to appeals, referrals, the making of an application under section 37(5), the making of submissions or observations to the Board under section 130, and requests for oral

hearings under section 134, and may provide for the payment of different fees in relation to different classes or descriptions of appeals and referrals, for exemption from the payment of fees in specified circumstances and for the waiver, remission or refund in whole or in part of fees in specified circumstances.

(2) The Board shall review the fees determined under subsection (1) from time to time, but at least every three years, having regard to any change in the consumer price index since the determination of the fees for the time being in force, and may amend the fees to reflect the results of that review, without the necessity of the Minister's approval under subsection (1).

(3) For the purposes of this section, "change in the consumer price index" means the difference between the All Items Consumer Price Index Number last published by the Central Statistics Office before the date of the determination under this section and the said number last published before the date of the review under subsection (2), expressed as a percentage of the last-mentioned number.

(4) Where the Board determines or amends fees in accordance with this section, it shall give notice of the fees in at least one newspaper circulating in the State, not less than 8 weeks before the fees come into effect.

(5) Fees determined in accordance with regulations under section 10(1) (b) of the Act of 1982 shall continue to be payable to the Board in accordance with those regulations until such time as the Board determines fees in accordance with this section.

(6) The Board shall specify fees for the making of copies under section 5(6)(a), not exceeding the cost of making the copies.

Note
Section 144 is new. It deals with the Board providing for the fees to be payable to it.

[285]–[290]
145. Expenses of appeal or referral
(1) Where an appeal or referral is made to the Board—

(a) the Board, if it so thinks proper and irrespective of the result of the appeal or referral, may direct the planning authority to pay—
  (i) to the appellant or person making the referral, such sum as the Board, in its absolute discretion, specifies as compensation for the expense occasioned to him or her in relation to the appeal or referral, and
  (ii) to the Board, such sum as the Board, in its absolute discretion, specifies as compensation to the Board towards the expense incurred by the Board in relation to the appeal or referral, and
(b) in case the decision of the planning authority in relation to an appeal or referral is confirmed or varied, if the Board in determining the appeal or referral does not accede in substance to the grounds of appeal or referral or if the Board considers that the appeal or referral was made with the intention of delaying the development or securing a monetary gain by a third party, the Board, if it so thinks proper, may direct the appellant or person making the referral to pay—
  (i) to the planning authority, such sum as the Board, in its absolute discretion, specifies as compensation to the planning authority for the expense occasioned to it in relation to the appeal or referral,

(ii) to any of the other parties to the appeal or referral, such sum as the Board, in its absolute discretion, specifies as compensation to the party for the expense occasioned to him or her in relation to the appeal or referral, and

(iii) to the Board, such sum as the Board, in its absolute discretion, specifies as compensation to the Board towards the expense incurred by the Board in relation to the appeal or referral.

(2) Any sum directed under this section to be paid shall, in default of being paid, be recoverable as a simple contract debt in any court of competent jurisdiction.

Note
Section 145 restates s 19 of LG(PD)A 1976.

[291]
146. Reports and documents of the Board
(1) The Board or an employee of the Board duly authorised by the Board may, in connection with the performance of any of the Board's functions under this Act, assign a person to report on any matter on behalf of the Board.

(2) A person assigned in accordance with subsection (1) shall make a written report on the matter to the Board, which shall include a recommendation, and the Board shall consider the report and recommendation before determining the matter.

(3) (a) The documents relating to any appeal or referral or to a decision of the Board under section 175 or Part XIV shall be made available at the offices of the Board for inspection by members of the public and may be made available at such other places as the Board may determine within 3 working days following the relevant decision.

(b) Copies of the documents, and of extracts from such documents shall be made available at the offices of the Board, or such other places as the Board may determine, for a fee not exceeding the reasonable cost of making the copy.

(4) The documents to which subsection (3) applies shall be made available for a period of at least 5 years commencing on the third working day following the decision of the Board in relation to the matter.

PART VII   DISCLOSURE OF INTERESTS, ETC.

Note
Part VII deals with the requirements on members and employees of planning authorities and the Board in relation to interests they have, which may have implications for their work.

This Part has not yet been commenced.

[292]
147. Declaration by members, etc. of certain interests
(1) It shall be the duty of a person to whom this section applies to give to the relevant body a declaration in the prescribed form, signed by him or her and containing particulars of every interest of his or hers which is an interest to which this section applies and for so long as he or she continues to be a person to whom this section

applies it shall be his or her duty where there is a change regarding an interest particulars of which are contained in the declaration or where he or she acquires any other interest to which this section applies, to give to the relevant body a fresh declaration.

(2) A declaration under this section shall be given at least once a year.

(3) (a) This section applies to the following persons:
    (i)　a member of the Board;
    (ii)　a member of a planning authority;
    (iii)　an employee of the Board or any other person—
        (I)　whose services are availed of by the Board, and
        (II)　who is of a class, description or grade prescribed for the purposes of this section;
    (iv)　an officer of a planning authority who is the holder of an office which is of a class, description or grade so prescribed.
(b)　This section applies to the following interests:
    (i)　any estate or interest which a person to whom this section applies has in any land, but excluding any interest in land consisting of any private home within the meaning of paragraph 1(4) of the Second Schedule to the Ethics in Public Office Act, 1995;
    (ii)　any business of dealing in or developing land in which such a person is engaged or employed and any such business carried on by a company or other body of which he or she, or any nominee of his or hers, is a member;
    (iii)　any profession, business or occupation in which such a person is engaged, whether on his or her own behalf or otherwise, and which relates to dealing in or developing land.

(4) A person to whom this section applies and who has an interest to which this section applies shall be regarded as complying with the requirements of subsection (1) if he or she gives to the relevant body a declaration referred to in that subsection:

(a)　within the period of twenty-eight days beginning on the day on which he or she becomes such a person,
(b)　in case there is a change regarding an interest particulars of which are contained in a declaration already given by the person or where the person acquires any other interest to which this section applies, on the day on which the change occurs or the other such interest is acquired.

(5) For the purposes of this section, a person to whom this section applies shall be regarded as having an estate or interest in land if he or she, or any nominee of his or hers, is a member of a company or other body which has an estate or interest in the land.

(6) For the purposes of this section, a person shall not be regarded as having an interest to which this section applies, if the interest is so remote or insignificant that it cannot reasonably be regarded as likely to influence a person in considering or discussing, or in voting on, any question with respect to any matter arising or coming before the Board or authority, as may be appropriate, or in performing any function in relation to any such matter.

(7) Where a person to whom this section applies has an interest to which this section applies by reason only of the beneficial ownership of shares in a company or other body by him or her or by his or her nominee and the total value of those shares does not exceed the lesser of—

(a) £10,000, or
(b) one-hundredth part of the total nominal value of either the issued share capital of the company or body or, where that capital is issued in shares of more than one class, the issued share capital of the class or classes of shares in which he or she has an interest,

subsection (1) shall not have effect in relation to that interest.

(8) The Board and each planning authority shall for the purposes of this section keep a register ("the register of interests") and shall enter therein the particulars contained in declarations given to the Board or the authority, as the case may be, pursuant to this section.

(9) The register of interests shall be kept at the offices of the Board or the planning authority, as the case may be, and shall be available for public inspection during office hours.

(10) Where a person ceases to be a person to whom this section applies, any particulars entered in the register of interests as a result of a declaration being given by the person to the relevant body pursuant to this section shall be removed, as soon as may be after the expiration of the period of five years beginning on the day on which the person ceases to be such a person, from the register of interests by that body.

(11) Subject to subsection (12), a person who fails to comply with subsections (1) and (2) or who, when purporting to comply with the requirements of subsection (1), gives particulars which are false or which to his or her knowledge are misleading in a material respect, shall be guilty of an offence.

(12) In any proceedings for an offence under this section it shall be a defence for the defendant to prove that at the relevant time he or she believed, in good faith and upon reasonable grounds, that—

(a) the relevant particulars were true,
(b) there was no matter as regards which he or she was then required to make a declaration under subsection (1), or
(c) that the matter in relation to which the offence is alleged was not one as regards which he or she was so required to make such a declaration.

(13) (a) For the purposes of this section and sections 148 and 149—
    (i) a manager shall be deemed to be an officer of every planning authority for which he or she is manager,
    (ii) an assistant county manager for a county shall be deemed to be an officer of every planning authority in the county, and
    (iii) an officer of a planning authority who, by virtue of an arrangement or agreement entered into under any enactment, is performing functions under another planning authority, shall be deemed to be also an officer of the other authority.

(b) In this section "relevant body" means—
  (i) in case a person to whom this section applies is either a member or employee of the Board, or other person whose services are availed of by the Board, the Board, and
  (ii) in case such a person is either a member or officer of a planning authority, the authority.

Note
Section 147 restates s 32 of LG(PD)A 1976 with amendments. Specifically a declaration under the section now needs to be given at least once a year (sub-s (2)); and ownership of a private home is no longer an interest to which the section relates. A private home is defined by reference to the Public Office Act 1995. The fines for an offence have been increased from IR£500 to IR£2,000 (sub-s (7)(a)) and there are other changes that are not material.

[293]
148. Requirements affecting members etc who have certain beneficial interests
(1) Where a member of the Board has a pecuniary or other beneficial interest in, or which is material to, any appeal, contribution, question, determination or dispute which falls to be decided or determined by the Board under any enactment, he or she shall comply with the following requirements:

(a) he or she shall disclose to the Board the nature of his or her interest;
(b) he or she shall take no part in the discussion or consideration of the matter;
(c) he or she shall not vote or otherwise act as a member of the Board in relation to the matter;
(d) he or she shall neither influence nor seek to influence a decision of the Board as regards the matter.

(2) Where, at a meeting of a planning authority or of any committee of a planning authority, a resolution, motion, question or other matter is proposed or otherwise arises either pursuant to, or as regards the performance by the authority of a function under this Act or in relation to the acquisition or disposal by the authority of land under or for the purposes of this Act or any other enactment, a member of the authority or committee present at the meeting shall, if he or she has a pecuniary or other beneficial interest in, or which is material to, the matter—

(a) at the meeting, and before discussion or consideration of the matter commences, disclose the nature of his or her interest, and
(b) withdraw from the meeting for so long as the matter is being discussed or considered,

and accordingly, he or she shall take no part in the discussion or consideration of the matter and shall refrain from voting in relation to it.

(3) A member of a planning authority or of any committee of a planning authority who has a pecuniary or other beneficial interest in, or which is material to, a matter arising either pursuant to, or as regards the performance by the authority of a function under this Act, or in relation to the acquisition or disposal by the authority of land under or for the purposes of this Act or any other enactment, shall neither influence nor seek to influence a decision of the authority as regards the matter.

(4) Where the manager of a planning authority has a pecuniary or other beneficial interest in, or which is material to, any matter which arises or comes before the authority either pursuant to, or as regards the performance by the authority of a function under this Act, or in relation to the acquisition or disposal by the authority of land under or for the purposes of this Act or any other enactment, he or she shall, as soon as may be, disclose to the members of the planning authority the nature of his or her interest.

(5) (a) Where an employee of the Board, a consultant or adviser engaged by the Board, or any other person whose services are availed of by the Board has a pecuniary or other beneficial interest in, or which is material to, any appeal, contribution, question or dispute which falls to be decided or determined by the Board, he or she shall comply with the following requirements:

    (i) he or she shall neither influence nor seek to influence a decision of the Board as regards the matter;

    (ii) in case, as such employee, consultant, adviser or other person, he or she is concerned with the matter, he or she shall disclose to the Board the nature of his or her interest and comply with any directions the Board may give him or her in relation to the matter.

(b) Where an officer of a planning authority, not being the manager, has a pecuniary or other beneficial interest in, or which is material to, any matter which arises or comes before the authority, either pursuant to, or as regards the performance by the authority of a function under this Act, or in relation to the acquisition or disposal of land by the authority under or for the purposes of this Act or any other enactment, he or she shall comply with the following requirements:

    (i) he or she shall neither influence nor seek to influence a decision of the authority as regards the matter; and

    (ii) in case, as such officer, he or she is concerned with the matter, he or she shall disclose to the manager of the authority the nature of his or her interest and comply with any directions the manager may give him or her in relation to the matter.

(6) For the purposes of this section but without prejudice to the generality of subsections (1) to (5), a person shall be regarded as having a beneficial interest if—

(a) he or she or his or her spouse, or any nominee of his or her or of his or her spouse, is a member of a company or any other body which has a beneficial interest in, or which is material to, a resolution, motion, question or other matter referred to in subsections (1) to (5),

(b) he or she or his or her spouse is in partnership with or is in the employment of a person who has a beneficial interest in, or which is material to, such a resolution, motion, question or other matter,

(c) he or she or his or her spouse is a party to any arrangement or agreement (whether or not enforceable) concerning land to which such a resolution, motion, question or other matter relates, or

(d) his or her spouse has a beneficial interest in, or which is material to, such a resolution, motion, question or other matter.

(7) For the purposes of this section, a person shall not be regarded as having a beneficial interest in, or which is material to, any resolution, motion, question or

other matter by reason only of an interest of his or her or of any company or of any other body or person referred to in subsection (6) which is so remote or insignificant that it cannot reasonably be regarded as likely to influence a person in considering or discussing, or in voting on, any question with respect to the matter, or in performing any function in relation to that matter.

(8) Where a person has a beneficial interest referred to in subsection (1), (2), (3), (4) or (5) by reason only of the beneficial ownership of shares in a company or other body by him or her or by his or her spouse and the total value of those shares does not exceed the lesser of—

(a) £10,000, or
(b) one-hundredth part of the total nominal value of either the issued share capital of the company or body or, where that capital is issued in shares of more than one class, the issued share capital of the class of shares in which he or she has an interest,

none of those subsections shall have effect in relation to that beneficial interest.

(9) Where at a meeting referred to in subsection (2) a disclosure is made under that subsection, particulars of the disclosure and of any subsequent withdrawal from the meeting pursuant to that subsection shall be recorded in the minutes of the meeting.

(10) Subject to subsection (11), a person who contravenes or fails to comply with a requirement of this section shall be guilty of an offence.

(11) In any proceedings for an offence under this section it shall be a defence for the defendant to prove that at the time of the alleged offence he or she did not know and had no reason to believe that a matter in which, or in relation to which, he or she had a beneficial interest had arisen or had come before, or was being considered by, the Board or the relevant planning authority or committee, as may be appropriate, or that the beneficial interest to which the alleged offence relates was one in relation to which a requirement of this section applied.

Notes
Section 148 restates s 33 of LG(PD)A 1976 with some changes. Specifically, the fine that may be imposed for an offence has increased from IR£500 to IR£10,000 (see s (8)(a)).

Sub-section (11) provides for a defence to a prosecution, and is new.

[294]
149. Supplemental provisions relating to sections 147 and 148
(1) Proceedings for an offence under section 147 or 148 shall not be instituted except by or with the consent of the Director of Public Prosecutions.

(2) Where a person is convicted of an offence under section 147 or 148—

(a) the person shall be disqualified from being a member of the Board,
(b) in case the person is a member of the Board, he or she shall on conviction accordingly cease to be a member of the Board,
(c) in case the person is a member of a planning authority or a member of any committee of a planning authority, he or she shall on conviction cease to be a member of the authority or the committee, as may be appropriate,

(d) in case the person is a member of both a planning authority and any one or more such committees, he or she shall on conviction cease to be a member of both the authority and every such committee, and

(e) in case the person by virtue of this subsection ceases to be a member of a planning authority or any such committee, he or she shall be disqualified for being a member of the authority or committee during the period which, but for the cessation of his or her membership of the authority or committee under this section, would be the remainder of his or her term.

(3) A disqualification under this section shall take effect on the expiry of the ordinary time for appeal from the conviction concerned or if an appeal is brought within that time, upon the final disposal of that appeal.

(4) In case a person contravenes or fails to comply with a requirement of section 147, 148 or 150, or acts as a member of the Board, a planning authority or committee of a planning authority while disqualified for membership by virtue of this section, the fact of the contravention or failure or of his or her so acting, as the case may be, shall not invalidate any act or proceeding of the Board, authority or committee.

(5) Where any body which is a company within the meaning of section 155 of the Companies Act, 1963, is deemed under that section to be a subsidiary of another or to be another such company's holding company, a person who is a member of the first-mentioned such company shall, for the purposes of sections 147 and 143 be deemed also to be a member of the other company.

Note
Section 149 restates s 34 of LG(PD)A 1976 with some modifications. Sub-section (3) is new.

[295]–[300]
150. Codes of conduct
(1) (a) Every planning authority, by resolution, and the Board shall adopt a code of conduct for dealing with conflicts of interest and promoting public confidence in the integrity of the conduct of its business which must be followed by those persons referred to in subsection (3).

(b) A code of conduct under this section shall be adopted within one year of the commencement of this section.

(2) A code of conduct shall consist of a written statement setting out the planning authority's or the Board's policy on at least the following matters:

(a) disclosure of interests and relationships where the interests and relationships are of relevance to the work of the authority or the Board, as appropriate;

(b) membership of other organisations, associations and bodies, professional or otherwise;

(c) membership of, or other financial interests in, companies, partnerships or other bodies;

(d) undertaking work, not being work on behalf of the authority or the Board, as the case may be, both during and after any period of employment with the authority or the Board, whether as a consultant, adviser or otherwise;

(e) acceptance of gifts, sponsorship, considerations or favours;

(f) disclosure of information concerning matters pertaining to the work of the authority or the Board, as appropriate;

(g) following of proper procedure in relation to the functions of the authority and the Board including the procedures for—

    (i)   (I)   the review, making and variation of development plans,

        (II) the review, making and amendment of local area plans,

        (III) the processing of planning applications and appeals, and

        (IV) the granting of permission which would materially contravene the development plan, including the use of resolutions referred to in section 34(A)(c),

      and

    (ii) the disclosure by members and employees of the authority or of the Board of any representations made to such members or employees whether in writing or otherwise in relation to those matters.

(3) This section shall apply to—

(a) a member of the Board,

(b) a member of a planning authority,

(c) an employee of the Board or any other person—

    (i) whose services are availed of by the Board, and

    (ii) who is of a class, description or grade prescribed for the purposes of this section, and

(d) an officer of a planning authority who is the holder of an office which is of a class, description or grade so prescribed.

(4) (a) It shall be a condition of appointment of persons listed at subsection (3)(a) that they shall comply with the code of conduct.

(b) It shall be a condition of taking up and holding office by persons listed at subsection (3)(b) that they shall comply with the code of conduct.

(c) It shall be a condition of employment of persons listed at subsection (3)(c) and (d) that they shall comply with the code of conduct.

(5) A planning authority or the Board may at any time review a code of conduct adopted under this section and may—

(a) amend the code of conduct, or

(b) adopt a new code of conduct.

Note
Section 150 is a new provision. It requires planning authorities and the Board to adopt rules of conduct for dealing with conflicts of interest and for promoting public confidence in the integrity of the conduct of its business. Compliance with the code of conduct will be a requirement for members and employees of planning authorities and the Board.

PART VIII   ENFORCEMENT

Note
This Part has not yet been commenced.

[301]
151. Offence
Any person who has carried out or is carrying out unauthorised development shall be guilty of an offence.

Note

Section 24 of LG(PD)A 1963 as amended by LG(PD)A 1976 (s 45) and LG(PD)A 1982 (s 15) said essentially the same. Note the definition of '*unauthorised development*' in the interpretation section (s 2).

[302]
152. Warning letter

(1) Where—

(a) a representation in writing is made to a planning authority by any person that unauthorised development may have been, is being or may be carried out, and it appears to the planning authority that the representation is not vexatious, frivolous or without substance or foundation, or

(b) it otherwise appears to the authority that unauthorised development may have been, is being or may be carried out,

the authority shall issue a warning letter to the owner, the occupier or any other person carrying out the development and may give a copy, at that time or thereafter, to any other person who in its opinion may be concerned with the matters to which the letter relates.

(2) Notwithstanding subsection (1), where the development in question is of a trivial or minor nature the planning authority may decide not to issue a warning letter.

(3) A planning authority shall issue the warning letter under subsection (1) as soon as may be but not later than 6 weeks after receipt of the representation under subsection (1).

(4) A warning letter shall refer to the land concerned and shall—

(a) state that it has come to the attention of the authority that unauthorised development may have been, is being or may be carried out,

(b) state that any person served with the letter may make submissions or observations in writing to the planning authority regarding the purported offence not later than four weeks from the date of the service of the warning letter,

(c) state that when a planning authority considers that unauthorised development has been, is being or may be carried out, an enforcement notice may be issued,

(d) state that officials of the planning authority may at all reasonable times enter on the land for the purposes of inspection,

(e) explain the possible penalties involved where there is an offence, and

(f) explain that any costs reasonably incurred by the planning authority in relation to enforcement proceedings may be recovered from a person on whom an enforcement notice is served or where court action is taken.

Note

Section 152 sets out the procedure for the issuing of warning letters. This is a new procedure not previously provided for in the planning legislation.

[303]
153. Decision on enforcement

(1) As soon as may be after the issue of a warning letter under section 152, the planning authority shall make such investigation as it considers necessary to enable it to make a decision on whether to issue an enforcement notice.

(2) (a) It shall be the duty of the planning authority to ensure that decisions on whether to issue an enforcement notice are taken as expeditiously as possible.
(b) Without prejudice to the generality of paragraph (a), it shall be the objective of the planning authority to ensure that the decision on whether to issue an enforcement notice shall be taken within 12 weeks of the issue of a warning letter.

(3) A planning authority, in deciding whether to issue an enforcement notice shall consider any representations made to it under section 152(1)(a) or submissions or observations made under section 152(4)(b) and any other material considerations.

(4) The decision made by the planning authority under subsection (1) including the reasons for it shall be entered by the authority in the register

(5) Failure to issue a warning letter under section 152 shall not prejudice the issue of an enforcement notice or any other proceedings that may be initiated by the planning authority.

Note
Section 153 is new. It provides that planning authorities shall investigate subsequent to the issuing of a warning letter, shall make a decision as to whether or not to serve an enforcement notice, and shall include the reasons for the decision in the planning register entry.

[304]
154. Enforcement notice

(1) (a) Where a decision to enforce is made under section 153 or where urgent action is required under section 155, the planning authority shall, as soon as may be, serve an enforcement notice under this section.
(b) Where an enforcement notice is served under this section, the planning authority shall notify any person who made representations under section 152(1)(a) and any other person, who in the opinion of the planning authority may be concerned with the matter to which the notice concerned relates, not being a person on whom the enforcement notice was served, of the service of the enforcement notice.

(2) Where the planning authority decides not to issue an enforcement notice, it shall notify any person to whom the warning letter was copied under section 152 and any other person who made a representation under that section of the decision in writing within 2 weeks of the making of that decision.

(3) (a) An enforcement notice under subsection (1) shall be served on the person carrying out the development and, where the planning authority considers it necessary, the owner or the occupier of the land or any other person who, in the opinion of the planning authority, may be concerned with the matters to which the notice relates.
(b) If, subsequent to the service of the enforcement notice, the planning authority

becomes aware that any other person may be carrying out development or is an owner or occupier of the land or may be affected by the notice, the notice may be served on that person and the period specie fled for compliance with the notice shall be extended as necessary to a maximum of 6 months, and the other person or persons on whom the notice had previously been served under paragraph (a) shall be informed in writing.

(4) An enforcement notice shall take effect on the date of the service thereof.

(5) An enforcement notice shall refer to the land concerned and shall—

(a) (i) in respect of a development where no permission has been granted, require that development to cease or not to commence, as appropriate, or

(ii) in respect of a development for which permission has been granted under Part III, require that the development will proceed in conformity with the permission, or with any condition to which the permission is subject,

(b) require such steps as may be specified in the notice to be taken within a specified period, including, where appropriate, the removal, demolition or alteration of any structure and the discontinuance of any use and, in so far as is practicable, the restoration of the land to its condition prior to the commencement of the development,

(c) warn the person or persons served with the enforcement notice that, if within the period specified under paragraph (b) or within such extended period (not being more than 6 months) as the planning authority may allow, the steps specified in the notice to be taken are not taken, the planning authority may enter on the land and take such steps, including the removal, demolition or alteration of any structure, and may recover any expenses reasonably incurred by them in that behalf,

(d) require the person or persons served with the notice to refund to the planning authority the costs and expenses reasonably incurred by the authority in relation to the investigation, detection and issue of the enforcement notice concerned and any warning letter under section 152, including costs incurred in respect of the remuneration and other expenses of employees, consultants and advisers, and the planning authority may recover these costs and expenses incurred by it in that behalf, and

(e) warn the person or persons served with the enforcement notice that if within the period specified by the notice or such extended period, not being more than 6 months, as the planning authority may allow, the steps specified in the notice to be taken are not taken, the person or persons may be guilty of an offence.

(6) If, within the period specified under subsection (5)(b) or within such extended period, not being more than 6 months, as the planning authority may allow, the steps specified in the notice to be taken are not taken, the planning authority may enter on the land and take such steps, including the demolition of any structure and the restoration of land, and may recover any expenses reasonably incurred by it in that behalf.

(7) Any expenses reasonably incurred by a planning authority under paragraphs (c) and (d) of subsection (5) and subsection (6) may be recovered—

(a) as a simple contract debt in any court of competent jurisdiction from the person or persons on whom the notice was served, or

(b) secured by—
   (i)   charging the land under the Registration of Title Act, 1964, or
   (ii) where the person on whom the enforcement notice was served is the owner of the land, an instrument vesting the ownership of the land in the authority subject to a right of redemption by the owner within five years.

(8) Any person on whom an enforcement notice is served under subsection (1) who fails to comply with the requirements of the notice (other than a notice which has been withdrawn under subsection (11)(a) or which has ceased to have effect) within the specified period or within such extended period as the planning authority may allow, not exceeding 6 months, shall be guilty of an offence.

(9) Any person who knowingly assists or permits the failure by another to comply with an enforcement notice shall be guilty of an offence.

(10) Particulars of an enforcement notice shall be entered in the register.

(11) (a) A planning authority may for stated reasons by notice in writing to any person served with the notice, and, where appropriate, any person who made a representation under section 152(1)(a), withdraw an enforcement notice served under this section.
   (b) Where an enforcement notice is withdrawn pursuant to this subsection by a planning authority or where a planning authority finds that an enforcement notice has been complied with, the fact that the enforcement notice was withdrawn and the reason for the withdrawal or that it was complied with, as appropriate, shall be recorded by the authority in the register.

(12) An enforcement notice shall cease to have effect 10 years from the date of service of the notice under subsection (1) or, if a notice is served under subsection (3)(b), 10 years from the date of service of the notice under that subsection.

(13) A person shall not question the validity of an enforcement notice by reason only that the person or any other person, not being the person on whom the enforcement notice was served, was not notified of the service of the enforcement notice.

(14) A report of a local authority under section 50 of the Local Government Act, 1991, shall contain details of the number of enforcement notices issued under this section, warning notices issued under section 153, prosecutions brought under section 157 and injunctions sought under section 160 by that authority.

Notes
Section 154 streamlines the enforcement notice procedure previously provided for by ss 31, 32, 33, 35 and 36 of LG(PD)A 1963 (as amended). Now, one form of enforcement notice can be used for the offences previously provided for under the aforementioned sections in LG(PD)A 1963.

Sub-section (3)(a) no longer makes it compulsory to serve the notice on the owner and occupier of the relevant lands as was previously the case (see also sub-s (13)).

Sub-section (4) is a new provision, which states that the enforcement notice takes effect as and from the date of service thereof.

Sub-section (12) states that an enforcement notice shall have effect for ten years from the date of its service.

Note the contents of sub-s (13) particularly in the context of the comments made above regarding sub-s (3)(a).

[305]–[310]
155. Issue of enforcement notice in cases of urgency
(1) Where, in the opinion of the planning authority, due to the nature of an unauthorised development and to any other material considerations, it is necessary to take urgent action with regard to the unauthorised development, notwithstanding sections 152 and 153, it may serve an enforcement notice under section 154.

(2) Where an enforcement notice is issued in accordance with subsection (1), any person who made a representation under section 152(1)(a) shall be notified in writing within two weeks of the service of the notice.

Note
Section 155 is a new provision allowing for the service of an enforcement notice without the need for a warning letter.

[311]
156. Penalties for offences
(1) A person who is guilty of an offence under sections 58(4), 63,151,154, 205, 230(3), 239 and 247 shall be liable -

(a) on conviction on indictment, to a fine not exceeding £10,000,000, or to imprisonment for a term not exceeding 2 years, or to both, or
(b) on summary conviction, to a fine not exceeding £1,500, or to imprisonment for a term not exceeding 6 months, or to both.

(2) Where a person is convicted of an offence referred to in subsection (1) and there is a continuation by him or her of the offence after his or her conviction, he or she shall be guilty of a further offence on every day on which the contravention continues and for each such offence shall be liable—

(a) on conviction on indictment, to a fine not exceeding £10,000 for each day on which the offence is so continued, or to imprisonment for a term not exceeding 2 years, or to both, provided that if a person is convicted in the same proceedings of 2 or more such further offences the aggregate term of imprisonment to which he or she shall be liable shall not exceed 2 years, or
(b) on summary conviction, to a fine not exceeding £400 for each day on which the offence is so continued or to imprisonment for a term not exceeding 6 months, or to both, provided that if a person is convicted in the same proceedings of 2 or more such further offences the aggregate term of imprisonment to which he or she shall be liable shall not exceed 6 months.

(3) Where a person is convicted of an offence referred to in subsection (1) involving the construction of an unauthorised structure, the minimum fine shall be—

(a) on conviction on indictment, the estimated cost of the construction of the structure or £10,000, whichever is less, or
(b) on summary conviction, the estimated cost of the construction of the structure or £500, whichever is less,

except where the person convicted can show to the court's satisfaction that he or she does not have the necessary financial means to pay the minimum fine.

(4) Any person who is guilty of an offence under this Act other than an offence referred to in subsection (1) (or a further offence under subsection (2)) shall be liable, on summary conviction, to a fine not exceeding £1,500 or, at the discretion of the court, to imprisonment for a term not exceeding 6 months or to both.

(5) If the contravention in respect of which a person is convicted under section 46(11), 208(2)(b) or 252(9) is continued after the conviction, that person shall be guilty of a further offence on every day on which the contravention continues and for each such offence he or she shall be liable on summary conviction to a fine not exceeding £400.

(6) In a prosecution for an offence under sections 151 and 154 it shall not be necessary for the prosecution to show, and it shall be assumed until the contrary is shown by the defendant, that the subject matter of the prosecution was development and was not exempted development.

(7) Where an enforcement notice has been served under section 154, it shall be a defence to a prosecution under section 151 or 154 if the defendant proves that he or she took all reasonable steps to secure compliance with the enforcement notice.

(8) On conviction of an offence under section 154, the court may, in addition to imposing the penalties specified in subsections (1) and (2), order the person convicted to take the steps specified in the enforcement order to be taken.

Note
Section 156 deals with penalties for offences and allows for an increase in fines in certain circumstances to IR£10,000,000. The penalties for continuing offences have also been increased. Elsewhere in PDA 2000, the offences that may be prosecuted on indictment are specified. Note in particular sub-s (6), which effectively reverses the onus of proof. See also the defence provisions at sub-s (7).

[312]
157. Prosecution of offences
(1) Subject to section 149, summary proceedings for an offence under this Act may be brought and prosecuted by a planning authority whether or not the offence is committed in the authority's functional area.

(2) Notwithstanding section 10(4) of the Petty Sessions (Ireland) Act, 1851, and subject to subsection (3) of this section, summary proceedings may be commenced—

(a) at any time within 6 months from the date on which the offence was committed, or
(b) at any time within 6 months from the date on which evidence sufficient, in the opinion of the person by whom the proceedings are initiated, to justify proceedings comes to that person's knowledge,

whichever is the later.

(3) For the purposes of this section, a certificate signed by or on behalf of the person initiating the proceedings as to the date or dates on which evidence described in sub-

section (2)(b) came to his or her knowledge shall be evidence of the date or dates and in any legal proceedings a document purporting to be a certificate under this section and to be so signed shall be deemed to be so signed and shall be admitted as evidence without proof of the signature of the person purporting to sign the certificate, unless the contrary is shown.

(4) (a) No warning letter or enforcement notice shall issue and no proceedings for an offence under this Part shall commence—

    (i)   in respect of a development where no permission has been granted, after seven years from the date of the commencement of the development;

    (ii)   in respect of a development for which permission has been granted under Part III, after seven years beginning on the expiration, as respects the permission authorising the development, of the appropriate period within the meaning of section 40 or, as the case may be, of the period as extended under section 42.

(b) Notwithstanding paragraph (a), proceedings may be commenced at any time in respect of any condition concerning the use of land to which the permission is subject.

(c) It shall be presumed until the contrary is proved that proceedings were commenced within the appropriate period.

(5) Proceedings for other offences under this Act shall not be initiated later than 7 years from the date on which the offence concerned was alleged to have been committed.

Notes

Section 157 provides that a planning authority may take summary proceedings for offences created under the Act whether or not the offence was committed in its area. Offences under ss 147 and 148 cannot be instituted except with the consent of the DPP. Sections 147 and 148 (referred to in s 149) relate to offences concerning declaration of interests etc (Pt VII of the Act.)

Sub-section (4)(a)(i) increases the five-year time limit previously introduced by LG(PD)A 1992 (s 19) with a seven-year limit. Note that this does not apply in respect of the use of land as set out at sub-s (4)(b).

[313]
158. Offences by bodies corporate

(1) Where an offence under this Act is committed by a body corporate or by a person acting on behalf of a body corporate and is proved to have been so committed with the consent, connivance or approval of, or to have been facilitated by any neglect on the part of a person being a director, manager, secretary or other officer of the body or a person who was purporting to act in any such capacity, that person shall also be guilty of an offence and shall be liable to be proceeded against and punished as if he or she were guilty of the first-mentioned offence.

(2) Where the affairs of a body corporate are managed by its members, subsection (1) shall apply in relation to the acts and defaults of a member in connection with his or her functions of management as if he or she were a director of the body corporate.

Note

Section 158 is in line with provisions already contained in environmental and waste management legislation.

[314]
159. Payment of fines to planning authorities

Where a court imposes a fine or affirms or varies a fine imposed by another court for an offence under this Act it shall provide by order for the payment of the amount of the fine to the planning authority and the payment may be enforced by the authority as if it were due to it on foot of a decree or order made by the court in civil proceedings.

Note
Section 159 is new and provides that fines imposed and costs awarded shall be paid to the relevant planning authority (see also s 161 below.)

[315]–[320]
160. Injunctions in relation to unauthorised development

(1) Where an unauthorised development has been, is being or is likely to be carried out or continued, the High Court or the Circuit Court may, on the application of a planning authority or any other person, whether or not the person has an interest in the land, by order require any person to do or not to do, or to cease to do, as the case may be, anything that the Court considers necessary and specifies in the order to ensure, as appropriate, the following:

(a) that the unauthorised development is not carried out or continued;
(b) in so far as is practicable, that any land is restored to its condition prior to the commencement of any unauthorised development;
(c) that any development is carried out in conformity with the permission pertaining to that development or any condition to which the permission is subject.

(2) In making an order under subsection (1), where appropriate, the Court may order the carrying out of any works, including the restoration, reconstruction, removal, demolition or alteration of any structure or other feature.

(3) (a) An application to the High Court or the Circuit Court for an order under this section shall be by motion and the Court when considering the matter may make such interim or interlocutory order (if any) as it considers appropriate.
(b) Subject to section 161, the order by which an application under this section is determined may contain such terms and conditions (if any) as to the payment of costs as the Court considers appropriate.

(4) (a) Rules of court may provide for an order under this section to be made against a person whose identity is unknown.
(b) Any relevant rules of Court made in respect of section 27 (inserted by section 19 of the Act of 1992) of the Act of 1976 shall apply to this section and shall be construed to that effect.

(5) (a) An application under this section to the Circuit Court shall be made to the judge of the Circuit Court for the circuit in which the land which is the subject of the application is situated.
(b) The Circuit Court shall have jurisdiction to hear and determine an application under this section where the rateable valuation of the land which is the subject of the application does not exceed £200.
(c) The Circuit Court may, for the purposes of paragraph (b), in relation to land that

has not been given a rateable valuation or is the subject with other land of a rateable valuation, determine that its rateable valuation would exceed, or would not exceed, £200.

(d) Where the rateable valuation of any land which is the subject of an application under this section exceeds £200, the Circuit Court shall, if an application is made to it in that behalf by any person having an interest in the proceedings, transfer the proceedings to the High Court, but any order made or act done in the course of such proceedings before the transfer shall be valid unless discharged or varied by the High Court by order.

(6) (a) An application to the High Court or Circuit Court for an order under this section shall not be made—

    (i) in respect of a development where no permission has been granted, after the expiration of a period of 7 years from the date of the commencement of the development, or

    (ii) in respect of a development for which permission has been granted under Part III, after the expiration of a period of 7 years beginning on the expiration, as respects the permission authorising the development, of the appropriate period (within the meaning of section 40) or, as the case may be, of the appropriate period as extended under section 42.

(b) Notwithstanding paragraph (a), an application for an order under this section may be made at any time in respect of any condition to which the development is subject concerning the ongoing use of the land.

(7) Where an order has been sought under this section, any other enforcement action under this Part may be commenced or continued.

Note

Section 160 restates with some amendments s 27 of LG(PD)A 1976 dealing with planning injunctions. Specifically, s 160 allows an application to be made for an injunction where 'an unauthorised development has been, is being, *or is likely to be* carried out or continued . . .'. This therefore allows the Court to grant quia timet relief in circumstances which the Supreme Court decided were not permissible in *Mahon v Butler* [1997] 3 IR 369.

Sub-section (2) is also new in allowing the court to make positive orders for the carrying out of works.

The relief can now be sought from the High Court, or the Circuit Court where the rateable valuation of the land the subject of the application does not exceed IR£200, or is so determined by the Circuit Court: see sub-s (5)(a)-(d).

Sub-section (6)(a)(i) and (ii) states that the relevant period is now seven years instead of five years as prescribed by s 27 of LG(PD)A 1976 as inserted by s 19 of LG(PD)A 1992. This does not apply where the development concerns the on-going use of land, and this provision is new.

[321]
161. Costs of prosecutions and applications for injunctions
(1) The court shall, unless it is satisfied that there are special and substantial reasons for not so doing, order the person to pay—

(a) where a person is convicted of an offence under this Part, to the planning authority, or

(b) where the person is the subject of an order under section 160, to the planning authority or to any other person as appropriate, the costs and expenses of the action, measured by the court

(2) Where costs or expenses are to be paid to the authority, they shall include any such costs or expenses reasonably incurred by the authority in relation to the investigation, detection and prosecution of the offence or order, as appropriate, including costs incurred in respect of the remuneration and other expenses of employees, consultants and advisers.

Note
Section 161 allows for fines to be paid to the planning authority and provides for costs or expenses as incurred by the planning authority in investigating and prosecuting the matter to be paid to them also. This is consistent with the 'polluter pays' principle and is mirrored in s 159 above.

[322]
162. Evidence of permission
(1) In any proceedings for an offence under this Act, the onus of proving the existence of any permission granted under Part III shall be on the defendant.

(2) Notwithstanding subsection (1) of this section, it shall not be a defence to a prosecution under this Part if the defendant proves that he or she has applied for or has been granted permission under section 34(12)—

(a) since the initiation of proceedings under this Part,
(b) since the date of the sending of a warning letter under section 152, or
(c) since the date of service of an enforcement notice in a case of urgency in accordance with section 155.

(3) No enforcement action under this Part (including an application under section 160) shall be stayed or withdrawn by reason of an application for retention of permission under section 34(12) or the grant of that permission.

Note
Section 162 is new. It provides that it shall be no defence to a prosecution for the defendant to show that he has applied for or been granted retention planning permission since the initiation of proceedings, since the date of any warning letter, or since the date of any enforcement notice.

[323]
163. Permission not required for any works required under this Act
Notwithstanding Part III, permission shall not be required in respect of development required by a notice under section 154 or an order under section 160 (disregarding development for which there is in fact permission under Part III).

Note
Section 163 states that planning permission will not be required for the carrying out of development required under an enforcement notice or required under an order made pursuant to s 160.

[324]
164. Transitional arrangements for offences

Notwithstanding any repeal of any enactment ("repealed enactment") by this Act, where proceedings have been initiated in respect of any offence under the repealed enactment, or an enforcement notice or a warning notice (within the meaning of the relevant provisions) has issued under any provision of the repealed enactment, or an application to a Court has been made under section 27 of the Act of 1976, the relevant provision which applied before the repeal shall continue to so apply until the proceedings have been finalised, the notices complied with or withdrawn or the application determined, as the case may be.

Note
These are the transitional provisions. Any proceedings issued pursuant to LG(PD)A 1963–1999 will be prosecuted in their entirety under the 'old' legislation.

PART IX   STRATEGIC DEVELOPMENT ZONES

Note
This Part introduces the new concept of Strategic Development Zones ('SDZ') into Irish law. The introduction of SDZs may be viewed as bringing Irish planning law in line with other jurisdictions where such zones are quite common. The Planning and Development Act, 2000 (Commencement) Order 2000 brought Pt IX into operation from 1 November 2000.

[325]–[330]
165. Interpretation

In this Part—

"development agency" means the Industrial Development Agency (Ireland), Enterprise Ireland, the Shannon Free Airport Development Company Limited, Udaras na Gaeltachta, the National Building Agency Limited, a local authority or such other person as may be prescribed by the Minister for the purposes of this Part:

"strategic development zone" means a site or sites to which a planning scheme made under section 169 applies.

Note
The definition of 'development agency' appears to be confined to authorities principally concerned with industrial development and does not, for example, include transportation bodies.

[331]
166. Designation of sites for strategic development zones

(1) Where, in the opinion of the Government, specified development is of economic or social importance to the State, the Government may by order, when so proposed by the Minister, designate one or more sites for the establishment, in accordance with the provisions of this Part, of a strategic development zone to facilitate such development.

(2) The Minister shall, before proposing the designation of a site or sites to the Government under subsection (1), consult with any relevant development agency or planning authority on the proposed designation.

(3) An order under subsection (1) shall—

(a) specify the development agency or development agencies for the purposes of section 168,

(b) specify the type or types of development that may be established in the strategic development zone, and

(c) state the reasons for specifying the development and for designating the site or sites.

(4) The Minister shall send a copy of any order made under this section to any relevant development agency, planning authority and regional authority and to the Board.

(5) Development that is specified in an order under subsection (3) shall be deemed to include development that is ancillary to, or required for, the purposes of development so specified, and may include any necessary infrastructural and community facilities and services.

(6) The Government may revoke or amend an order made under this section.

Notes
Section 166(1)
The designation of sites for strategic development is the responsibility of Government.

Section 166(2)
The Minister must consult with any relevant development agency or planning authority regarding the proposed designation before proposing it to Government.

Section 166(3)
Once an Order designating a site for an SDZ has been made, it must specify inter alia the development agency or agencies with responsibility for implementation of the Scheme for the SDZ.

Section 166(5)
This is a key provision. It states that a number of activities may be excluded from the requirement to obtain planning permission.

[332]
167. Acquisition of site for strategic development zone
(1) A planning authority may use any powers to acquire land that are available to it under any enactment, including any powers in relation to the compulsory acquisition of land, for the purposes of providing, securing or facilitating the provision of, a site referred to in section 166(1).

(2) Where a person, other than the relevant development agency, has an interest in land, or any part of land, on which a site or sites referred to in an order under section 166(1) is or are situated, the relevant development agency may enter into an agreement with that person for the purpose of facilitating the development of the land.

(3) An agreement made under subsection (2) with any person having an interest in land may be enforced by the relevant development agency against persons deriving title under that person in respect of that land.

Note
Section 167 confers wide powers of compulsory purchase relative to implementing an SDZ.

[333]
168. Planning scheme for strategic development zones

(1) Where a site is designated under section 166, the relevant development agency or, where an agreement referred to in section 167 has been made, the relevant development agency and any person who is a party to the agreement, may, as soon as may be and in any case not later than 2 years after the making of an order under section 166, prepare a draft planning scheme in respect of all or any part of the site and submit it to the relevant planning authority.

(2) A draft planning scheme under this section shall consist of a written statement and a plan indicating the manner in which it is intended that the site is to be developed and in particular—

(a) the type or types of development which may be permitted to establish on the site (subject to the order of the Government under section 166),

(b) the extent of any such proposed development,

(c) proposals in relation to the overall design of the proposed development, including the maximum heights, the external finishes of structures and the general appearance and design,

(d) proposals relating to transportation, including public transportation, the roads layout, the provision of parking spaces and traffic management,

(e) proposals relating to the provision of services on the site, including the provision of waste and sewerage facilities and water, electricity and telecommunications services, oil and gas pipelines, including storage facilities for oil or gas,

(f) proposals relating to minimising any adverse effects on the environment, including the natural and built environment, and on the amenities of the area, and

(g) where the scheme provides for residential development, proposals relating to the provision of amenities, facilities and services for the community, including schools, creches and other education and childcare services.

(3) A draft planning scheme shall also contain information on any likely significant impacts on the environment of implementing the planning scheme and to that effect it shall contain the information prescribed under section 177, in so far as such information is relevant to the detail contained in the scheme.

(4) (a) A draft planning scheme for residential development shall be consistent with the housing strategy prepared by the planning authority in accordance with Part V.

(b) Where land in a strategic development zone is to be used for residential development, an objective to secure the implementation of the housing strategy shall be included in the draft planning scheme as if it were a specific objective under section 95(1)(b).

(5) Where an area designated under section 166 is situated within the functional area of two or more planning authorities the functions conferred on a planning authority under this Part shall be exercised—

(a) jointly by the planning authorities concerned, or

(b) by one of the authorities, provided that the consent of the other authority or authorities, as appropriate, is obtained prior to the making of the scheme under section 169,

and the words "planning authority" shall be construed accordingly.

Note
Section 168(3)
Some commentators have concerns that the SDZ orders may facilitate development that could have adverse environmental consequences. This is counterbalanced to a certain degree by s 168(3), which requires that an environmental impact statement must be produced.

[334]
169. Making of planning scheme
(1) Where a draft planning scheme has been prepared and submitted to the planning authority in accordance with section 168, the planning authority shall, as soon as may be—

(a) send notice and copies of the draft scheme to the Minister, the Board and the prescribed authorities,
(b) publish notice of the preparation of the draft scheme in one or more newspapers circulating in its area.

(2) A notice under subsection (1) shall state—

(a) that a copy of the draft may be inspected at a stated place or places and at stated times during a stated period of not less than 6 weeks (and the copy shall be kept available for inspection accordingly), and
(b) that written submissions or observations with respect to the draft scheme made to the planning authority within the stated period will be taken into consideration in deciding upon the scheme.

(3) (a) Not longer than 12 weeks after giving notice under subsection (2) the manager of a planning authority shall prepare a report on any submissions or observations received under that subsection and submit the report to the members of the authority for their consideration.
(b) A report under paragraph (a) shall—
    (i) list the persons or bodies who made submissions or observations under this section.
    (ii) summarise the issues raised by the persons or bodies in the submissions or observations,
    (iii) give the response of the manager to the issues raised, taking account of the proper planning and sustainable development of the area, the statutory obligations of any local authority in the area and any relevant policies or objectives for the time being of the Government or of any Minister of the Government.

(4) (a) The members of a planning authority shall consider the draft planning scheme and the report of the manager prepared and submitted in accordance with subsection (3).
(b) The draft planning scheme shall be deemed to be made 6 weeks after the submission of that draft planning scheme and report to the members of the planning authority in accordance with subsection (3) unless the planning authority decides, by resolution, to—
    (i) make, subject to variations and modifications, the draft planning scheme, or
    (ii) decides not to make the draft planning scheme.

(c) Where a draft planning scheme is—
    (i)   deemed, in accordance with paragraph (b), to have been made, or
    (ii) made in accordance with paragraph (b)(i),
it shall have effect 4 weeks from the date of such making unless an appeal is brought to the Board under subsection (6)

(5) (a) Following the decision of the planning authority under subsection (4) the authority shall, as soon as may be, and in any case not later than 6 working days following the making of the decision—
    (i)   give notice of the decision of the planning authority to the Minister, the Board, the prescribed authorities and any person who made written submissions or observations on the draft scheme, and
    (ii) publish notice of the decision in one or more newspapers circulating in its area.
(b) A notice under paragraph (a) shall—
    (i)   give the date of the decision of the planning authority in respect of the draft planning scheme,
    (ii) state the nature of the decision,
    (iii) state that a copy of the planning scheme is available for inspection at a stated place or places (and the copy shall be kept available for inspection accordingly),
    (iv) state that any person who made submissions or observations regarding the draft scheme may appeal the decision of the planning authority to the Board within 4 weeks of the date of the planning authority's decision, and
    (v) contain such other information as may be prescribed.

(6) The development agency or any person who made submissions or observations in respect of the draft planning scheme may, for stated reasons, within 4 weeks of the date of the decision of the planning authority appeal the decision of the planning authority to the Board.

(7) (a) The Board may, following the consideration of an appeal made under this section, approve the making of the planning scheme, with or without modifications or it may refuse to approve it.
(b) Where the Board approves the making of a planning scheme in accordance with paragraph (a), the planning authority shall, as soon as practicable, publish notice of the approval of the scheme in at least one newspaper circulating in its area, and shall state that a copy of the planning scheme is available for inspection at a stated place or places (and a copy shall be kept available for inspection accordingly).

(8) In considering a draft planning scheme under this section a planning authority or the Board, as the case may be, shall consider the proper planning and sustainable development of the area and consider the provisions of the development plan, the provisions of the housing strategy, the provisions of any special amenity area order or the conservation and preservation of any European Site and, where appropriate—

(a) the effect the scheme would have on any neighbouring land to the land concerned,
(b) the effect the scheme would have on any place which is outside the area of the planning authority, and

(c) any other consideration relating to development outside the area of the planning authority, including any area outside the State.

(9) A planning scheme made under this section shall be deemed to form part of any development plan in force in the area of the scheme until the scheme is revoked, and any contrary provisions of the development plan shall be superseded.

Notes
Section 169(6)
Only the relevant development agency or any person who made submissions or observations on the draft planning scheme may appeal to the Board.

Section 169(9)
Where there is a conflict between the development plan and the provisions of the planning scheme the provisions of the planning scheme will take precedence.

[335]–[340]
170. Application for development in strategic development zone
(1) Where an application is made to a planning authority under section 34 for a development in a strategic development in that section and any permission regulations shall apply, subject to zone, the other provisions of this section.

(2) A planning authority shall grant permission in respect of an application for a development in a strategic development zone where it is satisfied that the development, where carried out in accordance with the application or subject to any conditions which the planning authority may attach to a permission, would be consistent with any planning scheme in force for the land in question, and no permission shall be granted for any development which would not be consistent with such a planning scheme.

(3) Notwithstanding section 37, no appeal shall lie to the Board against a decision of a planning authority on an application for permission in respect of a development in a strategic development zone.

(4) Where the planning authority decides to grant permission for a development in a strategic development zone, the grant shall be deemed to be given on the date of the decision.

Note
Section 170(1), (3)
Where an application is made to a planning authority for a development in an SDZ, the normal provisions governing planning permissions apply save that no appeal shall lie to the Board against a decision of a planning authority relative to a planning permission.

[341]
171. Revocation of planning scheme
(1) A planning authority may by resolution, with the consent of the relevant development agency, amend or revoke a planning scheme made under this Part.

(2) Where a planning authority proposes to amend a planning scheme under this section it shall comply with the procedure laid down in section 169 and that section shall be construed accordingly.

(3) Notice of the revocation of a planning scheme under this section shall be given in at least one newspaper circulating in the area of the planning authority.

(4) The amendment or revocation of a planning scheme shall not prejudice the validity of any planning permission granted or anything done in accordance with the terms of the scheme before it was amended or revoked except in accordance with the terms of this Act.

(5) Without prejudice to the generality of subsection (4), sections 40 and 42 shall apply to any permission granted under this Part.

PART X   ENVIRONMENTAL IMPACT ASSESSMENT

Note

It is useful to set out firstly the pre-existing regime in this area.

The European Communities (Environmental Impact Assessment) Regulations 1989, SI 349/1989, first introduced the requirements for environmental impact assessment in line with Ireland's obligations to implement Council Directive 85/337/EEC. Those regulations were amended in 1994 (SI 84/1994), 1996 (SI 101/1996), and 1998 (SI 351/1998). The European Communities (Environmental Impact Assessment) (Amendment) Regulations 1999, SI 93/1999, came into force on 1 May 1999 and had the objective of implementing amending Directive 97/11/EC. EC(EIA)(A)R 1999 replaced the First Schedule contained in EC(EIA)R 1989 (being the list of developments requiring an environmental impact assessment) and also replaced the Second Schedule to EC(EIA)R 1989 (detailing the contents of an environmental impact statement). Planning Regulations 1994–2000 incorporated the EIA process into the planning process.

Part X provides the basis for environmental impact assessment in *primary* legislation for the first time. It provides the framework for environmental impact assessment in the planning process. Regulations made under Pt X will provide the detail, and once in place, will supersede the pre-existing regime described above.

This part has not yet been commenced.

[342]
172. Requirement for environmental impact statement

(1) Where a planning application is made in respect of a development or class of development referred to in regulations under section 176, that application shall, in addition to meeting the requirements of the permission regulations, be accompanied by an environmental impact statement.

(2) In addition to the matters set out in section 33(2), the Minister may make permission regulations in relation to the submission of planning applications which are to be accompanied by environmental impact statements.

(3) (a) At the request of an applicant or of a person intending to apply for permission, the Board may, having afforded the planning authority concerned an opportunity to furnish observations on the request, and where the Board is satisfied that exceptional circumstances so warrant, grant in respect of a proposed development an exemption from a requirement of or under regulations under this section to prepare an environmental impact statement, except that no exemption may be granted in respect of a proposed development if another

Member State of the European Communities or other state party to the Transboundary Convention, having been informed about the proposed development and its likely effects on the environment in that State, has indicated that it intends to furnish views on those effects.

(b) The Board shall, in granting an exemption under paragraph (a), consider whether—

    (i) the effects, if any, of the proposed development on the environment should be assessed in some other manner, and

    (ii) the information arising from the assessment should be made available to the members of the public, and the Board may apply such requirements regarding these matters in relation to the application for permission as it considers necessary or appropriate.

(c) The Board shall, as soon as may be, notify the planning authority concerned of the Board's decision on any request made under paragraph (a), and of any requirements applied under paragraph (b).

(d) Notice of any exemption granted under paragraph (a), of the reasons for granting the exemption, and of any requirements applied under paragraph (b) shall, as soon as may be—

    (i) be published in Iris Oifigiúil and in at least one daily newspaper published in the State,

    (ii) be given, together with a copy of the information, if any, made available to the members of the public in accordance with paragraph (b), to the Commission of the European Communities.

(4) (a) A person who makes a request to the Board for an exemption under subsection (3) shall, as soon as may be, inform the planning authority concerned of the making of the request and the date on which it was made.

(b) Notwithstanding subsection (8) of section 34, the period for making a decision referred to in that subsection shall not, in a case in which a request is made to the Board under subsection (3) of this section, include the period beginning on the day of the making of the request and ending on the day of receipt by the planning authority concerned of notice of the Board's decision on the request.

(5) In addition to the matters provided for under Part VI, Chapter III, the Minister may prescribe additional requirements in relation to the submission of appeals to the Board which are to be accompanied by environmental impact statements.

Note

An environmental impact statement will have to be prepared where same is required by regulations that will replace EC(EIA)R 1999. This section provides for the making of regulations that will replace the regulations described above as the pre-existing regime (see also s 176 below). Sub-section (3) is a change from the pre-existing regime where the Minister had the power to grant an exemption from the requirement of an environmental impact statement in exceptional circumstances. This power is now given to the Board on the terms set out in the rest of that section.

[343]
173. Permission for development requiring environmental impact assessment

(1) In addition to the requirements of section 34(3), where an application in respect of which an environmental impact statement was submitted to the planning authority

in accordance with section 172, the planning authority, and the Board on appeal, shall have regard to the statement, any supplementary information furnished relating to the statement and any submissions or observations furnished concerning the effects on the environment of the proposed development.

(2) (a) If an applicant or a person intending to apply for permission so requests, the planning authority concerned shall give a written opinion on the information to be contained in an environmental impact statement, subject to any prescribed consultations to be carried out by the planning authority in relation to such an opinion, before that person submits the application for the grant of planning permission.

(b) The giving of a written opinion in accordance with paragraph (a) shall not prejudice the exercise by the planning authority concerned of its powers under this Act, or any regulations made thereunder, to require the person who made the request to submit further information regarding the application concerned.

(c) The Minister may, by regulations, provide for additional, incidental, consequential or supplementary matters as regards procedure in respect of the provision of a written opinion under paragraph (a).

(3) (a) Where a person is required by or under this Act to submit an environmental impact statement to the Board, he or she may, before submitting the statement, request the Board to provide him or her with its opinion as to the information that should be contained in such statement, and the Board shall on receipt of such a request provide such opinion in writing.

(b) The giving of a written opinion in accordance with paragraph (a) shall not prejudice the exercise by the Board of its powers pursuant to this Act or any regulations under this Act, to require the applicant to submit specified information in relation to any appeal to which the environmental impact statement relates.

(c) The Minister may make regulations in relation to the making of a request or providing an opinion to which this subsection relates.

Note

Section173(2) and (3) provide the opportunity for an applicant for permission, or a person intending to apply for permission, to seek and obtain a written opinion from the planning authority or the Board respectively relative to the information to be contained in an environmental impact statement. It is anticipated by sub-ss (2)(c), (3)(c), that the Minister may make regulations providing more detail on this procedure. This opinion procedure was first introduced by LG(PD)R 1999.

[344]
174. Transboundary environmental impacts

(1) (a) The Minister may make regulations in respect of applications for development which require the submission of an environmental impact statement, where the planning authority, or the Board on appeal, is aware that the development is likely to have significant effects on the environment in another Member State of the European Communities or a state which is a party to the Transboundary Convention or where the other State concerned considers that the development would be likely to have such effects.

(b) Without prejudice to the generality of paragraph (a), regulations under this subsection may make provision for the following:

   (i)   the notification of the Minister regarding the application;
   (ii) the submission of information to the Minister regarding the application;
   (iii) the notification of the other State involved and the provision of information
         to that State;
   (iv) the making of observations and submissions regarding the application from
         the other State involved and the entering into consultations with that State;
   (v)   the extension of time limits for the making of decisions under this Act.

(2) In addition to the requirements of sections 173(1) and 34(3), the planning authority or the Board, as the case may be, shall have regard, where appropriate, to the views of any Member State of the European Communities or other party to the Transboundary Convention in relation to the effects on the environment of the proposed development.

(3) Notwithstanding any other provisions of this Act, a planning authority or the Board, as the case may be, may, following the consideration of any submissions or observations received or any consultations entered into by a planning authority or the Board, impose conditions on a grant of permission in order to reduce or eliminate potential transboundary effects of any proposed development.

(4) Where a planning authority or a State authority requests, or in any other case where the Minister otherwise decides, the Minister may request another Member State of the European Communities or other party to the Transboundary Convention to forward information in respect of any development which is subject to the Council Directive or Transboundary Convention and which is likely to have significant environmental effects in Ireland.

(5) (a) The Minister or a State authority or planning authority having consulted with
         the Minister, may decide to forward submissions or observations to, or enter
         into discussions with, the other state involved in respect of the development
         referred to in subsection (4) regarding the potential transboundary effects of that
         development and the measures envisaged to reduce or eliminate those effects.
   (b) The Minister may make regulations regarding the provision of public notification of any environmental impact statement or other information received by the
         Minister, State authority or planning authority under subsection (4), and the
         making of submissions or observations regarding the information.

(6) The Minister may enter into an agreement with any other Member State of the European Communities or other party to the Transboundary Convention regarding the detailed procedures to be followed in respect of consultations regarding proposed developments which are likely to have significant transboundary effects.

Note
Section 174, dealing with transboundary environmental impacts, is essentially a restatement of pre-existing provisions in EC(EIA)R 1989. Again, the Minister may make regulations pursuant to this section as is referred to in sub-s (5)(b).

[345]–[350]
175. Environmental impact assessment of certain development carried out by or on behalf of local authorities
(1) Where development belonging to a class of development, identified for the purposes of section 176, is proposed to be carried out by or on

(a) by a local authority that is a planning authority, whether in its capacity as a planning authority or in any other capacity, or

(b) by some other person on behalf of, or jointly or in partnership with, such a local authority, pursuant to a contract entered into by that local authority whether in its capacity as a planning authority or in any other capacity,

within the functional area of the local authority concerned (hereafter in this section referred to as "proposed development"), the local authority shall prepare, or cause to be prepared, an environmental impact statement in respect thereof.

(2) Proposed development in respect of which an environmental impact statement has been prepared in accordance with subsection (1) shall not be carried out unless the Board has approved it with or without modifications.

(3) Where an environmental impact statement has been prepared pursuant to subsection (1), the local authority shall apply to the Board for approval.

(4) Before a local authority makes an application for approval under subsection (3), it shall—

(a) publish in one or more newspapers circulating in the area in which it is proposed to carry out the development a notice indicating the nature and location of the proposed development and—
  (i) stating that—
    (I) it proposes to seek the approval of the Board for the proposed development,
    (II) an environmental impact statement has been prepared in respect of the proposed development,
  (ii) specifying the times and places at which, and the period (not being less than 6 weeks) during which, a copy of the environmental impact statement may be inspected free of charge or purchased, and
  (iii) inviting the making, during such period, of submissions and observations to the Board relating to—
    (I) the implications of the proposed development for proper planning and sustainable development in the area concerned, and
    (II) the likely effects on the environment of the proposed development, if carried out,
  and
(b) send a copy of the application and the environmental impact statement to the prescribed authorities together with a notice stating that submissions or observations may, during the period referred to in paragraph (a)(ii), be made in writing to the Board in relation to—
  (i) the likely effects on the environment of the proposed development, and
  (ii) the implications of the proposed development for proper planning and sustainable development in the area concerned, if carried out.

(5) (a) The Board may, where it considers it necessary to do so, require a local authority that has applied for approval for a proposed development to furnish to the Board such further information in relation to the effects on the environment of the proposed development as the Board may specify.

(b) The Board shall, where it considers that the further information received pursuant to paragraph (a) contains significant additional data relating to—

    (i) the likely effects on the environment of the proposed development, and

    (ii) the likely consequences for proper planning and sustainable development in the area in which it is proposed to situate the said development of such development, require the local authority

        (I) to publish in one or more newspapers circulating in the area in which the proposed development would be situate a notice stating that further information in relation to the proposed development has been furnished to the Board, indicating the times at which, the period (which shall not be less than 3 weeks) during which and the place, or places, where a copy of the further information may be inspected free of charge or purchased and that submissions or observations in relation to the further information may be made to the Board before the expiration of the indicated period, and

        (II) to send notice of the furnishing of the further information to the Board, and a copy of the information furnished to any prescribed authority to which notice was given pursuant to subsection (4)(b), and to indicate to the authority that submissions or observations in relation to the further information may be made to the Board before the expiration of a period (which shall not be less than 3 weeks) beginning on the day on which the notice is sent to the prescribed authority by the local authority.

(6) Before making a decision in respect of a proposed development under this section, the Board shall consider—

(a) the environmental impact statement submitted pursuant to subsection (1), any submissions or observations made in accordance with subsection (4) and any other information furnished in accordance with subsection (5) relating to—

    (i) the likely effects on the environment of the proposed development, and

    (ii) the likely consequences for proper planning and sustainable development in the area in which it is proposed to situate the said development of such development,

(b) the views of any other Member State of the European Communities or a state which is a party to the Transboundary Convention to which a copy of the environmental impact statement was sent, and

(c) the report and any recommendations of the person conducting a hearing referred to in subsection (7) where evidence is heard at such a hearing relating to—

    (i) the likely effects on the environment of the proposed development, and

    (ii) the likely consequences for proper planning and sustainable development in the area in which it is proposed to situate the said development of such development.

(7) The person conducting an oral hearing in relation to the compulsory purchase of land which relates wholly or partly to a proposed development under this section in respect of which a local authority has applied for approval shall be entitled to hear evidence relating to—

(a) the likely effects on the environment of the proposed development, and

(b) the likely consequences for proper planning and sustainable development in the area in which it is proposed to situate the said development of such development.

(8) (a) The Board may where it is satisfied that exceptional circumstances so warrant, grant an exemption in respect of proposed development from a requirement under subsection (1) to prepare an environmental impact statement except that no exemption may be granted in respect of proposed development where another Member State of the European Communities or a State party to the Transboundary Convention has indicated that it wishes to furnish views on the effects on the environment in that State of the proposed development.

(b) The Board shall, in granting an exemption under paragraph (a), consider whether—

(i) the effects, if any, of the proposed development on the environment should be assessed in some other manner, and

(ii) the information arising from such an assessment should be made available to the members of the public,

and it may apply such requirements regarding these matters in relation to the application for approval as it considers necessary or appropriate.

(c) Notice of any exemption granted under paragraph (a) of the reasons for granting the exemption, and of any requirements applied under paragraph (b) shall, as soon as may be—

(i) be published in Iris Oifigiúil and in at least one daily newspaper published in the State, and

(ii) be given, together with a copy of the information, if any, made available to the members of the public in accordance with paragraph (b), to the Commission of the European Communities.

(9) The Board may—

(a) approve,

(b) approve, subject to conditions, or

(c) refuse to approve,

a proposed development under this section.

(10) (a) Where an application under this section relates to proposed development which comprises or is for the purposes of an activity for which an integrated pollution control licence or a waste licence is required, the Board shall not, where it decides to approve the proposed development, subject that approval to conditions which are for the purposes of—

(i) controlling emissions from the operation of the activity, including the prevention, limitation, elimination, abatement or reduction of those emissions, or

(ii) controlling emissions related to or following the cessation of the operation of the activity.

(b) Where an application under this section relates to proposed development which comprises or is for the purposes of an activity for which an integrated pollution control licence or a waste licence is required, the Board may, in respect of any proposed development comprising or for the purposes of the activity, decide to refuse the proposed development, where the Board considers that the develop-

ment, notwithstanding the licensing of the activity, is unacceptable on environmental grounds, having regard to the proper planning and sustainable development of the area in which the development is or will be situate.

(c) (i) Before making a decision in respect of proposed development comprising
or for the purposes of an activity, the Board may request the
Environmental Protection Agency to make observations within such
period (which period shall not in any case be less than 3 weeks from the
date of the request) as may be specified by the Board in relation to the proposed development.

(ii) When making its decision the Board shall have regard to the observations,
if any, received from the Agency within the period specified under subparagraph (i).

(d) The Board may, at any time after the expiration of the period specified by the
Board under paragraph (c)(i) for making observations, make its decision on the
application.

(e) The making of observations by the Agency under this section shall not prejudice
any other function of the Agency under this Act.

(11) (a) The Minister may make regulations to provide for such matters of procedure and administration as appear to the Minister to be necessary or expedient
in respect of applications for approval under this section.

(b) Without prejudice to the generality of paragraph (a), regulations under this subsection may make provision for—

(i) enabling a local authority to request the Board to give a written opinion on
the information to be contained in an environmental impact statement.

(ii) matters of procedure relating to the making of observations by the
Environmental Protection Agency under this section and matters connected therewith,

(iii) the notification of another Member State of the European Communities or
other parties to the Transboundary Convention in relation to proposed
development, receiving observations and submissions from the State or
party and entering into consultations with them, and

(iv) requiring the Board to give information in respect of its decision regarding
the proposed development for which approval is sought.

(12) In considering under subsection (6) information furnished relating to the likely
consequences for proper planning and sustainable development of a proposed development in the area in which it is proposed to situate such development, the Board
shall have regard to—

(a) the provisions of the development plan for the area,

(b) the provisions of any special amenity area order relating to the area,

(c) if the area or part of the area is a European site or an area prescribed for the purposes of section 10(2)(c), that fact,

(d) where relevant, the policies of the Government, the Minister or any other
Minister of the Government, and

(e) the provisions of this Act and regulations under this Act where relevant.

(13) A person who contravenes a condition imposed by the Board under this section
shall be guilty of an offence.

(14) This section shall not apply to proposed road development within the meaning of the Roads Act, 1993, by or on behalf of a road authority.

Note
Section 175 deals with environmental impact assessment of development carried out by local authorities. In line with the change made at s 172 above, the function of approving proposed development requiring an environmental impact statement has now passed to the Board from the Minister. This function passed to the Board with effect from 1 January 2001 pursuant to the LG(PD)(No 2)R, SI 458/2000. See also the EC(EIA)(A)R 2000, SI 450/2000. These provisions apply whether the development is carried out by a local authority, or on their behalf, jointly or in partnership with them. This section sets out in detail the procedure to be adopted.

[351]
176. Prescribed classes of development requiring assessment
(1) The Minister may, in connection with the Council Directive or otherwise, make regulations—

(a) identifying development which may have significant effects on the environment, and

(b) specifying the manner in which the likelihood that such development would have significant effects on the environment is to be determined.

(2) Without prejudice to the generality of subsection (1), regulations under that subsection may provide for all or any one or more of the following matters:

(a) the establishment of thresholds or criteria for the purpose of determining which classes of development are likely to have significant effects on the environment;

(b) the establishment of different such thresholds or criteria in respect of different classes of areas;

(c) the determination on a case-by-case basis, in conjunction with the use of thresholds or criteria, of the developments which are likely to have significant effects on the environment;

(d) where thresholds or criteria are not established, the determination on a case-by-case basis of the developments which are likely to have significant effects on the environment;

(e) the identification of selection criteria in relation to—

   (i)   the establishment of thresholds or criteria for the purpose of determining which classes of development are likely to have significant effects on the environment, or

   (ii) the determination on a case-by-case basis of the developments which are likely to have significant effects on the environment.

(3) Any reference in an enactment to development of a class specified under Article 24 of the European Communities (Environmental Impact Assessment) Regulations, 1989 (S.I. No. 349 of 1989), shall be deemed to be a reference to a class of development prescribed under this section.

Note

Section 176 empowers the Minister to make regulations in relation to environmental impact assessment. Sub-section (1) sets out the subject matter of those regulations and sub-s (2) sets out the matters that may particularly be provided for.

No regulations have been made under s 176 yet.

[352]
177. Prescribed information regarding environmental impact statements
(1) The Minister may prescribe the information that is to be contained in an environmental impact statement.

(2) Any reference in an enactment to the information to be contained in an environmental impact statement specified under Article 25 of the European Communities (Environmental Impact Assessment) Regulations, 1989, shall be deemed to be a reference to information prescribed under this section.

Note
Section 177 provides that the Minister may prescribe the information to be contained in the environmental impact statement and this will require regulations.

PART XI   DEVELOPMENT BY LOCAL AND STATE AUTHORITIES, ETC.

Note
Part XI deals with developments by local and state authorities. Developments by a local authority within its own functional area do not require planning permission. This part provides for certain restrictions on development by local authorities, the notification of local authority and state authority development, the taking in charge of housing estates and certain powers in relation to the erection of cables, wires and pipelines.

Section 182 commenced on 1 January 2001 (SI 449/2000). This is the only section in this part commenced to date.

[353]
178. Restrictions on development by certain local authorities
(1) The council of a county shall not effect any development in its functional area, exclusive of any borough or urban district which contravenes materially the development plan.

(2) The corporation of a county or other borough shall not effect any development in the borough which contravenes materially the development plan.

(3) The council of an urban district shall not effect any development in the district which contravenes materially the development plan.

Note
Section 178 restates s 39 of LG(PD)A 1963.

[354]
179. Local authority own development
(1) (a) The Minister may prescribe a development or a class of development for the purposes of this section where he or she is of the opinion that by reason of

the likely size, nature or effect on the surroundings of such development or class of development there should, in relation to any such development or development belonging to such class of development, be compliance with the provisions of this section and regulations under this section.

(b) Where a local authority that is a planning authority proposes to carry out development, or development belonging to a class of development prescribed under paragraph (a) (hereafter in this section referred to as "proposed development") it shall in relation to the proposed development comply with this section and any regulations under this section.

(c) The Minister may prescribe specified cases or classes of development by local authorities for the purposes of this section where he or she is of the opinion that it is necessary by reason of its size, nature or effect on its surroundings.

(d) This section shall also apply to proposed development which is carried out within the functional area of a local authority which is a planning authority, on behalf of, or in partnership with the local authority, pursuant to a contract with the local authority.

(2) The Minister shall make regulations providing for any or all of the following matters:

(a) the publication by a local authority of any specified notice with respect to proposed development;

(b) requiring local authorities to—
  (i) (I) notify prescribed authorities of such proposed development or classes of proposed development as may be prescribed, or
       (II) consult with them in respect thereof,
       and
  (ii) give to them such documents, particulars, plans or other information in respect thereof as may be prescribed;

(c) the making available for inspection, by members of the public, of any specified documents, particulars, plans or other information with respect to proposed development;

(d) the making of submissions or observations to a local authority with respect to proposed development.

(3) (a) The manager of a local authority shall, after the expiration of the period during which submissions or observations with respect to the proposed development may be made, in accordance with regulations under subsection (2), prepare a written report in relation to the proposed development and submit the report to the members of the authority.

(b) A report prepared in accordance with paragraph (a) shall—
  (i) describe the nature and extent of the proposed development and the principal features thereof, and shall include an appropriate plan of the development and appropriate map of the relevant area,
  (ii) evaluate whether or not the proposed development would be consistent with the proper planning and sustainable development of the area to which the development relates, having regard to the provisions of the development plan and giving the reasons and the considerations for the evaluation,
  (iii) list the persons or bodies who made submissions or observations with

respect to the proposed development in accordance with the regulations under subsection (2),

(iv) summarise the issues, with respect to the proper planning and sustainable development of the area in which the proposed development would be situated, raised in any such submissions or observations, and give the response of the manager thereto, and

(v) recommend whether or not the proposed development should be proceeded with as proposed, or as varied or modified as recommended in the report, or should not be proceeded with, as the case may be.

(4) (a) The members of a local authority shall, as soon as may be, consider the proposed development and the report of the manager under subsection (3).

(b) Following the consideration of the manager's report under paragraph (a), the proposed development may be carried out as recommended in the manager's report, unless the local authority, by resolution, decides to vary or modify the development, otherwise than as recommended in the manager's report, or decides not to proceed with the development.

(c) A resolution under paragraph (b) must be passed not later than 6 weeks after receipt of the manager's report.

(5) Sections 2, 3 and 4 of the City and County Management (Amendment) Act, 1955, shall not apply to development under this section.

(6) This section shall not apply to proposed development which—

(a) consists of works of maintenance or repair, other than works which would materially affect the character of a protected structure or proposed protected structure,

(b) is necessary for dealing urgently with any situation which the manager considers is an emergency situation calling for immediate action,

(c) consists of works which a local authority is required by or under statute or by order of a court to undertake, or

(d) is development in respect of which an environmental impact statement is required under section 175 or under any other enactment.

Note
Section 179 restates with modifications s 78 of LG(PD)A 1963, which provides that the Minister may make regulations regarding certain classes of development carried out by or on behalf of local authorities in their own functional areas. It provides for the public notification of certain developments that do not require an environmental impact statement under s 175, and incorporates some of the provisions contained in the Pt X procedure in the LG(PD)R 1994.

[355]–[360]
180. Taking in charge of estates
(1) Where a development for which permission is granted under section 34 or under Part IV of the Act of 1963 includes the construction of 2 or more houses and the provision of new roads, open spaces, car parks, sewers, watermains or drains, and the development has been completed to the satisfaction of the planning authority in accordance with the permission and any conditions to which the permission is sub-

ject, the authority shall, where requested by the person carrying out the development, or, subject to subsection (3), by the majority of the qualified electors who are owners or occupiers of the houses involved, as soon as may be, initiate the procedures under section 11 of the Roads Act, 1993.

(2) (a) Notwithstanding subsection (1), where the development has not been completed to the satisfaction of the planning authority and enforcement proceedings have not been commenced by the planning authority within seven years beginning on the expiration, as respects the permission authorising the development, of the appropriate period, within the meaning of section 40 or the period as extended under section 42, as the case may be, the authority shall, where requested by the majority of qualified electors who own or occupy the houses in question, comply with section 11 of the Roads Act, 1993, except that subsection (1) (b) (ii) of that section shall be disregarded.

(b) In complying with paragraph (a), the authority may apply any security given under section 34(4)(g) for the satisfactory completion of the development in question.

(3) (a) The planning authority may hold a plebiscite to ascertain the wishes of the qualified electors.

(b) The Minister may make or apply any regulations prescribing the procedure to be followed by the planning authority in ascertaining the wishes of the qualified electors.

(4) Where an order is made under section 11(1) of the Roads Act, 1993, in compliance with this section, the planning authority shall, in addition to the provisions of that section, take in charge any open spaces, car parks, sewers, watermains, or drains within the attendant grounds of the development

(5) Where a planning authority acts in compliance with this section, references in section 11 of the Roads Act, 1993, to a road authority shall be deemed to include references to a planning authority.

(6) In this section, "qualified electors" means every person who, in relation to the area of the dwelling houses in question, is registered as a local government elector in the register of local government electors for the time being in force.

Notes
Section 180 is new. It provides that where a housing estate has been completed in compliance with the conditions of a planning permission and to the satisfaction of the local authority, the local authority must, if requested by a majority of the residents, take the estate in charge.

Even if the estate has not been completed to the satisfaction of the local authority and no enforcement proceedings have been taken against the developer within seven years from the expiration of the planning permission, the local authority shall, if requested to do so by a majority of the residents, take the estate in charge.

It may apply any sums received from the developer as security on the granting of the permission towards the cost of completing the development. It is clear that if the development does not comply with the conditions of the planning permission, the local authority may, within seven years beginning on the expiration of the planning permission, take enforcement proceedings to compel the developer to complete the development fully.

The local authority may hold a plebiscite to ascertain the wishes of the residents.

[361]
181. Development by State authorities

(1) (a) The Minister may, by regulations, provide that, except for this section, the provisions of this Act shall not apply to any specified class or classes of development by or on behalf of a State authority where the development is, in the opinion of the Minister, in connection with or for the purposes of public safety or order, the administration of justice or national security or defence and, for so long as the regulations are in force, the provisions of this Act shall not apply to the specified class or classes of development.

(b) The Minister may, by regulations, provide for any or all of the following matters in relation to any class or classes of development to which regulations under paragraph (a) apply:

   (i) the publication by a State authority of any specified notice with respect to development that it proposes to carry out or to have carried out on its behalf;

   (ii) the giving by a State authority, to the planning authority for the area in which proposed development is to be carried out, or any other specified person, of any specified notice, documents, particulars, plans or other information with respect to the proposed development;

   (iii) the making available for inspection by members of the public of any specified documents, particulars, plans or other information with respect to the proposed development;

   (iv) the preparation of an environmental impact statement with respect to the proposed development, the contents of such a statement and the making available for inspection or purchase by members of the public of such a statement;

   (v) the making of submissions or observations to a State authority with respect to the proposed development;

   (vi) the reference to a specified person of any dispute or disagreement, with respect to the proposed development, between a State authority and the planning authority for the area in which the proposed development is to be carried out;

   (vii) requiring a State authority, in deciding whether the proposed development is to be carried out, to have regard to any specified matters or considerations.

(2) (a) Where development is proposed to be carried out by or on behalf of a Minister of the Government or the Commissioners, the Minister of the Government concerned or, in the case of development proposed to be carried out by or on behalf of the Commissioners, the Minister for Finance, may, if he or she is satisfied that the carrying out of the development is required by reason of an accident or emergency, by order provide that this Act or, as may be appropriate, any requirement or requirements of regulations under subsection (1)(b) specified in the order, shall not apply to the development, and for so long as such an order is in force this Act or the said requirement or requirements, as the case may be, shall not apply to the development.

(b) A Minister of the Government may by order revoke an order made by him or her under paragraph (a).

(c) A Minister of the Government shall cause an order made by him or her under this subsection to be published in Iris Oifigiúil and notice of the making of the order to be published in a newspaper circulating in the area of the development concerned.

Note
Section 181 restates s 2 of the LG(PD)A 1993.

[362]
182. Cables, wires and pipelines

(1) A local authority may, with the consent of the owner and occupier of any land not forming part of a public road, place, construct or lay, as may be appropriate, cables, wires or pipelines (including water pipes, sewers or drains) and any ancillary apparatus on, under or over the land, and may, from time to time, inspect, repair, alter, renew or remove any such cables, wires or pipelines.

(2) A local authority may, with the consent of the owner and of the occupier of any structure, attach to the structure any bracket or other fixture required for the carrying or support of any cable, wire or pipeline placed, erected or constructed under this section.

(3) A local authority may erect and maintain notices indicating the position of cables, wires or pipelines placed, erected or constructed under this section and may, with the consent of the owner and of the occupier of any structure, affix such a notice to the structure.

(4) Subsections (1) to (3) shall have effect subject to the proviso that—

(a) a consent for the purposes of any of them shall not be unreasonably withheld,
(b) if the local authority considers that such a consent has been unreasonably with-held. it may appeal to the Board, and
(c) if the Board determines that such a consent was unreasonably withheld, it shall be treated as having been given.

(5) The local authority may permit the use of any cables, wires or pipelines placed, erected or constructed under this section and of any apparatus incidental to the cables, wires or pipelines subject to such conditions and charges as it considers appropriate.

Notes
Section 182 restates s 85 of LG(PD)A 1963 as amended by s 14 of LG(PD)A 1976.

Note that s 199 provides that compensation for damage caused by local authority develop-ments under s 182 is limited to the amount of the reduction in value of the land, or for damage for disturbance, and is not related to the value of the easement itself.

PART XII COMPENSATION

Note
Part XII principally re-enacts the provisions of LG(PD)A 1990 relative to compensation. Sections 14, 20, 21, and 24 of LG(PD)A 1990 have not been re-enacted as they are considered redundant. Changes have been made to the Schedules, detailed at the end of this part.

This Part has not been commenced.

CHAPTER I   COMPENSATION GENERALLY

[363]
183. Compensation claims: time limits
(1) Subject to subsection (2), a claim for compensation under this Part shall be made not later than 6 months after—

(a) in the case of a claim under section 190, the date of the decision of the Board.

(b) in the case of a claim under section 195, the date of the decision of the planning authority or the Board, as the case may be,

(c) in the case of a claim under section 196, the removal or alteration of the structure,

(d) in the case of a claim under section 197, the discontinuance or compliance.

(e) in the case of a claim referred to in section 198, the date of the approval of a scheme under section 85 or the date of complying with a notice under section 88, as the case may be,

(f) in the case of a claim under section 199, the date on which the action of the planning authority occurred,

(g) in the case of a claim under section 200, the date on which the order creating the public right of way commences to have effect, and

(h) in the case of a claim under section 201, the date on which the damage is suffered.

(2) The High Court may, where it considers that the interests of justice so require, extend the period within which a claim for compensation under this Part may be brought, upon application being made to it in that behalf.

Note
Section 183 restates s 4 of LG(PD)A 1990.

[364]
184. Determination of compensation claim
A claim for compensation under this Part shall, in default of agreement, be determined by arbitration under the Acquisition of Land (Assessment of Compensation) Act, 1919, but subject to—

(a) the Second Schedule in respect of a reduction in the value of an interest in land,

(b) the proviso that the arbitrator shall have jurisdiction to make a nil award, and

(c) the application of the Second Schedule to a claim for compensation under Chapter III of this Part for a reduction in the value of an interest as if a reference to "the relevant decision under Part III" or to "the decision" was, in relation to each of the sections in that Chapter set out in column A of the Table to this section, a reference to the matter set out in column B of that Table opposite the reference in column A to that section.

TABLE

A	B
Section	
196	the removal or alteration of a structure consequent upon a notice under section 46.
197	the discontinuance with, or the compliance with conditions on the continuance, of the use of land consequent upon a notice under section 46.
198	the approval of a scheme under section 85 or the compliance with a notice under section 88.
199	the action by the planning authority under section 182.
200	the making by the planning authority of an order under section 207.

Note
Section 184 restates s 5 of LG(PD)A 1990.

[365]–[370]
185. Regulations in relation to compensation
The Minister may make regulations to provide for the following:

(a) the form in which claims for compensation are to be made;
(b) the provision by a claimant of evidence in support of his or her claim, and information as to his or her interest in the land to which the claim relates;
(c) a statement by a claimant of the names and addresses of all other persons (so far as they are known to him or her) having an interest in the land to which the claim relates and, unless the claim is withdrawn, the notification by the planning authority or the claimant of every other person (if any) appearing to it or him or her to have an interest in the land.

Note
Section 185 restates s 6 of LG(PD)A 1990 save that sub-ss (d) and (e) have not been repeated.

[371]
186. Prohibition of double compensation
Where a person would, but for this section, be entitled to compensation under this Part in respect of any matter or thing, and also to compensation under any other enactment in respect of the same matter or thing, he or she shall not be entitled to compensation in respect of the matter or thing both under this Part and under the other enactment, and shall not be entitled to any greater amount of compensation under this Part in respect of the matter or thing than the amount of the compensation to which he or she would be entitled under the other enactment in respect of the matter or thing.

Note
Section 186 restates s 7 of LG(PD)A 1990.

[372]
187. Recovery of compensation from planning authority
(1) All compensation payable under this Part by the planning authority shall, when the amount thereof has been determined by agreement or by arbitration in accordance with this Part, be recoverable from that authority as a simple contract debt in any court of competent jurisdiction.

(2) All costs and expenses of parties to an arbitration to determine the amount of any compensation shall, in so far as the costs and expenses are payable by the planning authority, be recoverable from that authority as a simple contract debt in any court of competent jurisdiction.

(3) Sections 69 to 79 of the Lands Clauses Consolidation Act, 1845, as amended or adapted by or under the Second Schedule to the Housing of the Working Classes Act, 1890, or any other Act, shall apply in relation to compensation by this section made recoverable as a simple contract debt, as if the compensation were a price or compensation under the Lands Clauses Consolidation Act, 1845, as so amended or adapted.

(4) Where money is paid into court by the planning authority under section 69 of the Lands Clauses Consolidation Act, 1845, as applied by this section, no costs shall be payable by that authority to any person in respect of any proceedings for the investment, payment of income, or payment of capital of that money.

Note
Section 187 restates s 8 of LG(PD)A 1990.

[373]
188. Registration of compensation
(1) Where, on a claim for compensation under Chapter II of this Part, compensation has become payable of an amount exceeding £500, the planning authority shall prepare and retain a statement of that fact, specifying the refusal of permission or grant of permission subject to conditions, or the revocation or modification of permission, the land to which the claim for compensation relates, and the amount of the compensation.

(2) (a) A planning authority shall enter in the register particulars of a statement prepared by it under this section.
(b) Every entry under paragraph (a) shall be made within the period of 2 weeks beginning on the day of the preparation of the statement.

Note
Section 188 restates s 9 of LG(PD)A 1990.

[374]
189. Recovery by planning authority of compensation on subsequent development
(1) No person shall carry out any development to which this section applies, on land in respect of which a statement (a "compensation statement") stands registered (whether under section 72 of the Act of 1963, section 9 of the Act of 1990 or section 188 of this Act) until that amount, as is recoverable under this section in respect of

the compensation specified in the compensation statement, has been paid or secured to the satisfaction of the planning authority.

(2) This section applies to any development (other than exempted development) of a kind specified in section 192(2), except that—

(a) this section shall not apply to any development by virtue of a permission to develop land under Part III referred to in section 192(5) where the permission was granted subject to conditions other than conditions of a class or description set out in the Fifth Schedule, and

(b) in a case where the compensation specified in the statement became payable in respect of the imposition of conditions on the granting of permission to develop land, this section shall not apply to the development for which that permission was granted.

(3) Subject to subsection (4), the amount recoverable under this section in respect of the compensation specified in a compensation statement—

(a) if the land on which the development is to be carried out (the "development area") is identical with, or includes (with other land) the whole of the land comprised in the compensation statement, shall be the amount of compensation specified in that statement, or

(b) if the development area forms part of the land comprised in the compensation statement, or includes part of that land together with other land not comprised in that statement, shall be so much of the amount of compensation specified in that statement as is attributable to land comprised in that statement and falling within the development area.

(4) The attribution of compensation under subsection (3)(b) shall be in accordance with the following—

(a) the planning authority shall (if it appears to it to be practicable to do so) apportion the amount of the compensation between the different parts of the land, according to the way in which those parts appear to it to be differently affected by the refusal of permission or grant of permission subject to conditions;

(b) if no apportionment is made, the amount of the compensation shall be treated as distributed rateably according to area over the land to which the statement relates;

(c) if an apportionment is made, the compensation shall be treated as distributed in accordance with that apportionment, as between the different parts of the land by reference to which the apportionment is made, and so much of the compensation as, in accordance with the apportionment, is attributed to a part of the land shall be treated as distributed rateably according to area over that part of the land;

(d) if any person disputes an apportionment under this subsection, the dispute shall be submitted to and decided by a property arbitrator nominated under the Property Values (Arbitration and Appeals) Act, 1960.

(5) Where, in connection with the development of any land, an amount becomes recoverable under this section in respect of the compensation specified in a compensation statement, then no amount shall be recoverable, in so far as it is attributable to that land, in connection with any subsequent development thereof.

(6) An amount recoverable under this section in respect of any compensation shall be payable to the planning authority, and—

(a) shall be so payable, either as a single capital payment or as a series of instalments of capital and interest combined (the interest being determined at the same rate as for a judgment debt), or as a series of other annual or periodical payments, of such amounts, and payable at such times, as the planning authority may direct, after taking into account any representations made by the person by whom the development is to be carried out, and

(b) except where the amount is payable as a single capital payment, shall be secured by that person in such manner (whether by mortgage, covenant or otherwise) as the planning authority may direct.

(7) If any person initiates any development to which this section applies in contravention of subsection (1), the planning authority may serve a notice upon him or her, specifying the amount appearing to it to be the amount recoverable under this section in respect of the compensation in question, and requiring him or her to pay that amount to the planning authority within such period, not being less than 12 weeks after the service of the notice, as may be specified in the notice, and, in default of the amount being paid to the planning authority within the period specified in the notice, it shall be recoverable as a simple contract debt in any court of competent jurisdiction.

Note
Section 189 restates s 10 of LG(PD)A 1990.

CHAPTER II   COMPENSATION IN RELATION TO DECISIONS UNDER PART III

[375]–[380]
190. Right to compensation
If, on a claim made to the planning authority, it is shown that, as a result of a decision on an appeal under Part III involving a refusal of permission to develop land or a grant of permission to develop land subject to conditions, the value of an interest of any person existing in the land to which the decision relates at the time of the decision is reduced, that person shall, subject to the other provisions of this Chapter, be entitled to be paid by the planning authority by way of compensation—

(a) such amount, representing the reduction in value, as may be agreed,
(b) in the absence of agreement, the amount of such reduction in value, determined in accordance with the Second Schedule, and
(c) in the case of the occupier of the land, the damage (if any) to his or her trade, business or profession carried out on the land.

Note
Section 190 restates s 11 of LG(PD)A 1990.

[381]
191. Restriction of compensation
(1) Compensation under section 190 shall not be payable in respect of the refusal of permission for any development—

(a)   of a class or description set out in the Third Schedule, or
(b)   if the reason or one of the reasons for the refusal is a reason set out in the Fourth Schedule.

(2) Compensation under section 190 shall not be payable in respect of the refusal of permission for any development based on any change of the zoning of any land as a result of the making of a new development plan under section 12.

(3) Compensation under section 190 shall not be payable in respect of the imposition, on the granting of permission to develop land, of any condition of a class or description set out in the Fifth Schedule.

(4) Compensation under section 190 shall not be payable in respect of the refusal of permission, or of the imposition of conditions on the granting of permission, for the retention on land of any unauthorised structures.

Note
Section 191 restates s 12 of LG(PD)A 1990, but note changes made to the Schedules detailed below.

[382]
192. Notice preventing compensation
(1) Where a claim for compensation is made under section 190, the planning authority concerned may, not later than 12 weeks after the claim is received, and having regard to all the circumstances of the case, serve a notice in such form as may be prescribed on the person by whom or on behalf of whom the claim has been made stating that, notwithstanding the refusal of permission to develop land or the grant of permission to develop land subject to conditions, the land in question is in its opinion capable of other development for which permission under Part III ought to be granted.

(2) For the purpose of subsection (1), "other development" means development of a residential, commercial or industrial character, consisting wholly or mainly of the construction of houses, shops or office premises, hotels, garages and petrol filling stations, theatres or structures for the purpose of entertainment, or industrial buildings (including warehouses), or any combination thereof.

(3) A notice under subsection (1) shall continue in force for a period of 5 years commencing on the day of service of the notice, unless before the expiration of that period—

(a)   the notice is withdrawn by the planning authority,
(b)   a permission is granted under Part III to develop the land to which the notice relates in a manner consistent with the other development specified in the notice, subject to no conditions or to conditions of a class or description set out in the Fifth Schedule, or
(c)   the notice is annulled by virtue of subsection (5).

(4) Compensation shall not be payable on a claim made under section 190 where—

(a)   a notice under subsection (1) is in force in relation to that claim,
(b)   a notice under subsection (1) was in force in relation to that claim but has ceased

to be in force by reason of the expiration of the period referred to in subsection (3), and an application for permission under Part III to develop the land to which the notice relates, in a manner consistent with the other development specified in the notice, has not been made within that period, or

(c) a notice under subsection (1) was in force in relation to the claim but has ceased to be in force by virtue of subsection (3) (b)

(5) A notice under subsection (1) shall be annulled where, upon an application for permission under Part III to develop the land to which the notice relates in a manner consistent with the other development specified in the notice, the permission is refused or is granted subject to conditions other than conditions of a class or description set out in the Fifth Schedule.

(6) No claim for compensation under section 190 shall lie in relation to a decision under Part III referred to in subsection (5).

Note
Section 192 restates s 13 of LG(PD)A 1990.

[383]
193. Special provision for structures substantially replacing structures demolished or destroyed by fire
(1) Nothing in section 191 shall prevent compensation being paid—

(a) in a case in which there has been a refusal of permission for the erection of a new structure substantially replacing a structure (other than an unauthorised structure) which has been demolished or destroyed by fire or otherwise than by an unlawful act of the owner or of the occupier with the agreement of the owner within the 2 years preceding the date of application for permission, or there has been imposed a condition in consequence of which the new structure may not be used for the purpose for which the demolished or destroyed structure was last used, or

(b) in a case in which there has been imposed a condition in consequence of which the new structure referred to in paragraph (a) or the front thereof, or the front of an existing structure (other than an unauthorised structure) which has been taken down in order to be re-erected or altered. is set back or forward.

(2) Every dispute and question as to whether a new structure would or does replace substantially within the meaning of subsection (1) a demolished or destroyed structure shall be referred to the Board for determination.

Note
Section 193 restates s 15 of LG(PD)A 1990; note the addition of sub-s (2).

[384]
194. Restriction on assignment of compensation under section 190
A person shall not be entitled to assign to any other person all or any part of any prospective compensation under section 190, under and every purported assignment or promise, express or implied, to pay any other person any money in respect of any such compensation is void.

Note
Section 194 restates s 16 of LG(PD)A 1990.

[385]–[390]
195. Compensation where permission is revoked or modified
(1) Where permission to develop land has been revoked or modified by a decision under section 44—

(a) if, on a claim made to the planning authority, it is shown that any person interested in the land has incurred expenditure or entered into a contract to incur expenditure in respect of works which are rendered abortive by the revocation or modification, the planning authority shall pay to that person compensation in respect of that expenditure or contract,
(b) the provisions of this Part shall apply in relation to the decision where it revoked the permission or modified it by the imposition of conditions—
   (i) in case it revoked the permission, as they apply in relation to refusal of permission to develop land, and
   (ii) in case it modified the permission by the imposition of conditions, as they apply in relation to a grant of permission to develop land subject to conditions.

(2) For the purposes of this section, any expenditure reasonably incurred in the preparation of plans for the purposes of any works or upon other similar matters preparatory thereto shall be deemed to be included in the expenditure incurred in carrying out those works but, no compensation shall be paid by virtue of this section in respect of any works carried out before the grant of the permission which is revoked or modified, or in respect of any other loss or damage arising out of anything done or omitted to be done before the grant of that permission.

Note
Section 195 restates s 17 of LG(PD)A 1990 with some amendments. Specifically, sub-s (1)(a) includes the extra words '. . . or entered into a contract to incur expenditure in respect of . . .' on the second line, and '. . . or contract' at the end of that sub-section. The deletion of the rider at the end of s 17(1)(b) of LG(PD)A 1990 is not material.

CHAPTER III   COMPENSATION IN RELATION TO SECTIONS 46, 85, 88, 182, 207 AND 252

[391]
196. Compensation regarding removal or alteration of structure
If, on a claim made to the planning authority, it is shown that as a result of the removal or alteration of any structure consequent upon a notice under section 46, the value of an interest of any person in the structure existing at the time of the confirmation of the notice is reduced, or that any person having an interest in the structure at that time has suffered damage by being disturbed in his or her enjoyment of the structure, that person shall, subject to the other provisions of this Part, be entitled to be paid by the planning authority by way of compensation the amount of the reduction in value or the amount of the damage.

Note
Section 196 restates s 18 of LG(PD)A 1990 save that s 18(2) of LG(PD)A 1990 has not been repeated in s 196.

[392]
197. Compensation regarding discontinuance of use

(1) If, on a claim made to the planning authority, it is shown that as a result of the discontinuance or the compliance with conditions on the continuance, of any use of land consequent upon a notice under section 46, the value of an interest of any person in the land existing at the time of the confirmation of the notice is reduced, or that any person having an interest in the land at that time has suffered damage by being disturbed in his or her enjoyment of the land, that person shall, subject to the other provisions in this Part, be entitled to be paid by the planning authority by way of compensation the amount of the reduction in value or the amount of the damage.

(2) Notwithstanding subsection (1), no compensation shall be paid under this section in relation to reduction in value or damage resulting from the imposition under section 46 of conditions on the continuance of the use of land, being conditions imposed in order to avoid or reduce serious water pollution or the danger of such pollution.

(3) Subsection (1) shall not apply where the use of land is for the exhibition of advertising unless at the time of the discontinuance or compliance, the land has been used for the exhibition of advertising for less than 5 years, whether the use was continuous or intermittent or whether or not, while the land was being so used. advertising was exhibited at the same place on the land.

Note
Section 197 restates s 19 of LG(PD)A 1990 save that s 19(3) of LG(PD)A 1990 is not repeated.

[393]
198. Compensation claim relating to area of special planning control

If, on a claim made to a planning authority, it is shown that—

(a) the value of an interest of any person in land in an area of special planning control has been reduced, or

(b) as a result of complying with a notice under section 88, the value of an interest of any person in the land existing at the time of the notice has been reduced, or that any person, having an interest in the land at the time, has suffered damage by being disturbed in his or her enjoyment of the structure or other land, that person shall be paid by the planning authority, by way of compensation, a sum equal to the amount of the reduction in value or a sum in respect of the damage suffered.

Note
Section 198 is new and provides for compensation claims relative to areas of special planning control.

[394]
199. Compensation regarding cables, wires and pipelines

If, on a claim made to the local authority, it is shown that, as a result of the action of the authority pursuant to section 182 in placing, renewing or removing any cable, wire or pipeline, attaching any bracket or fixture or affixing any notice, the value of an interest of any person in the land or structure existing at the time of the action of the planning authority is reduced, or that any person having an interest in the land or structure at that time has suffered damage by being disturbed in his or her enjoyment of the land or structure, that person shall, subject to the other provisions of this Part, be entitled to be paid by the local authority by way of compensation the amount of the reduction in value or the amount of the damage.

Note
Section 199 restates s 24 of LG(PD)A 1990.

[395]–[400]
200. Compensation regarding creation of public rights of way
If, on a claim made to the planning authority, it is shown that the value of an interest of any person in land, being land over which a public right of way has been created by an order under section 207 made by that authority, is reduced, or that any person having an interest in the land has suffered damage by being disturbed in his or her enjoyment of the land, in consequence of the creation of the public right of way, that person shall, subject to the other provisions of this Part, be entitled to be paid by the planning authority by way of compensation the amount of the reduction in value or the amount of the damage.

Note
Section 200 restates s 22 of LG(PD)A 1990.

[401]
201. Compensation regarding entry on land
If, on a claim made to the planning authority, it is shown that, as a result of anything done under section 252 or 253, any person has suffered damage, the person shall, subject to the other provisions of this Part, be entitled to be paid by the planning authority by way of compensation the amount of the damage.

Note
Section 201 restates s 23 of LG(PD)A 1990.

PART XIII   AMENITIES

Notes
Part XIII re-enacts the provisions of Pt V of LG(PD)A 1963 with some changes.

This Part has not been commenced.

[402]
202. Area of special amenity
(1) Where, in the opinion of the planning authority, by reason of—

(a) its outstanding natural beauty, or
(b) its special recreational value,

and having regard to any benefits for nature conservation, an area should be declared under this section to be an area of special amenity, it may, by resolution,

make an order to do so and the order may state the objective of the planning authority in relation to the preservation or enhancement of the character or special features
of the area, including objectives for the prevention or limitation of development in
the area.

(2) Where it appears to the Minister that an area should be declared under this section to be an area of special amenity by reason of—

(a) its outstanding natural beauty, or
(b) its special recreational value,

and having regard to any benefits for nature conservation, he or she may, if he or she
considers it necessary, direct a planning authority to make an order under this section
in relation to an area specified in the direction and may, if he or she thinks fit, require
that objectives specified in the direction be included by the planning authority in the
order in respect of matters and in a manner so specified, and if the Minister gives a
direction under this subsection the planning authority concerned shall comply with
the direction.

(3) An order made pursuant to a direction under subsection (2) shall be revoked or
amended only with the consent of the Minister.

(4) An order under this section shall come into operation on being confirmed,
whether with or without modification, under section 203.

(5) Where the functional areas of two planning authorities are contiguous, either
authority may, with the consent of the other, make an order under this section in
respect of an area in or partly in the functional area of the other.

(6) Any order under this section may be revoked or varied by a subsequent order
under this section.

(7) Subject to subsection (3), a planning authority may, from time to time, review an
order made under this section (excepting any order merely revoking a previous
order), for the purpose of deciding whether it is desirable to revoke or amend the
order.

Note
Section 202 restates s 46 of LG(PD)A 1963 with some changes. See in particular the changed
reference to nature conservation and the explicit statement of the Minister's objectives in
sub-s (2).

[403]
203. Confirmation of order under section 202
(1) As soon as may be after it has made an order under section 202, a planning
authority shall publish in one or more newspapers circulating in the area to which the
order relates a notice—

(a) stating the fact of the order having been made, and describing the area to which
it relates,
(b) naming a place where a copy of the order and of any map referred to therein may
be seen during office hours,

(c) specifying the period (not being less than 4 weeks) within which, and the manner in which, objections to the order may be made to the planning authority, and
(d) specifying that the order requires confirmation by the Board and that, where any objections are duly made to the order and are not withdrawn, an oral hearing will be held and the objections will be considered before the order is confirmed.

(2) As soon as may be after the period for making objections has expired, the planning authority may submit the order made under section 202 to the Board for confirmation, and, when making any such submission, it shall also submit to the Board any objections to the order which have been duly made and have not been withdrawn

(3) (a) If no objection is duly made to the order, or if all objections so made are withdrawn, the Board may confirm the order made under section 202, with or without modifications, or refuse to confirm it.
(b) Where any objections to the order are not withdrawn, the Board shall hold an oral hearing and shall consider the objections, and may then confirm the order, with or without modifications, or refuse to confirm it.

(4) Any reference in this Act, or any other enactment, to a special amenity area order shall be construed as a reference to an order confirmed under this section.

Note
Section 203 restates s 43 of LG(PD)A 1963 with the principal change being that the function of confirming a special amenity order has now passed to the Board from the Minister.

[404]
204. Landscape conservation areas
(1) A planning authority may, by order, for the purposes of the preservation of the landscape, designate any area or place within the functional area of the authority as a landscape conservation area.

(2) (a) Notwithstanding any exemption granted under section 4 or under any regulations made under that section, the Minister may prescribe development for the purpose of this section, which shall not be exempted development.
(b) Development prescribed under paragraph (a) may be subject to any conditions or restrictions that the Minister may prescribe.

(3) An order made by a planning authority under this section may specify, in relation to all or any part of the landscape conservation area, that any development prescribed by the Minister under subsection (2) shall be considered not to be exempted development in that area.

(4) Where a planning authority proposes to make an order under this section, it shall cause notice of the proposed order to be published in one or more newspapers circulating in the area of the proposed landscape conservation area.

(5) A notice under subsection (4) shall state that—

(a) the planning authority proposes to make an order designating a landscape conservation area, indicating the place or places and times at which a map outlining the area may be inspected, and shall give details of the location of the area and any prescribed development which it proposes to specify in the order, and
(b) submissions or observations regarding the proposed order may be made to the

planning authority within a stated period of not less than 6 weeks, and that the submissions or observations will be taken into consideration by the planning authority.

(6) The members of a planning authority, having considered the proposed order and any submissions or observations made in respect of it, may, as they consider appropriate, by resolution, make the order, with or without modifications, or refuse to make the order.

(7) Where a planning authority wishes to amend or revoke an order made under this section, the planning authority shall give notice of its intention to amend or revoke the order, as the case may be.

(8) A notice under subsection (7) (which shall include particulars of the proposed amendment or revocation of the order) shall be published in one or more newspapers circulating in the landscape conservation area.

(9) A notice under subsection (7) shall state that—

(a) the planning authority proposes to amend or revoke the order, and
(b) submissions or observations regarding the proposed amendment or revocation of the order may be made to the planning authority within a stated period of not less than 6 weeks, and that the submissions or observations will be taken into consideration by the planning authority.

(10) The planning authority, having considered the proposed amendment or revocation of the order and any submissions or observations made in respect of it, may by resolution, as it considers appropriate, revoke the order or amend the order, with or without modifications, or refuse to make the order, as the case may be.

(11) Before making an order under this section, the planning authority shall consult with any State authority where it considers that any order relates to the functions of that State authority.

(12) (a) A planning authority shall give notice of any order made under this section in at least one newspaper circulating in its functional area, and the notice shall give details of any prescribed development which is specified in the order.
(b) Notice under this subsection shall also be given to the Board and to any other prescribed body which in the opinion of the planning authority has an interest in such notice.

(13) Where 2 or more planning authorities propose to jointly designate any area or place, which is situated within the combined functional area of the planning authorities concerned, as a landscape conservation area, the functions conferred on a planning authority under this section shall be performed jointly by the planning authorities concerned, and any reference to "planning authority" shall be construed accordingly.

(14) Particulars of an order under this section shall be entered in the register.

Note

This is a new power that provides for the designation of landscape conservation areas by planning authorities. Section 204 sets out the procedure that has to be followed and prescribes that development within such areas will not be exempt where otherwise it would be pursuant to s 4 of PDA 2000.

[405]–[410]
205. Tree preservation orders

(1) If it appears to the planning authority that it is expedient, in the interests of amenity or the environment, to make provision for the preservation of any tree, trees, group of trees or wood lands, it may, for that purpose and for stated reasons, make an order with respect to any such tree, trees, group of trees or woodlands as may be specified in the order.

(2) Without prejudice to the generality of subsection (1), an order under this section may—

(a) prohibit (subject to any conditions or exemptions for which provision may be made by the order) the cutting down, topping, lopping or wilful destruction of trees, and

(b) require the owner and occupier of the land affected by the order to enter into an agreement with the planning authority to ensure the proper management of any trees, group of trees or woodlands (including the replanting of trees), subject to the planning authority providing assistance, including financial assistance, towards such management as may be agreed.

(3) (a) Where a planning authority proposes to make an order under this section, it shall—

    (i) serve a notice (which shall include particulars of the proposed order) of its intention to do so on the owner and the occupier of the land affected by the order, and

    (ii) cause notice of the proposed order to be published in one or more newspapers circulating in its functional area.

(b) A notice under paragraph (a)(i) shall be accompanied by a map indicating the tree, trees, group of trees or woodland to be preserved.

(4) A notice under subsection (3) shall state that—

(a) the planning authority proposes to make an order preserving the tree, trees, group of trees or woodlands,

(b) submissions or observations regarding the proposed order may be made to the planning authority within a stated period of not less than 6 weeks, and that the submissions or observations will be taken into consideration by the planning authority, and

(c) any person who contravenes an order or, pending the decision of a planning authority, a proposed order under this section, shall be guilty of an offence.

(5) The planning authority, having considered the proposal and any submissions or observations made in respect of it, may by resolution, as it considers appropriate, make the order, with or without modifications, or refuse to make the order, and any person on whom notice has been served under subsection (3) shall be notified accordingly

(6) Where a planning authority intends to amend or revoke an order made under this section, the planning authority shall give notice of its intention to amend or revoke the order, as the case may be.

(7) (a) A notice under subsection (6) (which shall include particulars of the proposed order) shall be—

    (i)   served on the owner and the occupier of the land affected by the order, and on any other person on whom a notice was served under subsection (3), and

    (ii)   published in one or more newspapers circulating in the functional area of the planning authority.

(b) A notice under subsection (6) shall be accompanied by a map indicating the tree, trees, group of trees or woodland to be affected by the amendment or revocation of the order.

(8) A notice under subsection (6) shall state that—

(a) the planning authority proposes to amend or revoke the order, and

(b) submissions or observations regarding the proposal may be made to the planning authority within a stated period of not less than 6 weeks, and that the submissions or observations will be taken into consideration by the planning authority.

(9) The planning authority, having considered the proposal and any submissions or observations made in respect of it, may by resolution, as it considers appropriate, revoke the order or amend the order, with or without modifications, or refuse to make the order, as the case may be, and any person on whom notice has been served under subsection (7) shall be notified accordingly.

(10) Any person who contravenes an order or, pending the decision of a planning authority, a proposed order under this section, shall be guilty of an offence.

(11) Without prejudice to any other exemption for which provision may be made by an order under this section, no such order shall apply to the cutting down, topping or lopping of trees which are dying or dead or have become dangerous, or the cutting down, topping or lopping of any trees in compliance with any obligation imposed by or under any enactment or so far as may be necessary for the prevention or abatement of a nuisance or hazard.

(12) Particulars of an order under this section shall be entered in the register.

Note
Section 205 replaces s 45 of LG(PD)A 1963 as amended by LG(PD)A 1976 relative to the making of tree preservation orders. Submissions can be made in relation to proposed orders to the planning authority who must consider same. There is no longer any right of appeal to the Board.

[411]
206. Creation of public rights of way agreement
(1) A planning authority may enter into an agreement with any person having the necessary power in that behalf for the creation, by dedication by that person, of a public right of way over land.

(2) An agreement made under this section shall be on such terms as to payment or otherwise as may be specified in the agreement, and may, if it is so agreed, provide for limitations or conditions affecting the public right of way.

(3) Where an agreement has been made under this section, it shall be the duty of the planning authority to take all necessary steps for securing that the creation of the public right of way is effected in accordance with the agreement.

(4) Particulars of an agreement made under this section shall be entered in the register.

Note
Section 206 restates s 47 of LG(PD)A 1963.

207. Compulsory powers for creation of pubic rights of way
(1) If it appears to the planning authority that there is need for a public right of way over any land, the planning authority may, by resolution, make an order creating a public right of way over the land.

(2) (a) Where a planning authority proposes to make an order under this section, it shall—
    (i) serve a notice (which shall include particulars of the proposed order) of its intention to do so on the owner and the occupier of the land over which the public right of way is proposed to be created and on any other person who in its opinion will be affected by the creation of the public right of way, and
    (ii) cause notice of the proposed order to be published in one or more newspapers circulating in its functional area.
(b) A notice under paragraph (a)(i) shall be accompanied by a map indicating the public right of way to be created.

(3) A notice under subsection (2) shall state that—

(a) the planning authority proposes to make an order creating the public right of way, and
(b) submissions or observations regarding the proposed order may be made to the planning authority within a stated period of not less than 6 weeks and that the submissions or observations will be taken into consideration by the planning authority.

(4) The planning authority, having considered the proposal and any submissions or observations made in respect of it, may by resolution, as it considers appropriate, make the order, with or without modifications, or refuse to make the order and any person on whom notice has been served under subsection (2) shall be notified accordingly.

(5) Any person who has been notified of the making of an order under subsection (4) may appeal to the Board against the order within 4 weeks of being notified under that subsection.

(6) Where an appeal is brought under this section against an order, the Board may confirm the order with or without modifications or annul the order.

(7) An order under this section (other than an order which is annulled) shall take effect—

(a) in case no appeal against it is taken or every appeal against it is withdrawn before the expiration of the period for taking an appeal, on the expiration of the period for taking an appeal, or
(b) in case an appeal or appeals is or are taken against it and the appeal or appeals is or are not withdrawn during the period for taking an appeal, when every appeal not so withdrawn has been either withdrawn or determined.

(8) Particulars of a right of way created under this section shall be entered in the register.

(9) Any public right of way created under an enactment repealed by this Act that was in force immediately before the commencement of this section shall be deemed to have been made under this section.

Note
Section 207 restates s 48 of LG(PD)A 1963 with the addition of sub-s (2)(a)(ii) and (2)(b). Note the appeal period.

[413]
208. Supplemental provisions with respect to public right of way
(1) Where a public right of way is created pursuant to this Act, or where a provision in a development plan in force on the commencement of this section relates to the preservation of a public right of way, the way shall be maintained by the planning authority.

(2) (a) Where a right of way is required by this section to be maintained by the plan- ning authority, a person shall not damage or obstruct the way, or hinder or inter- fere with the exercise of the right of way.
(b) A person who contravenes this subsection shall be guilty of an offence.

(3) Where, in the case of a right of way required by this section to be maintained by the planning authority, the way is damaged or obstructed by any person, the planning authority maintaining the right of way may repair the damage or remove the obstruc- tion, and the expenses incurred by it in the repair or removal shall be paid to them by that person and, in default of being so paid, shall be recover able from him or her as a simple contract debt in any court of competent jurisdiction.

Note
Section 208 restates s 49 of LG(PD)A 1963.

[414]
209. Repair and tidying of advertisement structures and advertisement
(1) If it appears to a planning authority that, having regard to the interests of public safety or amenity, an advertisement structure or advertisement in its area should be repaired or tidied, the planning authority may serve on the person having control of the structure or advertisement a notice requiring that person to repair or tidy the advertisement structure or advertisement within a specified period.

(2) If it appears to a planning authority that any advertisement structure or adver- tisement is derelict, the planning authority may serve on the person having control of the structure or advertisement a notice requiring that person to remove the advertise- ment structure or advertisement within a specified period.

(3) If within the period specified in a notice under this section, the advertisement structure or advertisement is not repaired or tidied, or removed, as the case may be, the planning authority may enter on the land on which the structure is situate or the advertisement is exhibited and repair, tidy or remove the structure or advertisement and may recover as a simple contract debt in any court of competent jurisdiction

from the person having control of the structure or advertisement any expenses reasonably incurred by it in that behalf.

Note

Section 209 restates s 54 of LG(PD)A 1963 and grants a new power at sub-s (2) whereby a planning authority can require a person having control of a structure or advertisement to remove same. Sub-s (3) provides that if this is not done, the local authority can do so and recover the cost of the simple contract debt.

PART XIV   ACQUISITION OF LAND, ETC.

Note

Part XIV restates with modifications certain provisions of Pt VII of LG(PD)A 1963 regarding the powers of local authorities relative to the acquisition of land. Part XIV commenced on 1 January 2001 pursuant to SI 449/2000.

[415]–[420]
210. Appropriation of land for local authority purposes
(1) Where—

(a) land is vested in a local authority for the purposes of its functions under this or any other enactment, and
(b) the local authority is satisfied that the land should be made available for the purposes of any of those functions, the local authority may appropriate the land for those purposes.

(2) Where land is vested in a local authority by means of compulsory acquisition under any enactment, no claim shall be made for compensation or additional compensation and the acquisition shall not be challenged on account of any appropriation of land in accordance with subsection (1).

Note

Section 210 amends s 74 of the LG(PD)A 1963.

[421]
211. Disposal of land by local authority
(1) Any land acquired for the purposes of or appropriated under this Act or any other Act or acquired otherwise, by a local authority, may be sold, leased or exchanged, subject to such conditions as it may consider necessary where it no longer requires the land for any of its functions, or in order to secure—

(a) the best use of that or other land, and any structures or works which have been, or are to be, constructed, erected, made or carried out on, in or under that or other land, or
(b) the construction, erection, making or carrying out of any structures or works appearing to it to be needed for the proper planning and sustainable development of its functional area.

(2) The consent of the Minister shall, subject to subsection (3), be required for any sale, lease or exchange under subsection (1) in case the price or rent, or what is obtained by the local authority on the exchange, is not the best reasonably obtainable,

but in any other case, shall not be required notwithstanding the provisions of any other enactment.

(3) The Minister may by regulations provide for the disposal of land under subsection (1) without the consent of the Minister as required by subsection (2) in such circumstances as may be specified in the regulations and subject to compliance with such conditions (including conditions for the giving of public notice) as may be so specified.

(4) Capital money arising from the disposal of land under subsection (1) shall be applied for a capital purpose for which capital money may be properly applied.

(5) (a) Where, as respects any land acquired for the purposes of or appropriated under this or any other Act or acquired otherwise by a local authority, the authority considers that it will not require the use of the land for any of its functions for a particular period, the authority may grant a lease of the land for that period or any lesser period and the lease shall be expressed as a lease granted for the purposes of this subsection.

(b) The Landlord and Tenant Acts, 1967 to 1994, shall not apply in relation to a lease granted under paragraph (a) for the purposes of this subsection.

Note
Section 211 is effectively a restatement of s 75 of LG(PD)A 1963 with some modifications. In particular, see s 211(3).

[422]
212. Development by planning authority etc
(1) A planning authority may develop or secure or facilitate the development of land and, in particular and without prejudice to the generality of the foregoing, may do one or more of the following:

(a) secure, facilitate and control the improvement of the frontage of any public road by widening, opening, enlarging or otherwise improving;

(b) develop any land in the vicinity of any road or public transport facility which it is proposed to improve or construct;

(c) provide areas with roads, infrastructure facilitating public transport and such services and works as may be needed for development;

(d) provide, secure or facilitate the provision of areas of convenient shape and size for development;

(e) secure, facilitate or carry out the development and renewal of areas in need of physical, social or economic regeneration and provide open spaces and other public am entities;

(f) secure the preservation of any view or prospect, any protected structure or other structure, any architectural conservation area or natural physical feature, any trees or woodlands or any site of archaeological, geological, historical, scientific or ecological interest.

(2) A planning authority may provide or arrange for the provision of—

(a) sites for the establishment or relocation of industries, businesses (including hotels, motels and guesthouses), houses, offices, shops, schools, churches,

leisure facilities and other community facilities and of such buildings, premises, houses, parks and structures as are referred to in paragraph (b),
(b) factory buildings, office premises, shop premises, houses, amusement parks and structures for the purpose of entertainment, caravan parks, buildings for the purpose of providing accommodation, meals and refreshments, buildings for the purpose of providing trade and professional services and advertisement structures,
(c) transport facilities, including public and air transport facilities, and
(d) any services which it considers ancillary to anything which is referred to in paragraph (a), (b) or (c), and may maintain and manage any such site, building, premises, house, park, structure or service and may make any charges which it considers reasonable in relation to the provision, maintenance or management thereof.

(3) A planning authority may, in connection with any of its functions under this Act, make and carry out arrangements or enter into agreements with any person or body for the development or management of land, and may incorporate a company for those purposes.

(4) A planning authority may use any of the powers available to it under any enactment, including any powers in relation to the compulsory acquisition of land, in relation to its functions under this section and in particular in order to facilitate the assembly of sites for the purposes of the orderly development of land.

Note
This section effectively restates s 77 of LG(PD)A 1963 with some minor amendments.

[423]
213. Land acquisition by local authorities
(1) The power conferred on a local authority under any enactment to acquire land shall be construed in accordance with this section.

(2) (a) A local authority may, for the purposes of performing any of its functions (whether conferred by or under this Act, or any other enactment passed before or after the passing of this Act), including giving effect to or facilitating the implementation of its development plan or its housing strategy under section 94, do all or any of the following:
    (i) acquire land, permanently or temporarily, by agreement or compulsorily,
    (ii) acquire, permanently or temporarily, by agreement or compulsorily, any easement, way-leave, water-right or other right over or in respect of any land or water or any substratum of land,
    (iii) restrict or otherwise interfere with, permanently or temporarily, by agreement or compulsorily, any easement, way-leave, water-right or other right over or in respect of any land or water or any substratum of land,
    and the performance of all or any of the functions referred to in subparagraphs (i), (ii) and (iii) are referred to in this Act as an "acquisition of land".
(b) A reference in paragraph (a) to acquisition by agreement shall include acquisition by way of purchase, lease, exchange or otherwise.
(c) The functions conferred on a local authority by paragraph (a) may be performed in relation to—

(i) land, or

(ii) any easement, way-leave, water-right or other right to which that paragraph applies,

whether situated or exercisable, as the case may be, inside or outside the functional area of the local authority concerned.

(3) (a) The acquisition may be effected by agreement or compulsorily in respect of land not immediately required for a particular purpose if, in the opinion of the local authority, the land will be required by the authority for that purpose in the future.

(b) The acquisition may be effected by agreement in respect of any land which, in the opinion of the local authority, it will require in the future for the purposes of any of its functions notwithstanding that the authority has not determined the manner in which or the purpose for which it will use the land.

(c) Paragraphs (a) and (b) shall apply and have effect in relation to any power to acquire land conferred on a local authority by virtue of this Act or any other enactment whether enacted before or after this Act.

(4) A local authority may be authorised by compulsory purchase order to acquire land for any of the purposes referred to in subsection (2) of this section and section 10 (as amended by section 86 of the Housing Act, 1966) of the Local Government (No. 2) Act, 1960, shall be construed so as to apply accordingly and the reference to "purposes" in section 10(1)(a) of that Act shall be construed as including purposes referred to in subsection (2) of this section.

Note
Section 213 states that where a local authority has a power to acquire land under any existing legislation then the provisions of s 213 shall apply to those powers. A local authority is given the power for the purpose of performing any of its functions including giving effect to facilitating the implementation of its development plan or its housing strategy, to acquire land temporarily or permanently and by agreement or compulsorily. It may also acquire any easements, way leaves or other rights or may restrict or curtail permanently or temporarily and by agreement or compulsorily any existing easements, way leaves or other rights whether or not the land in question is within or outside the functional area of the local authority and whether or not the land is immediately required.

[424]
214. Transfer of Minister's functions in relation to compulsory acquisition of land to Board
(1) The functions conferred on the Minister in relation to the compulsory acquisition of land by a local authority under the following enactments are hereby transferred to, and vested in, the Board and any reference in any relevant provision of those Acts to the Minister, or construed to be a reference to the Minister, shall be deemed to be a reference to the Board except that any powers under those enactments to make regulations or to prescribe any matter shall remain with the Minister:

Public Health (Ireland) Act, 1878;
Local Government (Ireland) Act, 1898;
Local Government Act, 1925;
Water Supplies Act, 1942;

Local Government (No. 2) Act, 1960;
Local Government (Sanitary Services) Act, 1964;
Housing Act, 1966;
Derelict Sites Act, 1990;
Roads Acts, 1993 and 1998;
Dublin Docklands Development Authority Act, 1997.

(2) For the purposes of the compulsory acquisition of land by a local authority the following constructions shall apply:

(a) the references construed to be references to the Minister in section 203 of the Public Health (Ireland) Act, 1878, shall be construed as referring to the Board and any connected references shall be construed accordingly;

(b) the references to the Minister in section 68 of, and in the Sixth Schedule to, the Local Government Act, 1925, shall be construed as referring to the Board and any connected references shall be construed accordingly;

(c) the references to the Minister in sections 4, 8, 9 and 10 of, and in the Schedule to, the Water Supplies Act, 1942, shall be construed as referring to the Board and any connected references shall be construed accordingly;

(d) the references to the Minister, or to the appropriate Minister, in section 10 (as amended by section 86 of the Housing Act, 1966) of the Local Government (No. 2) Act, 1960, shall be construed as referring to the Board and any connected references shall be construed accordingly;

(e) the references to the Minister in sections 7, 8, 9 and 16 of the Local Government (Sanitary Services) Act, 1964, shall be construed as referring to the Board and any connected references shall be construed accordingly;

(f) (i) the references to the Minister, or to the appropriate Minister, in sections 76, 77, 78, 80 and 85 of, and the Third Schedule to, the Housing Act, 1966, shall be construed as referring to the Board and any connected references shall be construed accordingly;

    (ii) section 85 of the Housing Act, 1966, shall be construed as if subsections (2) and (3) were deleted;

(g) the references to the Minister in sections 16 and 17 of the Derelict Sites Act, 1990, shall be construed as referring to the Board and any connected references shall be construed accordingly;

(h) the references to the Minister in section 27(1) of the Dublin Docklands Development Authority Act, 1997, shall be construed as referring to the Board and any connected references shall be construed accordingly.

(3) The transfer of the Minister's functions to the Board in relation to the compulsory purchase of land in accordance with subsection (1) shall include the transfer of all necessary ancillary powers in relation to substrata, easements, rights over land (including public rights of way), rights of access to land, the revocation or modification of planning permissions or other such functions as may be necessary in order to ensure that the Board can fully carry out its functions in relation to the enactments referred to in subsection (1).

(4) In this section and section 216, "local authority" includes the Dublin Docklands Development Authority.

Note
The functions which were conferred on the Minister for the Environment in relation to compulsory acquisition of land by a local authority under certain legislation as set out in s 214 are now conferred on An Bord Pleanála.

[425]–[430]
215. Transfer of Ministerial functions under Road Acts, 1993 and 1998, to Board

(1) The functions of the Minister in relation to a scheme or certain proposed road development under sections 49, 50 and 51 of the Roads Act, 1993, are hereby transferred to and vested in the Board and relevant references in that Act to the Minister shall be construed as references to the Board and any connected references shall be construed accordingly, except that any powers under those sections to make regulations or to prescribe any matter shall remain with the Minister.

(2) The references to the Minister in section 19(7) and paragraphs (a), (c), (e) and (f) of section 20(1) of the Roads Act, 1993, shall be deemed to be references to the Board.

Note
The functions of the Minister under the Roads Acts 1993 to 1998 are now transferred from the Minister to the Board.

[431]
216. Confirmation of compulsory purchase order objections

(1) Where a compulsory purchase order is made in respect of the acquisition of land by a local authority in accordance with any of the enactments referred to in section 214(1) and—

(a) no objections are received by the Board or the local authority, as the case may be, within the period provided for making objections,
(b) any objection received is subsequently withdrawn at any time before the Board makes its decision. or
(c) the Board is of opinion that any objection received relates exclusively to matters which can be dealt with by a property arbitrator, the Board shall, where appropriate, inform the local authority and the local authority shall, as soon as may be, confirm the order with or without modification, or it may refuse to confirm the order.

(2) Subsection (1) shall not prejudice any requirement to obtain approval for a scheme in accordance with section 49 of the Roads Act, 1993, or proposed road development in accordance with section 51 of the Roads Act, 1993, or for proposed development under section 175 of this Act.

(3) This section shall not apply with respect to a compulsory purchase under the Derelict Sites Act, 1990.

Note
Section 216 is a new provision which states that where there are no objections or objections are withdrawn or where objections relate exclusively to matters that could be dealt with by a property arbitrator then a local authority is enabled to confirm a compulsory purchase order without seeking the Board's confirmation.

[432]
217. Certain time limits in respect of purchase of land, etc

(1) Where an objection is made to a sanitary authority in accordance with section 6 of the Water Supplies Act, 1942, and not withdrawn, the sanitary authority shall, within 6 weeks of receiving the objection, apply to the Board for a provisional order in accordance with section 8 of that Act.

(2) Where an objection is made to a sanitary authority in accordance with section 8 of the Local Government (Sanitary Services) Act, 1964, and not withdrawn, the sanitary authority shall, within 6 weeks of receiving the objection, apply to the Board for its consent to the compulsory acquisition of the land in accordance with that section.

(3) Subject to section 216, where a local authority complies with the notification provisions in relation to a compulsory purchase order under paragraph 4 of the Third Schedule to the Housing Act, 1966, it shall, within 6 weeks of complying with those provisions, submit the compulsory purchase order to the Board for confirmation.

(4) Where a road authority complies with the notification provisions in relation to a scheme in accordance with section 48 of the Roads Act, 1993, it shall, within 6 weeks of complying with those provisions, submit the scheme to the Board for approval.

(5) A notice of the making of a confirmation order to be published or served, as the case may be, in accordance with section 78(1) of the Housing Act, 1966, shall be published or served within 12 weeks of the making of the confirmation order.

(6) Notwithstanding section 123 of the Lands Clauses Consolidation Act, 1845, where a compulsory purchase order or provisional order is confirmed by a local authority or the Board and becomes operative and the local authority decides to acquire land to which the order relates, the local authority shall serve any notice required under any enactment to be served in order to treat for the purchase of the several interests in the land (including under section 79 of the Housing Act, 1966) within 18 months of the order becoming operative.

(7) (a) A decision of the Board made in the performance of a function transferred to it under section 214 or 215 shall become operative 3 weeks from the date on which notice of the decision is first published.

(b) Subsections (8) and (9) of section 52 of the Roads Act, 1993 (as inserted by section 5 of the Roads (Amendment) Act, 1998) and subsections (2) to (4) of section 78 of the Housing Act, 1966, shall not apply in relation to decisions of the Board under this Part.

Note
Section 217 is new and provides for time limits for the submission of proposed CPOs to the Board for its confirmation.

[433]
218. Oral hearings in relation to compulsorily acquisition of land

(1) Where, as a result of the transfer of functions under sections 214 and 215, the Board would otherwise be required to hold a local inquiry or public local inquiry in regard to any of its transferred functions, it shall instead hold an oral hearing.

(2) For the avoidance of doubt, it is hereby declared that the provisions of the Local Government Acts, 1941, 1946, 1955 and 1991, in relation to public local inquiries shall not apply in relation to oral hearings held by the Board in accordance with subsection (1).

(3) For the purposes of this Part, the references to local inquiries or public local inquiries in the following provisions shall be deemed to be references to oral hearings under this section:

(a) section 10 of the Local Government (No. 2) Act, 1960;
(b) section 78 of, and the Third Schedule to, the Housing Act, 1966;
(c) Part IV of the Roads Act, 1993.

(4) Sections 135, 143 and 146 shall apply and have effect in relation to the functions transferred to the Board under sections 214 and 215 and those sections shall be construed accordingly.

Note
This new section provides that where objections to the CPO are received, an oral hearing rather than a local inquiry or a public local inquiry shall be held.

[434]
219. Power to direct payment of certain costs in relation to oral hearing
(1) Where an oral hearing is held under section 218, the Board may in its absolute discretion direct the payment of such sum as it considers reasonable by a local authority concerned in the oral hearing—

(a) to the Board towards the costs incurred by the Board in holding the hearing,
(b) to any person appearing at the hearing as a contribution towards the costs, other than the costs referred to in section 135, incurred by that person,

and the local authority shall pay the sum.

(2) A reference to costs in subsection (1) shall be construed and have effect as a reference to such costs as the Board in its absolute discretion considers to be reasonable costs.

(3) Where a local authority fails to pay a sum as directed in accordance with subsection (1), the Board or any other person concerned (as may be appropriate) may recover the sum as a simple contract debt in any court of competent jurisdiction.

Note
The Board has a discretion under this new section to order that the costs of parties in an oral hearing to be paid by the local authority.

[435]–[440]
220. Certain procedures to run in parallel
(1) The person holding an oral hearing in relation to the compulsory acquisition of land, which relates wholly or in part to proposed development by a local authority which is required to comply with section 175 or any other statutory provision to comply with procedures for giving effect to the Council Directive, shall be entitled to hear evidence in relation to the likely effects on the environment of such development.

(2) Where an application for the approval of a proposed development which is required to comply with section 175 is made to the Board and a compulsory purchase order or provisional order has been submitted to the Board for confirmation and where the proposed development relates wholly or in part to the same proposed development, the Board shall, where objections have been received in relation to the compulsory purchase order, make a decision on the confirmation of the compulsory purchase order at the same time.

Note
Where an oral hearing is being conducted in respect of the compulsory purchase of land which relates wholly or partly to local authority development for which an EIA is required, the person conducting the oral hearing shall be entitled to hear evidence relating to the likely effects of the proposed development on the environment.

[441]
221. Objective of the Board in relation to transferred functions
(1) It shall be the duty of the Board to ensure that any matters submitted in accordance with the functions transferred to it under sections 214 and 215 are disposed of as expeditiously as may be and, for that purpose, to take all such steps as are open to it to ensure that, in so far as is practicable, there are no avoidable delays at any stage in the determination of those matters.

(2) Without prejudice to the generality of subsection (1) and subject to subsections (3), (4), (5) and (6), it shall be the objective of the Board to ensure that—

(a) the matter is determined within a period of 18 weeks beginning on the last day for making objections, observations or submissions, as the case may be, in accordance with the relevant enactment referred to in section 214 or 215, or

(b) the matter is determined within such other period as the Minister may prescribe in relation to paragraph (a), either generally or in respect of a particular class or classes of matter.

(3) (a) Where it appears to the Board that it would not be possible or appropriate, because of the particular circumstances of the matter with which the Board is concerned, to determine the matter within the period prescribed under subsection (2), the Board shall, by notice in writing served on any local authority involved and any other person who submitted objections, representations, submissions or observations in relation to the matter before the expiration of that period, inform the authority and those persons of the reasons why it would not be possible or appropriate to determine the matter within that period and shall specify the date before which the Board intends that the matter shall be determined.

(b) Where a notice has been served under paragraph (a), the Board shall take all such steps as are open to it to ensure that the matter is determined before the date specified in the notice.

(4) The Minister may by regulations vary the period as specified in subsection (2) either generally or in respect of a particular class or classes of matters with which the Board is concerned, in accordance with the transferred functions under this Part, where it appears to him or her to be necessary, by virtue of exceptional circumstances, to do so and, for so long as the regulations are in force, this section shall be construed and have effect in accordance therewith.

(5) Where the Minister considers it to be necessary or expedient that certain functions of the Board (being functions transferred under section 214 or 215) performable in relation to matters of a class or classes that—

(a) are of special strategic, economic or social importance to the State, and
(b) are submitted to the Board for the performance by it of such functions, be performed as expeditiously as is consistent with proper planning and sustainable development, he or she may give a direction to the Board that in the performance of the functions concerned priority be given to matters of the class or classes concerned, and the Board shall comply with such direction.

(6) Subsection (2) shall not apply in relation to the functions under the Public Health (Ireland) Act, 1878, the Local Government Act, 1925, or the Water Supplies Act, 1942, which are transferred to the Board under section 214.

(7) For the purposes of meeting its duty under this section, the chairperson may, or shall when so directed by the Minister, assign the functions transferred to the Board under sections 214 and 215 to a particular division of the Board in accordance with section 112.

(8) The Board shall include in each report made under section 118 a statement of the number of matters which the Board has determined within a period referred to in paragraph (a) or (b) of subsection (2) and such other information as to the time taken to determine such matters as the Minister may direct.

Note
Section 221 provides that the Board should, in relation to the new functions that have been transferred to it under Pt XIV, try and deal with those matters as expeditiously as possible. This section also provides that the Minister may where he or she considers it necessary or expedient give a direction to the Board that in the performance of its functions (pursuant to ss 214 and 215), priority should be given to certain matters of a particular class or classes.

[442]
222. Amendment of section 10 of Local Government (No. 2) Act, 1960
Section 10 (inserted by section 86 of the Housing Act, 1966) of the Local Government (No. 2) Act, 1960 is hereby amended—

(a) by the deletion of subsection (2), and
(b) in subsection (4), by the substitution for paragraph (d) of the following paragraph:

"(d) Where—
    (i)   an order is made by virtue of this section, and
    (ii) there is a public right of way over the land to which the order relates or any part thereof or
over land adjacent to or associated with the land or any part thereof, the order may authorise the local authority, by order made by them after they have acquired such land or part, to extinguish the right of way.".

Note
Section 222 amends s 10 of the Local Government (No 2) Act 1960. Formerly, motorway schemes did allow for extinguishment under the roads legislation but other CPOs did not and now this clarifies the position.

[443]
223. References to transferred function in regulations etc

(1) A reference in any regulations, prescribed forms or other instruments made under the enactments referred to in section 214 or 215 to the Minister, and which relate to the functions transferred under those sections, shall be deemed to be references to the Board.

(2) A reference in any regulations, prescribed forms or other instruments made under the enactments referred to in section 214 or 215 to local inquiries or public local inquiries, and which relate to functions transferred to the Board under those sections, shall be deemed to be references to oral hearings by the Board.

Note
Section 223 states that a reference in any regulations relative to the transfer of functions from the Minister to the Board pursuant to s 214 or 215 shall be deemed to be references to the Board and not the Minister.

PART XV   DEVELOPMENT ON THE FORESHORE

Note
This Part is a new section which has been introduced into the planning legislation.

Part XV has not yet commenced.

[444]
224. Definition
In this Part—

"development" includes development consisting of the reclamation of any land on the foreshore;

"foreshore" has the meaning assigned to it by the Foreshore Act, 1933, but includes land between the line of high water of ordinary or medium tides and land within the functional area of the planning authority concerned that adjoins the first-mentioned land.

Note
The Foreshore Act 1933 defines 'Foreshore' as 'The bed and shore below the line of high water, of ordinary or medium tides, of the sea and every tidal river and tidal estuary and every channel, creek and bay of the sea of any such river or estuary'.

[445]–[450]
225. Obligation to obtain permission in development on foreshore
(1) Subject to the provisions of this Act, permission shall be required under Part III in respect of development on the foreshore not being exempted development, in circumstances where, were such development carried out, it would adjoin—

(a) the functional area of a planning authority, or
(b) any reclaimed land adjoining such functional area,

and accordingly, that part of the foreshore on which it is proposed to carry out the development shall for the purposes of making an application for permission in respect of such development be deemed to be within the functional area of that planning authority.

(2) That part of the foreshore on which a development has been commenced or completed pursuant to permission granted under Part III shall, for the purposes of this Act or any other enactment, whether passed before or after the passing of this Act, be deemed to be within the functional area of the planning authority that granted such permission.

(3) This section shall not apply to—

(a) development to which section 226 applies, or
(b) development consisting of underwater cables, wires, pipelines or other similar apparatus used for the purpose of—
  (i) transmitting electricity or telecommunications signals, or
  (ii) carrying gas, petroleum, oil or water,
  or development connected to land within the functional area of a planning authority solely by means of any such cable, wire, pipeline or apparatus.

(4) This section is in addition to and not in substitution for the Foreshore Acts, 1933 to 1998.

Note
Section 225 requires permission under Pt III of PDA 2000 in respect of development of the foreshore, not being exempted development, in circumstances where were such development carried out, it would adjoin (a) the functional area of the planning authority or (b) any reclaimed land adjoining such functional area. Section 225 also provides that apart from obtaining planning permission in respect of development on the foreshore one will also have to obtain the necessary licences as required under other provisions of the Foreshore Acts 1933 to 1998.

[451]
226. Local authority development on foreshore
(1) Where development is proposed to be carried out wholly or partly on the foreshore—

(a) by a local authority that is a planning authority, whether in its capacity as a planning authority or otherwise, or
(b) by some other person on behalf of, or jointly or in partnership with, a local authority that is a planning authority, pursuant to an agreement entered into by that local authority whether in its capacity as a planning authority or otherwise, (hereafter in this section referred to as "proposed development"), the local authority concerned shall apply to the Board for approval of the proposed development.

(2) The Board may approve, approve subject to conditions, or refuse to approve a proposed development.

(3) Section 175 shall apply to proposed development belonging to a class of development, identified for the purposes of section 176, subject to—

(a) the modification that the local authority concerned shall not be required to apply for approval under subsection (3) of the said section 175 in respect of the proposed development,

(b) the modification that the reference in subsection (4) to approval under subsection (3) shall be construed as a reference to approval under subsection (1) of this section,

(c) any modifications consequential upon paragraph (a), and

(d) any other necessary modifications.

(4) Subsections (4), (5), (6), (7), (9), (10), (11)(a), (11)(b)(ii), (11)(b)(iii), (12), (13) and (14) of section 175 shall apply to a proposed development other than one referred to in subsection (3), subject to—

(a) the modification that the reference in subsection (4) of the said section 175 to approval under subsection (3) shall be construed as a reference to approval under subsection (1) of this section,

(b) the modification that—

   (i) references in subsections (4) and (5) of the said section 175 to environmental impact statement shall be construed as references to such documents, particulars, plans or other information relating to the proposed development as may be prescribed,

   (ii) references to likely effects on the environment shall be disregarded, and

   (iii) the reference in subsection (lI)(a) of the said section 175 to applications for approval under this section shall be construed as references to applications for approval under subsection (1) of this section, and

(c) any other necessary modifications.

(5) Sections 32 and 179 shall not apply to a proposed development.

(6) This section shall apply to proposed development that—

(a) if carried out wholly within the functional area of a local authority that is a planning authority, would be subject to the provisions of section 175, or

(b) is prescribed for the purposes of this section.

Notes

Section 226 deals with development that is proposed to be carried out in whole or in part on the foreshore by a local authority or by some person on behalf of or jointly or in partnership with a local authority that is a planning authority. The local authority in respect of any proposed development on the foreshore must apply to the Board for approval for the proposed development.

Sub-section (3) deals with the requirement of the local authority to prepare an EIS in respect of certain classes of development on the foreshore.

[452]
227. Acquisition of land etc on foreshore

(1) The powers of a local authority to compulsorily acquire land under the enactments specified in section 214(1) shall, where the local authority concerned is a planning authority and for the purposes specified in those enactments, extend to that part of the foreshore that adjoins the functional area of the local authority concerned.

(2) The functions of a road authority under sections 49, 50 and 51 of the Roads Act, 1993, shall extend to the foreshore adjoining the functional area of the road authority concerned.

(3) The functions transferred to the Board under section 214 shall be performable by the Board in relation to any compulsory acquisition of land to which subsection (1) applies.

(4) The functions transferred to the Board under section 215 shall be performable in relation to any scheme approved under section 49 of the Roads Act, 1993, relating to the foreshore.

(5) Where a local authority—

(a)   applies for approval under section 226,
(b)   in relation to land on the foreshore, submits any matter (howsoever described under the enactment concerned) to the Board in relation to which it falls to the Board to perform functions in respect thereof under an enactment specified in section 214, or
(c)   submits a scheme under section 49 of the Roads Act, 1993, it shall send copies of all maps, documents (including any environmental impact statement) and other materials sent to the Board in connection with the application or scheme concerned to the Minister for the Marine and Natural Resources.

(6) The Board shall, before performing any function conferred on it by section 226 or (in respect of land on the foreshore) under an enactment specified in section 214(1) or referred to in subsection (5), by notice in writing, invite observations in relation to the application or scheme concerned from the Minister for the Marine and Natural Resources within such period as may be specified in the notice being a period of not less than 8 weeks from the date of receipt of the notice.

(7) The Board shall in the performance of the functions referred to in subsection (6) have regard to any observations made pursuant to a notice under that subsection.

(8) The Foreshore Acts, 1933 to 1998, shall not apply in relation to any application to the Board under section 226, or matters to which subsection (5)(b) applies or a scheme submitted under section 49 of the Roads Act, 1993.

(9) The Board may, notwithstanding any other enactment, attach such conditions relating to the protection of the marine environment, as it considers appropriate, to—

(a)   the confirmation of any compulsory purchase order, or
(b)   the approval of any scheme under section 49 of the Roads Act, 1993, relating to the foreshore, and the local authority concerned shall comply with any such conditions.

(10) Nothing in the State Property Act, 1954, shall operate to prevent a local authority compulsorily acquiring land on the foreshore.

(11) This section shall not apply to any application to the Minister for the Marine and Natural Resources for a lease under section 2 of the Foreshore Act, 1933, or for a licence under section 3 of that Act made before the coming into operation of this section.

Note
Section 227 sets out the procedure where a local authority wants to compulsorily acquire land on the foreshore.

[453]
228. Entering on foreshore for certain purposes

(1) Where a local authority proposes to enter onto the foreshore for the purposes of carrying out site investigations, it shall not later than 4 weeks before the carrying out of such investigations—

(a) publish in at least one newspaper circulating in the area of the proposed site investigations, and

(b) serve on the Minister for the Marine and Natural Resources and to the pre-scribed bodies,

a notice of its intention to so do, and where any such site investigations would involve excavations, borings or other tests that would be capable of causing distur-bance to the marine environment, it shall inform that Minister and those bodies of the details of the proposed investigations.

(2) The Minister for the Marine and Natural Resources may make recommendations to the local authority concerned in relation to investigations referred to in sub-section (1) and the local authority shall have regard to any such recommendations when carrying out such investigations.

(3) Where there has been compliance with this section, section 252 shall not apply in relation to entry onto the foreshore for the purposes specified in subsection (1).

(4) Compliance with this section shall, in relation to entry onto the foreshore for the said purposes, constitute compliance with any other enactment requiring the giving of notice of entry on land by a local authority.

Note
Section 228 provides that a local authority shall publish a notice in a newspaper and notify cer-tain prescribed bodies of its intention to enter onto the foreshore for the purposes of carrying out site investigations.

PART XVI   EVENTS AND FUNFAIRS

Note
This is a new provision in the planning legislation and it provides for the licensing of certain outdoor activities and funfairs. Draft regulations to put the actual procedure in place for out-door events are currently before the Oireachtas. The Licensing of Indoor Events Bill 2001 was also recently published and introduces a new licensing system for indoor pop concerts and other entertainment events.

[454]
229. Interpretation

In this Part—

"event" means—

(a) a public performance which takes place wholly or mainly in the open air or in a structure with no roof or a partial, temporary or retractable roof, a tent or similar temporary structure and which is comprised of music, dancing, dis-plays of public entertainment or any activity of a like kind, and

(b) any other event as prescribed by the Minister under section 241;

"funfair" has the meaning assigned to it by section 239;

"licence" means a licence granted by a local authority under section 231;

"local authority" means—

(a) in the case of a county, the council of the county, and
(b) in the case of a county borough, the corporation of the borough.

Note
'Local authority' is defined such that county councils and larger borough corporations will have responsibility for licensing these events.

[455]–[460]
230. Obligation to obtain a licence for holding of an event
(1) Subject to subsection (4), a licence shall be required in respect of the holding of an event or class of event prescribed for the purpose of this section.

(2) When prescribing events or classes of events under subsection (1), the Minister shall have regard to the size, location, nature or other attributes of the event or class of event.

(3) Any person who—

(a) organises, promotes, holds or is otherwise materially involved in the organisation of an event to which this section applies, or
(b) is in control of land on which an event to which this section applies is held,

other than under and in accordance with a licence, shall be guilty of an offence.

(4) A licence shall not be required for the holding of an event prescribed in accordance with subsection (1) by a local authority.

Note
Section 230(3)
It will be an offence to hold an event without a licence or to be in control of land when an unlicensed event is held.

[461]
231. Grant of licence
(1) The Minister may by regulations provide for matters of procedure and administration in relation to applications for and the grant of licences for events.

(2) Without prejudice to the generality of subsection (1), regulations under this section may make provision for—

(a) requiring the publication of a notice of intention to make an application for a licence,
(b) requiring the notification of prescribed persons or bodies,
(c) the form and content of an application for a licence,
(d) the plans, documents and information to be submitted with an application for a licence,
(e) the persons and bodies which must be consulted in relation to a licence,
(f) enabling persons to make submissions or observations within a prescribed time,

(g) requiring the applicant to submit any further information with respect to their application, and

(h) the time within which a decision on an application for a licence must be made.

(3) (a) Where an application for a licence is made in accordance with regulations under this section, the local authority may decide to grant the licence, grant the licence subject to such conditions as it considers appropriate or refuse the licence.

(b) In considering an application for a licence under this section, the local authority shall have regard to—

   (i) any information relating to the application furnished to it by the applicant in accordance with subsection (2)(d) or (g),

   (ii) any consultations under subsection (2)(e),

   (iii) any submissions or observations made to it in accordance with subsection (2)(f),

   (iv) whether events have previously been held on the land concerned,

   (v) the matters referred to in subsection (4), and

   (vi) any guidelines or codes of practice issued by the Minister or by any other Minister of the Government.

(4) Without prejudice to the generality of subsection (3)(a), conditions subject to which a licence is granted may relate to all or any of the following—

(a) compliance with any guidelines or codes of practice issued by the Minister or any other Minister of the Government, or with any provisions of those guidelines or codes of practice;

(b) securing the safety of persons at the place in connection with the event;

(c) the provision of adequate facilities for the health and welfare of persons at the place in connection with the event, including the provision of sanitary facilities;

(d) the protection of the environment in which the event is to be held, including the control of litter;

(e) the maintenance of public order;

(f) the avoidance or minimisation of disruption to the neighbourhood in which the event is to take place;

(g) ensuring the provision of adequate means of transport to and from the place in which the event is to be held;

(h) the number of events which are permitted at a venue within a specified period not exceeding one year;

(i) the payment of a financial contribution to the authority of a specified amount or an amount calculated on a specified basis towards the estimated cost to the local authority of measures taken by the authority in connection with the event;

(j) the payment of a financial contribution to a person or body consulted in accordance with subsection (2)(e) of a specified amount or an amount calculated on a specified basis towards the estimated cost to that person or body of measures taken by the person or body in connection with the event;

(k) maintaining public liability insurance;

(l) the display of notices for persons attending the event as to their obligations and conduct at the event.

(5) Conditions under subsection (4)(i) or (j) requiring the payment of a financial contribution may only relate to an event which is held wholly or mainly for profit.

(6) A person shall not be entitled solely by reason of a licence under this section to hold an event.

Notes
Section 231(1)
These regulations are not yet implemented.

Section 231(4)
This sub-section sets out the conditions that may be attached to a licence.

Section 231(6)
If an applicant for a licence requires to comply with other legislation in order to hold the event then the licence granted under this section will not be sufficient until such time as other legislation/provisions are also complied with fully.

[462]
232. Codes of practice in relation to events
(1) The Minister or any Minister of the Government may draw up and issue codes of practice for the purpose of providing practical guidance with respect to the requirements of any of the relevant provisions of or under this Part.

(2) The Minister or any Minister of the Government, as appropriate, shall, before issuing a code of practice, consult any other Minister of the Government or other person or body that appears to that Minister to be appropriate.

(3) The Minister or any Minister of the Government, as appropriate, may amend or revoke any code of practice, following consultation with any other Minister of the Government or any other person or body that appears to the Minister to be appropriate.

Note
Section 232(1)
A number of these codes of practice have been drawn up already by the Minister.

[463]
233. Service of notice in relation to events
(1) Where a local authority has reason to believe that an event in respect of which a licence under section 230 is required is occurring or is likely to occur—

(a)   without such a licence, or
(b)   in contravention of the terms of such a licence, the authority may serve a notice under this section.

(2) A notice may require, as appropriate—

(a)   the immediate cessation of any event or the discontinuation or alteration of any preparations which are being made in relation to an event,
(b)   the removal of any temporary buildings, structures, plant, machinery or the like from land which the authority believes is intended to be used as the location of an event, and
(c)   the restoration of the land to its prior condition.

(3) Any person who fails to comply with the requirements of the notice served under subsection (1) shall be guilty of an offence.

[464]
234. General obligations with regard to safety at events

(1) A person to whom a licence is granted under section 231 shall take such care as is reasonable in all the circumstances, having regard to the care which a person attending the event may reasonably be expected to take for his or her own safety and, if the person is at the event in the company of another person, the extent of the supervision and control the latter person may be expected to exercise over the former person's activities, to ensure that persons on the land in connection with the event do not suffer injury or damage by reason of any danger arising out of the licensed event or associated activities.

(2) It shall be the duty of every person, being on land in connection with an event to which this section applies, to conduct himself or herself in such a way as to ensure that as far as reasonably practicable any person on the land is not exposed to danger as a consequence of any act or omission of his or hers.

Note
Section 234 imposes a duty on the holders of events and on persons attending events to take reasonable care for the safety of themselves other persons.

[465]–[470]
235. Powers of inspection in connection with events

(1) An authorised person (subject to the production by him or her, if so requested, of his or her authority in writing) or a member of the Garda Síochána shall be entitled at all reasonable times to enter and inspect any land or any structure for any purpose connected with this Part.

(2) Without prejudice to the generality of subsection (1), an authorised person or a member of the Garda Síochána shall, in the performance of his or her functions under subsection (1), be entitled to—

(a) require the person in control of the land or structure concerned to—
   (i) inform him or her of any matter which the authorised person or the member of the Garda Síochána considers to be relevant, or
   (ii) provide such plans, documentation or other information as are necessary to establish that the requirements of this Part and any regulations made under this Part or any licence or any conditions to which the licence is subject are being complied with,
(b) take with him or her on to land such persons and equipment as he or she considers necessary and to carry out such tests or to do such other things which he or she considers necessary for the purposes referred to in subsection (1).

(3) Any person who—

(a) refuses to allow an authorised person or a member of the Garda Síochána to enter any land in exercise of his or her powers under this section,
(b) obstructs or impedes an authorised person or a member of the Garda Síochána in exercise of his or her powers under this section, or
(c) wilfully or recklessly gives, either to an authorised person or a member of the Garda Síochána, information which is false or misleading in a material respect,

shall be guilty of an offence.

(4) In this section, "authorised person" means a person authorised for the purposes of this Act by a local authority.

[471]
236. Limitation of civil proceedings
(1) No action or other proceeding shall lie or be maintainable against the Minister or a local authority or any other officer or employee of a local authority or any person engaged by a local authority or a member of the Garda Síochána for the recovery of damages in respect of any injury to persons, damage to property or other loss alleged to have been caused or contributed to by a failure to exercise any function conferred or imposed on the local authority by or under this Part.

(2) A person shall not be entitled to bring any civil proceedings pursuant to this Part by reason only of the contravention of any provision of this Part, or of any regulations made thereunder.

Note
Section 236 limits the civil liability of the Minister and local authorities in relation to the application of this section. Some commentators have queried the constitutionality of these provisions and there is a possibility that this may be challenged in the future.

[472]
237. Consequential provisions for offences
(1) The local authority by whom a licence under section 231 was granted may revoke it if the person to whom the licence is granted is convicted of an offence under this Part.

(2) Proceedings for an offence under this Part may be brought by the local authority in whose area the offence is committed.

Note
Section 237 provides for the revocation of a licence when a person holding a licence is convicted of an offence under this part.

[473]
238. Holding of event by local authority
(1) An event that is prescribed in accordance with section 230(1) and is proposed to be carried out by a local authority (in this section referred to as a "proposed event") shall be carried out in accordance with this section and any regulations made under subsection (2).

(2) The Minister may make regulations providing for—

(a) the publication by the local authority of any specified notice with respect to the proposed event,
(b) the notification or consultation by the local authority of any specified person or persons,
(c) the making available for inspection, by members of the public, of any specified documents, particulars, plans or other information with respect to the proposed event, and

(d) the making of submissions or observations to the local authority within a prescribed time with respect to the proposed event.

(3) (a) The manager of a local authority shall, after the expiration of the period prescribed under subsection (2)(d) for the making of submissions or observations, prepare a written report in relation to the proposed event and submit the report to the members of the local authority.

(b) A report prepared in accordance with paragraph (a) shall—
    (i) specify the proposed event,
    (ii) specify the matters referred to in section 231(4) to which the holding of the proposed event will be subject,
    (iii) list the persons or bodies who made submissions or observations with respect to the proposed event in accordance with the regulations made under subsection (2),
    (iv) summarise the issues raised in any such submissions or observations and state the response of the manager to them, and
    (v) recommend whether or not the proposed event should be held.

(c) The members of the local authority shall, as soon as may be, consider the proposed event and the report of the manager under paragraph (a).

(d) Following the consideration of the manager's report under paragraph (c), the proposed event may be carried out as recommended in the manager's report, unless the local authority, by resolution, decides to vary or modify the event, otherwise than as recommended in the manager's report, or decides not to proceed with the event.

(e) A resolution under paragraph (d) must be passed not later than 6 weeks after receipt of the manager's report.

Note
Section 238 makes provision for the holding of a proposed event by a local authority and enables the Minister to make certain regulations in relation to the holding of such proposed events.

[474]
239. Control of funfairs
(1) In this section—

"fairground equipment" includes any fairground ride or any similar equipment which is designed to be in motion for entertainment purposes with members of the public on or inside it, any equipment which is designed to be used by members of the public for entertainment purposes either as a slide or for bouncing upon, and any swings, dodgems and other equipment which is designed to be in motion wholly or partly under the control of, or to be put in motion by, a member of the public or any equipment which may be prescribed, in the interests of public safety, for the purposes of this section;

"funfair" means an entertainment where fairground equipment is used.

(2) The organiser of a funfair and the owner of fairground equipment used at a funfair shall take such care as is reasonable in the circumstances, having regard to the care which a person attending the funfair may reasonably be expected to take for his or her own safety, and, if the person is at the event in the company of another person,

the extent of the supervision and control the latter person may be expected to exercise over the former person's activities to ensure that persons on the land in connection with the funfair do not suffer injury or damage by reason of any danger arising out of the funfair or associated activities.

(3) It shall be the duty of every person being on land in connection with a funfair to which this section applies to conduct himself or herself in such a way as to ensure that as far as is reasonably practicable any person on the land is not exposed to danger as a consequence of any act or omission of his or hers.

(4) (a) An organiser of a funfair or an owner of fairground equipment shall not make available for use by the public any fairground equipment unless such equipment has a valid certificate of safety in accordance with regulations made under subsection (5).

(b) An organiser of a funfair or owner of fairground equipment who makes available for use by the public any fairground equipment otherwise than in accordance with paragraph (a), shall be guilty of an offence.

(5) The Minister shall by regulations provide for such matters of procedure, administration and control as appear to the Minister to be necessary or expedient in relation to applications for and the grant of certificates of safety for fairground equipment.

(6) Without prejudice to the generality of subsection (5), regulations under that subsection may provide for—

(a) the class or classes of persons who are entitled to grant certificates of safety,
(b) the matters to be taken into account in determining applications for safety certificates,
(c) the payment of a prescribed fee for an application for a certificate of safety,
(d) the period of validity of a certificate of safety, and
(e) any class of fairground equipment to be exempt from the provisions of this section.

(7) (a) A person who intends to hold or organise a funfair, other than at a place where the operation of funfair equipment has been authorised by a permission under Part III of this Act or Part IV of the Act of 1963 or is not otherwise an unauthorised use, shall give 2 weeks notice (or such other period of notice as may be prescribed) in writing to the local authority in whose functional area the funfair is to be held.

(b) The notice referred to in paragraph (a) shall be accompanied by a valid certificate of safety for the fair ground equipment to be used at the funfair and shall give details of the names of the organiser of the funfair, the owner or owners of the fairground equipment to be used at the funfair and the location and dates on which the funfair is to be held.

(8) (a) Where a local authority has reason to believe that a funfair is taking place, or is likely to take place, which is not in compliance with subsection (4) or (7), the authority may serve a notice on any person it believes to be holding, organising or otherwise materially involved in the organisation of the funfair.

(b) A notice under paragraph (a) may require, as appropriate—

(i)   the immediate cessation of any activity or any preparations which are being made in relation to the fun fair within a specified time,

(ii)   the immediate cessation of the use of any fairground equipment without a valid certificate of safety,

(iii)   the removal, within a specified time, of any fairground equipment, temporary buildings or structures, plant, machinery or similar equipment which the authority believes is intended to be used in relation to the funfair, and

(iv)   the restoration of the land to its prior condition within a specified time.

(c)   A person who is served with a notice under paragraph (a) and who fails to comply with the requirements of the notice shall be guilty of an offence.

(d)   Where a person fails to comply with a notice served on the person under this section, the local authority concerned may, through its employees or agents—

(i)   give effect to the terms of the notice, and

(ii)   where necessary for that purpose, enter on the land concerned,

and may recover the expenditure reasonably incurred by it in so doing from the person as a simple contract debt in any court of competent jurisdiction.

(e)   A person who obstructs or impedes the local authority in the performance of its functions under paragraph (d) shall be guilty of an offence.

Note

Persons planning to organise funfairs or owning fairground equipment and persons attending funfairs will have to take reasonable care for the safety of other persons attending the funfair. A person intending to hold a funfair will have to notify the local authority in advance and show a certificate of safety for the fairground equipment to be used. The requirements for the certificate of safety may be set out by the Minister in regulations. The person who organises the funfair or who owns equipment used at a funfair that does not comply with the requirements of this section commits an offence. Local authorities can serve a notice to prevent an unauthorised funfair and to do any works required in the notice itself if necessary. Any person who disobeys the notice or impedes the authority in doing such works commits an offence.

[475]–[480]
240. Exclusion of events and funfairs from planning control

(1) Subject to subsection (2), the holding of an event to which this Part applies and works directly or solely relating to the holding of such an event shall not be construed as "development" within the meaning of this Act.

(2) (a)   Notwithstanding section 230 or 239, the provisions of this Part shall not affect the validity of any planning permission granted under Part IV of the Act of 1963 for the holding of an event or events or for a funfair.

(b)   Where a planning permission referred to in paragraph (a) has been granted for the holding of an event or events in respect of land, a licence under this Part shall be required for the holding of any additional event on the land concerned.

Note

Section 240 provides that holding an event or funfair or works relating to the holding of an event or funfair will not be development as defined in PDA 2000 and will therefore not require planning permission.

[481]
241. Regulations for event
The Minister may make regulations providing that any activity or class of activity to which the public have access and which takes place wholly or mainly in the open air or in a structure with no roof or a partial, temporary or retractable roof, a tent or other similar temporary structure to be an event for the purposes of this Part.

PART XVII   FINANCIAL PROVISIONS

Note
This part deals with financial provisions and is a restatement of LG(PD)A 1963 and LG(PD)A 1982, with modifications. None of the sections in Pt XVII have been commenced to date.

[482]
242. Expenses of administration of Minister
The expenses incurred by the Minister in the administration of this Act shall, to such extent as may be sanctioned by the Minister for Finance, be paid out of moneys provided by the Oireachtas.

Note
Section 242 restates s 12 of LG(PD)A 1963.

[483]
243. Charging of expenses of planning authority that is council of a county
Expenses under this Act of a planning authority that is the council of a county shall be charged on the county (exclusive of every borough and urban district therein).

Note
Section 243 restates s 13 of LG(PD)A 1963.

[484]
244. Apportionment of joint expenses of planning
(1) Two or more planning authorities may, by resolution, make and carry out an agreement for sharing the cost of performing all or any of their functions under this Act and, where an agreement has been made under this subsection, the planning authorities concerned may, by resolution, terminate it at any time if they so agree.

(2) Where a planning authority proposes to perform in its functional area a function under this Act at the request of or wholly or partially in the interests of the area of another planning authority (being a planning authority whose area is contiguous with the area of the first-mentioned planning authority), the other planning authority shall defray the cost of the performance of the function to such extent as may be agreed upon between the authorities or, in default of agreement, as may be determined by the Minister.

Note
Section 244 restates s 16(1) and 16(2) of LG(PD)A 1963, but omits s 16(3), which provides that the making of an agreement by local authorities to apportion their joint expenses is a reserved function.

[485]–[490]
245. Power to set-off

Where a sum is due under this Act to any person by a planning authority and, at the same time, another sum under this Act is due by that person to that authority, the former sum may be set-off against the latter either, as may be appropriate, in whole or in part.

Note

Section 245 restates s 17 of LG(PD)A 1963.

[491]
246. Fees payable to planning authorities

(1) The Minister may make regulations providing for—

(a) the payment to planning authorities of prescribed fees in relation to applications for—
   (i) permission under Part III, or
   (ii) extensions or further extensions under section 42,
(b) the payment to planning authorities of prescribed fees in relation to the making of submissions or observations respecting applications for permission referred to in paragraph (a),
(c) the payment to planning authorities of prescribed fees in relation to requests for declarations under section 5,
(d) the payment to local authorities of prescribed fees in relation to applications for grants of licences under section 231 or for certificates of safety under section 239, and
(e) the payment to planning authorities of prescribed fees in relation to applications for grants of licences under section 254,

and the regulations may provide for the payment of different fees in relation to cases of different classes or descriptions, for exemption from the payment of fees in specified circumstances, for the waiver, remission or refund (in whole or in part) of fees in specified circumstances and for the manner in which fees are to be disposed of.

(2) The Minister may prescribe that the fee payable to the authority for an application for permission under section 34(12) shall be an amount which shall be related to the estimated cost of the development, or the unauthorised part thereof, as the case may be.

(3) (a) Where, under regulations made under this section, a fee is payable to a planning authority or local authority by an applicant in respect of an application under paragraph (a), (d) or (e) of subsection (1) or by a person making a request for a declaration under paragraph (c) of subsection (1), the application shall not be decided, or the declaration issued, unless the authority is in receipt of the fee.

(b) With regard to applications under paragraph (a) of subsection (1), notwithstanding anything contained in section 34(8) or 42(2), a decision of a planning authority shall not be regarded, pursuant to any of those sections, as having been given on a day which is earlier than that which is 8 weeks after the day on which the authority is in receipt of the fee, and sections 34(8) and 42(2) shall be construed subject to and in accordance with the provisions of this paragraph.

(4) Where under regulations under this section a fee is payable to a planning authority or local authority and the person by whom the fee is payable is not the applicant for a permission, approval or licence, submissions or observations made, as regards the relevant application, appeal or referral by or on behalf of the person by whom the fee is payable, shall not be considered by the planning authority or local authority unless the fee has been received by the authority.

(5) A planning authority shall specify fees for the making of copies under sections 7, 16(1) and 38(4), not exceeding the reasonable cost of making such copies.

Notes
Section 246(1)
This sub-section dispenses with the need for the Minister for the Environment and Local Government to obtain the permission of the Minister for Finance in order to prescribe fees to be paid to local authorities. This sub-section restates s 10 of LG(PD)A 1982, but with the following additional provisions:

– It allows for fees to be charged for the making of observations and submissions on planning applications and appeals.
– The local authority may also charge fees for the provision of licences for events and funfairs, and for the laying of cables and other appliances on public roads.

Section 246(2)
This sub-section is new. It provides that the planning authority may prescribe a fee for the application under s 34(12) for retention permission, and that it may be an amount related to the estimated cost of the development. The explanatory memorandum to the Bill suggested a rate of 10% of the estimated cost of the development. This could amount to a considerable sum of money and act as a deterrent to applications for retention permission. Regulation 91 of LG(PD)R 1994 applied a cap on the amount that could be charged in relation to applications for retention permission.

Section 246(3)–(5)
The remaining sub-sections of s 246 restate s 10 of LG(PD)A 1982, with the only modification being the change in sub-s (3)(b) from two months to eight weeks.

PART XVIII   MISCELLANEOUS

Note
This part deals with, inter alia, consultations in relation to proposed developments, information to be provided in electronic form, additional requirements for public notifications, service of notices, calculation of time periods over holidays, powers of authorised persons to enter onto land, licensing of appliances and cables, performance of functions by planning authorities and amendment of certain legislation. This part is not in force yet save for s 262 which relates to the power of the Minister to make regulations.

[492]
247. Consultations in relation to proposed development
(1) A person who has an interest in land and who intends to make a planning application may, with the agreement of the planning authority concerned (which shall not be unreasonably withheld), enter into consultations with the planning authority in order to discuss any proposed development in relation to the land and the planning authority may give advice to that person regarding the proposed application.

(2) In any consultations under subsection (1), the planning authority shall advise the person concerned of the procedures involved in considering a planning application, including any requirements of the permission regulations, and shall, as far as possible, indicate the relevant objectives of the development plan which may have a bearing on the decision of the planning authority.

(3) The carrying out of consultations shall not prejudice the performance by a planning authority of any other of its functions under this Act, or any regulations made under this Act and cannot be relied upon in the formal planning process or in legal proceedings.

(4) (a) In order to satisfy the requirements of this section, a planning authority may specify that consultations may be held at particular times and at particular locations and the authority shall not be obliged to enter into consultations otherwise than as specified by it.

(b) Where a planning authority decides to hold consultations in accordance with paragraph (a) it shall, at least once in each year, publish notice of the times and locations at which consultations are held in one or more newspapers circulating in the area of the authority.

(5) The planning authority shall keep a record in writing of any consultations under this section that relate to a proposed development, including the names of those who participated in the consultations, and a copy of such record shall be placed and kept with the documents to which any planning application in respect of the proposed development relates.

(6) A member or official of a planning authority is guilty of an offence if he or she takes or seeks any favour, benefit or payment, direct or indirect (on his or her own behalf or on behalf of any other person or body), in connection with any consultation entered into or any advice given under this section.

Note
Section 247 is a new provision. It puts on a statutory footing a practice/procedure that has been ongoing for a number of years between the local authorities and planning applicants.

[493]
248. Information to be provided in electronic form
(1) Subject to subsection (2), any document or other information that is required or permitted to be given in writing under this Act or any regulations made under this Act by the Minister, the planning authority, the Board or any other person, may be given in electronic form.

(2) A document or information referred to in subsection (1) may be given in electronic form only—

(a) if at the time it was given it was reasonable to expect that it would be readily accessible to the planning authority, Board or other person to whom it was directed, for subsequent reference or use,
(b) where such document or information is required or permitted to be given to a

planning authority or the Board and the planning authority or the Board consents to the giving of the information in that form, but requires—

(i)   the information to be given in accordance with particular information technology and procedural requirements, or

(ii) that a particular action be taken by way of verifying the receipt of the information,

if the requirements of the planning authority or the Board have been met and those requirements have been made public and are objective, transparent, proportionate and non-discriminatory, and

(c) where such document or such information is required or permitted to be given to a person who is neither a planning authority nor the Board, if the person to whom the document or other information is required or permitted to be given consents to the information being given in that form.

(3) A document or information that the planning authority or the Board is required or permitted to retain or to produce, whether for a particular period or otherwise, and whether in its original form or otherwise, may be so retained or produced, as the case may be, in electronic form.

(4) Subsections (1), (2) and (3) are without prejudice to any other law requiring or permitting documents or other information to be given, retained or produced, as the case may be, in accordance with specified procedural requirements or particular information technology.

(5) The Minister may make regulations providing for or requiring the use of particular information technology or other procedural requirements in relation to the giving, retaining or production of a specified class or classes of documents or other information in electronic form.

(6) Without prejudice to the generality of subsection (5), the regulations may apply to a particular class or classes of documents or other information, or for a particular period.

(7) This section applies to a requirement or permission to give documents or other information whether the word "give", "make", "make available", "submit", "produce" or similar word or expression is used.

(8) (a) This section is without prejudice to the requirements under section 250 in relation to the service or giving of a notice or copy of an order unless prescribed in regulations made under paragraph (b).

(b) The Minister may by regulation extend the application of this section to the service or giving of a notice or copy of an order under section 250, where the Minister is of the opinion that the public interest would not be prejudiced by so doing and the section as so extended shall apply accordingly.

(9) In this section—

"documents or other information" includes but is not limited to—

(a) a development plan or any draft or variation of it,

(b) an application for permission or any other document specified in section 38(1),

(c)   any map, plan or other drawing, and

(d)   written submissions or observations;

"electronic form" means information that is generated, communicated, processed, sent, received, recorded, stored or displayed by electronic means and is capable of being used to make a legible copy or reproduction of that communicated information but does not include information communicated in the form of speech and such electronic means includes electrical, digital, magnetic, optical, electro-magnetic, biometric, photonic and any other form of related technology.

Note
Section 248 provides that any information required under the provisions of PDA 2000 or regulations *may* be provided in electronic form.

[494]
249.   Additional requirements for public notifications
(1)   Where any provision of this Act requires notice to be given in one or more newspapers circulating in the area of a planning authority, the planning authority may, in addition to the requirements of the particular provision and to the extent they consider appropriate, give the notice or draw the attention of the public to the notice through other forms of media including the broadcast media and the use of electronic forms for the provision of information.

(2)   Where any provision of this Act requires notice to be given to any person who has made representations, submissions or observations to a planning authority, the planning authority may dispense with that requirement where—

(a)   a large number of representations, submissions or observations are made to the planning authority as part of an organised campaign, or

(b)   it is not possible to readily ascertain with certainty the full name and address of those persons who made the representations, submissions or observations,

provided that the authority uses some other means of giving notice to the public that the authority is satisfied can adequately draw the attention of the public to that notice including, in the case of an organised campaign referred to in paragraph (a), giving notice to any person who, in the opinion of the planning authority, organised the campaign.

Note
Section 249 states that where any provision of PDA 2000 requires notice to be given to any person who has made representations or observations the planning authority may dispense with the requirement to notify where a large number of representations are made as part of an organised campaign or it is not possible to readily ascertain the full name and address of those who made representations provided that the authority is happy that it can use some other means to sufficiently draw the attention of the public to the notice.

[495]–[500]
250.   Service of notices etc
(1)   Where a notice or copy of an order is required or authorised by this Act or any order or regulation made thereunder to be served on or given to a person, it shall be addressed to him or her and shall be served on or given to him or her in one of the following ways—

(a) where it is addressed to him or her by name, by delivering it to him or her;

(b) by leaving it at the address at which he or she ordinarily resides or, in a case in which an address for service has been furnished, at that address;

(c) by sending it by post in a prepaid registered letter addressed to him or her at the address at which he or she ordinarily resides or, in a case in which an address for service has been furnished, at that address;

(d) where the address at which he or she ordinarily resides cannot be ascertained by reasonable inquiry and the notice or copy is so required or authorised to be given or served in respect of any land or premises, by delivering it to some person over the age of 16 years resident or employed on the land or premises or by affixing it in a conspicuous place on or near the land or premises;

(e) in addition to the methods of service provided for in paragraphs (a), (b), (c) and (d), by delivering it (in the case of an enforcement notice) to some person over the age of 16 years who is employed, or otherwise engaged, in connection with the carrying out of the development to which the notice relates, or by affixing it in a conspicuous place on the land or premises concerned.

(2) Where a notice or copy of an order is required by this Act or any order or regulation made under this Act to be served on or given to the owner or to the occupier of any land or premises and the name of the owner or of the occupier cannot be ascertained by reasonable inquiry, it may be addressed to "the owner" or "the occupier", as the case may require, without naming him or her.

(3) For the purposes of this section, a company registered under the Companies Acts, 1963 to 1999, shall be deemed to be ordinarily resident at its registered office, and every other body corporate and every unincorporated body shall be deemed to be ordinarily resident at its principal office or place of business.

(4) Where a notice or copy of an order is served on or given to a person by affixing it under subsection (1)(d), a copy of the notice or order shall, within two weeks thereafter, be published in at least one newspaper circulating in the area in which the person is last known to have resided.

(5) A person who, at any time during the period of 12 weeks after a notice is affixed under subsection (1)(d), removes, damages or defaces the notice without lawful authority shall be guilty of an offence.

(6) A person who, without lawful authority, removes, damages or defaces a notice required to be erected at the site of a development under the permission regulations or by the Board under section 142(4), shall be guilty of an offence.

(7) Where the Minister or the Board is satisfied that reasonable grounds exist for dispensing with the serving or giving under this Act or under any order or regulation made under this Act of a notice or copy of an order and that dispensing with the serving or giving of the notice or copy will not cause injury or wrong, the Minister or the Board may dispense with the serving or giving of the notice or copy and every such dispensation shall have effect according to the tenor thereof.

(8) A dispensation under subsection (7) may be given either before or after the time when the notice or copy would, but for the dispensation, be required to be served or

given and either before or after the doing of any act to which the notice or copy would, but for the dispensation, be a condition precedent.

(9) In this section, "notice" includes a warning letter.

Note
Section 250 effectively restates s 7 of LG(PD)A 1963.

[501]
251. Calculation of appropriate period and other time limits over holidays
(1) Where calculating any appropriate period or other time limit referred to in this Act or in any regulations made under this appropriate period Act, the period between the 24th day of December and the first day of January, both days inclusive, shall be disregarded.

(2) Subsection (1) shall not apply to any time period specified in Part II of this Act.

Note
Section 251 provides that where a period has to be calculated which includes the nine days between 24 December and 1 January then these dates will be disregarded.

[502]
252. Power of authorised person to enter on land
(1) An authorised person may, subject to the other provisions of this section, enter on any land at all reasonable times between the hours of 9 a.m. and 6 p.m., or during business hours in respect of a premises which is normally open outside those hours, for any purpose connected with this Act.

(2) An authorised person entering on land under this section may do all things reasonably necessary for the purpose for which the entry is made and, in particular, may survey, carry out inspections, make plans, take photographs, take levels, make excavations, and examine the depth and nature of the subsoil.

(3) Before an authorised person enters under this section on any land, the appropriate authority shall either obtain the consent (in the case of occupied land) of the occupier or (in the case of unoccupied land) the owner or shall give to the owner or occupier, as the case may be, not less than 14 days' notice in writing of the intention to make the entry.

(4) A person to whom a notice of intention to enter on land has been given under this section by the appropriate authority may, not later than 14 days after the giving of the notice, apply, on notice to the authority, to the judge of the District Court having jurisdiction in the district court district in which the land or part of the land is situated for an order prohibiting the entry, and, upon the hearing of the application, the judge may either wholly prohibit the entry or specify conditions to be observed by the person making the entry.

(5) Where a judge of the District Court prohibits under this section a proposed entry on land, it shall not be lawful for any person to enter under this section on the land, and where a judge of the District Court specifies conditions to be observed by persons entering on land, every person who enters under this section on the land shall observe the conditions so specified.

(6) (a) Where (in the case of occupied land) the occupier or (in the case of unoccupied land) the owner refuses to permit the exercise of a power conferred by this section on an authorised person, the appropriate authority may apply to the District Court to approve of the entry.

(b) An application under this subsection shall be made, on notice to the person who refused to permit the exercise of the power of entry, to the judge of the District Court having jurisdiction in the district court district in which the land or part of the land is situated.

(7) Subsections (3), (4) and (5) shall not apply to entry for the purposes of Part III and, in a case in which any such entry is proposed, if the occupier (in the case of occupied land) or the owner (in the case of unoccupied land) refuses to permit the entry—

(a) the entry shall not be effected unless it has been authorised by an order of the judge of the District Court having jurisdiction in the district court district in which the land or part of the land is situate and, in the case of occupied land, until after at least 24 hours' notice of the intended entry, and of the object thereof, has been given to the occupier,

(b) an application for such an order shall be made on notice (in the case of occupied land) to the occupier or (in the case of unoccupied land) to the owner.

(8) An authorised person may, in the exercise of any power conferred on him or her by this Act, where he or she anticipates any obstruction in the exercise of any other power conferred on him or her by or under this Act, request a member of the Garda Síochána to assist him or her in the exercise of such a power and any member of the Garda Síochána of whom he or she makes such a request shall comply therewith.

(9) Every person who, by act or omission, obstructs an authorised person in the lawful exercise of the powers conferred by this section shall be guilty of an offence.

(10) Every authorised person shall be furnished with a certificate of his or her appointment and when exercising any power conferred on him or her by or under this Act, the authorised person shall, if requested by any person affected, produce the certificate to that person.

(11) In this section and section 253—

"appropriate authority" means—

(a) in a case in which the authorised person was appointed by a local authority—that authority,

(b) in a case in which the authorised person was appointed by the Minister—the Minister, and

(c) in a case in which the authorised person was appointed by the Board—the Board;

"authorised person" means a member of the Board or a person who is appointed by a local authority, the Minister or the Board to be an authorised person for the purposes of this section and section 253.

Note
Section 252 restates with some amendments s 81 and s 83 of LG(PD)A 1963.

[503]
253. Powers of entry in relation to enforcement

(1) Notwithstanding section 252, an authorised person may, for any purpose connected with Part VIII, at all reasonable times, or at any time if he or she has reasonable grounds for believing that an unauthorised development has been, is being or is likely to be carried out, enter any premises and bring thereon such other persons (including members of the Garda Síochána) or equipment as he or she may consider necessary for the purpose.

(2) Subject to subsection (4), an authorised person shall not, other than with the consent of the occupier, enter into a private house under subsection (1) unless he or she has given to the occupier of the house not less than 24 hours' notice in writing of his or her intended entry.

(3) Whenever an authorised person enters any premises pursuant to subsection (1), the authorised person may exercise the powers set out in section 252(2) and, as appropriate, in addition—

(a) require from an occupier of the premises or any person employed on the premises or any other person on the premises, such information, or

(b) require the production of and inspect such records and documents, and take copies of or extracts from, or take away, if it is considered necessary for the purposes of inspection or examination, any such records or documents,

as the authorised person, having regard to all the circumstances, considers necessary for the purposes of exercising any power conferred on him or her by or under this Act.

(4) (a) Where an authorised person in the exercise of his or her powers under subsection (1) is prevented from entering any premises or has reason to believe that evidence related to a suspected offence under this Act may be present in any premises and that the evidence may be removed therefrom or destroyed or that any particular structure may be damaged or destroyed, the authorised person or the person by whom he or she was appointed may apply to a judge of the District Court for a warrant under this subsection authorising the entry by the authorised person in the premises.

(b) If on application being made to him or her under this subsection, a judge of the District Court is satisfied, on the sworn information of the applicant, that the authorised person concerned has been prevented from entering a premises or that the authorised person has reasonable grounds for believing the other matters referred to in paragraph (a), the judge may issue a warrant under his or her hand authorising that person, accompanied, if the judge considers it appropriate so to provide, by such number of members of the Garda Síochána as may be specified in the warrant, at any time within 4 weeks from the date of the issue of the warrant, on production, if so requested, of the warrant, to enter, if need be by force, the premises concerned and exercise the powers referred to in subsection (3).

Note
Section 253(1) and (3) which are new provisions, provide that persons shall have additional powers of entry when this is required in relation to enforcement provisions under Pt VIII of the Act.

[504]
254. Licensing of appliances and cables, etc., on public roads

(1) Subject to subsection (2), a person shall not erect, construct, place or maintain—

(a) a vending machine,
(b) a town or landscape map for indicating directions or places,
(c) a hoarding, fence or scaffold,
(d) an advertisement structure,
(e) a cable, wire or pipeline,
(f) a telephone kiosk or pedestal, or
(g) any other appliance, apparatus or structure, which may be prescribed as requiring a licence under this section,

on, under, over or along a public road save in accordance with a licence granted by a planning authority under this section.

(2) This section shall not apply to the following—

(a) an appliance, apparatus or structure which is authorised in accordance with a planning permission granted under Part III;
(b) a temporary hoarding, fence or scaffold erected in accordance with a condition of planning permission granted under Part III;
(c) the erection, construction, placing or maintenance under a public road of a cable, wire or pipeline by a statutory undertaker.

(3) A person applying for a licence under this section shall furnish to the planning authority such plans and other information concerning the position, design and capacity of the appliance, apparatus or structure as the authority may require.

(4) A licence may be granted under this section by the planning authority for such period and upon such conditions as the authority may specify, including conditions in relation to location and design, and where in the opinion of the planning authority by reason of the increase or alteration of traffic on the road or of the widening of the road or of any improvement of or relating to the road, the appliance, apparatus or structure causes an obstruction or becomes dangerous, the authority may by notice in writing withdraw the licence and require the licensee to remove the appliance, apparatus or structure at his or her own expense.

(5) In considering an application for a licence under this section a planning authority, or the Board on appeal, shall have regard to—

(a) the proper planning and sustainable development of the area,
(b) any relevant provisions of the development plan, or a local area plan,
(c) the number and location of existing appliances, apparatuses or structures on, under, over or along the public road, and
(d) the convenience and safety of road users including pedestrians.

(6) (a) Any person may, in relation to the granting, refusing, withdrawing or continuing of a licence under this section or to the conditions specified by the planning authority for such a licence, appeal to the Board.
(b) Where an appeal under this section is allowed, the Board shall give such directions with respect to the withdrawing, granting or altering of a licence under this

section as may be appropriate, and the planning authority shall comply there-with.

(7) Development carried out in accordance with a licence under this section shall be exempted development for the purposes of this Act.

(8) A person shall not be entitled solely by reason of a licence under this section to erect, construct, place or maintain on, under, over or along a public road any appliance, apparatus or structure.

(9) Subject to subsection (10), any person who—

(a) erects, constructs, places or maintains an appliance, apparatus or structure referred to in subsection (1) on, under, over or along any public road without having a licence under this section to do so,

(b) erects, constructs, places or maintains such an appliance, apparatus or structure on, under, over or along any public road otherwise than in accordance with a licence under this section, or

(c) contravenes any condition subject to which a licence has been granted to him or her under this section,

shall be guilty of an offence.

(10) (a) A planning authority may, by virtue of this subsection, itself erect, construct, place or maintain, on, under, over or along a public road any appliance, apparatus or structure referred to in subsection (1), and it shall not be necessary for the planning authority to have a licence under this section.

(b) Nothing in this subsection shall be construed as empowering a planning authority to hinder the reasonable use of a public road by the public or any person entitled to use it or as empowering a planning authority to create a nuisance to the owner or occupier of premises adjacent to the public road.

(11) Where a planning authority is not the road authority for the purposes of national or regional roads in its area, it shall not grant a licence under this section in respect of any appliance, apparatus or structure on, under, over or along a national or regional road or erect, construct or place any appliance, apparatus or structure on, under, over or along a national or regional road except after consultation with the authority which is the road authority for those purposes.

Note
Section 254 restates with modifications s 89 of LG(PD)A 1963.

[505]–[510]
255. Performance of functions by planning authorities
(1) A planning authority shall supply the Minister with such information relating to the performance of its functions as he or she may from time to time request.

(2) (a) A planning authority shall conduct, at such intervals as it thinks fit or the Minister directs, reviews of its organisation and of the systems and procedures used by it in relation to its functions under this Act.

(b) Where the Minister gives a direction under this subsection, the planning authority shall report to the Minister the results of the review conducted pursuant to the direction and shall comply with any directive which the Minister may, after consultation with the planning authority as regards those results, give in relation to all or any of the matters which were the subject of the review.

(3) The Minister may appoint a person or body, not being the planning authority concerned, to carry out a review in accordance with subsection (2).

(4) Without prejudice to the powers of the Minister under the Local Government Act, 1941, if the Minister has formed the opinion from information available to him or her that—

(a) a planning authority may not be carrying out its functions in accordance with the requirements of or under this Act,
(b) a planning authority is not in compliance with guidelines issued under section 23, a directive issued under section 29, or a direction issued under section 31,
(c) there may be impropriety in the conduct of any of its functions by a planning authority, or
(d) there are serious diseconomies or inefficiencies in the conduct of its functions by a planning authority,

he or she may, where he or she considers it necessary or appropriate, for stated reasons appoint a commissioner to carry out and have full responsibility for all or any one or more of the functions of the planning authority under this Act and in doing so may distinguish between reserved functions and other functions.

(5) In considering whether it is necessary or expedient to appoint a commissioner under this section, the Minister may have regard to any loss of public confidence in the carrying out of its functions by the planning authority and the need to restore that confidence.

(6) A commissioner appointed under this section shall be appointed in accordance with such terms and conditions and for such period as may be specified by the Minister.

(7) A planning authority may on stated grounds based on the provisions of subsection (4), by resolution, request the Minister to appoint a commissioner to carry out all or any of the functions of the authority under this Act and the Minister shall have regard to any such request

(8) It shall be the duty of every member and every official of a planning authority to co-operate with any commissioner appointed under this section.

Note
Section 255 is a new provision which gives the Minister an overseeing and supervisory role relative to the powers and duties of local authorities.

[511]
256. Amendment of Environmental Protection Agency Act, 1992
The Environmental Protection Agency Act, 1992, is hereby amended in section 98—

(a) by the substitution for subsection (1) of the following subsections—

"(1) Notwithstanding section 34 of the Planning and Development Act, 2000, or any other provision of that Act, where a licence or revised licence under this Part has been granted or is or will be required in relation to an activity, a planning authority or An Bord Pleanála shall not, where it decides to grant a permission under section 34 of that Act in respect of any development comprising the activity or for the purposes of the activity, subject the permission to conditions which are for the purposes of—

(a) controlling emissions from the operation of the activity, including the prevention, limitation, elimination, abatement or reduction of those emissions, or

(b) controlling emissions related to or following the cessation of the operation of the activity.

(1A) Where a licence or revised licence under this Part has been granted or is or will be required in relation to an activity, a planning authority or An Bord Pleanála may, in respect of any development comprising the activity or for the purposes of the activity, decide to refuse a grant of permission under section 34 of the Planning and Development Act, 2000, where the authority or An Bord Pleanála considers that the development, notwithstanding the licensing of the activity under this Part, is unacceptable on environmental grounds, having regard to the proper planning and sustainable development of the area in which the development is or will be situate.

(1B) (a) Before making a decision in respect of a development comprising or for the purposes of an activity, a planning authority or An Bord Pleanála may request the Agency to make observations within such period (which period shall not in any case be less than 3 weeks from the date of the request) as may be specified by the authority or the Board in relation to the development, including in relation to any environmental impact statement submitted.

(b) When making its decision, the authority or An Bord Pleanála, as the case may be, shall have regard to the observations, if any, received from the Agency within the period specified under paragraph (a).

(1C) The planning authority or An Bord Pleanála may, at any time after the expiration of the period specified by the authority or An Bord Pleanála under subsection (1B)(a) for making observations, make its decision on the application or appeal.

(1D) The Minister may make regulations making such incidental, consequential, or supplementary provision as may appear to him or her to be necessary or proper to give full effect to any of the provisions of this section.

(1E) Without prejudice to the generality of subsection (1D), regulations made under this section may provide for matters of procedure in relation to the request for or the making of observations from or by the Agency under this section and related matters.

(1F) The making of observations by the Agency under this section shall not prejudice any other function of the Agency under this Act.",

and

(b) in subsection (3)(a), by the substitution for "Part IV of the Act of 1963" of "section 34 of the Planning and Development Act, 2000".

Note
Section 256 amends s 98 of the EPAA 1992. It clarifies the position/relationship of the planning authorities and the EPA in relation to development which requires an IPC licence.

[512]
257. Amendment of Waste Management Act 1996
The Waste Management Act, 1996, is hereby amended in section 54—

(a) by the substitution for subsection (3) of the following subsections:

"(3) Notwithstanding section 34 of the Planning and Development Act, 2000, or any other provision of that Act, where a waste licence has been granted or is or will be required in relation to an activity, a planning authority or An Bord Pleanála shall not, where it decides to grant a permission under section 34 of that Act in respect of any development comprising the activity or for the purposes of the activity, subject the permission to conditions which are for the purposes of—

(a) controlling emissions from the operation of the activity, including the prevention, limitation, elimination, abatement or reduction of those emissions, or

(b) controlling emissions related to or following the cessation of the operation of the activity.

(3A) Where a waste licence has been granted under this Part or is or will be required in relation to an activity, a planning authority or An Bord Pleanála may, in respect of any development comprising the activity or for the purposes of the activity, decide to refuse a grant of permission under section 34 of the Planning and Development Act, 2000, where the authority or An Bord Pleanála considers that the development, notwithstanding the licensing of the activity under this Part, is unacceptable on environmental grounds, having regard to the proper planning and sustainable development of the area in which the development is or will be situate.

(3B) (a) Before making a decision in respect of a development comprising or for the purposes of an activity, a planning authority or An Bord Pleanála may request the Agency to make observations within such period (which period shall not in any case be less than 3 weeks from the date of the request) as may be specified by the authority or the Board in relation to the development, including in relation to any environmental impact statement submitted.

(b) When making its decision, the authority or An Bord Pleanála, as the case may be, shall have regard to the observations, if any, received from the Agency within the period specified under paragraph (a).

(3C) The planning authority or An Bord Pleanála may, at any time after the expiration of the period specified by the authority or An Bord Pleanála under subsection (3B)(a) for making observations, make its decision on the application or appeal.

(3D) The Minister may make regulations making such incidental, consequential, or supplementary provision as may appear to him or her to be necessary or proper to give full effect to any of the provisions of this section.

(3E) Without prejudice to the generality of subsection (3D), regulations made under this section may provide for matters of procedure in relation to the request for or the making of observations from or by the Agency under this section and related matters

(3F) The making of observations by the Agency under this section shall not prejudice any other function of the Agency under this Act.",

(b) in subsection (4), by the substitution for "Part IV of the Act of 1963" of "section 34 of the Planning and Development Act, 2000" in each place it occurs, and
(c) in subsection (5), by the substitution for "the Local Government (Planning and Development) Acts, 1963 to 1993, and a condition attached to a permission granted under Part IV of the Act of 1963" of "the Planning and Development Act, 2000, and a condition attached to a permission under section 34 of that Act".

Note
Section 257 is similar to s 256 in that it clarifies the relationship between a planning authority and the EPA relevant to development which requires a waste licence. This section amends s 54 of the WMA 1996.

[513]
258. Limitation on connection to sanitary authority
(1) This section shall apply to any structure which is constructed, erected or made on or after the 10th day of June, 1990, or which is not connected to a sewer of a sanitary authority.

(2) Section 27 of the Public Health (Ireland) Act, 1878, shall not apply in relation to a structure to which this section applies.

(3) Notwithstanding section 23 of the Public Health (Ireland) Act, 1878, or any other enactment, the owner or occupier of a structure to which this section applies shall not be entitled to connect his or her drains to any sewer of the sanitary authority in whose functional area the structure is situated except with the consent of the sanitary authority, which may be given subject to such conditions as the sanitary authority considers reasonable.

(4) Any person who connects a drain or causes it to be connected to a sewer of a sanitary authority in contravention of subsection (3) shall be guilty of an offence.

(5) The sanitary authority may close any connection between a drain and sewer made in contravention of subsection (3) and may recover from the person who made the connection or who caused the connection to be made any expenses incurred by the authority under this subsection and in default of the expenses being paid to the authority, they shall be recoverable as a simple contract debt in any court of competent jurisdiction.

(6) Where a notice under section 8(1) of the Local Government (Sanitary Services) Act, 1962, takes effect in relation to any premises, a consent of the sanitary authority by whom the notice has been served shall not be required under subsection (3) of this section for the connection of the structure to the appropriate sewer of the sanitary authority.

(7) Unless otherwise indicated, the grant of a permission under Part III in relation to a structure to which this section applies shall be taken to include the consent of the sanitary authority under subsection (3) to the connection of that structure to the appropriate sewer of the sanitary authority.

(8) In considering whether to give consent under subsection (3), a sanitary authority shall be entitled to have regard to the constraints described at paragraph 1 of the Fourth Schedule in so far as these may apply to the provision of sewerage facilities by them.

(9) In this section, "drain", "sanitary authority" and "sewer" have the meanings assigned to them in the Local Government (Sanitary Services) Acts, 1878 to 1995.

Note
Section 258 restates s 25 of LG(PD)A 1990.

[514]
259. Limitation of section 53 of Waterworks Clauses Act 1847
(1) Section 53 of the Waterworks Clauses Act, 1847, and other enactment which confers a right to a supply of water for domestic purposes, shall not apply in relation to a house which is an unauthorised structure or the use of which constitutes an unauthorised use.

(2) Nothing in this section shall restrict the operation of section 8(2) of the Local Government (Sanitary Services) Act, 1962.

Note
Section 259 restates s 26 of LG(PD)A 1990.

[515]–[520]
260. Saving for national monuments
Nothing in this Act shall restrict, prejudice, or affect the functions of the Minister for Arts, Heritage, Gaeltacht and the Islands under the National Monuments Acts, 1930 to 1994, in relation to national monuments as defined by those Acts or any particular monuments.

Note
Section 260 restates with modifications s 90 of LG(PD)A 1963.

[521]
261. Control of quarries
(1) The owner or operator of a quarry to which this section applies shall, not later than one year from the coming into operation of this section, provide to the planning authority, in whose functional area the quarry is situated, information relating to the operation of the quarry at the commencement of this section, and on receipt of such information the planning authority shall, in accordance with section 7, enter it in the register.

(2) Without prejudice to the generality of subsection (1), information provided under that subsection shall specify the following—

(a) the area of the quarry, including the extracted area delineated on a map,

(b) the material being extracted and processed (if at all),

(c) the date when quarrying operations commenced on the land (where known),

(d) the hours of the day during which the quarry is in operation,

(e) the traffic generated by the operation of the quarry including the type and frequency of vehicles entering and leaving the quarry,

(f) the levels of noise and dust generated by the operations in the quarry,

(g) any material changes in the particulars referred to in paragraphs (a) to (f) during the period commencing on the commencement of this section and the date on which the information is provided,

(h) whether—

  (i) planning permission under Part IV of the Act of 1963 was granted in respect of the quarry and if so, the conditions, if any, to which the permission is subject, or

  (ii) the operation of the quarry commenced before 1 October 1964, and

(i) such other matters in relation to the operations of the quarry as may be prescribed.

(3) A planning authority may require a person who has submitted information in accordance with this section to submit such further information as it may specify, within such period as it may specify, relating to the operation of the quarry concerned and, on receipt thereof, the planning authority shall enter the information in the register.

(4) (a) A planning authority shall, not later than 6 months from the registration of a quarry in accordance with this section, publish notice of the registration in one or more newspapers circulating in the area within which the quarry is situated.

(b) A notice under paragraph (a) shall state—

  (i) that the quarry has been registered in accordance with this section,

  (ii) where planning permission has been granted in respect of the quarry, that it has been so granted and whether the planning authority is considering restating, modifying or adding to conditions attached to the planning permission in accordance with subsection (6)(a)(ii), or

  (iii) where planning permission has not been granted in respect of the quarry, that it has not been so granted and whether the planning authority is considering—

    (I) imposing conditions on the operation of the quarry in accordance with subsection (6)(a)(i), or

    (II) requiring the making of a planning application and the preparation of an environmental impact statement in respect of the quarry in accordance with subsection (7),

  (iv) the place or places and times at which the register may be inspected,

  (v) that submissions or observations regarding the operation of the quarry may be made to the planning authority within 4 weeks from the date of publication of the notice.

(c) A notice under this subsection may relate to one or more quarries registered in accordance with this section.

(5) (a) Where a planning authority proposes to—

  (i) impose, restate, modify or add to conditions on the operation of the quarry under this section, or

(ii) require, under subsection (7), a planning application to be made and an environmental impact statement to be submitted in respect of the quarry in accordance with this section, it shall, as soon as may be after the expiration of the period for making observations or submissions pursuant to a notice under subsection (4)(b), serve notice of its proposals on the owner or operator of the quarry.

(b) A notice referred to in paragraph (a), shall state—
    (i) the reasons for the proposals, and
    (ii) that submissions or observations regarding the proposals may be made by the owner or operator of the quarry to the planning authority within such period as may be specified in the notice, being not less than 6 weeks from the service of the notice.

(c) Submissions or observations made pursuant to a notice under paragraph (b) shall be taken into consideration by a planning authority when performing its functions under subsection (6) or (7).

(6) (a) Not later than 2 years from the registration of a quarry under this section, a planning authority may, in the interests of proper planning and sustainable development, and having regard to the development plan and submissions or observations (if any) made pursuant to a notice under subsection (4) or (5)—
    (i) in relation to a quarry which commenced operation before 1 October 1964, impose conditions on the operation of that quarry, or
    (ii) in relation to a quarry in respect of which planning permission was granted under Part IV of the Act of 1963 restate, modify or add to conditions imposed on the operation of that quarry,
and the owner and operator of the quarry concerned shall as soon as may be thereafter be notified in writing thereof.

(b) Where, in relation to a grant of planning permission conditions have been restated, modified or added in accordance with paragraph (a), the planning permission shall be deemed, for the purposes of this Act, to have been granted under section 34, and any condition so restated, modified or added shall have effect as if imposed under section 34.

(c) Notwithstanding paragraph (a), where an integrated pollution control licence has been granted in relation to a quarry, a planning authority or the Board on appeal shall not restate, modify, add to or impose conditions under this subsection relating to—
    (i) the control (including the prevention, limitation, elimination, abatement or reduction) of emissions from the quarry, or
    (ii) the control of emissions related to or following the cessation of the operation of the quarry.

(7) (a) Where the continued operation of a quarry—
    (i) (I) the extracted area of which is greater than 5 hectares, or
        (II) that is situated on a European site or any other area prescribed for the purpose of section 10(2)(c), or land to which an order under section 15, 16 or 17 of the Wildlife Act, 1976, applies, and
    (ii) that commenced operation before 1 October 1964,
would be likely to have significant effects on the environment (having regard to any selection criteria prescribed by the Minister under section 176(2)(e)), a plan-

ning authority shall not impose conditions on the operation of a quarry under subsection (6), but shall, not later than one year after the date of the registration of the quarry, require, by notice in writing, the owner or operator of the quarry to apply for planning permission and to submit an environmental impact statement to the planning authority not later than 6 months from the date of service of the notice, or such other period as may be agreed with the planning authority.

(b) Section 172(1) shall not apply to development to which an application made pursuant to a requirement under paragraph (a) applies.

(c) A planning authority, or the Board on appeal, shall, in considering an application for planning permission made pursuant to a requirement under paragraph (a), have regard to the existing use of the land as a quarry.

(8) (a) Where, in relation to a quarry for which permission was granted under Part IV of the Act of 1963, a planning authority adds or modifies conditions under this section that are more restrictive than existing conditions imposed in relation to that permission, the owner or operator of the quarry may claim compensation under section 197 and references in that section to compliance with conditions on the continuance of any use of land consequent upon a notice under section 46 shall be construed as including references to compliance with conditions so added or modified, save that no such claim may be made in respect of any condition relating to a matter specified in paragraph (a), (b) or (c) of section 34(4), or in respect of a condition relating to the prevention, limitation or control of emissions from the quarry, or the reinstatement of land on which the quarry is situated.

(b) Where, in relation to a quarry to which subsection (7) applies, a planning authority, or the Board on appeal, refuses permission for development under section 34 or grants permission thereunder subject to conditions on the operation of the quarry, the owner or operator of the quarry shall be entitled to claim compensation under section 197 and for that purpose the reference in subsection (1) of that section to a notice under section 46 shall be construed as a reference to a decision under section 34 and the reference in section 197(2) to section 46 shall be construed as a reference to section 34 save that no such claim may be made in respect of any condition relating to a matter specified in paragraph (a), (b) or (c) of section 34(4), or in respect of a condition relating to the prevention, limitation or control of emissions from the quarry, or the reinstatement of land on which the quarry is situated.

(9) (a) A person who provides information to a planning authority in accordance with subsection (1) or in compliance with a requirement under subsection (3) may appeal a decision of the planning authority to impose, restate, add to or modify conditions in accordance with subsection (6) to the Board within 4 weeks from the date of receipt of notification by the authority of those conditions.

(b) The Board may at the determination of an appeal under paragraph (a) confirm with or without modifications the decision of the planning authority or annul that decision.

(10) (a) A quarry to which this section applies in respect of which the owner or operator fails to provide information in relation to the operations of the quarry

in accordance with subsection (1) or in accordance with a requirement under subsection (3) shall be unauthorised development.

(b) Any quarry in respect of which a notification under subsection (7) applies shall, unless a planning application in respect of the quarry is submitted to the planning authority within the period referred to in that subsection, be unauthorised development.

(11) This section shall apply to—

(a) a quarry in respect of which planning permission under Part IV of the Act of 1963 was granted more than 5 years before the coming into operation of this section, and

(b) any other quarry in operation on or after the coming into operation of this section, being a quarry in respect of which planning permission was not granted under that Part.

(12) The Minister may issue guidelines to planning authorities . regarding the performance of their functions under this section and a planning authority shall have regard to any such guidelines.

(13) In this section—

"emission" means—

(a) an emission into the atmosphere of a pollutant within the meaning of the Air Pollution Act, 1987,

(b) a discharge of polluting matter, sewage effluent or trade effluent within the meaning of the Local Government (Water Pollution) Act, 1977, to waters or sewers within the meaning of that Act,

(c) the disposal of waste, or

(d) noise;

"operator" means a person who at all material times is in charge of the carrying on of quarrying activities at a quarry or under whose direction such activities are carried out;

"quarry" has the meaning assigned to it by section 3 of the Mines and Quarries Act, 1965.

Note

Section 261 refers to the control of quarries and provides that owners and operators must comply with certain requirements and obligations relevant to their continued operations of a quarry. These are new provisions. It is also expected that Department of the Environment will produce guidelines in relation to this section.

[522]
262. Regulations generally

(1) The Minister may make regulations for prescribing any matter referred to in this Act as prescribed or to be prescribed, or in relation to any matter referred to in this Act as the subject of regulations.

(2) Regulations under this Act may contain such incidental, supplemental and consequential provisions as appear to the Minister to be necessary or expedient.

(3) Before making any regulations under this Act, the Minister shall consult with any relevant State authority where the regulations relate to the functions of that State authority.

(4) Where regulations are proposed to be made under section 4(2), 19(3), 25(5), 100(1)(b), (c) or (d), 126(4), 176, 179(1), 181(1), 221(4), 230(1) or 246, a draft of the regulations shall be laid before both Houses of the Oireachtas and the regulations shall not be made unless a resolution approving the draft has been passed by each such House.

(5) Every regulation made under this Act (other than a regulation referred to in subsection (4)) shall be laid before each House of the Oireachtas as soon as may be after it is made and, if a resolution annulling the regulation is passed by either such House within the next 21 days on which that House has sat after the regulation is laid before it, the regulation shall be annulled accordingly but without prejudice to the validity of anything previously done thereunder.

Note
Section 522 refers to the Minister's powers to make regulations under PDA 2000. This section is now in force.

PART XIX   COMMENCEMENT, REPEALS AND CONTINUANCE

Note
Part XIX deals with the transitional provisions that are to apply and also deals with the commencement of PDA 2000.

[523]
263. Interpretation
In this Part, "repealed enactments" means the enactments specified in column (2) of the Sixth Schedule.

[524]
264. Repeals
The enactments specified in column (2) of the Sixth Schedule are hereby repealed to the extent specified in column (3) of that Schedule.

[525]–[530]
265. Continuity of repealed enactments
(1) (a) Nothing in this Act shall affect the validity of any thing done under the Local Government (Planning and Development) Acts, 1963 to 1999, or under any regulations made under those Acts.
(b) Any order, regulation or policy directive made, or any other thing done, under the Local Government (Planning and Development) Acts, 1963 to 1999, that could have been made or done under a corresponding provision of this Act, shall not be invalidated by any repeal effected by this Act but shall, if in force immediately before that repeal was effected, have effect as if made or done under the corresponding provision of this Act, unless otherwise provided.

(2) The continuity of the operation of the law relating to the matters provided for in the repealed enactments shall not be affected by the substitution of this Act for those enactments, and—

(a)   so much of any enactment or document (including enactments contained in this Act) as refers, whether expressly or by implication, to, or to things done or falling to be done under or for the purposes of, any provision of this Act, shall, if and so far as the nature of the subject matter of the enactment or document permits, be construed as including, in relation to the times, years or periods, circumstances or purposes in relation to which the corresponding provision in the repealed enactments has or had effect, a reference to, or, as the case may be, to things done or falling to be done under or for the purposes of, that corresponding provision.

(b)   so much of any enactment or document (including repealed enactments and enactments and documents passed or made after the commencement of this Act) as refers, whether expressly or by implication, to, or to things done or falling to be done under or for the purposes of, any provision of the repealed enactments shall, if and so far as the nature of the subject matter of the enactment or document permits, be construed as including, in relation to the times, years or periods, circumstances or purposes in relation to which the corresponding provision of this Act has effect, a reference to, or, as the case may be, to things done or deemed to be done or falling to be done under or for the purposes of, that corresponding provision.

(3) Section 2 of the Acquisition of Land (Assessment of Compensation) Act, 1919, as amended by section 69(1) of the Act of 1963 shall, notwithstanding the repeal of section 69 of the Act of 1963 by the Act of 1990, apply to every case, other than a case under this Act or the Act of 1990, where any compensation assessed will be payable by a planning authority or any other local authority.

(4) In the case of any application to a planning authority, or any appeal or any other matter with which the Board is concerned which is received by the planning authority or the Board, as the case may be, before the repeal of the relevant provisions or the revocation of any associated regulations, the provisions of the Local Government (Planning and Development) Acts, 1963 to 1999, and regulations made thereunder shall continue to apply to the application, appeal or other matter notwithstanding the repeal of any enactment or revocation of any regulation.

Notes
Section 265(1)(a)
This sub-section provides that the provisions of PDA 2000 do not have retrospective effect.

Section 265(2)(a)
If any enactment or document refers to things done or falling to be done relative to provisions of the previous Planning Acts, they are to be construed as if referring to the corresponding provisions in PDA 2000.

Section 265(4)
Any planning application lodged prior to the coming into force of Pt III will be governed by previous legislation. The situation is similar in relation to any appeal before the Board at the time Pt III is commenced. It seems that there may be some uncertainty about the situation where a decision on an application is given by a planning authority after the coming into force

of Pt III. Is the appeal on this decision governed by the new Act or not? The regulations to be implemented under this section may clarify the position.

[531]
266. Transitional provisions regarding development plans
(1) (a) Notwithstanding the repeal of any enactment by this Act, development plans made under Part III of the Act of 1963 shall continue in force and shall be deemed to have been made under and in compliance with this Act.

(b) Notwithstanding the repeal of any enactment by this Act, where a planning authority has given notice under section 21 of the Act of 1963 of the preparation of a draft development plan, Part III of the Act of 1963 shall continue to apply in respect of that draft development plan until the making of such plan.

(2) (a) Where, on the commencement of Part II, a development plan is in force for longer than 4 years, the planning authority concerned shall, not later than one year after such commencement, initiate the notification procedures under section 11.

(b) Except as is provided for in paragraph (a) and in subsection (1)(b), the provisions of Part II in relation to the review of development plans and the preparation of new plans shall apply to all existing development plans.

(c) For the purposes of paragraphs (a) and (b), the reference to the development plan shall be a reference to the development plan in force for the functional area of the planning authority which covers all, or the greater part of, that functional area and—
   (i) a development plan for a scheduled town, within the meaning of section 2 of the Act of 1963, or
   (ii) a development plan covering part only of the functional area of the authority (not being the greater part),
   shall be deemed not to be a development plan for the purposes of those paragraphs.

(3) A reference in any enactment or instrument to a development plan shall be deemed to be a reference to a development plan as defined in this Act.

Notes
Section 266(1)(a)
Development plans made under the previous legislation shall continue in force and be deemed to have been made under the Act.

Section 266(2)(a)
If on 1 January 2001, a development plan was four years old or more, the relevant planning authority must within one year from 1 January 2001 give notice of the preparation of a new plan.

[532]
267. Transitional provisions respecting acquisition of land
(1) Where, before the transfer of functions to the Board in accordance with sections 214 and 215, any matter was to be determined by the Minister under the enactments referred to in those sections, the Board shall, in lieu of the Minister, determine the matter in accordance with those sections.

(2) Sections 217, 218, 219, 220, 221 and 222 shall not apply to matters referred to in subsection (1) to be determined by the Board in accordance with that subsection.

[533]
268. Miscellaneous transitional provisions

(1) Notwithstanding the repeal of any enactment by this Act—

(a) subsections (2) to (5) of section 38 of the Act of 1999 continue to apply to a planning authority until the planning authority has made the decisions required by those subsections and served them on the appropriate owners and occupiers,

(b) a scheme for the granting of pensions, gratuities or other allowances in respect of the chairperson and ordinary members or in respect of wholetime employees of the Board under an Act repealed by this Act shall continue in force and shall be deemed to be a scheme under section 119 or 121, as appropriate,

(c) a special amenity area order or tree preservation order confirmed or made under an Act repealed by this Act that is in force immediately before the commencement of this section shall be deemed to have been confirmed or made under section 203 or 205, as appropriate,

(d) paragraph 12 of the Third Schedule to the Act of 1990 shall continue to apply for a period of 3 years from the commencement of this section, and

(e) section 55A (inserted by the Roads (Amendment) Act, 1998) of the Roads Act, 1993 (as inserted by section 6 of the Roads (Amendment) Act, 1998) shall continue to apply in relation to an order of the Minister under section 49(3) or 51(6) of that Act.

(2) Any codes of practice concerning the holding of events issued by the Minister or any other Minister of the Government prior to the coming into force of this Act shall be deemed to be codes of practice under section 232.

(3) (a) Notwithstanding section 191, compensation shall be payable under section 190 where there has been a refusal of permission under Part III on the grounds specified in paragraph 5 of the Fourth Schedule, and where—

(i) the development plan contained, prior to the coming into operation of section 10, an objective for the zoning of the land to which the application concerned related for use solely or primarily for the purpose for which the application was made, and

(ii) the application for permission was made not later than 3 years after the coming into operation of this section.

(b) Paragraph (a) shall not apply to a refusal of permission if—

(i) the development is of a class or description set out in the Third Schedule, or

(ii) the refusal was on grounds specified in the Fourth Schedule (other than paragraph (a)).

[534]
269. Regulations to remove difficulties

If any difficulty arises during the period of 3 years from the commencement of this Act in bringing any provision of this Act into operation or in relation to the operation of any provision, the Minister may by regulations do anything which appears to the

Minister to be necessary or expedient for the purposes of removing the difficulty, bringing that provision into operation, or securing or facilitating its operation.

Note
The Minister may by regulation do anything that appears to him/her necessary to remove any difficulty for the operation of PDA 2000 within the first three years of its commencement.

[535]–[540]
270. Commencement
(1) This Act shall come into operation on such day or days as the Minister may appoint by order or orders either generally or with reference to any particular purpose or provision, and different days may be so fixed for different purposes and provisions.

(2) An order under subsection (1) may, in respect of the repeals effected by section 264 of the enactments mentioned in the Sixth Schedule, fix different days for the repeal of different enactments or for the repeal for different purposes of any enactment.

Note
Section 270(1)
PDA 2000 is being commenced on a stage by stage basis. Two commencement orders have been made to date:

(a) Planning and Development Act 2000 (Commencment) Order 2000, SI 349/2000.
(b) Planning and Development Act 2000 (Commencement) (No 2) Order 2000, SI 449/2000.

PART XX   AMENDMENTS OF ROADS ACT, 1993
Note
Part XX contains minor amendments to Pt V of the Roads Act 1993, which relates to toll roads and the making of toll schemes. The most substantial change to the previous legislation is that the roads authority no longer needs the consent or approval of the Minister in relation to the preparation and carrying out of any toll scheme. Approval of the Board is not required.

Part XX was commenced in its entirety on 1 January 2001 (SI 449/2000).

It should be noted that s 215 of PDA 2000 transfers some of the Minister's functions *only* under ss 49, 50 and 51 the Roads Act 1993 (as amended by the Roads (Amendment) Act 1998) to the Board. Those sections deal with proposed motorways, busways and protected roads schemes, and not to the toll schemes referred to in this part.

The Roads Act 1993 refers to the 'road authority'. In the case of a national road, this means the National Roads Authority, established under the Roads Act 1993. In the case of regional or local roads, it means the local authority department with responsibility for the development and maintenance of local roads.

[541]
271. Amendment of section 57 of Roads Act, 1993
Section 57 of the Roads Act, 1993, is hereby amended—

(a) by the substitution of the following for subsection (1):

"(1) A road authority may prepare a scheme for the establishment of a system of tolls in respect of the use of a public road.",

(b) in subsection (2), by the substitution for "In making a toll scheme" of "In preparing a scheme under subsection (1)",

(c) in subsection (3), by the substitution for "toll scheme" of "scheme prepared under subsection (1)",

(d) in subsection (4), by the substitution for "toll scheme" of "scheme under subsection (1)",

(e) by the substitution of the following for subsection (5):

"(5) A road authority may prepare a scheme amending a toll scheme adopted by it under section 58.",

(f) in subsection (6), by the substitution for "toll scheme" of "scheme prepared under subsection (1)", and

(g) by the substitution of the following for subsection (7):

"(7) (a) The Authority shall, before adopting, under section 58, a scheme prepared under subsection (1) in relation to a national road, send a copy of the scheme to the appropriate road authority under section 13 and serve a notice on the road authority stating—
   (i) that a scheme under subsection (1) has been prepared, and
   (ii) that representations may be made in writing to the Authority in relation to the scheme before such date as is specified in the notice (being not less than 6 weeks from the date of service of the notice).

(b) The Authority shall consider any representations made to it pursuant to a notice under paragraph (a).

(c) The making of representations by a road authority under this subsection shall be a reserved function and shall be without prejudice to the right of that authority to make objections to the Authority under section 58.".

Note

Section 271 amends s 57 of the Roads Act 1993 by substituting the words 'make a scheme (a "toll scheme")' with 'prepare a scheme for the establishment of a system of tolls'. The scheme no longer requires ministerial approval for the preparation of a scheme.

Section 271(7) provides that if it is a scheme prepared by the National Roads Authority, the local authority may now make objections or submissions directly to the National Roads Authority, and not to the Minister, as was previously the case in s 58 of the Roads Act 1993.

In the event of an objection to a scheme, the roads authority may appoint an appropriate person to conduct an oral hearing into the matters to which the objection relates. It was previously the case that an oral hearing could be held into the scheme in its entirety *and* into the matters to which the objection related.

[542]
272. Scheme prepared under section 57 of Roads Act 1993 be adopted by road authority

The Roads Act, 1993, is hereby amended by the substitution of the following section for section 58:

"**58.** (1) A road authority shall publish in one or more newspapers circulating in the area where the proposed toll road is located or is to be located a notice—

(a) stating that a draft toll scheme has been prepared,

(b) indicating the times at which, the period (being a period of not less than one month from the first publication of the notice) during which, and the place at which a copy of the scheme prepared under section 57, any map referred to therein and the explanatory statement relating to the scheme may be inspected, and

(c) stating that objections to the draft toll scheme may be made in writing to the road authority before such date as is specified in the notice (being not less than 2 weeks from the end of the period for inspection referred to in paragraph (b)).

(2) (a) Subject to paragraph (b), a road authority may adopt a scheme prepared by it under subsection (1), with or without modifications and, subject to subsection (3), a scheme so adopted is hereafter in this Act referred to as a "toll scheme".

(b) If an objection to a draft toll scheme is made to the road authority and the objection is not withdrawn, the road authority shall, before deciding whether to adopt the draft toll scheme or not, cause an oral hearing to be held into the matters to which the objection relates, by a person appointed by the road authority, and shall consider the report of and any recommendation made by the person so appointed.

(3) (a) A toll scheme adopted by the road authority under this section shall come into force with the modifications, if any, therein made by the road authority on such day as may be determined by the road authority.

(b) Notice of the day on which a toll scheme is to come into force shall be published by the road authority at least one month before such day in one or more newspapers circulating in the area in which the toll road to which the scheme relates is located or will be located.".

Note

Section 272 amends s 58 of the Roads Act 1993 by removing the requirement for Ministerial approval for the adoption of a scheme. A toll scheme may now be adopted by the roads authority itself, subject to the procedural requirements in sub-s (2)(b) relating to objections.

Section 58(2)(b) of the Roads Act 1993 referred to objections made 'in writing'. The amended section merely refers to 'an objection'.

Section 272 deletes s 58(2)(c) of the Roads Act 1993.

[543]
273. Amendment of section 60 of Roads Act 1993
Section 60 of the Roads Act, 1993, is hereby amended by the substitution of the following for that section:

"**60.** (1) A road authority may by order revoke a toll scheme adopted by it under section 58.

(2) Where a road authority proposes to make an order under subsection (1) it shall, before so making the order, publish in one or more newspapers circulating in the area where the toll road is located a notice—

(a) stating that it proposes to revoke the scheme,

(b) indicating the times at which, the period (being not less than one month from the first publication of the notice) during which, and the place at which, a copy of the proposal may be inspected,

(c) stating that objections or representations may be made in writing to the road authority in relation to the proposal before such date as is specified in the notice (being a date that falls not less than 2 weeks from the end of the period for inspection of the proposal).

(3) Before making an order under subsection (1), the road authority shall consider any objections or representations made to it in accordance with a notice under sub-section (2).

(4) A road authority may at its discretion cause an oral hearing to be held into any matter to which objections or representations, made in accordance with a notice under subsection (2) and not withdrawn, relate, by a person appointed by the road authority, and where a road authority causes an oral hearing to be so held it shall, before revoking the toll scheme under subsection (3), consider the report of and any recommendation made by that person.

(5) The road authority shall publish in one or more newspapers circulating in the area where the toll road is located notice of the making of any order under subsection (1).

(6) The making of an order under this section in relation to a regional road or a local road shall be a reserved function.".

Notes
Section 273 restates s 60 of the Roads Act 1993 with the following modifications:

(a) The requirement for Ministerial approval for the revocation of a toll scheme is deleted from sub-s (1). The roads authority may make the order to revoke a toll scheme without approval.

(b) Sub-section (4), which sets out the procedure to be followed when an objection is made to the revocation of a toll scheme, provides that the roads authority may cause an oral hearing to be held by an appointed person, and that it shall consider the report and any recommendations made by that person. The Roads Act 1993 merely provided that a public local inquiry be held.

[544]
274. Amendment of section 61 of Roads Act, 1993
Section 61 of the Roads Act, 1993, is hereby amended—

(a) by the deletion of subsection (5),

(b) by the substitution of the following subsection for subsection (6):

"(6) Before making bye-laws, a road authority shall publish in one or more newspapers circulating in the area where the toll road to which the bye-laws relate is located or is to be located a notice—

(a) indicating that it is proposed to make such byelaws and stating the purpose of the bye-laws,

    (b) indicating the times at which, the period (being a period of not less than one month from the date of the first publication of the notice) during which, and the place at which, a copy of the draft bye-laws may be inspected,

    (c) stating that objections or representations may be made in writing to the road authority in relation to the draft bye-laws before such date as is specified in the notice (being a date that falls not less than 2 weeks from the end of the period for inspection of the draft bye-laws), and

    (d) stating that a copy of the draft bye-laws may be purchased on payment of such fee as is specified in the notice not exceeding the reasonable cost incurred in the making of such copy.",

(c) by the substitution of the following subsection for subsection (7):

"(7) Before making bye-laws the road authority shall consider any objections or representations which have been made to it in accordance with a notice under subsection (6) and not withdrawn.",

(d) by the substitution of the following subsection for subsection (8):

"(8) Bye-laws made by a road authority under this section shall come into effect on such date as is specified in those bye-laws.",

and

(e) in subsection (9), by the substitution for "approved" of "made".

Notes

Section 274 deletes s 61(5) of the Roads Act 1993, which stated that bye-laws under sub-s (1) would have no effect unless and until the Minister approved them.

Section 61 (as amended by s 274) requires that the newspaper notice must include:

(a) the fact that it is proposed to make bye-laws, and what their purpose will be, and
(b) the fee to be paid for a copy of the draft bye-law.

[545]–[550]
275. Amendment of section 63 of Roads Act 1993
Section 63 of the Roads Act, 1993, is hereby amended—

(a) in subsection (1), by the substitution for "Where a toll scheme is approved by the Minister, a road authority may, with the consent of the Minister," of "Where a toll scheme is adopted by a road authority, the road authority may", and

(b) in subsection (3), by the deletion of ", with the consent of the Minister,".

Note

Section 275 makes minor modifications to the wording of s 63 of the Roads Act 1993 to remove the requirement for Ministerial approval.

[551]
276. Amendment of section 65 of Roads Act 1993
The Roads Act, 1993, is hereby amended in section 65 by the substitution for "section 57" of "section 58".

Note

Section 276 amends s 65 of the Roads Act 1993, which provides that the Minister may make regulations to enable a toll scheme to go ahead. The 1993 Act referred to a toll scheme under s 57 but that is amended so that the reference is to s 58, the section that provides for the adoption, as opposed to the preparation, of a toll scheme.

[552]–[580]
277. Further amendment of Part V of Roads Act 1993

Part V of the Roads Act, 1993, is hereby amended by the insertion after section 66 of the following sections—

"66A. Ministerial policy directives on road tolling

(1) The Minister may, from time to time, issue policy directives to road authorities regarding the exercise of any of their functions under Part V or any matter connected therewith and road authorities shall comply with any such directives.

(2) The Minister may revoke or amend a policy directive issued under this section.

(3) The Minister shall cause a copy of any policy directive issued under this section to be laid before each House of the Oireachtas.

(4) A road authority shall make available for inspection by members of the public any policy directive issued to it under this section.

(5) The Minister shall not issue a directive relating to a particular tolling scheme.

66B. Continuance of bye-laws and agreements

Notwithstanding this Part, every agreement entered into and every toll scheme or bye law made by a road authority and in force immediately before the commencement of this section shall continue in force as if made or entered into under this Part as amended by the Planning and Development Act, 2000.

66C. Transitional provisions regarding toll schemes

Where, before the commencement of Part XX of the Planning and Development Act, 2000, any toll scheme, proposal to revoke a toll scheme or bye-law has been submitted to the Minister under Part V and the matter has not been determined by the Minister, the determination of the matter shall continue to rest with the Minister and Part V as amended by Part XX of the Planning and Development Act, 2000, shall not apply with respect to the matter.".

Note

Section 277 inserts a new provision (s 66A) into the Roads Act 1993. It provides for the making of Ministerial Policy Directives. Policy Directives may be issued by the Minister in relation to any general planning matter, but they may not be issued in relation to a particular toll scheme, or a particular planning decision.

FIRST SCHEDULE   (Section 10)
PURPOSES FOR WHICH OBJECTIVES MAY BE INDICATED IN
DEVELOPMENT PLAN

PART I   LOCATION AND PATTERN OF DEVELOPMENT

[581]
1. Reserving or allocating any particular land, or all land in any particular area, for development of a specified class or classes, or prohibiting or restricting, either permanently or temporarily, development on any specified land.

2. Promoting sustainable settlement and transportation strategies in urban and rural areas.

3. Preserving the quality and character of urban or rural areas.

4. Regulating, restricting or controlling retail development.

5. Regulating, promoting or controlling tourism development.

6. Regulating, restricting or controlling development in areas at risk of flooding (whether inland or coastal), erosion and other natural hazards.

7. Regulating, restricting and controlling the development of coastal areas and development in the vicinity of inland waterways.

8. Regulating, restricting and controlling development on the foreshore, or any part of the foreshore.

9. Giving effect to the European Spatial Development Perspective towards balanced and sustainable development of the territory of the European Union, adopted by the meeting of Ministers responsible for Regional/Spatial Planning of the European Union at Potsdam, 10 and 11 May, 1999.

10. Regulating, restricting or controlling development in order to reduce the risk of serious danger to human health or the environment.

11. Regulating, promoting or controlling the exploitation of natural resources.

PART II   CONTROL OF AREAS AND STRUCTURES

[582]
1. Regulating and controlling the layout of areas and structures, including density, spacing, grouping and orientation of structures in relation to roads, open spaces and other structures.

2. Regulating and controlling the design, colour and materials of structures and groups of structures, including streets and townscapes, and structures and groups of structures in rural areas.

3. Promoting design in structures for the purposes of flexible and sustainable use, including conservation of energy and resources.

4. Limiting the number of structures, or the number of structures of a specified class, which may be constructed, erected or made on, in or under any area.

5. Regulating and controlling, either generally or in particular areas, all or any of the following matters:

(a) the size, height, floor area and character of structures;
(b) building lines, coverage and the space about houses and other structures;
(c) the extent of parking places required in, on or under structures of a particular class or size, or services or facilities for the parking, loading, unloading or fuelling of vehicles;
(d) the objects which may be affixed to structures;
(e) the purposes for and the manner in which structures may be used or occupied, including, in the case of a house, the letting thereof in separate units.

6. Regulating and controlling, in accordance with the principles of proper planning and sustainable development, the following:

(a) the disposition or layout of land and structures or structures of any specified class, including the reservation of sufficient open space in relation to the number, class and character of structures in any particular development proposal, road layout, landscaping and planting;
(b) the provision of water, waste water, waste and public lighting facilities:
(c) the provision of service roads and the location and design of means of access to transport networks, including public transport:
(d) the provision of facilities for parking, unloading, loading and fuelling of vehicles on any land.

7. The removal or alteration of structures which are inconsistent with the development plan.

PART III   COMMUNITY FACILITIES

[583]
1. Facilitating the provision and siting of services and facilities necessary for the community, including the following:

(a) hospitals and other healthcare facilities;
(b) centres for the social, economic, recreational, cultural, environmental, or general development of the community;
(c) facilities for the elderly and for persons with disabilities;
(d) places of public worship and meeting halls;
(e) recreational facilities and open spaces, including caravan and camping parks, sports grounds and playgrounds;
(f) shopping and banking facilities.

2. Ensuring the provision and siting of sanitary services.

3. Reserving of land for burial grounds.

PART IV   ENVIRONMENT AND AMENITIES

[584]

1. Protecting and preserving the quality of the environment, including the prevention, limitation, elimination, abatement or reduction of environmental pollution and the protection of waters, groundwater, the seashore and the atmosphere.

2. Securing the reduction or prevention of noise emissions or vibrations.

3. Prohibiting, regulating or controlling the deposit or disposal of waste materials, refuse and litter, the disposal of sewage and the pollution of waters.

4. Protecting features of the landscape which are of major importance for wild fauna and flora.

5. (a) Preserving and protecting flora, fauna and ecological diversity.
(b) Preserving and protecting trees, shrubs, plants and flowers.

6. Protecting and preserving (either in situ or by record) places, caves, sites, features and other objects of archaeological, geological, historical, scientific or ecological interest.

7. Preserving the character of the landscape, including views and prospects, and the amenities of places and features of natural beauty or interest.

8. Preserving any existing public right of way, including, in particular, rights of way which give access to seashore, mountain, lakeshore, riverbank or other place of natural beauty or recreational utility.

9. Reserving land as open spaces, whether public or private (other than open spaces reserved under Part II of this Schedule) or as a public park, public garden or public recreation space.

10. Prohibiting, restricting or controlling, either generally or in particular places or within a specified distance of the centre line of all roads or any specified road, the erection of all or any particular forms of advertisement structure or the exhibition of all or any particular forms of advertisement.

11. Preventing, remedying or removing injury to amenities arising from the ruinous or neglected condition of any structure or from the objectionable or neglected condition of any land.

PART V   INFRASTRUCTURE AND TRANSPORT

[585]–[590]

1. Reserving land for transport networks, including roads, rail, light rail and air and sea transport, for communication networks, for energy generation and for energy networks, including renewable energy, and for other networks, and for ancillary facilities to service those networks.

2. Facilitating the provision of sustainable integrated transport, public transport and road traffic systems and promoting the development of local transport plans.

3. Securing the greater convenience and safety of users of all transport networks and of pedestrians and cyclists.

4. Establishment of public rights of way and extinguishment of public and private rights of way.

5. Construction, alteration, closure or diversion of roads, including cycleways and busways.

6. Establishing—

(a)   the line, width, level and construction of,
(b)   the means of access to and egress from, and
(c)   the general dimensions and character of,

roads, including cycleways and busways, and, where appropriate, other transport networks, whether new or existing.

7. Providing for the management and control of traffic, including the provision and control of parking areas.

8. Providing for works incidental to the making, improvement or landscaping of any transport, communication, energy or other network.

SECOND SCHEDULE   (Section 184)
RULES FOR THE DETERMINATION OF THE AMOUNT OF
COMPENSATION

[591]
1. The reduction in value shall, subject to the other provisions of this Schedule, be determined by reference to the difference between the antecedent and subsequent values of the land, where—

(a)   the antecedent value of the land is the amount which the land, if sold in the open market by a willing seller immediately prior to the relevant decision under Part III (and assuming that the relevant application for permission had not been made), might have been expected to realise, and
(b)   the subsequent value of the land is the amount which the land, if sold in the open market by a willing seller immediately after that decision, might be expected to realise.

2. In determining the antecedent value and subsequent value of the land for the purposes of paragraph I—

(a)   regard shall be had to—
    (i)   any contribution which a planning authority might have required or might require as a condition precedent to development of the land,
    (ii) any restriction on the development of the land which, without conferring a right to compensation, could have been or could be imposed under any Act or under any order, regulations, rule or bye-law made under any Act,

   (iii) the fact that exempted development might have been or may be carried out on the land, and
   (iv) the open market value of comparable land, if any, in the vicinity of the land whose values are being determined;
(b) no account shall be taken of—
   (i)   any part of the value of the land attributable to subsidies or grants available from public moneys, or to any tax or rating allowances in respect of development, from which development of the land might benefit,
   (ii) the special suitability or adaptability of the land for any purpose if that purpose is a purpose to which it could be applied only in pursuance of statutory powers, or for which there is no market apart from the special needs of a particular purchaser or the requirements of any statutory body as defined in paragraph 5:

   Provided that any bona fide offer for the purchase of the land which may be brought to the notice of the arbitrator shall be taken into consideration,

   (iii) any increase in the value of land attributable to the SCH. 2 use thereof or of any structure thereon in a manner which could be restrained by any court, or is contrary to law, or detrimental to the health of the inmates of the structure, or to public health or safety, or to the environment,
   (iv) any depreciation or increase in value attributable to the land, or any land in the vicinity, being reserved for a particular purpose in a development plan,
   (v)   any value attributable to any unauthorised structure or unauthorised use,
   (vi) the existence of proposals for development of the land or any other land by a statutory body, or
   (vii) the possibility or probability of the land or other land becoming subject to a scheme of development undertaken by a statutory body;
   and
(c) all returns and assessments of capital value for taxation made or acquiesced in by the claimant may be considered.

3. (1) In assessing the possibilities, if any, for developing the land, for the purposes of determining its antecedent value, regard shall be had only to such reasonable possibilities as, having regard to all material considerations, could be judged to have existed immediately prior to the relevant decision under Part III.

(2) Material considerations for the purposes of subparagraph (1) shall, without prejudice to the generality thereof, include—

(a) the nature and location of the land,
(b) the likelihood or unlikelihood, as the case may be, of obtaining permission or further permission, to develop the land in the light of the provisions of the development plan,
(c) the assumption that, if any permission to develop the land were to be granted, any conditions which might reasonably be imposed in relation to matters referred to in the Fifth Schedule (but no other conditions) would be imposed, and
(d) any permission to develop the land, not being permission for the development of a kind specified in section 192(2), already existing at the time of the relevant decision under Part III.

4. (1) In determining the subsequent value of the land in a case in which there has been a refusal of permission—

(a) it shall be assumed, subject to subparagraph (2), that, after the refusal, permission under Part III would not be granted for any development of a kind specified in section 192(2),
(b) regard shall be had to any conditions in relation to matters referred to in the Fifth Schedule (but no other conditions) which might reasonably be imposed in the grant of permission to develop the land.

(2) In a case in which there has been a refusal of permission in relation to land in respect of which there is in force an undertaking under Part VI of the Act of 1963, it shall be assumed in determining the subsequent value of the land that, after the refusal, permission under Part III of this Act would not be granted for any development other than development to which the undertaking relates.

5. (1) In paragraph 2, "statutory body" means—

(a) a Minister of the Government,
(b) the Commissioners,
(c) a local authority within the meaning of the Local Government Act, 1941,
(d) a harbour authority within the meaning of the Harbours Act, 1946,
(e) a health board established under the Health Act, 1970, a vocational education committee within the meaning of the Vocational Education Act, 1930,
(g) a board or other body established by or under statute,
(h) a company in which all the shares are held by, or on behalf of, or by directors appointed by, a Minister of the Government, or
(i) a company in which all the shares are held by a board, company, or other body referred to in subparagraph (g) or (h).

(2) In clauses (h) and (i) of subparagraph (1), "company" means a company within the meaning of section 2 of the Companies Act, 1963.

Note
This Schedule restates the First Schedule of LG(PD)A 1990 regarding the rules of determination of compensation.

THIRD SCHEDULE   (Section 191)
DEVELOPMENT IN RESPECT OF WHICH A REFUSAL OF PERMISSION WILL NOT ATTRACT COMPENSATION

[592]
1. Any development that consists of or includes the making of any material change in the use of any structures or other land.

2. The demolition of a habitable house.

3. Any development which would materially affect a protected structure or proposed protected structure.

4. The erection of any advertisement structure.

5. The use of land for the exhibition of any advertisement.

6. Development in an area to which a special amenity area order relates.

7. Any development on land with respect to which there is available (notwithstanding the refusal of permission) a grant of permission under Part III for any development of a residential, commercial or industrial character, if the development consists wholly or mainly of the construction of houses, shops or office premises, hotels, garages and petrol filling stations, theatres or structures for the purpose of entertainment, or industrial buildings (including warehouses), or any combination thereof, subject to no conditions other than conditions of the kind referred to in the Fifth Schedule.

8. Any development on land with respect to which compensation has already been paid under section 190, section 11 of the Act of 1990 or under section 55 of the Act of 1963, by reference to a previous decision under Part III of this Act or under Part IV of the Act of 1963 involving a refusal of permission.

Note
This Schedule restates the Second Schedule of LG(PD)A 1990 and sets out the types of development for which a refusal of permission will not attract compensation.

FOURTH SCHEDULE   (Section 191)
REASONS FOR THE REFUSAL OF PERMISSION WHICH EXCLUDE
COMPENSATION

[593]
1. Development of the kind proposed on the land would be premature by reference to any one or combination of the following constraints and the period within which the constraints involved may reasonably be expected to cease—

(a) an existing deficiency in the provision of water supplies or sewerage facilities,
(b) the capacity of existing or prospective water supplies or sewerage facilities being required for prospective development as regards which a grant of a permission under Part III of this Act, an undertaking under Part VI of the Act of 1963 or a notice under section 13 of the Act of 1990 or section 192 of this Act exists,
(c) the capacity of existing or prospective water supplies or sewerage facilities being required for the prospective development of another part of the functional area of the planning authority, as indicated in the development plan,
(d) the capacity of existing or prospective water supplies or sewerage facilities being required for any other prospective development or for any development objective, as indicated in the development plan,
(e) any existing deficiency in the road network serving the area of the proposed development, including considerations of capacity, width, alignment, or the surface or structural condition of the pavement, which would render that network, or any part of it, unsuitable to carry the increased road traffic likely to result from the development,
(f) any prospective deficiency (including the considerations specified in sub-

paragraph (e)) in the road network serving the area of the proposed development which—

(i) would arise because of the increased road traffic likely to result from that development and from prospective development as regards which a grant of permission under Part III, an undertaking under Part VI of the Act of 1963 or a notice under section 13 of the Act of 1990 or section 192 exists, or

(ii) would arise because of the increased road traffic likely to result from that development and from any other prospective development or from any development objective, as indicated in the development plan, and

would render that road network, or any part of it, unsuitable to carry the increased road traffic likely to result from the proposed development.

2. Development of the kind proposed would be premature pending the determination by the planning authority or the road authority of a road layout for the area or any part thereof.

3. Development of the kind proposed would be premature by reference to the order of priority, if any, for development indicated in the development plan or pending the adoption of a local area plan in accordance with the development plan.

4. The proposed development would endanger public safety by reason of traffic hazard or obstruction of road users or otherwise.

5. The proposed development—

(a) could, due to the risk of a major accident or if a major accident were to occur, lead to serious danger to human health or the environment, or

(b) is in an area where it is necessary to limit the risk of there being any serious danger to human health or the environment.

6. The proposed development is in an area which is at risk of flooding.

7. The proposed development, by itself or by the precedent which the grant of permission for it would set for other relevant development, would adversely affect the use of a national road or other major road by traffic.

8. The proposed development would interfere with the character of the landscape or with a view or prospect of special amenity value or natural interest or beauty, any of which it is necessary to preserve.

9. The proposed development would cause serious air pollution, water pollution, noise pollution or vibration or pollution connected with the disposal of waste.

10. In the case of development including any structure or any addition to or extension of a structure, the structure, addition or extension would—

(a) infringe an existing building line or, where none exists, a building line determined by the planning authority or by the Board,

(b) be under a public road,

(c) seriously injure the amenities, or depreciate the value, of property in the vicinity,

(d) tend to create any serious traffic congestion,

(e) endanger or interfere with the safety of aircraft or the safe and efficient navigation thereof,

(f) endanger the health or safety of persons occupying or employed in the structure or any adjoining structure, or

(g) be prejudicial to public health.

11. The development would contravene materially a condition attached to an existing permission for development.

12. The proposed development would injure or interfere with a historic monument which stands registered in the Register of Historic Monuments under section 5 of the National Monuments (Amendment) Act, 1987, or which is situated in an archaeological area so registered.

13. The proposed development would adversely affect an architectural conservation area.

14. The proposed development would adversely affect the linguistic or cultural heritage of the Gaeltacht.

15. The proposed development would materially contravene an objective indicated in a local area plan for the area.

16. The proposed development would be contrary to any Ministerial guidelines issued to planning authorities under section 28 or any Ministerial policy directive issued to planning authorities under section 29.

17. The proposed development would adversely affect a landscape conservation area.

18. In accordance with section 35, the planning authority considers that there is a real and substantial risk that the development in respect of which permission is sought would not be completed in accordance with any permission or any condition to which such a permission would be subject.

19. The proposed development—

(a) would contravene materially a development objective indicated in the development plan for the conservation and preservation of a European site insofar as the proposed development would adversely affect one or more specific—
    (i)   (I)   natural habitat types in Annex I of the Habitats Directive, or
          (II) species in Annex II of the Habitats Directive which the site hosts, and which have been selected by the Minister for Arts, Heritage, Gaeltacht and the Islands in accordance with Annex III (Stage 1) of that Directive,
    (ii) species of bird or their habitat or other habitat specified in Article 4 of the Birds Directive, which formed the basis of the classification of that site, or
(b) would have a significant adverse effect on any other areas prescribed for the purpose of section 10(2)(c).

20. The development would contravene materially a development objective indicated in the development plan for the zoning of land for the use solely or primarily of particular areas for particular purposes (whether residential, commercial, industrial, agricultural, recreational, as open space or otherwise or a mixture of such uses).

21. (a) Subject to paragraph 22, paragraphs 19 and 20 shall not apply in a case where a development objective for the use specified in paragraph 20 applied to the land at any time during the period of a development plan and the develop-

ment objective of which was changed as a result of a variation of the plan during such period prior to the date on which the relevant application for permission was made to develop the land, and the development would not have contravened materially that development objective.

(b) Paragraph 20 shall not apply in a case where, as a result of a direction by the Minister under section 31(2) given within one year of the making of a development plan, a planning authority amends or revokes a development objective referred to in paragraph 19 but without prejudice to any right of compensation which may otherwise arise in respect of any refusal of permission under Part III in respect of an application made before such direction was issued by the Minister.

22. Paragraph 21 shall not apply in a case where a person acquired his or her interest in the land—

(a) after the objective referred to in paragraph 19 or 20 has come into operation, or

(b) after notice has been published,

(i) in accordance with section 12 or 13, of a proposed new development plan or of proposed variations of a development plan, as the case may be, or

(ii) in accordance with section 12, of a material alteration of the draft concerned,

indicating in draft the development objective referred to in paragraph 19 or 20, or

(c) in the case of paragraph 19, after notice has been published by the Minister for Arts, Heritage, Gaeltacht and the Islands of his or her intention to propose that the land be selected as a European site.

23. For the purposes of paragraph 22, the onus shall be on a person to prove all relevant facts relating to his or her interest in the land to the satisfaction of the planning authority.

24. In this Schedule, "road authority" and "national road" have the meanings assigned to them in the Roads Act, 1993.

Note

This Fourth Schedule restates the Third Schedule of LG(PD)A 1990 with amendments. The Schedule sets out the reasons for refusal of permission which exclude the payment of compensation. This list has been extended by the addition of a number of reasons as follows:- 5(a) and (b); 6; 12–21 inclusive; 22 is a revised version of the pre-existing 13; and clauses 23 and 24 are a restatement of 14 and 15 in the previous Schedule. The provisions of clauses 21 and 22 are of particular importance in prescribing circumstances where compensation will nevertheless be payable.

FIFTH SCHEDULE   (Section 191)
CONDITIONS WHICH MAY BE IMPOSED, ON THE GRANTING OF PERMISSION TO DEVELOP LAND, WITHOUT COMPENSATION

[594]

1. A condition, under paragraphs (g) and (j) of section 34(4), requiring the giving of security for satisfactory completion of the proposed development (including mainte-

nance until taken in charge by the local authority concerned of roads, open spaces, carparks, sewers, watermains or drains).

2. A condition, included in a grant of permission pursuant to section 48 or 49, requiring the payment of a contribution for public infrastructure benefitting the development.

3. A condition, under paragraph (a) of section 34(4), requiring the removal of an advertisement structure.

4. Any condition under paragraph (a) of section 34(4) in a case in which the relevant application for permission relates to a temporary structure.

5. Any condition relating to the reservation or allocation of any particular land, or all land in any particular area, for development of a specified class or classes, or the prohibition or restriction either permanently or temporarily, of development on any specified land.

6. Any condition relating to the preservation of the quality and character of urban or rural areas.

7. Any condition relating to the regulation, restriction and control of development of coastal areas or development in the vicinity of inland waterways.

8. Any provision relating to the protection of the linguistic or cultural heritage of the Gaeltacht.

9. Any condition relating to reducing the risk or limiting the consequences of a major accident, or limiting the risk of there being any serious danger to human health or the environment.

10. Any condition regulating, restricting or controlling development in areas at risk of flooding.

11. Any condition relating to—

(a) the regulation and control of the layout of areas and structures, including density, spacing, grouping and orientation of structures in relation to roads, open spaces and other structures,
(b) the regulation and control of the design, colour and materials of structures and groups of structures,
(c) the promotion of design in structures for the purposes of flexible and sustainable use, including conservation of energy and resources.

12. Any condition limiting the number of structures or the number of structures of a specified class which may be constructed, erected or made on, in or under any area.

13. Any condition regulating and controlling all or any of the following matters—

(a) the size, height, floor area and character of structures;
(b) building lines, coverage and the space about houses and other structures;
(c) the extent of parking places required in, on or under structures of a particular class or size or services or facilities for the parking, loading, unloading or fuelling of vehicles;
(d) the objects which may be affixed to structures;

(e)   the purposes for and the manner in which structures may be used or occupied, including, in the case of dwellings, the letting thereof in separate units.

14. Any condition relating to the alteration or removal of unauthorised structures.

15. Any condition relating to the provision and siting of sanitary services and waste facilities, recreational facilities and open spaces.

16. Any condition relating to the protection and conservation of the environment including the prevention of environmental pollution and the protection of waters, groundwater, the seashore and the atmosphere.

17. Any condition relating to measures to reduce or prevent the emission or the intrusion of noise or vibration.

18. Any condition prohibiting, regulating or controlling the deposit or disposal of waste materials and refuse, the disposal of sewage and the pollution of rivers, lakes, ponds, gullies and the seashore.

19. Any condition relating to the protection of features of the landscape which are of major importance for wild fauna and flora.

20. Any condition relating to the preservation and protection of trees, shrubs, plants and flowers.

21. Any condition relating to the preservation (either in situ or by record) of places, caves, sites, features or other objects of archaeological, geological, historical, scientific or ecological interest.

22. Any condition relating to the conservation and preservation of—

(a)   one or more specific—
   (i)   (I)   natural habitat types in Annex I of the Habitats Directive, or
          (II)   species in Annex II of the Habitats Directive which the site hosts, contained in a European site selected by the Minister for Arts, Heritage, Gaeltacht and the Islands in accordance with Annex III (Stage 1) of that Directive,
   (ii)   species of bird or their habitat or other habitat contained in a European site specified in Article 4 of the Birds Directive, which formed the basis of the classification of that site, or
(b)   any other area prescribed for the purpose of section 10(2) (c).

23. Any condition relating to the preservation of the landscape in general, or a landscape conservation order in particular, including views and prospects and amenities of places and features of natural beauty or interest.

24. Any condition for preserving any existing public right of way.

25. Any condition reserving, as a public park, public garden or public recreation space, land normally used as such.

26. Any condition prohibiting, restricting or controlling, either generally or within a specified distance of the centre line of any specified road, the erection of all or any particular forms of advertisement structure or the exhibition of all or any particular forms of advertisement.

27. Any condition preventing, remedying or removing injury to amenities arising from the ruinous or neglected condition of any structure, or from the objectionable or neglected condition of any land attached to a structure or abutting on a public road or situate in a residential area.

28. Any condition relating to a matter in respect of which a requirement could have been imposed under any other Act, or under any order, regulation, rule or bye-law made under any other Act, without liability for compensation.

29. Any condition prohibiting the demolition of a habitable house.

30. Any condition relating to the filling of land.

31. Any condition in the interest of ensuring the safety of aircraft or the safe and efficient navigation thereof.

32. Any condition determining the sequence in which works shall be carried out or specifying a period within which works shall be completed.

33. Any condition restricting the occupation of any structure included in a development until the completion of other works included in the development or until any other specified condition is complied with or until the planning authority consents to such occupation.

34. Any conditions relating to the protection of a protected structure or a proposed protected structure.

Note
This Fifth Schedule restates the Fourth Schedule of LG(PD)A 1990 with modifications to take account of changes made in PDA 2000, eg new power to remove advertising structures (3); conditions relating to reducing the risk or limiting the consequences of a major accident (9); conditions relating to the protection of features of the landscape (19); conditions in relation to the conservation or preservation of habitats pursuant to the Habitats Directive; and conditions relating to measures to reduce or prevent the emission or the intrusion of noise and vibration (25).

SIXTH SCHEDULE   (Section 264)
ENACTMENTS REPEALED

[595]–[800]

Number and Year (1)	Short Title (2)	Extent of Repeal (3)
No. 28 of 1963	Local Government (Planning and Development) Act, 1963	The whole Act.
No. 20 of 1976	Local Government (Planning and Development) Act, 1976	The whole Act.
No. 21 of 1982	Local Government (Planning and Development) Act, 1982	The whole Act, other than section 6.

Number and Year (1)	Short Title (2)	Extent of Repeal (3)
No. 28 of 1983	Local Government (Planning and Development) Act, 1983	The whole Act.
No. 11 of 1990	Local Government (Planning and Development) Act, 1990	The whole Act.
No. 11 of 1991	Local Government Act, 1991	Sections 44 and 45.
No. 14 of 1992	Local Government (Planning and Development) Act, 1992	The whole Act.
No. 12 of 1993	Local Government (Planning and Development) Act, 1993	The whole Act, other than section 4.
No. 14 of 1993	Roads Act, 1993	Section 55A (as inserted by section 6 of the Roads (Amendment) Act, 1998).
No. 9 of 1998	Local Government (Planning and Development) Act, 1998	The whole Act.
No. 17 of 1999	Local Government (Planning and Development) Act, 1999	The whole Act.

Index

Note: References are to paragraph numbers

'ACCOMMODATION NEEDS',
HOUSING SUPPLY 183

ACQUISITION OF LAND 415–43
appeals, open space and control of
development 85–90
architectural conservation areas 163
capital money and disposal of land 421
compensation claims and open space
85–90
compulsory acquisition 424
foreshore development 452
local authority 423
compulsory acquisition 424
oral hearings 433, 434, 435–40
compulsory purchase order 423
confirmation of objections 431
parallel procedures 435–40
disposal of land 421
purposes 415–20
Local Government (No. 2), Act 1960,
amendment of section 10 442
open space 85–90
parallel procedures 435–40
planning authority development 422
regulations, references to transferred
functions 443
Road Acts 1993 and 1998 425–30
time limits in respect of purchase 432
transferred functions
and objective of Board 441
referred to in regulations 443

ADMINISTRATION EXPENSES,
FINANCIAL PROVISIONS 482

ADVERTISEMENT STRUCTURES
amenities 414
environment and amenities (first schedule
part IV) 584
granting of permission to develop land,
without compensation (fifth
schedule) 594
licensing of appliances on public roads
504
refusal of permission will not attract
compensation (third schedule) 592

'AFFORDABLE HOUSING' 183, 184, 191
allocation 193
amount paid to planning authority 191
application for a certificate 192
controls on resale 194
convictions for forgery or alteration 192
development to which section 96 does
not apply 192
disputes 191
exceptions 191
expiry of date from grant of permission
191
'forged or altered certificate' 192
houses or sites 191
housing authority and planning authority
201
housing supply 183, 184, 191
land or sites 191
'owner' (definition) 191
ownership transferred to planning
authority 191
planning applications 191
property arbitrator 191
regulations 195–200
'the court' 192

AGREEMENTS REGULATING
DEVELOPMENT OR USE OF LAND
92

AIRCRAFT, GRANTING OF
PERMISSION TO DEVELOP LAND,
WITHOUT COMPENSATION
(FIFTH SCHEDULE) 594

AMENDMENTS, ROADS ACT, 1993
541–80

AMENITIES 402–14
advertisement structures 414
and environment, purposes for which
objectives may be indicated in the
Development Plan (first schedule)
584
area of special amenity 402
confirmation of order under section 202
403
landscape conservation areas 404
joint planning authorities 404
notices to be published 404
order amended or revoked 404
State authority functions 404
public rights of way agreement 411
appeals 412
compulsory powers for creating 412
supplemental provisions 413
tree preservation orders 405–10

AMOUNT RECOVERABLE,
COMPENSATION 374

AN BORD PLEANÁLA 202–91
accounts and audits 232
annual report 233
appeal procedures
discretion of Board 273
duty and objective of Board 251
expenses determined by Board 285–
90
fees payable 284
in relation to appeals and referrals
245–51
power to request submissions or
observations 261
power to require submission of
documents 262
power to where notice is served 263
regard for objectives of public
authorities 283

reports and documents of the Board
291
submissions or observations
by other parties 254
by persons other than parties
255–60
chairperson
appointment and removal from office
204, 205–10
role to ensure efficient discharge of
business 215–20, 221
committee 205–10, 211
communications in relation to appeals
224
constitution 204, 205–10
consultants and advisers 244
continuation of the Board 202
deputy chairperson 212
disclosure of information 223
divisions of Board 222
employees of the Board 120
superannuation 241
environmental impact assessment 345–50
establishment and constitution 202–13
grants 231
indemnification 225–30
meetings and procedure 221
membership of either House of the
Oireachtas 243
Ministerial powers 205–10, 211, 242
ordinary members 211
organisation 214–44
performance of Board 214
prohibitions 223–24
quorum vacancies 213
staffing 214–44
superannuation
of employees 241
of members 234
to be corporate body 203
voting on decisions 221
see also appeal procedures

ANNUITY PAYMENTS PURCHASE,
ACQUISITION OF LAND FOR
OPEN SPACE 85–90

APPEAL PROCEDURES 245–91
An Bord Pleanála
discretion to dismiss appeals or
referrals 273
duty and objective of Board 251
expenses determined by Board 285–90

fees payable 284
in relation to appeals and referrals
	245–51
power to request submissions or
	observations 261
power to require submission of
	documents 262
power to where notice is served 263
regard for objectives of public
	authorities 283
reports and documents of the Board
	291
appeals against conditions 274
control of development, reviews 95–100
dismissal of appeals or referrals 273
matters other than those raised by parties
	272
objectives of public authorities 283
oral hearings 264, 265–70
planning authorities, documents
	submitted 253
provisions as to making appeals or
	referrals 252
referrals, convening of meetings on 271
regulations 282
specified classes 251
submission of documents 253, 262
submissions or observations
	An Bord Pleanála's power to request
		261
	by other parties 254
	by persons other than parties 255–60
supplemental provisions relating to oral
	hearings, offences 265–70
time and specified period 281
where notice is served under section 131
	or 132 263
withdrawals 275–80
see also appeals

APPEALS
acquisition of land for open space 85–90
against notices, protected structures 121
Bord Pleanála, communications in
	relation to appeals 224
public rights of way agreement 412
removal or alteration of structure or
	discontinuance of use 91
strategic development zones 334
see also appeal procedures

APPLIANCES AND CABLES ON
	PUBLIC ROADS, LICENSING 504

APPLICATIONS
for a certificate, 'affordable housing' 192
for injunctions and prosecutions,
	enforcement 321
for permission, regulations and control of
	development 63
strategic development zones 340

'APPROPRIATE AUTHORITY'
	(DEFINITION), POWER TO ENTER
	ON LAND 502

ARCHITECTURAL CONSERVATION
	AREAS 161–63
definition 161
acquisition of structure or other land in
	area 163
development 162
protected structures 115–20
refusal of permission which excludes
	compensation (fourth schedule) 593
special planning control 164
	'city' (definition) 164
	development 172–82
	notice relating to structures or other
		land 173–80
	objectives 164, 165–70
	owner or occupier's requests 172
	rescission or variation of a declaration
		172
	scheme 164, 165–71
	'town' (definition) 164

ARCHITECTURAL HERITAGE 101–82

AREA OF SPECIAL AMENITY 402

AREA OF SPECIAL PLANNING
	CONTROL, COMPENSATION 393

AREAS AND STRUCTURES, CONTROL
	OF, PURPOSES FOR WHICH
	OBJECTIVES MAY BE INDICATED
	IN THE DEVELOPMENT PLAN
	(FIRST SCHEDULE, PART II) 582

AREAS OF SPECIAL PLANNING
	CONTROL 164–73

ATTRIBUTION OF COMPENSATION
	374

'AUTHORISED PERSON'
(definition) 502
events 465–70
power to enter on land 502, 503

BANKING FACILITIES, COMMUNITY
FACILITIES (FIRST SCHEDULE
PART III) 583

BOARD *SEE* AN BORD PLEANÁLA

BURIAL GROUNDS, COMMUNITY
FACILITIES (FIRST SCHEDULE
PART III) 583

CABLES, WIRES AND PIPELINES
compensation 394
licensing of appliances and cables on
public roads 504

CAPITAL MONEY, ACQUISITION AND
DISPOSAL OF LAND 421

CERTIFICATE, 'AFFORDABLE
HOUSING' 192
'forged or altered certificate' 192

CHAIRPERSON, AN BORD PLEANÁLA
204, 205–10, 221

CHANGE OF USE, REFUSAL OF
PERMISSION WILL NOT ATTRACT
COMPENSATION (THIRD
SCHEDULE) 592

CITY AND COUNTY MANAGEMENT
(AMENDMENT) ACT 1955,
CONTROL OF DEVELOPMENT 64

'CITY' (DEFINITION),
ARCHITECTURAL
CONSERVATION AREAS 164

CIVIL PROCEEDINGS, LIMITATIONS,
EVENTS 471

CLAIMS FOR COMPENSATION *SEE*
COMPENSATION

CLASSES OF DEVELOPMENT
environmental impact assessment 351

specified classes, appeal procedures 251
supplementary development contribution
schemes 94

COASTAL AREAS
granting of permission to develop land,
without compensation (fifth
schedule) 594
location end pattern of development (first
schedule, part 1) 581

CODES OF CONDUCT, DISCLOSURE
OF INTERESTS 295–300

CODES OF PRACTICE, EVENTS 462

COMMENCEMENT, REPEALS AND
CONTINUANCE 523–40
interpretation 523
commencement 535–40
continuity of repealed enactments 525–30
regulations to remove difficulties 534
repeals 524
transitional provisions
miscellaneous 533
regarding development plans 531
respecting acquisition of land 532

COMMITTEE, AN BORD PLEANÁLA
205–10, 211

COMMUNITY FACILITIES, PURPOSES
FOR WHICH OBJECTIVES MAY BE
INDICATED IN THE
DEVELOPMENT PLAN (FIRST
SCHEDULE PART III) 583

COMPENSATION 363–401
acquisition of land for open space 85–90
amount recoverable 374
application of section 189 374
attribution of compensation 374
claims
determination of claim 364
time limits 363
contravention 374
determination of amount and value of
compensation (second schedule) 591
double compensation prohibited 371
entry on land 401
granting of permission to develop land,
without compensation (fifth
schedule) 594

in relation to divisions under Part III 375–90
notice preventing compensation 382
permission revoked or modified 385–90
restriction of compensation 381
restriction under section 190 384
right to compensation 375–80
special provisions for fire damage 383
structures destroyed by fire 383
in relation to sections 46. 85. 88. 182 207 and 252 391–401
area of special planning control 393
cables, wires and pipelines 394
creation of public rights of way 395–400
discontinuance of use 392
entry on land 401
removal or alteration of structure 391
protected structures 152
recovery by planning authority on subsequent development 374
'compensation statement' 374
recovery from planning authority 372
refusal of permission which excludes compensation (fourth schedule) 593
refusal of permission will not attract compensation (third schedule) 592
registration 373
regulations 365–70

COMPULSORY ACQUISITION OF LAND 424
costs in relation to oral hearings 434
transfer of Ministerial functions to Board 424

COMPULSORY ACQUISITION ORDER, PROTECTED STRUCTURES 142–43

COMPULSORY POWERS, PUBLIC RIGHTS OF WAY AGREEMENT 412

COMPULSORY PURCHASE ORDER
acquisition of land 423
confirmation of objections 431
local authorities 423
parallel procedures 435–40

CONDITIONS WHICH MAY BE IMPOSED ON THE GRANTING OF PERMISSION TO DEVELOP LAND, WITHOUT COMPENSATION, (FIFTH SCHEDULE) 594

CONNECTION, LIMITATION ON CONNECTION TO SANITARY AUTHORITY 513

CONSEQUENTIAL PROVISIONS FOR OFFENCES, EVENTS 472

CONSERVATION *SEE* PRESERVATION

CONSTITUTION, AN BORD PLEANÁLA 204, 205–10

CONSULTANTS AND ADVISERS, AN BORD PLEANÁLA 244

CONSULTATIONS, PROPOSED DEVELOPMENTS 492

CONTENT
development plans 15–20
regional planning guidelines 43

CONTRAVENTION, COMPENSATION 374

CONTRIBUTIONS *SEE* DEVELOPMENT CONTRIBUTIONS

CONTROL OF AREAS, PURPOSES FOR WHICH OBJECTIVES MAY BE INDICATED IN THE DEVELOPMENT PLAN (FIRST SCHEDULE PART II) 582

CONTROL OF DEVELOPMENT 62–100
acquisition of land for open space 85–90
appeals 85–90
compensation claims 85–90
purchase annuity payments 85–90
registration of title 85–90
scope of definition of 'open space' 85–90
agreements regulating development or use of land 92
appeal to the An Bord Pleanála 72
expiration of appropriate period 72
interest in adjoining land 72

availability of documents relating to planning applications 73
development contributions 93
appeals 93
phased payment of contributions 93
public infrastructure and facilities (definition) 93
publication of scheme 93
schemes for payment (definition) 93
special contribution (definition) 93
development in respect of which a refusal of planning permission for past failures to comply 65–70
general obligations to obtain permission 62
judicial reviews of appeals, referrals and other matters 95–100
application to apply for judicial review 95–100
application to stay the proceedings 95–100
European Communities Member State 95–100
Transboundary Convention 95–100
limit of duration of permission 75–80
outline permission 71
permission for development 64
conditions under subsection 64
contravention of development plan 64
extension of period of decision-making 64
the City and County Management (Amendment) Act 1955 64
power to extend appropriate period 82
power to vary appropriate period 81
quarries 521
regulations regarding applications for permission 63
regulations regarding sections 40, 41, 42 83
requiring removal or alteration of structure or discontinuance of use 91
appeal 91
confirmation of notice 91
expenses payable 91
failure to comply 91
planning authority's powers within specified period 91
unauthorised development 91
revocation or modification of permission 84
supplemental provisions as to grant of permission 74

supplementary development contribution schemes 94
agreements of planning authority 94
amount and manner of payment 94
classes of development 94
functional area of the planning authority 94
public infrastructure project or service 94

CONTROLS ON RESALE, 'AFFORDABLE HOUSING' 194

CORPORATE BODIES, ENFORCEMENT OFFENCES 313

COSTS OF PROSECUTIONS AND APPLICATIONS FOR INJUNCTIONS, ENFORCEMENT 321

CYCLISTS, INFRASTRUCTURE AND TRANSPORT (FIRST SCHEDULE PART V) 585–90

DECLARATION AND REFERRAL 5

DECLARATIONS, WORKS AFFECTING CHARACTER OF PROTECTED STRUCTURES 112

DEMOLITION OF A HABITABLE HOUSE, REFUSAL OF PERMISSION WILL NOT ATTRACT COMPENSATION (THIRD SCHEDULE) 592

DEPUTY CHAIRPERSON, AN BORD PLEANÁLA 212

DEVELOPMENT, GENERAL 3

'DEVELOPMENT AGENCY', STRATEGIC DEVELOPMENT ZONES 325–30

DEVELOPMENT CONTRIBUTIONS, CONTROL OF DEVELOPMENT 93
supplementary schemes 94

'DEVELOPMENT OBJECTIVE' (DEFINITION), PROTECTED STRUCTURES 102

DEVELOPMENT PLANS 14–32
  and regional planning guidelines 52
  content 15–20
    additional objectives 15
  copies of development plans 31
  draft development plan 21
  evidence of development plans 17
  general duty of planning authority to
    secure objectives 25–30
  making of development plan 22
  obligation to make development plans 14
  public rights of way 24
  purposes for which objectives may be
    indicated in the Development Plan
    (first schedule) 581–90
  variation of development plan 23

DISABLED PERSONS' FACILITIES,
  COMMUNITY FACILITIES (FIRST
  SCHEDULE PART III) 583

DISCLOSURE OF INFORMATION, AN
  BORD PLEANÁLA 223

DISCLOSURE OF INTERESTS 292–300
  declaration by members 292
    beneficial interests 293
    failure to comply 292
    'register of interests' 292
    supplemental provisions 294

DISCONTINUANCE OF USE,
  COMPENSATION 392

DISMISSAL OF APPEALS OR
  REFERRALS, APPEAL
  PROCEDURES 273

DISPOSAL OF LAND 421

DISPUTES, 'AFFORDABLE HOUSING'
  191

DISTRICT COURT, PROTECTED
  STRUCTURES 125–30, 131, 132

DIVISIONS UNDER PART III,
  COMPENSATION 375–90, 382

'DOCUMENTS OR OTHER
  INFORMATION' (DEFINITION) 493

DOUBLE COMPENSATION
  PROHIBITED 371

DRAFT DEVELOPMENT PLAN,
  PREPARATION 21

DRAFT PLANNING SCHEME,
  STRATEGIC DEVELOPMENT
  ZONES 333, 334

DRAINS, LIMITATION ON
  CONNECTION TO SANITARY
  AUTHORITY 513

ELDERLY PERSONS' FACILITIES,
  COMMUNITY FACILITIES (FIRST
  SCHEDULE PART III) 583

ELECTRONIC FORMAT, INFORMATION
  TO BE PROVIDED IN 493

'ELIGIBLE PERSON', HOUSING
  SUPPLY 183

EMPLOYEES OF THE BOARD, AN
  BORD PLEANÁLA 120, 241

ENACTMENTS REPEALED, (SIXTH
  SCHEDULE) 595–800

ENDANGERED STRUCTURES
  application for contribution to cost of
    work 132
  duty of owners to protect 113
  exemption from development 133
  notice to require works to be carried out
    114
  offences relating to endangerment 123
  owner's powers in relation to notices
    concerning restoration 124
  planning authority's recovery of expenses
    for work 135–40
  protected 113–14, 123, 124
    exemption from development 133

ENFORCEMENT 301–24
  costs of prosecutions and applications for
    injunctions 321
  decision on enforcement 303
  enforcement notice 304, 305–10
    failure to comply 304
    planning authority's recovery of
      expenses incurred 304
    register 304
    urgent cases 305–10

fines, payment of to planning authorities
314
injunctions
costs of 321
in relation to unauthorised
development 315–20
offences 301
corporate bodies 313
penalties 311
prosecution 312
transitional arrangement 324
permission
evidence of 322
not required 323
transitional arrangement for offences 324
unauthorised development, injunctions
315–20
warning letter 302, 312

ENTRY ON LAND, COMPENSATION
401

ENVIRONMENT AND AMENITIES,
PURPOSES FOR WHICH
OBJECTIVES MAY BE INDICATED
IN THE DEVELOPMENT PLAN
(FIRST SCHEDULE PART IV) 584

ENVIRONMENTAL IMPACT
ASSESSMENT 342–52
classes of development 351
environmental impact statement 342
prescribed information 352
local authorities development 345–50
approval of the Board 345–50
exemptions granted by the Board
345–50
information to be supplied to the
Board 345–50
notices of proposed development
345–50
oral hearings 345–50
proposals considered by the Board
345–50
regulations 345–50
permission for development 343
prescribed classes of development
requiring assessment 351
transboundary environmental impacts 344

ENVIRONMENTAL PROTECTION
AGENCY ACT, 1992, AMENDMENT
511

EUROPEAN SITES, REFUSAL OF
PERMISSION WHICH EXCLUDES
COMPENSATION (FOURTH
SCHEDULE) 593

EUROPEAN SPATIAL DEVELOPMENT
PERSPECTIVE, LOCATION END
PATTERN OF DEVELOPMENT
(FIRST SCHEDULE, PART 1) 581

EVENTS 454–81
'authorised person' 465–70
codes of practice 462
consequential provisions for offences
472
exclusion from planning control 475–80
funfairs 474–80
grant of licence 461
inspection of land and structures 465–70
interpretation 454
licence for 455–61
limitation of civil proceedings 471
local authority holds event 473
regulations 481
safety obligations 464
service of notice 463

EXCLUSION FROM PLANNING
CONTROL, EVENTS 475–80

EXEMPTED DEVELOPMENT 4
declaration and referral 5
endangered structures 133
ministerial powers 4
other state authority 4
references in the Act 4

EXPENSES
expenses determined, appeal procedures
285–90
expenses incurred, recovery of,
enforcement notice 304
expenses payable, control of
development 91
see also financial provisions

EXPIRATION OF APPROPRIATE
PERIOD, CONTROL OF
DEVELOPMENT 72

FAILURE TO COMPLY, CONTROL OF
DEVELOPMENT 91

FAIRGROUND EQUIPMENT
(DEFINITION), CONTROL OF
FUNFAIRS 474

FEES PAYABLE
appeal procedures 284
to planning authorities, financial
provisions 491

FENCES, LICENSING OF APPLIANCES
AND CABLES ON PUBLIC ROADS
504

FIFTH SCHEDULE, CONDITIONS
WHICH MAY BE IMPOSED ON
THE GRANTING OF PERMISSION
TO DEVELOP LAND, WITHOUT
COMPENSATION 594

FINANCIAL PROVISIONS 482–91
administration expenses 482
apportionment of joint expenses 484
expenses of planning authority 483
fees payable to planning authorities 491
power to set-off 485–90

FINES, PAYMENT OF TO PLANNING
AUTHORITIES, ENFORCEMENT
314

FIRE DAMAGE, COMPENSATION,
SPECIAL PROVISIONS 383

FIRST SCHEDULE, PURPOSES FOR
WHICH OBJECTIVES MAY BE
INDICATED IN THE
DEVELOPMENT PLAN 581–90
location end pattern of development (part
I) 581
control of areas and structures (part II)
582
community facilities (part III) 583
environment and amenities (part IV) 584
infrastructure and transport (part V)
585–90

FLOODING CONTROL
granting of permission to develop land,
without compensation (fifth
schedule) 594
location end pattern of development (first
schedule, part I) 581
refusal of permission which excludes
compensation (fourth schedule) 593

FLORA AND FAUNA
environment and amenities (first schedule
part IV) 584
granting of permission to develop land,
without compensation (fifth
schedule) 594

FORESHORE ACT 1933, LEASE UNDER
SECTION 2 452

FORESHORE DEVELOPMENT 444–53
definitions 444
acquisition of land 452
'development' (definition) 444
entering for certain purposes 453
Foreshore Act 1933, lease under section
2 452
'foreshore' (definition) 444
functions transferred to the Board 452
local authority development 451
location end pattern of development (first
schedule, part I) 581
permission to be obtained 445–50
road authority 452
State Property Act, 1954 452

FORGERY OR ALTERATION,
CONVICTIONS FOR AND
'AFFORDABLE HOUSING'
192

FOURTH SCHEDULE, REFUSAL OF
PERMISSION WHICH EXCLUDES
COMPENSATION 593

FUNFAIRS 474–80
definition 454
exclusion from planning control 475–80
see also events

GAELTACHT
granting of permission to develop land,
without compensation (fifth
schedule) 594
refusal of permission which excludes
compensation (fourth schedule)
593

GRANTS, AN BORD PLEANÁLA 231

GUIDELINES AND DIRECTIVES 53–61
limitations on ministerial power 55–60

ministerial directions regarding
  development plans 61
ministerial guidelines 53
ministerial policy directives 54

'HABITABLE HOUSE', REFUSAL OF
  PERMISSION WILL NOT ATTRACT
  COMPENSATION (THIRD
  SCHEDULE) 592

HEALTH AND THE ENVIRONMENT,
  LOCATION END PATTERN OF
  DEVELOPMENT (FIRST
  SCHEDULE, PART I) 581

HISTORIC MONUMENTS, REFUSAL OF
  PERMISSION WHICH EXCLUDES
  COMPENSATION (FOURTH
  SCHEDULE) 593

HOARDINGS, LICENSING OF
  APPLIANCES AND CABLES ON
  PUBLIC ROADS 504

HOSPITALS AND HEALTHCARE
  FACILITIES, COMMUNITY
  FACILITIES (FIRST SCHEDULE
  PART III) 583

HOUSING
  'affordable housing' 201
  'habitable house', refusal of permission
    will not attract compensation (third
    schedule) 592

'HOUSING STRATEGY',
  DEVELOPMENT PLANS 183, 184

HOUSING SUPPLY 183–201
  'accommodation needs' 183
  'affordable housing' 183, 184, 191
  development plans 185–90
  'eligible person' 183
  estimate of amount of housing 184
  'housing strategy' 183, 184
  interpretation 183
  'market value' 183
  'mortgage' 183
  objectives of planning authority 185–90
  social and affordable housing provision
    191

INDEMNIFICATION, AN BORD
  PLEANÁLA 225–30

INFORMATION
  electronic format 493
  obligation to give information to local
    authority 13

INFRASTRUCTURE AND TRANSPORT,
  PURPOSES FOR WHICH
  OBJECTIVES MAY BE INDICATED
  IN THE DEVELOPMENT PLAN
  (FIRST SCHEDULE PART V) 585–90

INJUNCTIONS
  cost of enforcement 321
  enforcement 315–20
  prosecutions and enforcement 321

INLAND WATERWAYS, LOCATION
  END PATTERN OF
  DEVELOPMENT (FIRST
  SCHEDULE, PART I) 581

INSPECTION OF LAND AND
  STRUCTURES, EVENTS 465–70

INTERESTS, DISCLOSURE OF 292–300

INTERPRETATIONS 2
  commencement, repeals and continuance
    523
  defined terms 2
  events 454
  housing supply 183
  references 2
  reserved functions 2
  strategic development zones 325–30
  terminology 2

INVESTIGATION, POWER OF
  EXAMINATION, INVESTIGATION
  AND SURVEY 11

JOINT EXPENSES, FINANCIAL
  PROVISIONS 484

JOINT PLANNING AUTHORITIES
  apportionment of expenses 484
  landscape conservation areas 404
  strategic development zones 333

JUDICIAL REVIEWS OF APPEALS, REFERRALS AND OTHER MATTERS, CONTROL OF DEVELOPMENT 95–100

LAND
acquisition of 415–43
for open space 85–90
foreshore development 452
local authority and disposal of land 421
agreements regulating development or use of land 92
'authorised person's' power to enter on land 502, 503
determination of the amount and value of compensation (second schedule) 591
entry on land, compensation 401
granting of permission to develop land, without compensation (fifth schedule) 594
interest in adjoining land, control of development 72

LAND OR SITES, 'AFFORDABLE HOUSING' 191

LANDSCAPE CONSERVATION AREAS, AMENITIES 404

LANDSCAPE PROTECTION
environment and amenities (first schedule part IV) 584
refusal of permission which excludes compensation (fourth schedule) 593

LEASE OF LAND, ACQUISITION AND DISPOSAL OF LAND 421

LICENCE
definition 454
appliances and cables on public roads 504
events 455–61
not applicable 504

LIMITATIONS
civil proceedings, events 471
duration of permission, control of development 75–80
ministerial power 55–60
see also time

LOCAL AREA PLANS 33
application and content 34
consultation and adoption 35–40

LOCAL AUTHORITIES
acquisition of land 423
compulsory acquisition 424
oral hearings 433, 434, 435–40
compulsory purchase order 423
confirmation of objections 431
parallel procedures 435–40
disposal of land 421
capital money 421
lease of land 421
purposes 415–20
cables, wires and pipelines 362
development by local authority 353–60
exceptions 354
notice of development 354
own development 354
report on proposed development 354
restrictions 353
environmental impact assessment 345–50
events 473
definition of local authority 454
foreshore development 451
objectives and appeal procedures 283
obligation to give information to local authority 13
taking in charge of estates 355–60
'qualified electors' 355–60
see also State authorities

LOCAL GOVERNMENT (NO. 2), ACT 1960, AMENDMENT OF SECTION 10 442

LOCATION END PATTERN OF DEVELOPMENT, PURPOSES FOR WHICH OBJECTIVES MAY BE INDICATED IN THE DEVELOPMENT PLAN (FIRST SCHEDULE PART I) 581

MAPS, LICENSING OF APPLIANCES AND CABLES ON PUBLIC ROADS 504

'MARKET VALUE' (INTERPRETATION), HOUSING SUPPLY 183

MEETING HALLS, COMMUNITY
FACILITIES (FIRST SCHEDULE
PART III) 583

MINISTER FOR ARTS HERITAGE,
GAELTACHT AND THE ISLANDS,
PROTECTED STRUCTURES 102

MINISTERIAL DIRECTIONS,
DEVELOPMENT PLANS 61

MINISTERIAL GUIDELINES 53

MINISTERIAL POLICY DIRECTIVES 54

MINISTERIAL POWER
An Bord Pleanála 205–10, 211
limitations 55–60

'MORTGAGE' (INTERPRETATION),
HOUSING SUPPLY 183

NATIONAL MONUMENTS 515–20

'NATIONAL ROAD' (DEFINITION),
REFUSAL OF PERMISSION WHICH
EXCLUDES COMPENSATION
(FOURTH SCHEDULE) 593

NATURAL RESOURCES,
EXPOLOITATION, LOCATION END
PATTERN OF DEVELOPMENT
(FIRST SCHEDULE, PART I) 581

NEGLECTED AMENITIES,
ENVIRONMENT AND AMENITIES
(FIRST SCHEDULE PART IV) 584

NOISE EMISSIONS
environment and amenities (first schedule
part IV) 584
granting of permission to develop land,
without compensation (fifth
schedule) 594
see also pollution

NOTICES
additional requirements for public
notification 494
architectural conservation areas 173–80
compliance with the notice
compulsory 175–80
failure to comply is an offence 181
implementation of the notice 174
permission not required for any
development 182
relating to structures or other land
173–80
service of notice 173
confirmation of notice requiring removal
or alteration of structure or
discontinuance of use 91
events 463
preventing compensation 382
protected structures
effective date of notices 122
to require restoration of character
115–20
to require works to be carried out 114
service of notices 495–500
special planning control 173–80
to require works to be carried out,
endangered structures 114

OBJECTIONS, COMPULSORY
ACQUISITION ORDER,
PROTECTED STRUCTURES 142–43

OBJECTIVES
and appeal procedures, public authorities
283
of planning authority, housing supply
185–90
regional planning guidelines 43

OBLIGATION
to give information 13
to make development plans 14

OCCUPIER
'authorised person's' power to enter on
land 502, 503
duty to protect structure 113
requests, special planning control 172
written request, works affecting character
of protected structures 112
see also owner

OFFENCES
endangerment of protected structures 123
enforcement 301
penalties 311
transitional arrangement for offences
324

OPEN SPACE, ACQUISITION OF LAND
   FOR OPEN SPACE
   annuity payments purchase 85–90
   appeals 85–90
   community facilities (first schedule part
      III) 583
   compensation claims 85–90
   control of development 85–90
   environment and amenities (first schedule
      part IV) 584
   scope of definition 85–90

ORAL HEARINGS
   appeal procedures 264, 265–70
   environmental impact assessment 345–50

ORDERS, TREE PRESERVATION
   405–10

OUTLINE PERMISSION, CONTROL OF
   DEVELOPMENT 71

OWNER
   definition of, 'affordable housing' 191
   'authorised person's' power to enter on
      land 502
   owner or occupier's requests,
      architectural conservation areas 172
   powers in relation to notices concerning
      endangerment restoration 124
   protected structures
      compulsory acquisition order 142, 143
      duty to protect structure 113
      written request and works affecting
         character of structures 112
   see also occupier

PARALLEL PROCEDURES,
   ACQUISITION OF LAND 435–40

PEDESTRIANS, INFRASTRUCTURE
   AND TRANSPORT (FIRST
   SCHEDULE PART V) 585–90

PENALTIES, ENFORCEMENT
   OFFENCES 311

PERIOD OF TIME *SEE* TIME

PERMISSION *SEE* PLANNING
   PERMISSION

PIPELINES *SEE* CABLES, WIRES AND
   PIPELINES

PLACES OF WORSHIP
   community facilities (first schedule part
      III) 583
   works affecting character of protected
      structures 112

PLANNING APPLICATIONS
   'affordable housing' 191
   availability of documents 73

PLANNING AUTHORITIES
   'affordable housing' 201
      amount paid to authority 191
   appeal procedures, documents submitted
      253
   development and acquisition of land 422
   endangered structures 135–40
   enforcement notice, recovery of expenses
      incurred 304
   financial provisions 483, 491
   general duty to secure objectives 25–30
   housing supply 185–90
   obligation to make development plans 14
   performance of functions 505–10
   powers within specified period 91
   protected structures 135–40, 155–60
   regional planning guidelines 42
   strategic development zones 333
   supplementary development contribution
      schemes 94
   see also An Bord Pleanála

PLANNING PERMISSION
   compensation, permission revoked or
      modified 385–90
   control of development 64
      outline permission 71
      refusal of for past failures to comply
         65–70
      regulations regarding applications for
         permission 63
   enforcement
      evidence of permission 322
      permission not required 323
   environmental impact assessment 343
   foreshore development 445–50
   refusal of permission which excludes
      compensation (fourth schedule) 593

PLANNING REGISTER 12

PLANNING SCHEME, STRATEGIC
    DEVELOPMENT ZONES 333–34

POLLUTION
    environment and amenities (first schedule
        part IV) 584
    granting of permission to develop land,
        without compensation (fifth
        schedule) 594
    refusal of permission which excludes
        compensation (fourth schedule)
        593
    see also noise emissions

POWER
    An Bord Pleanála 261, 262, 263
        Ministerial powers 205–10, 211, 242
    compulsory powers and public rights of
        way agreement 412
    of owner, notices concerning
        endangerment restoration 124
    of planning authority
        to acquire protected structure 141–52
        to carry out works 134
        to extend appropriate period 82
        within specified period 91
    power of entry, 'authorised persons' 502,
        503
    power of examination, investigation and
        survey 11
    power to extend appropriate period,
        control of development 82
    to enter on land of appropriate authority
        502
    to make the regional planning guidelines
        41
    to set-off, financial provisions 485–90
    to vary appropriate period, control of
        development 81

PRESCRIBED CLASSES REQUIRING
    ASSESSMENT, ENVIRONMENTAL
    IMPACT ASSESSMENT 351

PRESERVATION
    environment and amenities (first schedule
        part IV) 584
    granting of permission to develop land,
        without compensation (fifth
        schedule) 594

PROHIBITIONS, AN BORD PLEANÁLA
    223–24

PROPERTY ARBITRATOR,
    'AFFORDABLE HOUSING' 191

PROSECUTIONS AND APPLICATIONS
    FOR INJUNCTIONS,
    ENFORCEMENT OFFENCES 321

PROTECTED STRUCTURES 101–60
    additions or deletions from record of
        protected structures 104, 105–10
    appeals against notices 121
    application to District Court
        for consent 125–30
        for contribution to cost of works 132
    architectural conservation areas 115–20
    compensation for interest in protected
        structures 152
    compulsory acquisition order 142–43
    'development objective' (definition) 102
    District Court 125–30, 131, 132
    duty of owners and occupiers to protect
        structure 113
    effective date of notices 122
    endangered structures 113–14, 123, 124
        application for contribution to cost of
            work 132
        duty of owners to protect 113
        exemption from development 133
        notice to require works to be carried
            out 114
        offences relating to endangerment 123
        owner's powers in relation to notices
            concerning restoration 124
        planning authority's recovery of
            expenses for work 135–40
    grants to planning authorities 155–60
    guidelines by Minister for Arts Heritage,
        Gaeltacht and the Islands 102
    notice to require restoration of character
        of protected structures 115–20
    notice to require works to be carried out
        114
    objection to compulsory acquisition order
        143
    offence relating to endangerment of
        protected structures 123
    owner and compulsory acquisition order
        142, 143
    owners' powers in relation to notices
        concerning endangerment
        restoration of structures 124
    planning authority
        compulsory acquisition notice 142–43

grants in respect of functions 155–60
power to acquire protected structure
    141–52
power to carry out works 134
recovery of expenses 135–40
use of protected structure 153
procedure for making additions and
    deletions 105–10
recommendations to planning authorities
    103
record of protected structures 101, 104,
    105–10
registration of acquired title and
    amendment of vesting order 151
Registration of Title Act 1964 111
sanitary authorities' obligations 154
specific structures 103
vesting order 144–52
    annual payments to the Minister of
        Agriculture, Food and Rural
        Development 145–50
    form and effect 145–50
    registration of acquired title and
        amendment of vesting order 151
works affecting character of protected
    structures 112
    declarations 112
    owner or occupier's written request
        112
    places of worship 112
'works' (definition) 115–20

PUBLIC AUTHORITIES, OBJECTIVES
    AND APPEAL PROCEDURES 283

PUBLIC INFRASTRUCTURE
    development contributions 93
    'public infrastructure project or service'
        (definition) 94
    supplementary development contribution
        schemes 94

PUBLIC NOTIFICATION, ADDITIONAL
    REQUIREMENTS 494

PUBLIC RIGHTS OF WAY
    amenities agreement 411
    appeals agreement 412
    compensation 395–400
    development plans 24
    environment and amenities (first schedule
        part IV) 584

infrastructure and transport (first schedule
    part V) 585–90

PURCHASE ANNUITY PAYMENTS,
    ACQUISITION OF LAND FOR
    OPEN SPACE 85–90

PURPOSES FOR WHICH OBJECTIVES
    MAY BE INDICATED IN THE
    DEVELOPMENT PLAN (FIRST
    SCHEDULE) 581–90

QUARRIES, CONTROL OF
    DEVELOPMENT 521
    'emission' (definition) 521
    'operator' (definition) 521

QUORUM VACANCIES, AN BORD
    PLEANÁLA 213

RECREATIONAL FACILITIES
    community facilities (first schedule part
        III) 583
    granting of permission to develop land,
        without compensation (fifth
        schedule) 594

REFERRAL *SEE* APPEAL
    PROCEDURES; DECLARATION
    AND REFERRAL

REFUSAL OF PERMISSION WHICH
    EXCLUDES COMPENSATION
    (FOURTH SCHEDULE) 593

REFUSAL OF PERMISSION WILL NOT
    ATTRACT COMPENSATION
    (THIRD SCHEDULE) 592

REFUSAL OF PLANNING PERMISSION,
    CONTROL OF DEVELOPMENT
    65–70

REGIONAL PLANNING GUIDELINES
    41–52
    and development plans 52
    co-operation of planning authorities with
        regional authority 42
    consultation 44
    content and objectives 43

power to make the regional planning
guidelines 41
procedure for making guidelines 45–50
review 51

REGISTER, ENFORCEMENT NOTICE
304

REGISTRATION OF ACQUIRED TITLE,
AMENDMENT OF VESTING
ORDER AND PROTECTED
STRUCTURES 151

REGISTRATION OF TITLE,
ACQUISITION OF LAND FOR
OPEN SPACE 85–90

REGULATIONS
acquisition of land, transferred functions
443
'affordable housing' 195–200
appeal procedures 282
control of development
applications for permission 63
sections 40, 41, 42 83
environmental impact assessment 345–50
events 481
Planning and Development Act 2000,
general regulations 522

REPEALS *SEE* COMMENCEMENT,
REPEALS AND CONTINUANCE

RESCISSION OR VARIATION OF A
DECLARATION, SPECIAL
PLANNING CONTROL 172

RESTRICTION OF COMPENSATION
381, 384

RETAIL DEVELOPMENT, LOCATION
END PATTERN OF
DEVELOPMENT (FIRST
SCHEDULE, PART I) 581

RETAIL FACILITIES DEVELOPMENT,
COMMUNITY FACILITIES (FIRST
SCHEDULE PART III) 583

REVIEWS OF APPEALS *SEE* APPEAL
PROCEDURES; DECLARATION
AND REFERRAL

REVOCATION OR MODIFICATION OF
PERMISSION, CONTROL OF
DEVELOPMENT 84

RIGHT TO COMPENSATION 375–80

RIGHTS OF WAY *SEE* PUBLIC RIGHTS
OF WAY

ROAD ACTS 1993 AND 1998,
ACQUISITION OF LAND 425–30

ROAD AUTHORITY
definition, refusal of permission which
excludes compensation (fourth
schedule) 593
foreshore development and land
acquisition 452

ROAD TOLLING, ROADS ACT 1993
541–44, 552–80

ROADS
infrastructure and transport
granting of permission to develop
land, without compensation (fifth
schedule) 594
refusal of permission which excludes
compensation (fourth schedule)
593
infrastructure and transport (first
schedule) 585–90

ROADS ACT 1993
amendments 541–80
further amendments of Part V 552–80
section 57 541, 542
section 58 541
section 60 543
section 61 544
section 63 545–50
section 65 551
sections 66A, 66B, 66C 552–80
road tolling 541–44, 552–80

RULES FOR THE DETERMINATION OF
THE AMOUNT AND VALUE OF
COMPENSATION (SECOND
SCHEDULE) 591

RURAL AREAS, LOCATION END
PATTERN OF DEVELOPMENT
(FIRST SCHEDULE, PART I) 581

SAFETY OBLIGATIONS, EVENTS 464

SANITARY SERVICES
community facilities (first schedule part III) 583
limitation on connection 513

SCAFFOLDS, LICENSING OF APPLIANCES AND CABLES ON PUBLIC ROADS 504

SCHEDULES ONE TO SIX OF THE PLANNING AND DEVELOPMENT ACT 2000 581–800

SCHEMES
planning scheme, strategic development zones 333, 334
schemes for payment (definition), development contributions 93
special planning control 164, 165–71

SECOND SCHEDULE, RULES FOR THE DETERMINATION OF THE AMOUNT AND VALUE OF COMPENSATION 591

SETTLEMENT DEVELOPMENT, LOCATION END PATTERN OF DEVELOPMENT (FIRST SCHEDULE, PART I) 581

SEWAGE DISPOSAL
environment and amenities (first schedule part IV) 584
granting of permission to develop land, without compensation (fifth schedule) 594
refusal of permission which excludes compensation (fourth schedule) 593
sewers and the limitation on connection to sanitary authority 513

SHOPPING FACILITIES, COMMUNITY FACILITIES (FIRST SCHEDULE PART III) 583

SITES
'affordable housing' 191
strategic development zones 331, 332

SITES OF SPECIAL INTEREST, PROTECTION AND PRESERVATION, ENVIRONMENT AND AMENITIES (FIRST SCHEDULE PART IV) 584

SIXTH SCHEDULE, ENACTMENTS REPEALED 595–800

SOCIAL AND AFFORDABLE HOUSING PROVISION 191

SPECIAL AMENITIES
development on respect of which a refusal of permission will not attract compensation (third schedule) 592
refusal of permission which excludes compensation (fourth schedule) 593

SPECIAL CONTRIBUTION (DEFINITION), CONTROL OF DEVELOPMENT 93

SPECIAL PLANNING CONTROL
architectural conservation areas 164–73
notice relating to structures or other land 173–80
owner or occupier's requests 172
rescission or variation of a declaration 172
scheme 164, 165–71
'town' (definition) 164

SPECIFIED CLASSES, APPEAL PROCEDURES 251

STAFFING, AN BORD PLEANÁLA 214–44

STATE AUTHORITIES
development 361
functions, landscape conservation areas 404
see also local authorities

STATE PROPERTY ACT, 1954, FORESHORE DEVELOPMENT 452

'STATUTORY BODY' (DEFINITION), DETERMINATION OF THE AMOUNT AND VALUE OF COMPENSATION (SECOND SCHEDULE) 591

STRATEGIC DEVELOPMENT ZONES
301–24, 325–30
interpretation 325–30
appeals and planning scheme 334
application for development 340
decisions of planning authority 334
'development agency' 325–30
draft planning scheme 333, 334
planning authorities, two or more 333
planning scheme 333–34
refusal of permission which excludes
compensation (fourth schedule) 593
report on submissions to planning
scheme 334
revocation of planning scheme 341
sites
acquisition 332
designation 331

STRUCTURES
acquisition of , in architectural
conservation areas 163
granting of permission to develop land,
without compensation (fifth
schedule) 594
refusal of permission which excludes
compensation (fourth schedule) 593
refusal of permission will not attract
compensation (third schedule) 592
removal or alteration of structure or
discontinuance of use 91
special planning control 173–80

STRUCTURES, CONTROL OF AREAS
AND STRUCTURES, PURPOSES
FOR WHICH OBJECTIVES MAY BE
INDICATED IN THE
DEVELOPMENT PLAN (FIRST
SCHEDULE PART II) 582

SUBMISSION OF DOCUMENTS,
APPEAL PROCEDURES, AN BORD
PLEANÁLA'S POWER TO
REQUIRE 262

SUBMISSIONS OR OBSERVATIONS,
APPEAL PROCEDURES, AN BORD
PLEANÁLA'S POWER TO
REQUEST 261

SUPERANNUATION, AN BORD
PLEANÁLA
of employees 241
of members 234

SUPPLEMENTAL PROVISIONS AS TO
GRANT OF PERMISSION,
CONTROL OF DEVELOPMENT
74

SUPPLEMENTARY DEVELOPMENT
CONTRIBUTION SCHEMES,
CONTROL OF DEVELOPMENT
94

SURVEY, POWER OF EXAMINATION,
INVESTIGATION AND SURVEY 11

TELEPHONE KIOSKS, LICENSING OF
APPLIANCES AND CABLES ON
PUBLIC ROADS 504

THIRD SCHEDULE, REFUSAL OF
PERMISSION WILL NOT ATTRACT
COMPENSATION 592

TIME
calculation of periods and limits 501
control of development 64, 72, 75–80, 91
expiration of appropriate period 72
limit of duration of permission 75–80
period of decision-making extended,
permission for development 64
periods and limits, in respect of purchase,
acquisition of land 432
permission and period of decision-
making extended 64
power to extend appropriate period 82
power to vary appropriate period 81
powers of planning authority, within
specified period 91
specified period, appeal procedures 281
see also limitations

TITLE OF ACT 1

TOLL ROADS AND TOLL SCHEMES,
AMENDMENTS TO ROADS ACT
1993 541–44, 552–80

TOURISM DEVELOPMENT, LOCATION
END PATTERN OF
DEVELOPMENT (FIRST
SCHEDULE, PART I) 581

'TOWN' (DEFINITION), SPECIAL
PLANNING CONTROL 164

TRAFFIC CONTROL,
INFRASTRUCTURE AND
TRANSPORT (FIRST SCHEDULE
PART V) 585–90

TRANSBOUNDARY ENVIRONMENTAL
IMPACTS, ENVIRONMENTAL
IMPACT ASSESSMENT 344

TRANSFER OF OWNERSHIP TO
PLANNING AUTHORITY,
'AFFORDABLE HOUSING' 191

TRANSFERRED FUNCTIONS,
ACQUISITION OF LAND
objective of An Bord Pleanála 441
referred to in regulations 443

TRANSITIONAL ARRANGEMENT FOR
OFFENCES, ENFORCEMENT 324

TRANSPORT
and infrastructure (first schedule part V)
585–90
location end pattern of development (first
schedule, part I) 581

TREE PRESERVATION ORDERS
amended or revoked order 405–10
amenities 405–10
contravention of order 405–10
exemptions 405–10

UNAUTHORISED DEVELOPMENT
control of development 91
enforcement and injunctions 315–20

URBAN AREAS, LOCATION END
PATTERN OF DEVELOPMENT
(FIRST SCHEDULE, PART I) 581

VENDING MACHINES, LICENSING OF
APPLIANCES AND CABLES ON
PUBLIC ROADS 504

VESTING ORDER, PROTECTED
STRUCTURES 151

VOTING, AN BORD PLEANÁLA 221

WARNING LETTERS
enforcement 302, 312
service of notices 495–500

WASTE MANAGEMENT ACT 1996,
AMENDMENT 512

WASTE MATERIALS
environment and amenities (first schedule
part IV) 584
granting of permission to develop land,
without compensation (fifth
schedule) 594

WATER SUPPLIES
environment and amenities (first schedule
part IV) 584
granting of permission to develop land,
without compensation (fifth
schedule) 594
refusal of permission which excludes
compensation (fourth schedule)
593

WATERWAYS, GRANTING OF
PERMISSION TO DEVELOP LAND,
WITHOUT COMPENSATION
(FIFTH SCHEDULE) 594

WATERWORKS CLAUSES ACT 1847,
LIMITATION OF SECTION 53 514

WIRES *SEE* CABLES, WIRES AND
PIPELINES

WITHDRAWALS, APPEAL
PROCEDURES 275–80

WORKS AFFECTING CHARACTER OF
PROTECTED STRUCTURES 112